Public Relations Campaigns and Techniques

Building Bridges into the 21st Century

Fran R. Matera

Arizona State University

Ray J. Artigue

Senior Vice President of Marketing Communications
NBA Phoenix Suns

Allyn and Bacon

Boston ■ London ■ Toronto ■ Sydney ■ Tokyo ■ Singapore

Vice President, Education: *Paul A. Smith*
Senior Editor: *Karon Bowers*
Editorial Assistant: *Jennifer Becker*
Marketing Manager: *Jackie Aaron*
Editorial Production Service: *Chestnut Hill Enterprises, Inc.*
Manufacturing Buyer: *Julie McNeill*
Cover Administrator: *Jennifer Hart*
Electronic Composition: *Omegatype Typography, Inc.*

Internet: www.abacon.com

Between the time web site information is gathered and published, some sites may have
closed. Also, the transcription of URLs can result in typographical errors. The publisher would
appreciate notification where these occur so that they may be corrected in subsequent editions.

Library of Congress Cataloging-in-Publication Data

Matera, Fran R.
    Public relations campaigns and techniques : building bridges into the 21st century /
Fran R. Matera, Ray J. Artigue.
        p.   cm.
    Includes bibliographical references and index.
    ISBN 0-205-15815-3
    1. Public relations.   I. Artigue, Ray J.
HM1221.M37   1999
659.2—dc21   99-048412
                                                                      CIP

Printed in the United States of America

10   9   8   7   6   5   4   3   04   03   02

CONTENTS

PREFACE

If public relations (PR) is emerging as the bridge to the twenty-first century in a figurative sense, then the literal link is the optic fiber. It denotes the expanding influence of technology as a channel of communication. Together—public relations with its persuasive messages and technology with its global reach—they create an even greater need for informed and ethical decision making on the part of current and future practitioners.

This book is intended to help bridge the expanse between yesterday and tomorrow as they relate to public relations. It is primarily designed for both undergraduate and graduate students interested in the techniques and applications of the field.

Public Relations Campaigns and Techniques serves the student by offering a way for the instructor to combine elements of public relations, technology, design, marketing, and advertising in an integrated approach. The *Instructor's Manual* will mirror the textbook by offering traditional components found in other guides as well as exercises sensitive to the ever-changing role and pace of public relations found on the hundreds of thousands of web sites worldwide.

We would like to thank the following reviewers: Jeanne Brittingham, University of Nebraska–Omaha; Erica Weintraub Austin, Washington State University; Melvin Sharpe, Ball State University; Jack Detweiler, University of Florida–Gainesville; Gerald Schwarty, G.S. Schwarty & Co., Inc.; Richard Nelson; and Karen Miller, University of Georgia.

FOREWORD

With greater recognition of public relations and a constantly growing need for public relations services, it's essential to have more useful textbook material to serve as a guide for current and future practitioners.

In recent years, there has been a series of books by public relations executives in which they recount their personal experiences. We've also seen a volume that's an exposé on one public relations firm. Meanwhile, there has been just a handful of new basic textbooks on public relations practice.

A survey undertaken by our firm of professors at business schools throughout the United States showed that a substantial number recognized the increasing importance of public relations for business. But most of them acknowledge that instruction on the use of public relations in business had not yet been included in their curricula.

At this time, the preponderance of education in the public relations field is carried out through public relations courses in universities around the country. Students are generally exposed to a broad liberal arts education in the first two years of college and then move into classes covering technical aspects of public relations practice during their junior and senior years. In some instances, a graduate degree is also offered.

There's still a burning need for public relations courses to penetrate the business schools of America. At the same time, professionals in the field have to continue to encourage officials at the most prestigious universities in the nation to include at least some optional courses on public relations.

It is in the context of the need for greater educational materials on the practice of public relations that I welcome this new textbook, *Public Relations Campaigns and Techniques: Building Bridges into the 21st Century,* written by Dr. Fran Matera, associate professor at the Walter Cronkite School of Journalism and Telecommunication at Arizona State University, and public relations counselor Ray J. Artigue, APR of Phoenix. It is designed for undergraduate-level instruction on public relations campaigns. The book is unique in that it includes commentaries at the conclusion of a number of chapters by noted public relations experts who are knowledgeable on the various subjects covered in the text.

As I review the nearly half-century since I got involved in the public relations business, I feel the greatest sense of gratification that we've come so far in terms of awareness of our field and that there is a constantly growing sense of the need for our services. The pioneers were Ivy Lee, John Hill, Carl Byoir, and the venerable Ed Bernays. But it was really after the Second World War that public relations began to show up on the table of organization in larger companies. Meanwhile, new firms like our own opened their doors and began to provide public relations services to companies, trade associations, and charitable institutions. There's been a continuing growth in the number of people in the business and the budgets provided for public relations. We're on our own unique growth curve: We're providing more services in more areas.

There's been an increase in specialization. Particularly in the larger public relations firms, there are teams of people organized into specialty groups in such areas as health, medical, and pharmaceutical issues; high technology; consumer products; finances; government relations; public affairs; business-to-business marketing; professional services; tourism; the environment; and crisis communications. There are also specialists in both media training and the production of videos and publications.

Another major development is internationalization. Multinational companies are increasingly looking for a public relations firm that can service their needs in all parts of the world. The leading U.S.-based firms have offices in Europe, Canada, Asia Pacific, and South America. They're opening up new offices in Central America, Eastern Europe, and China. Global service capability is essential today. But as we keep reminding our staff, you have to live by the old adage: "Think global, act local." You have to adapt to varied regulations in different parts of the world. It's essential to adjust copy to the type of product offered in a given country; you have to tailor campaigns to local needs.

There's been a gradual but clearly defined expansion of the challenge to public relations in the marketing field. Clients are looking to their public relations firm to come up with creative ideas that serve as a major promotional vehicle to be both employed in sales promotion and widely publicized through the public relations team. In our experience, there have been a number of occasions in which the public relations concept was so appealing that the client literally adopted it as the primary advertising vehicle!

As a longtime specialist in marketing public relations, I am greatly encouraged by the growing appreciation of the tangible values of public relations. One of our clients reported to management in an internal memo that news coverage of several products "is generating public awareness that has a positive impact on sales." Citing third-party credibility of the public relations message, he reported that after one national broadcast reporting on one of the company's products, there were numerous inquiries that directly led to sales. He cited a number of other comparable examples and added: "It has been demonstrated repeatedly that public relations is a cost-effective marketing tool that reaches broad, targeted audiences with specific product messages."

Another client in the medical field circulated an internal memo crediting the public relations campaign for positioning its new product in such a way that it achieved leadership in the category in the first days after introduction and has continued to gain market share with each new public relations campaign subsequently introduced.

A chief executive of U.S. operations of a Japanese company told us before returning to headquarters in Tokyo after a decade in the United States that our firm had put the company and its products "on the map in the United States." Our late client Charlie Lubin of Sara Lee Bakeries often reported publicly that "public relations was worth one thousand times the advertising" in getting Sara Lee's message to consumer and trade audiences. Dr. A. J. F. O'Reilly, chairman and chief executive officer of H. J. Heinz Company, told his communications people: "Dynamic companies are increasingly using imaginative public relations to give their products a competitive edge where advertising and promotion suffer from the law of diminishing returns."

Political candidates have long recognized the power of public relations. Ross Perot became an overnight "brand name" through interviews on national cable and TV networks and articles in national magazines. Bill Clinton emerged as a new national figure by taking local media interviews and even appearing on MTV. He held town meetings and stopped to greet people on the street when he jogged. He emerged as a fresh voice with new ideas and went on to win the White House twice.

It's my own prediction that we've only just begun to see how far public relations can go. Its roots are firmly planted; its continuing growth is inevitable. Its prospects are rosier than ever as we move toward the end of the decade and into the twenty-first century. In recent years, there have been unfortunate incidents that have served to remind those of us who practice in the public relations field that our only limitation on future growth may be excessive greed and the loosening of our commitment to the highest standards of ethical practice. We've seen representations of dubious and controversial clients, a reversion to the discredited use of front organizations, and a falling into the gray area of serving political and commercial interests where conflict of interest is inevitable. These developments led to a drumbeat of negative coverage, both on top network TV programs and in leading newspapers, focusing on public relations as selling out to rich, unsavory clients and buying influence. It's very gratifying to me that we seem to have passed this critical period in the history of public relations. We realize that we don't have to be "hired guns"; we can make choices with regard to clients we want to represent. There is a renewed commitment that we're going to abide by our own code of ethics and maintain the highest moral standards of service.

I'm a great optimist with regard to the future of public relations. We're attracting more quality people. We must continue to broaden our horizons, build our expertise, and commit ourselves to making a real contribution. We're engaged in one of the most stimulating and most interesting professional fields. Its future is unlimited.

Daniel J. Edelman, Founder, Chairman, & CEO
Edelman Public Relations Worldwide

1 Public Relations in the Twenty-First Century

Bridging Yesterday and Tomorrow

CHAPTER OUTLINE

World Climate
Mass Media Climate
Evolution of PR

CHAPTER OBJECTIVES

When you have completed this chapter, you should be able to:

- Understand the challenges/opportunities PR practitioners face
- Recognize the effect of organizational structures on the workplace
- Know why internal publics are increasingly important
- Identify new global markets
- Identify bases of power

The new millennium, like the old, offers a unique array of opportunities. No doubt the twenty-first century will be fraught with challenges not even imagined. Tomorrow's professionals will benefit from a range of resources unavailable to yesterday's PR practitioners, if they do their homework.

The tangible benefits of the new century will be technology (particularly data retrieval and delivery systems), fiber optics, new media, and a well-defined body of knowledge. Nearly two decades ago, veteran practitioner Betsy Ann Plank predicted that PR practitioners would "capture the new communications technologies," which would in turn expand their influence within their organizations. However, this did not happen as quickly as she had hoped.

In the early 1980s, researchers found limited use for computer technology. Bleecker and Lento pointed out that "managers, marketers and accountants within corporations make daily use of communications technology. How much respect can a public relations practitioner, whose work is communications, expect from them if he or she refuses to take advantage of the very advances that could transform the PR function?"

Change still moves at a crawl, according to Anderson and Reagan. In their study of practitioners and their uses of technology, they conclude that "use of such job-enhancing technologies as online data bases, electronic bulletin boards, computer conferencing and spreadsheet programs is low." They suggest further research into why practitioners are more like laggards than leaders in technology adoption. "The costs involved in adopting new technologies are substantial. But the real cost to the practitioner is losing his or her competitive edge to those who have mastered computer-age technology." As late as 1994, a survey by Gorman of the top fifty public relations agencies in the United States found that computer technology was primarily used for word processing; when online database research was employed, it was to monitor breaking news and client press coverage.

The 1970's blue sky promise of a "wired nation" where information is at the fingertips of every man, woman, and child is now feasible, affordable, and realistic. But it's a fact that information does not equal knowledge. And perhaps knowledge, and how it is conveyed, will best define the PR practitioner of the new century.

According to James Quella, vice chairman of Mercer Management Consulting, because of the competitive nature of surviving in business, knowledge has become a highly valued asset. "Knowledge is information that adds value. True knowledge management . . . collects, codifies and disseminates critical information about customers, competitors and internal processes to support short-term operations, execution decisions and long-term strategic decisions." He notes that, in the future, speed and knowledge, not size and scale, will be the gold standard. "There will be a premium on a person's willingness to change and the ability to learn. With so much more information and knowledge available, the PR professional will be more tapped in to what is going on and less restricted by the accessibility of senior leadership." However, he cautions there could be a downside to this deluge of data. It may make it harder to determine where to tap in and what to say to the outside world.

The intangibles, such as public opinion, will emerge as the change agents of tomorrow. If this is true, then consensus building among those target audiences, both internal and external, will become the engine that drives public relations.

This "people" focus is not new. Warren Bennis, a communications theorist, believes that an organization is its people. However, this approach was overlooked in the Industrial Revolution's headlong embrace of Max Weber's bureaucracy model with its fixed division of labor, a hierarchy of offices, and separation of personal from official property and rights.

Weber believed this rational approach would solve problems. However, Bennis dubs this structure as one of "organizations without people." Bennis predicts that the most advanced organizations would move toward postbureaucratic forms, away from hierarchical arrangements, "beyond bureaucracy," or "from bureaucracy to ad-hocracy." Scott writes that "futurists and social commentators such as Bennis and . . . Toffler agree that the new organizational forms require highly educated, self-directed, and flexible participants in order to function."

It appears that they are right. "Employees are taking over the workplace, and corporate communicators who don't abet the revolution may wind up keeping their jobs, but losing their budgets and staff. Hierarchical structures are crumbling. The explicit and even implicit contracts between employer and employee are being rewritten," says Matthew Gonring, former director of corporate communications at USG Corporation, now managing partner at Arthur Andersen and Company in Chicago. Another practitioner writes, "Times have clearly changed. Company after company has come to the realization that employees who are well-informed and encouraged are the key to survival in an increasingly competitive environment."

Bridging the gap between workers and employers with employee involvement (EI) programs has become a critical goal. EI programs empower employees while satisfying demands for a commitment to organizational goals. "Maintaining or winning back the loyalty and commitment of employees—and gaining their cooperation— . . . will be the greatest challenge facing corporate communicators in the next few years," says Alvie Smith, former director of corporate communications at General Motors. However, a commitment from management is needed for programs and policies to work. A study by the International Association of Business Communicators (IABC) Research Foundation found that the corporate culture of an organization determines its commitment; programs flourish in a participatory environment. "The participative culture . . . is characterized by teamwork, and shared power and decision-making with work guided by common goals and the organization as a whole open to new ideas," Gonring writes.

Many PR counselors now think "small is good," regardless of the size of the organization. John Graham, chairman and CEO of Fleishman-Hillard, recommends PR firms make their employees a priority to avert staff turnover, develop a set of corporate values, and watch the bottom line but don't be obsessed with it.

Wisdom and experience have taught us that it is unreasonable to assume individuals can make decisions bereft of any emotion, with no thought to the consequences of their actions. In fact, Thomas Harrison, director of the public relations division of the Russ Reid Company and a former vice president with Daniel J. Edelman, writes that "Nonprofits are noticing that corporate America is responding to concerns of the marketplace in a new way. . . . This reawakening of concern for humanity, the environment, and the quality of life is a reflection of something much larger happening."

This human relations perspective is as practical as it is altruistic. It recognizes that it is the meshing of human cogs in a corporate wheel that makes the organization work. Burger King, Coca-Cola, and Coors are spending millions annually on literacy and education programs. McDonald's operates a network of more than 125 Ronald McDonald Houses worldwide, which provide care and comfort for terminally ill children and their families. Ultimately, these programs show up on the bottom line, both tangibly and intangibly, as increased profits and customer loyalty—elements that construct favorable public opinion.

This "construction" is aided by public relations, advertising, direct marketing, promotions, and a host of other tactics. In the past, these areas have functioned individually or in combination; this is because some organizational charts regard communications as a discrete function, an afterthought. In other cases, advertising and public relations firms have tended to protect their own turf and have suggested solutions using methods with which they themselves are most familiar. "Integrated communications boils down to delivering the right messages to the right people through the right medium to elicit the desired response," writes James Foster, president and CEO of Brouillard/LGFE. Although this seems ideal and obvious, Foster points out that integrated campaigns are not common.

However, if corporations are going to work smarter (not harder) and get the job done more efficiently, more effectively, and at a lower cost with fewer people, then integrated campaigns would appear to be, if not the best solution, at least a front-runner.

World Climate

The contemporary world milieu is characterized by much higher levels of interdependence and complexity than have ever existed. This has led to a much higher level of uncertainty or turbulence. Organizations, governments, and individuals alike sense what Emery and Trist call "the ground in motion." McCann and Selsky identify another environment, one they term hyperturbulence. It describes a situation in which instability is so dangerously accelerated that it has overwhelmed the capacities of some members of the environment to adapt and threatens the survival of the rest. Examples of this are the National Aeronautics and Space Administration's reorganization after the *Challenger* disaster and Johnson & Johnson's handling of the cyanide-laced Tylenol deaths. In each case, a period of great instability occurred prior to the actual or feared collapse of the entire entity.

What made the difference? Absorbing uncertainty through collaboration and reordering resources. This tactic allows information managers to impose structure upon and clarify ambiguous events, to provide direction, and to allow decision making. It also gives rise to effective communication and defines reality. This, in turn, creates conditions for action.

Edward Stanton, chairman and CEO of Manning, Selvage and Lee, is in charge of the firm's worldwide operations. He says that "we are moving into a stage of worldwide consolidation, in which the largest firms, and the small niche firms, are expected to be the survivors, along with specialty agencies." To be a survivor then, public relations must reduce uncertainty, embrace true globalization, and adapt to the sensitivities of different nationalities and of different groups within nations. Stanton believes this can only be accomplished through worldwide, integrated communications—a comprehensive, cross-cultural plan that tailors its messages to myriad publics.

Public relations is uniquely positioned to balance the needs and benefits of the world's audiences while taking the initiative and striking down at least some barriers to communication. By involving practitioners in foreign countries and by mastering technology, languages, and customs, PR can galvanize its role in any new world order. It can shift the balance of power, so to speak, in its own favor by filling a communications void. Power has been defined as a reservoir of potential influence by Cartwright and Zander and is identified by three elements:

- The degree of uncertainty in the situation
- The importance of the activity to the larger organization
- The prominence of the individual actor who has a "stake in the decision"

Patchen writes that the relationship between uncertainty and power is related to "the kind of uncertainty upon which depends the life of the organization." These arguments are consistent with Hickson, who stresses that it is the coping with uncertainty that is the real basis of power—a concise and precise job description of a public relations professional. Given the criteria for increasing power, complex global relationships provide public relations practitioners with unique opportunities to identify common ground and build consensus.

"Power imbalances not only undermine trust, they can inhibit both the weaker and to a lesser extent the stronger party, such that they do not advance their respective views in a clear and forceful manner," Walton writes. This environment could also elevate the profession to the point at which PR practitioners "win a place at top management's table," PR counselor Davis Young claims.

PRoActive

Curriculum

"The newly formed Commission on Public Relations Education will provide curricular recommendations to prepare students for careers in the 21st Century." This article asserts that there will be three phenomena that will directly influence future PR practice—societal, technological, and professional.

Societal

The role and function of public relations will be impacted by societal changes that will occur for a host of reasons, but particularly by the social impact of communication and transportation technology. All practice will become international and multicultural because society will have become global. These societal changes will affect the role and function of U.S. practitioners in at least two ways:

- They will need to satisfactorily nurture for the U.S.-based organizations, not only a greater number of public relationships, but also relationships that are far more complex because of cultural and related factors.
- They will have to reconcile norms and expectations of multinational organizations—helping institutions as well as people worldwide to

resolve problems associated with rapid and dramatic social change, including the creation of new publics that will inevitably and irrevocably emerge within a global society.

Technological

Most societal changes will revolve around information and how it will be communicated instantaneously through time and space. Technological advances will affect the role and function of U.S. practitioners in at least two ways:

- As media to be understood and to be used effectively in communicating with a range of publics.
- As intervening variables affecting—in the most McLuhanesque sense—an organization's relationships with existing and new publics.

Professional

While an able and growing body of scholars is contributing to the literature of public relations, research is still minuscule compared to that of other professional occupations. The number of Ph.D. degree–granting institutions in public relations also remains insufficient.

Source: Adapted From Dean Kruckeberg. "The Future of PR Education: Some Recommendations." *Public Relations Review* 24 (Summer 1998): 235–248.

To do so, however, means that practitioners must confront reality, warns practitioner and editor Philip Lesly. "We in public relations could be on the threshold of a boom—if we prepare ourselves and use our persuasive skills to steer the frame of mind of our populace toward discipline, restraint, recognition of demands for better performance—in other words, toward reality."

Chester Burger, counsel at Arnold & Truitt in New York, cites what he believes will be "significant signals" in heralding change in the next century. The first is a science and technology signal that will alter where we work. Thanks to inexpensive data transmission via fiber optics and corporate downsizing, organizations will reduce their need for space, thereby encouraging working at home. Selecting precise channels of communication will be possible, making postal and messenger services obsolete. Lastly, Burger believes the mass media will disappear. Many mass media researchers agree with his last assessment.

The potential audience for PR's messages is enormous. The creation of the European Economic Community in 1992 created a market of about 320 million people, 7 percent of the world's population. January 1999 ushered in the introduction of the Euro dollar, one currency balancing the exchange rate of twelve nations. Eastern Europe's open markets swell population estimates to 520 million and a gross national product of $5 trillion, more than double that of Japan. The North American Free Trade Agreement (NAFTA) involving the United States, Canada, and Mexico is changing the face of our domestic marketplace, specifically privatization. With the transition of the former Soviet Union to, at present, capitalism and democracy, messages once manipulated and compressed may now switch from propagandizing to publicizing.

"New" Europe

According to Susan Fry Bovet, "Stepped-up demand for cross-border public relations from clients both within and outside Europe has increased competition among worldwide firms, global networks and independents and enhanced opportunities for all. Growth potential is emerging primarily from health care, consumer products and business-to-business communication." Privatization is also a prime target as industries, at one time run by the governments, need public relations assistance to attract investors and foreign dollars in addition to learning how to communicate effectively with employees and external publics. Among the European Community, France, Germany, and the United Kingdom retain the most clout, each exerting influence over political and financial policies. The media will remain a major concern for practitioners in the "new" Europe in that the levels of sophistication vary widely (see Exhibit 1.1). Richard Edelman, president and chief operating officer of Edelman Public Relations Worldwide, suggests that "Narrowcasting is something we can learn from Europe. Wire the home and lease space to commercial ventures."

Latin America

Privatization is also emerging as a means for economic growth in the free market regions of Latin America—Mexico, Argentina, Brazil, Chile, and Venezuela. Many believe that Latin America will be the success story of the era, leading the way for public relations to grow at unprecedented levels in order to help reach a market that by some estimates will exceed 500

EXHIBIT **1.1**

**U.S. and European Corporate Clients
Share Three Major Concerns**

As they look to the year 2000 and beyond, corporate public relations directors surveyed on both sides of the Atlantic share many common concerns. Global competition, government regulation, and environmental issues will have an impact on the overseas operations of both U.S. and European companies. The 1992 survey conducted by Fleishman-Hillard, Inc., a public relations firm based in St. Louis, Missouri, reported key findings:

- Global competition, government regulation, and the environment ranked in the top five when 113 European and 80 U.S. practitioners were asked to identify issues that would have a major impact on their operations.
- U.S. executives also viewed a single, unified European market and the opening of Eastern Europe as significant business influences, the survey found. European clients considered trade protectionism and currency exchange rates as significant issues affecting their operations in the United States.
- Two-thirds of all respondents thought the worldwide economic situation would have the greatest impact on global competition. Technological innovation also ranked high with both groups surveyed.
- About one in five (22 percent) U.S. executives and three of ten Europeans said the greatest obstacle in conducting transatlantic business is understanding and breaking through cultural barriers.
- Forty-six percent of all respondents believed public relations will become more strategic and international in scope and involved both in investor/government/media relations and with other groups in their companies.

Source: Adapted from Susan Fry Baret. "Trends in the 'New' Europe." *Public Relations Journal* 49(9) (September 1993): 18–24.

million people by 2010. Raymond Kotcher, senior partner, president, and COO of Ketchum Public Relations Worldwide, writes that "Economic growth, democratization, a changing media environment, and rising consumerism are creating tremendous public relations opportunities in Latin America." A proposed thirty-nation Free Trade Area of the Americas may mean "the twenty-first century will be marked by free trade among all nations of the Western Hemisphere."

As with Europe, media channels are a concern; however, many U.S.-based conglomerates are making inroads. Kotcher notes that "media in Latin America are increasingly sophisticated," with an emergence of specialized media including trade publications. Technology is breaking down the geographic barrier to communication. Satellite dishes and cable TV bring foreign programs to the area. NBC and Fox have committed their resources to establishing networks there. *Fortune, Time, Newsweek,* and *Business Week* sell briskly to influentials in the region. Sharlach correctly notes that it is these "highly educated . . . business people" who will be important media targets for many public relations programs in the future (see Exhibit 1.2).

EXHIBIT 1.2

Doing Public Relations in Latin America

- Work with local people who know the market and the media in the country you want to reach.
- Use indigenous translators. Materials must be sensitive to cultural differences and subtle linguistic changes.

- Slow down. Don't plan to rush out of a lunch meeting after an hour for your next appointment.
- Be sure you have a concrete assignment, with budgets and deadlines confirmed in writing, before you start work.

Source: Adapted from Jeffrey R. Sharlach, "A New Era in Latin America." *Public Relations Journal* 49(9) (September 1993): 26–28.

Mass Media Climate

The mass media have long served as the information conduits to target audiences. However, the latter decades of the twentieth century have redefined Americans' sense of credible information sources. Media are no longer confined to network television, radio stations, and newspapers. In addition to cable, there are satellite systems and telephone companies (telcos), which can deliver voice, data, and video signals simultaneously over the same fiber-optic cable.

As long ago as 1972, Smith listed some uses of cable communication's "powerful technology"—home library retrieval, facsimile, delivery of mail, crime detection and prevention, and the reduced need for travel as well as "religious programs, school activities, county fairs, fundraising drives, sports, cultural events, political debates, public hearings, school board meetings, children's programs and daily variety shows."

In 1989, Markoff wrote that visionaries foresee such things as home banking, electronic mail, picture telephones, and customized television feeds becoming standard home fare. John Burgess, in an article in the *Washington Post,* suggested that fiber-optic lines will become "a network of 'information highways' crisscrossing the country, conveying commercial and private data galore in the same way that asphalt arteries convey goods and services." Others predicted colleges without walls. Some of these benefits have materialized; others remain elusive.

Television

Post–World War II prosperity and bulging advertising revenues fueled the television network news machine. Network news grew in sophistication, budgets, news staffs, foreign bureaus, correspondents, and news-gathering technologies. At one time, network television news ranked as the most used and most credible source of information for the American public. But by the mid-1980s, new owners had taken control of the networks and "imposed strong, bottom-line directives which led to a massive number of firings," according to Small. "Those giddy days of yore when [ratings] were in the low 90 percentiles" were gone. By 1993, network evening news ratings had dropped to 60 percent; by 1995, viewership had slipped to 48 percent and by 1997 had declined again, to 42 percent.

News departments were not immune to the budget cuts. As the networks' ability to reach audiences plummeted, so did ad revenues, taking many news operations with them. "Newsroom costs are being scrutinized in ways that are altering the newsgathering process," a *Broadcasting* article asserted. The most serious changes are pooled coverage and the shrinking or disappearance of domestic and foreign news bureaus. "In some cases, that has translated into a lone correspondent and/or producer in a city that once housed a full bureau. Technicians are being switched from fulltime to freelance or are being replaced by free-lancers." These changes have taken place even though 88 percent of the U.S. public turns to TV as their source of news about national and international issues, according to a 1997 study conducted by the Pew Research Center for the People & the Press.

Cable, Wireless, and DBS

In mid-1991, the Federal Communication Commission's Office of Plans and Policy predicted a gloomy future for broadcast TV. "The broadcast industry has suffered an irreversible long-term decline in audience and revenue shares, which will continue through the current decade." The reason? According to the report, it's cable television. That medium serves 65 percent of U.S. homes, according to Nielsen Media Research, and continues to attract audiences and advertisers. In 1994, the National Cable Television Association reported that there were more than 11,351 cable systems in the nation, compared to just 2,490 in 1970. Three years later, the number grew to 11,800 systems serving 34,000 communities. By 1996, the U.S. Bureau of the Census said 68.8 percent of TV households watched cable, generating in excess of $25 billion in basic and pay revenues and $5 billion in advertising. "The change in fortunes in broadcasting and cable will likely force massive cost-cutting by networks, affiliates and independents," the FCC conceded.

As network descends, cable ascends. By 1991, Ted Turner's Cable News Network staff members "soared from its original 225 to more than 1,700." While networks were consolidating or closing bureaus, CNN spent $2 million in 1991 to open 3 new offices, bringing the network's bureaus to 27, domestic and worldwide. In 1999, CNN bureaus number 32—9 in major U.S. cities and 23 at international sites. CNN and CNNI together are seen in more than 170 million households in 210 countries and territories, with distribution to 70 million domestic and 110 million international households. Cable television has launched an array of basic and pay channels, including ESPN, C-SPAN, the Weather Channel, Headline News, CNBC, and MTV.

Unlike its hardwired counterpart, a wireless cable system uses a microwave transmitter to send video programming to antennas of individual subscribers and offers similar programs to those an audience would see via cable. Currently, the Wireless Cable Association reports there are 252 systems available.

In 1994, the direct broadcast satellite (DBS) introduced yet another way to receive programming transmitting: through high-power satellites to small antennas on the ground. Mid-power DBS systems also transmit via satellite but require bigger land-bound antennas.

Radio

Of the 12,227 radio stations operating in the United States at the end of 1997, 4,762 were commercial AMs. The lion's share of stations were on the FM dial, with 5,542 commercial and 1,923 noncommercial FMs. News and news/talk formats nationwide numbered 809 and 1,083, respectively; talk was king on just 686 stations. Americans ranked the country music format as their favorite, with adult contemporary music close behind. In 1997, the Radio Advertising Bureau estimated that 99 percent of U.S. homes were radio-equipped, with 70 percent of the audience listening to FM. This means that although the medium is portable and inexpensive; music saturates the airwaves. Radio extended its reach via the Internet in all 50 states, the District of Columbia, Puerto Rico, Guam, the Virgin Islands, and Canada. The key to the development of Internet radio was the 1995 arrival of "streaming." Before streaming, or audio in real time, a listener would wait several minutes to download an audio file before it could be played. Now the user can click on a word or icon to access a program or station. The audio is then brought directly into the user's computer where it can be played, rewound, or fast-forwarded. Most often, Internet radio is used by existing radio stations to reach a new or geographically broader audience. However, there are cases where Internet radio stations exist solely on the Internet. Their low start-up costs coupled with no regulation by the FCC allow virtually anyone with encoding software and a Web server to create a radio station and broadcast worldwide.

Newspapers

Print media sailed into its own rough waters. In 1946, there were 1,763 dailies; by 1992, the number had slid to 1,586, with adult readership dropping from 78 percent in 1970 to 62.6 percent. Newspaper employment also dipped, according to estimates by the U.S. Bureau of Labor Statistics. The number of weekly newspapers decreased from 8,174 in 1960 to 7,417 in 1992. Minority representation on staffs accounted for just 18 percent of the U.S. daily newspaper workforce, and major dailies suffered from sagging ad revenues and subscriptions. Tabloids and metros alike stopped the presses forever. By 1997, 1,516 dailies were published, with a total circulation of about 63 million; there were about 7,400 weekly papers, averaging 7,500 each. Magazine publishing increased from 2,500 in the mid-1980s to more than 4,000 by 1998. Daily newspapers also ventured into online versions, complementing rather than duplicating their print news product and generating a new revenue stream by charging for online database and archive searches of the stories.

Telcos

In July 1991, the seven Regional Bell Operating Companies (RBOCs), a result of the breakup of American Telephone & Telegraph (AT&T), won the right to enter into the information services business. This action put the telcos into direct competition with cable and broadcast television outside their service areas. A National Association of Broadcasters' response to the decision by U.S. District Judge Harold Greene said that "it will clearly have broad legal, regulatory, legislative and business implications." That was correct. In the decade of the 1990s, telephone companies such as USWest are entering the cable business, and cable companies like Cox Communications are vying for telephone and Internet access customers.

PRoSpeak
Public Relations in the Twenty-First Century

The twenty-first century is here. What this means to the practice of public relations can be expected to change continually, not only with the arrival of the millennium but also with the passing of each year, each month, and even each day, as our society evolves and unfolds. Changes in the way we communicate and relate as a people have been profoundly altered by technology. And the rate of these changes surely will continue to accelerate in the twenty-first century.

Marshall McLuhan was often described as twenty-five years ahead of his time when he wrote: "The new electronic interdependence recreates the world in the image of a global village."

He was certainly light-years ahead of our first president, George Washington, who said in his farewell address at the close of the eighteenth century:

> Against the insidious wiles of foreign influence . . . the jealousy of a free people ought to be constantly awake, since history and experience prove that foreign influence is one of the most baneful foes of republican government.

Washington's view dominated the American experience until 1945: Distracted by populating and developing a vast continent, distant from foreign languages and cultures, lacking much colonial experience—America's world role did not really begin until the end of the Second World War.

Were George Washington here at the end of the twentieth century, his use of the term "foreign" in a modern context would seem less clear or relevant. But our first president didn't have a hot line or *Air Force One;* he didn't relax in a hideaway office in the old Executive Office Building watching CNN, or send e-mail to John Adams in Boston. He never counted down a space shot, imagined men on the moon, or thought of this fragile planet, spaceship Earth, as an electronic global village.

Yet Mr. Washington would surely recognize that our nation and our world are in transition. The changes in America are pronounced and profound, reaching from Wall Street to Main Street, from the

James E. Arnold
Chairman and CEO
Arnold & Truitt, New York

shop floor to the board room. Consider a few relevant statistics:

- 10 percent of our workforce is employed by non-U.S. owned firms.
- 50 percent of all purchases in the U.S. are from non-U.S. companies.
- Every public relations professional today uses products or services from outside the U.S.—videotape technology, or personal computers, or fax machines—each of which represents lost or transferred jobs from local communities.

Today we are told in books, articles, and speeches about the communications revolution, the eventual convergence of national cultures, and ultimately the melding of consumer tastes and aspirations. We are reminded of the growth of satellite and cable television, the emergence of interactive television, McDonald's in Moscow, Pepsi Cola in India, Coca Cola and American Express everywhere.

(continued)

PRoSpeak Continued

We're told that needs and wants are being both homogenized and globalized, that the age of the global market and brand is with us. The twenty-first century is at hand. We are no longer citizens of Hometown, U.S.A., but citizens of Planet Earth. It's a wonderful life.

But hold on there, fellow practitioners of public relations. Our world is in transition: not to an easier and simpler world but rather an increasingly complicated and complex one. It will be increasingly possible to communicate round the world instantly, but in many other aspects it will become increasingly difficult and complex to practice the profession of public relations in the next century.

As public relations professionals we are thrilled that the communications revolution makes possible simple global telephone calls; real-time television broadcasts from Tiananmen Square, the Berlin Wall or Iraq; or even fax machines that wake up to receive transmissions in the night.

But these are the media of communication—the hardware. And it is true that the hardware—satellites, television, fiber-optic cable, and all the other wonderful breakthroughs—have greatly improved the speed, accuracy, and ease of communication. It is now possible for millions to receive the same message simultaneously.

But what of the message? Will millions interpret it in the same way? Will they understand it? I am not so concerned about getting the message delivered, but I am concerned about the failure to understand, to be understood, to get through, to make sense, to reach agreement. This is the "software" aspect of the communications revolution—the message, the interpretation of the message, and the response of the audience to the message.

It is probably the case that the greater the extension of communications hardware, the more complex and challenging the role of the public relations counselor. It is far more difficult to use subtlety, nuance, inflection, inference, or metaphor to an audience of several million than to a far smaller audience whose minds you know well.

We are entering the global village and we are right to look forward to it with great expectations. But there is no such place as "Global." People do not drink "Global" wines or admire "Global's" beautiful beaches. Great wines and beaches will continue to belong to countries, regions, and hometowns. That's where real people live. And those real people are our audiences—to reach, influence, and motivate.

Public relations skills will be in great demand in the twenty-first century because ours is a profession that focuses on audiences and aims to affect behavior over time. Our profession must transcend communications hardware and reach for the hopes, fears, wants, and wishes of each individual person we would influence. We rely not merely on the media but all the attendant knowledge and sensitivity required to make a communication personal and most effective.

In 2000 and beyond, public relations will be a renewed profession, with new people, new ideas, new technologies, new leaders. The words of Arthur W. Page, AT&T's first vice president of public relations, will continue to light the way for those who follow us into the future:

> All business in a democratic society begins with public permission and exists by public approval. If that be true, it follows that business should be cheerfully willing to tell the public what its policies are, what it is doing, and what it hopes to do. This seems to me practically a duty.

Evolution of PR

When Edward Bernays penned *Crystallizing Public Opinion* in 1927, he coined the term public relations and set in motion forces that would evolve into what he called "a vital tool of adjustment, interpretation, and integration between individuals, groups, and society. . . . We are enmeshed with our world through a two-way process. . . . Through this process, we come to understand or misunderstand the world around us. And through it we are understood or misunderstood." The "father of PR" supported a multidisciplinary, cross-cultural approach to the craft decades ago. Yet in practice, the field would not approach this concept until now. The nephew of psychoanalyst Sigmund Freud, Bernays discovered the benefits of combining principles of anthropology, sociology, and psychology to arrive at solutions for his clients.

Modern-day PR evolution began in the postwar years of the 1930s when publicity reigned. Its practitioners came from the ranks of newspapers where they plied the media on behalf of their clients and counted clips. This seat-of-the-pants approach later gave way to counseling functions and strategic planning as well as incorporating specialists, lawyers, accountants, scientists, and government officials, who are now selecting PR as a second career.

However, the activities associated with PR remain unchanged and have been articulated by the Public Relations Society of America:

- Publicity
- Communication
- Public affairs
- Issues management
- Government relations
- Financial public relations
- Community relations
- Industry relations
- Minority relations
- Advertising
- Press agentry
- Promotion
- Media relations
- Propaganda

Public relations is still about performance but "will depend on understanding and tackling the big social, economic and political issues in our communities, in the nation and around the globe," writes Robert Dilenschneider, former president and CEO of Hill and Knowlton, who now runs the Dilenschneider Group, Inc., in New York. Businesses will spend more time analyzing information on a continual basis "to launch first-strike programs." Knowledge will focus on the need for sampling and perhaps pioneering the use of "artificial intelligence in solving qualitative problems."

James Dowling, former president and CEO of Burson-Marsteller and now managing director of its Latin American operations in Miami, says that practitioners of the future must learn to work in a new environment characterized by five trends:

1. Creation of new and improbable strategic alliances
2. Development of new multinational corporate cultures
3. Multiple interactive solutions
4. Reregulation and government intervention
5. Changing business landscape (which means continuation of corporate restructuring requiring cultivation of employee commitment to the organization)

Innovations have redefined, and will continue to redefine, the role of the media in public relations. As the world gets smaller, the Roman maxim *"vox populi, vox dei"* (the voice of the people is the voice of God) takes on added meaning. Perhaps the public relations industry must accord itself the status of a "special public." Cutlip, Center, and Broom define a special public as a segment of the population that can mobilize its forces to generate change. Normally, special publics promote action on issues by means of boycotting, protesting, or voting. However, the definition could be expanded to include promoting changes in old opinions and creating new ones on behalf of clients. In this way, public relations, in tandem with controlled and uncontrolled media, could set the public agenda and influence public opinion.

How will these changes affect the relationship between public relations and the media? Perhaps for the better. The walls that have created an adversarial relationship between PR and media practitioners may come tumbling down in the future. Smaller, less experienced staffs and fewer resources may force journalists to reconsider their assumptions about public relations practitioners. It may turn out that market forces have conferred on PR practitioners a gatekeeper status in that the information-gathering process and methods of dissemination in the future will rest with organizations that can get to the public directly without media middlemen. As Eugene Marlow writes, "Electronic public relations may be the *way* public relations gets done. . . . It is not a matter of whether public relations professionals use electronic media or not in the future; it will be a matter of *how well* they use these media."

Summary

Public relations practitioners in the twenty-first century must acquire skill in using technology while at the same time balancing their knowledge with multicultural sensitivity in order to reach global audiences. Changes in the marketplace and advances in science and technology will propel PR practitioners to the forefront where they must exercise applied social science to retain their effectiveness. Dilenschneider also cites the need for wise PR counsel that is sensitive to social responsibility and "to convince corporate leaders that . . . they need to restrain their pursuit of even larger profits by assuming greater responsibility for the lives their businesses affect." Adams concludes that ethical behavior is where PR practitioners should focus their efforts "transcending mere persuasion and sometimes willing to supercede what's in the organization's best interests."

QUESTIONS

1. What are some examples of a turbulent environment?

2. What elements does integrated communication encompass?

3. What implications does "caller ID" pose?

4. How will technology affect the way practitioners communicate with their publics?

READINGS

William Adams, "Resolutions for the New Millenium." *The Public Relations Strategist* vol 5, no. 1 (Spring 1999); 27–29.

Ronald Anderson and Joey Reagan. "Practitioner Roles and Uses of New Technologies." *Journalism Quarterly* 69, no. 1 (Spring 1992): 156–165.

Warren Bennis. "Leadership Theory and Administrative Behavior." *Administrative Science Quarterly* 4 (December 1959): 259–301.

_____ *Changing Organizations.* New York: Mc-Graw-Hill, 1966.

Warren Bennis and Philip Slater. *The Temporary Society.* New York: Harper & Row, 1968.

Edward Bernays. *Crystallizing Public Opinion.* 1927. New York: Boni and Liveright, 192.

Susan Fry Bovet. "Trends in the 'New' Europe." *Public Relations Journal* 49, no. 9 (September 1993): 18–24.

Broadcasting & Cable Yearbook 1998, vol. 1. New Providence, NJ: A Broadcasting & Cable/R. R. Bowker Publication.

Robert L. Dilenschneider. "A 'Make-or-Break' Decade." *Public Relations Journal* 46, no. 1 (January 1990): 7.

_____. "Public Relations for the New Millenium." *Public Relations Strategist,* 5, no. 1 (Spring, 1999): 12–17.

Fred E. Emery and Eric L. Trist. "The Causal Texture of Organizational Environments." *Human Relations* 18 (February 1965): 21–32.

Dan Forbush and Patricia A. Foster. "Building Coherent Communications." *Case Currents* 16, no. 3 (1990): 44–46.

James Foster. "Working Together: How Companies Are Integrating Their Corporate Communications." *Public Relations Journal* 46, no. 9 (September 1990): 18–19.

Donald Godfrey and Frederic Leigh. *Historical Dictionary of American Radio.* Westport, CT: Greenwood Press, 1998.

Julie Gorman. Uses and Appeals of Communication Techniques in the Practice of Public Relations: A Survey of the 50 Largest U.S. Public Relations Agencies. (An applied project for the Master of Mass Communication, Arizona State University,

Walter Cronkite School of Journalism and Telecommunication, 1995.)

John Graham. "A 10-Point Plan to Manage for the Future." *Public Relations Journal* 47, no. 6 (June 1991): 39–40.

William A. Hachten. *The Troubles of Journalism: A Critical Look at What's Right and Wrong with the Press.* Mahwah, NJ: Lawrence Erlbaum Associates, 1998.

David Hickson, C. R. Hinings, C. A. Lee, R. E. Schneck, and J. M. Pennings. "A Strategic Contingencies Theory of Interorganizational Power." *Administrative Science Quarterly* 16 (June 1971): 216–229.

Raymond L. Kotcher. "The Changing Role of PR in Latin America." *Public Relations Tactics* 5, no. 3 (March 1998): 26.

Philip Lesly. "Public Relations in the Turbulent New Human Climate." *Public Relations Review* 17, no. 1 (Spring 1991): 1–8.

"The Management of Knowledge: New Key to Growth." *Public Relations Strategist* (Summer 1998): 1, 33–35.

Eugene Marlow. *Electronic Public Relations.* Belmont, CA: Wadsworth Publishing Company, 1996.

Joseph McCann and John Selsky. "Hyperturbulence and the Emergence of Type 5 Environments." *Academy of Management Review* 9 (1984): 460–470.

Martin Patchen. *The Choice of Wage Comparisons.* Englewood Cliffs, NJ: Prentice-Hall, 1961.

W. Richard Scott. *Organizations: Rational. Natural, and Open Systems.* Englewood Cliffs, NJ: Prentice-Hall, 1981.

Jeffrey R. Sharlach. "A New Era in Latin America." *Public Relations Journal* (September 1993): 26–28.

Max Weber. *The Theory of Social and Economic Organizations,* ed. A. H. Henderson and Talcott Parsons. Glencoe, IL: Free Press, 1947.

DEFINITIONS

bureaucracy: Weber's bureaucratic organization is characterized by a fixed division of labor; a hierarchy of offices; a set of rules governing performance; a separation of personal from official property and rights; a selection of employees based on technical qualifications; and employment viewed as a career by workers.

human relations perspective: It recognizes that individual workers are complex beings with multiple motives and values who are driven by feelings and facts. Mayo describes them as not behaving like individual, isolated actors but as members of a social group in which loyalties outweigh self-interest.

hyperturbulence: McCann and Selsky describe this as a situation in which instability is so dangerously accelerated that it can overwhelm the capacity of the environment to adapt, thereby threatening its survival.

integrated communications: The evolution of communication strategies that effectively and efficiently blend public relations, advertising, marketing, sales promotion, and direct promotion.

Regional Bell Operating Company (RBOC): There are seven in the United States.

telcos: An abbreviation for telephone companies.

turbulence: What researchers Emery and Trist term "the ground in motion"; a condition characterized by high levels of uncertainty.

2 Public Relations and Technology

Choices and Challenges

CHAPTER OUTLINE

CHAPTER OBJECTIVES

When you have completed this chapter, you should be able to:

- Understand terminology of technology
- Identify software programs used in public relations
- Identify application of public relations techniques

Technology—from laptop computers to facsimile machines, from voice mail systems to cellular phones—is dramatically changing the way public relations people do their jobs. According to Middleberg, the business penetration of communication technology is nearing 100 percent.

Throughout the public relations field, for the most part, the days of typewriters are gone. Today, computers let public relations practitioners manipulate and store data in complex ways. Research, too, has been simplified, as online databases supply a wealth of information on almost any subject. Software is available both to manage media lists and news clippings and to analyze publicity results.

All of this technology enables communicators to do their jobs faster and more efficiently, and it takes fewer people to produce more quality work. "Buffeted by staff cutbacks, tumbling budgets, and media that are being sliced into finer and finer shards, many public relations practitioners are relying on technology to pick up the slack," writes Wiesendanger.

Almost anything can be done faster, more easily, and more accurately by flicking a modem switch or pressing a fax machine button. As the prices of computer hardware, software, and technological services are reduced, public relations practitioners are getting more bang for their buck and are seeing greater returns on their investment. Some even say these new tools are as cheap as or cheaper than the older mailing, clipping, and monitoring methods, especially if savings in staff time are factored into the equation.

According to Capps, "The value of the new technology will come from a practitioner's skill to integrate it into the proven relationship techniques already being practiced." In *The Practice of Public Relations,* Seitel discusses the following as some of the more useful technologies available to public relations professionals:

- Laptops provide everything communicators need to write and edit at home or on the road. Modems, which let two computers exchange information over telephone lines, allow laptops to transfer and retrieve data; to access electronic mail, databases, and news monitoring services; and to send documents to a facsimile machine. To support laptops, there are now docking stations that provide full-size monitors and keyboards in offices as well as portable printers, copiers, and fax machines.
- Electronic publishing, or desktop publishing, enables public relations practitioners to create documents—from simple news releases to flashy brochures—with vivid charts, drawings, and tables. Producing material in-house can save a great deal of money. Internal production means more time spent working on a project rather than routing material between the office and outside design firms.
- The facsimile machine, which transmits documents via telephone lines, is as common as the office copier. Whereas mail delivery can take days, facsimile technology can transmit information in less than a minute. Bovet states that fax on-demand services are an excellent way to provide targeted distribution of press releases. In addition, an increasingly popular alternative to sending mass mailings through the mail is broadcast fax, in which a single document is simultaneously transmitted to hundreds of recipients. In fact, there are companies, such as PR Newswire, that will provide bulk fax distribution for public relations divisions and firms.
- Computer-based voice mail systems can answer phone calls and dispense information 24 hours a day. Unlike regular answering machines, voice mail systems can take a message even when the phone is in use, eliminating the frustration of busy signals and "telephone tag." Messages can be transferred from one person to another or circulated like memos. Users also can send copies of the same message to many people at once by pressing a button or two on the phone. In this fashion, important messages can be distributed quickly. Voice mail, always on duty, is particularly useful for people communicating across time zones.
- Electronic mail, or e-mail, allows subscribers to transmit information—from short memos to long reports—to other people's computers. Company e-mail networks, called intranets, are usually internal, although some have been linked to external e-mail systems. Professionals can use e-mail to send news releases directly to

reporters' terminals. The key to e-mail is that messages are delivered to people wherever they are instead of to places. Fax machines and telephones do not contact people; they contact devices that are location-dependent. Electronic mail is well suited to a crisis where the need is to bring people together rapidly, wherever they are.

"Changes inside public relations offices will be every bit as great as those in the outside world," predicts Brody, coauthor of *New Technology and Public Relations: On to the Future.* "Survival in many cases may depend on a practitioner's ability to apply the new and emerging technologies. Inability to quickly access a database and extract information needed by a client or employer will be a crippling handicap to the practitioners of the 21st century," writes Calloway.

Computer-based communication tools and multimedia technologies have already begun to influence how leading organizations craft their messages for select audiences. Today's digital technologies bring multimedia and global communication capabilities right to your desktop PC and Mac. As consumer multimedia and other convergence-created utilities begin to enter the mainstream and capture the popular imagination, companies and agencies will move to adopt the technology for business use. Even so, it's not just a matter of techno-cultural trends driving business adoption; agencies will seize on multimedia for the competitive edge they provide, according to Duffy and Palmer.

In a world of just-in-time information technology, containing CNN, fax, mobile full-broadcast satellite systems, videoconferencing, and mundane technologies like e-mail, Calloway says it seems necessary to ask whether public relations people are limiting their own productivity. A public relations organization without enough telephones is handcuffed. Yet in today's networked world, a public relations organization without laptop computers, e-mail, and a video downlink from headquarters may also be a public relations organization that is handcuffed and handicapped. Good communication is no guarantee of good public relations; poor communication is a certain guarantee of poor public relations.

Computer-based technology has been the catalyst for change in the business environment. The changes have occurred so swiftly that critics view them as "revolutionary rather than evolutionary," according to Goltz. This is especially true when comparing the last two decades to the past 100 years.

Computer-based technology is also altering the working environment and skills necessary to succeed in public relations. As late as 1994, public relations lagged behind most other business functions in computer literacy, in participating in the technology and its benefits. Part of this problem had been the reluctance of public relations professionals to embrace technology. However, the reluctance has been replaced by the ever-growing presence of technology, its increased simplicity and access, its decreased costs, and systems dedicated to public relations.

Public relations is a field that has traditionally favored the personal touch in communications. Most public relations executives describe themselves as "people-oriented," "nuts and bolts" individuals with little experience using advanced telecommunications technology, according to O'Donnell. In reality, the industry has long since grown in scope and sophistication, and getting the word out frequently takes precedence over the handshake. This is especially true in fast-moving situations where timing is critical or where the audience is too large or geographically dispersed to receive individual attention.

According to O'Donnell, the term *Information Age* describes more than the ability to process vast quantities of information; it describes the need to. There is, quite simply, more information to be gathered and to be disseminated. As the general public insists on more information on which to base its personal, social, and marketing decisions, and as the move toward participative management grows, the challenge to public relations will be to develop a variety of methods or channels to communicate with its constituencies. Technology provides the means.

One of the main concerns is that in this drive to automate the process, some of the personal touches so prized by the public relations practitioner will be sacrificed. Computer technology is intended to enhance, not supplant, the basic public relations function. Teleconferencing and toll-free numbers, for instance, do not replace direct contact, O'Donnell notes. Rather, they make it possible to reach and include an audience that might otherwise be inaccessible. Telecommunications services are relatively easy to implement, allow for a range of creative applications, and will continue to represent a good return in improved public relations.

The Information Age

The first step toward joining the Information Age is understanding how society got to where it is today. The Industrial Age permeated the working world gradually. In less than 100 years, human society changed on a massive scale. To live between 1890 and 1920, for instance, was to live with the introduction of electricity, telephones, radios, automobiles, and airplanes.

Traditional economics courses defined the cornerstones of an economy as land, labor, capital, and the entrepreneurial spirit. That traditional definition is now challenged. Today, there are references to a fifth key economic element: information. As we evolve from an industrial to an information society, jobs are changing from physical to mental labor. Just as people moved physically from farms to factories in the Industrial Age, so today people are shifting from muscle power to brain power in a computer-based society, observes O'Leary and O'Leary.

The start of the Information Age might be traced to many events earlier this century, including the invention of television. Slow and steady marked its pace up through the 1950s, when the miniaturization of electronic components, such as transistors, enabled production of the first personal computers, also called microcomputers, in the 1970s. From that point, the pace of the Information Age increased to fast and furious, and its impact extended to each individual in our society. One need only look at how the number of personal computers in business has skyrocketed. At the end of 1987, the year personal computers took off, there were about 11 million personal computers in use in business. The number of units climbed to more than 31 million by 1991 and tripled again by the end of the decade.

Compared to the Industrial Revolution, the Information Age is evolving much more rapidly. The amount of information in the world is purportedly doubling every six to seven years. If this assessment is accurate, a grasp of technology is essential in order to keep up with the burgeoning body of information.

The Computer Age

The remarkable thing about the computer age is that so much has happened in so short a time. Four generations of technology have evolved in about forty years—a span of time whose events are within the memories of many people today. The first three computer "generations" are pinned to three technological developments: the vacuum tube, the transistor, and the integrated circuit. Each has drastically changed the nature of computers. The timing of each generation is defined according to the beginning of commercial delivery of the hardware technology. Defining subsequent generations has become more complicated because the entire industry has become more complex.

The First Generation, 1951–1958: The Vacuum Tube

Many regard June 14, 1951, as the beginning of the commercial computer age. This was the date the first UNIVAC (UNIVersal Automatic Computer) was delivered to the U.S. Bureau of the Census for use in tabulating the previous year's data. The date also marked the first time that a computer had been built for business applications rather than for military, scientific, or engineering use. The first UNIVAC sold to a private company was purchased by General Electric Corporation.

In the first generation, vacuum tubes—electronic tubes about the size of lightbulbs—were used as the internal computer components. However, because thousands of such tubes were required, they generated a great deal of heat, causing problems in temperature regulation and climate control. In addition, tubes were subject to frequent burnout, and the computer operators often did not know whether the problem was in the programming or the machine.

Another drawback was that the language used in programming was machine language, which is number based. Using numbers alone made programming the computer difficult and time-consuming. The UNIVAC used magnetic cores to create memory. These consisted of small, doughnut-shaped rings about the size of pinheads, which were strung like beads on intersecting thin wires. To supplement primary storage, first-generation computers stored data on punched cards. In 1957, magnetic tape was introduced as a faster, more compact method of storing data.

The Second Generation, 1959–1964: The Transistor

Three Bell Lab scientists developed the transistor, a small device that transfers electric signals across a resistor. The name transistor began as a trademark concocted from "transfer" plus "resistor." The scientists, J. Bardeen, H. Brattain, and W. Shockley, later received the Nobel Prize for their invention. The transistor revolutionized electronics in general and computers in particular. They were small in size, needed no warm-up, consumed less energy, and were faster and more reliable.

During the second generation, another important development was the move from machine language to assembly language, also called symbolic language. Abbreviations, rather than numbers, were used for instructions. This made programming less cumbersome.

After the development of symbolic languages came high-level languages, such as Fortran (1954) and Cobol (1959). Both languages, still widely used today, are more English-like than assembly languages. High-level languages allowed programmers to give more attention to solving problems. Also in 1962, the first removable disk pack was marketed. Disk storage supplemented magnetic tape systems and enabled users to gain fast access to desired data.

All these developments made the second generation of computers less costly to operate and thus began a surge of growth in computer systems. Throughout this period, computers were used principally by business, university, and government organizations; they had not filtered down to the general public. The most profound phase of the revolution was about to begin.

The Third Generation, 1965–1970: The Integrated Circuit

One of the most abundant elements in the earth's crust is silicon, a nonmetallic substance found in common beach sand as well as in practically all rocks and clay. The importance of this element to Santa Clara County, which is about thirty miles south of San Francisco, is responsible for the county's nickname: Silicon Valley. In 1965, Silicon Valley became the principal site for the manufacture of the so-called silicon chip: the integrated circuit.

The Fourth Generation, 1971–Present:
The Microprocessor

Throughout the 1970s, computers gained dramatically in the areas of speed, reliability, and storage capacity, but entry into the fourth generation was evolutionary rather than revolutionary. The fourth generation was, in fact, an extension of third-generation technology. In the early part of the third generation, specialized chips were developed for computer memory and logic. Thus, all the ingredients were in place for the next technological development, the general-purpose processor-on-a-chip—otherwise known as the microprocessor—which became commercially available in 1971. The first microprocessor chip, the Intel 4004, contained more than 2,000 transistors on a three millimeter by four millimeter silicon chip.

Nowhere is the pervasiveness of computer power more apparent than in the explosive use of the microprocessor. In addition to the common applications of digital watches, pocket calculators, and personal computers, microprocessors can be found in virtually every machine in the home or business, including microwave ovens, cars, copy machines, and television sets. Computers today are 100 times smaller than those of the first generation, and a single chip is far more powerful than the ENIAC mainframe. The microprocessor chip rearranged an entire industry. The microprocessor combines all the essential elements of a computer—a processor, memory, and input/output circuits—all on one small piece of silicon.

The Fifth Generation: Japan's Challenge

The term fifth generation was coined to describe the machines the Japanese wanted to create by the mid-1990s—"intelligent" machines more powerful than those on the market so far. However, now it has become an umbrella term encompassing many research fields in the computer industry. Key areas of ongoing research are: artificial intelligence, expert systems, and natural language.

The Personal Computer Age

The personal computer age officially began in January 1974. That month, *Popular Electronics* magazine featured the MITS Altair computer on its cover. Offering the computer in a kit allowed MITS to enter the computer business with only minimal manufacturing facilities and helped keep the costs of the computer down to $397. The Altair used an Intel 8080 and had a front panel covered with lights and switches. However, it didn't have a keyboard, video display, disk drive, or tape storage unit. Users would enter their programs one instruction at a time, using the switches on the front panel.

The Apple and Macintosh PCs

It took two teenagers, Steve Jobs and Steve Wozniak, to capture the imagination of the public with the first Apple computer. They built it in a garage, using the $1,300 proceeds from the sale of an old Volkswagen. Designed for home use, the Apple was the first to offer an easy-to-use keyboard and screen. Founded in 1977, Apple Computer was immediately and wildly successful. When its stock was offered to the public in December 1980, it started a stampede among investors who were eager to buy shares.

Introduced in January 1984, the Macintosh computer was an almost instant success. It had a graphical user interface (GUI) instead of the text-based display of the Apple II, and it also used a mouse. The Mac's operating system was designed to ensure that all application programs operated in a similar fashion. The Macintosh saved Apple from extinction. The Macintosh is still with us today, and Apple has retained its place among the world's top PC makers. Apple weathered the storm caused by IBM's arrival in the small computer business. Apple has introduced an increasingly powerful line of computers, including the Power Macintosh and the iMac, which continues to sell well.

The IBM PC Phenomenon

On August 12, 1981, the personal computer industry, not yet a decade old, changed forever. On that day, mainframe computer giant IBM announced its own personal computer. IBM captured the top market share in just eighteen months; even more important, its machine became the industry standard.

IBM did many things right, such as including the possibility of adding memory. IBM also provided internal expansion slots, so that peripheral equipment manufacturers could build accessories for the IBM PC. In addition, IBM provided hardware schematics and software listings to companies that wanted to build products in conjunction with the new PC. Many of the new products accelerated demand for the IBM machine. As a result, IBM was able to announce a large variety of application programs for the PC from day one, including the leading word processor, spreadsheet, and database manager programs.

The story of personal computer history is ongoing, with daily fluctuations reflected in the trade press. The effects of personal computers are far-reaching, and they remain a key topic in the computer industry.

Personal Computers.   The smallest computers, personal computers, are also known as microcomputers, or home computers. For many years, the computer industry was on a quest for the next biggest computer. The search was always for more power and greater capacity.

Forecasters who suggested a niche for a smaller computer were ridiculed by people who, as it turned out, could not have been more wrong. By 1993, more than 87 million personal computers had been sold worldwide, 31 million to U.S. customers. In 1997, the U.S. Department of Commerce and Trade and the International Trade Administration projected that there would be 47 million portable and desktop computers in use, and by 2001, the figure will rise to 53 million.

Software: The Big Five

In the past, when people thought about computers, they thought about machines. The tapping on the keyboard, the clacking of the printers, the rumble of a whirling disk drive, the changing flashes of color on a computer screen—these are the attention getters. However, it is really the software—the planned, step-by-step instructions required to turn data into information—that makes a computer useful. The software is the brain of a computer; it defines the instructions the computer is to carry out. Until a program has been loaded into the computer's memory, the computer is like a body without a brain, unable to perform any actions.

The collective set of business problems is limited, and the number of ways to solve these problems is limited as well. Thus, the problems and the software solutions fall, for the most part, into just a few categories. These categories can be found in most business environments. Because of their widespread use, the main categories are often called the Big Five: word processing/desktop publishing, electronic spreadsheets, database management, graphics, and data communications.

Carr lists integrated software programs as an additional category. Integrated software programs combine in a single package capabilities often found only in separately purchased, stand-alone programs. Their main advantage is that they allow the public relations professional to own a number of sophisticated applications at an affordable price, with the added convenience of having them all on one disk or in one program.

Word Processing/Desktop Publishing.   Word processing programs are the oldest and most frequently used application for computers. This software allows the user to create, edit, format, store, and print text and graphics in one document. Using this definition, the word that makes word processing different from plain typing is "store." Since a diskette is used to store the typed memo or document, it can be retrieved at another time, changed, or reprinted. Word processing can cut days off preparation time, especially in the case of massive texts such as speeches and reports. It can increase accuracy by eliminating errors during retyping and through the use of spell checkers. By freeing the writer from mechanical constraints, it can improve the quality of writing.

Communicators have quickly picked up on the word processing applications. The ease with which copy can be created and edited makes the computer an indispensable part of the workplace. The primary tangible output of most public relations offices is the written word, as Gorman found in her 1994 study of the top fifty public relations agencies in the United States (see PRoActive). Specific applications for public relations professionals include using text manipulation capabilities for moving text and boilerplate material while writing proposals, using a mail merge function for repetitive letter-writing campaigns, or using a custom-designed, industry-specific spell checker. Thus, word processing is by far the most important application of the new technology, and the only one offering hope for significant short-run gains in productivity.

PRoActive
Practitioners' Use of Technology in Top Fifty U.S. PR Firms

GORMAN'S SURVEY RESPONSES 1994–95
21 surveys returned = 42% response rate

1. *Do you use communication technologies in your practice of public relations?*

   All 21 respondents said yes (100%).

   Number of firms using specific systems:

System	# of Firms	Percentage
IBM	15	71%
Mac	14	67%
Power Mac	7	33%
Unix	3	14%
NeXT	2	10%
Amiga	0	0%
Other	1	5%
*IBM & Mac	11	52%

   *all firms using more than 1 system use both IBM & Mac.

   Number of different systems used per firm:

# of Systems	# of Firms	Percentage
Use 1 system	10 firms	48%
Use 2 systems	7 firms	33%
Use 3 systems	3 firms	14%
Use 4 systems	1 firm	5%
		100%

2. *Which computer systems do you use?*

Specific Systems Used	# of Systems	Specific Systems Used	# of Systems
IBM, Mac	2 systems	IBM, Mac	2 systems
IBM	1 system	IBM, Mac,	2 systems
IBM, Mac, Power Mac, Unix, NeXT	4 systems	Unix	1 system
		IBM, Mac, NeXT	3 systems
IBM	1 system	IBM	1 system
IBM, Mac, Power Mac, Unix	3 systems	Mac	1 system
		Mac, Power Mac	1 system
Mac, Power Mac	1 system	Mac	1 system
IBM, Mac	2 systems	IBM, Power Mac	2 systems
IBM	1 system	IBM, Mac, Power Mac, D13C	3 systems
IBM, Mac	2 systems		
IBM, Mac	2 systems	IBM	1 system

3. *Additional hardware used:*

Fax machine	21	100%
Modem	21	100%
Floppy disks	21	100%
Laptop computer	20	95%
CD-ROM	15	71%
Scanner	14	67%
External drive	12	57%
Digital tablet	2	10%
Electronic camera	1	5%

4. *Software and telecommunications services used:*

Services	# of Firms	Percentage
Word processing	21	100%
Online information & retrieval services	21	100%
Desktop publishing	19	90%
Graphic design	17	81%
Database searches/research	17	81%
Electronic spreadsheets	17	81%
Fax transmission services	17	81%
Database management	16	76%
Electronic mail/telex services	16	76%
Media monitoring (clipping services)	14	67%
Communications	12	57%
Media relations	10	48%
Teleconferencing services	7	33%
Language translation	1	5%

5. *Online services used:*

Services	# of Firms	Percentage
CompuServe	19	90%
Internet	10	48%
America Online	7	33%
Prodigy	1	5%
Delphi	1	5%
E-World	1	5%
GEnie	0	0%
None	0	0%

Number of online services used per agency:

# of Services	# of Firms	Percentage
None	2	10%
One	8	38%
Two	5	24%
Three	4	19%
Four	2	10%

(continued)

PRoActive   Continued

6. *Specific PR software used:*

   As indicated in question 7.

   Bacon's CD-ROM, Datatimes

   The majority of agencies said none.

7. *Do you use computer technologies to conduct research?*

   All 21 respondents said yes (100%).

   What specific services/online databases do you use?

Database	# of Firms	Percentage
Lexis/Nexis	18	86%
Associated Press	12	57%
Dow-Jones News	12	57%
DIALOG	8	38%
Datatimes	7	33%
Reuters	6	29%
Dunn & Bradstreet	5	24%
InvesText	3	14%
NewsNat	3	14%
Dialcom	1	5%
Facts on File	0	0%
BRS Info Tech	0	0%

   Number of online databases used per agency:

Databases	# of Firms	Percentage
None	0	0%
One	3	14%
Two	4	19%
Three	3	14%
Four	5	24%
Five	3	14%
Six	2	10%
Seven	0	0%
Eight	0	0%
Nine	1	5%

8. *How do you use databases in your research efforts?*

Percentage	# of Firms	Uses of Databases for Research
76%	16	Monitor breaking news and client press coverage
71%	15	Research new clients for business pitches
62%	13	Prospect for new business
57%	12	Keep track of key issues and social trends
43%	9	Monitor client competition
33%	7	Help win better media coverage by indicating how/where efforts should be directed

9. *What software do you use for media relations research?*

Percentage	# of Firms	Software
29%	6	Bacon's Directory on Disk
24%	5	Media Manager by MediaMap
10%	2	Burrelle's Media Directory—Electronic Format
10%	2	Spin Control by SpinWare
5%	1	Targeter by Media Distribution Services
5%	1	Automated Broadcast Retrieval System by Radio/TV Reports
0%	0	Media Relations Manager by Turrikey
0%	0	Press Access Directories & Databases for High-Tech PR

How many media relations programs used per firm?

# of Programs	# of Firms	Percentage
None	10	48%
One	8	38%
Two	2	10%
Six	1	5%

10. *Do you use computer technologies for planning the following?*

Percentage	# of Firms	Planning Methods
62%	13	Crisis management
38%	8	Environmental issues
38%	8	Media training
33%	7	Crisis management
33%	7	Issues management/strategic planning
29%	6	Legislative/regulatory
24%	5	Information campaigns
14%	3	Product promotion campaigns
14%	3	Risk management
14%	3	Sports/special-event tie-ins
10%	2	Fund-raising
5%	1	Speakers bureau

11. *How does your organization use computer technology for planning?*

- To keep track of social trends and the thoughts/opinions of selected interest groups.
- By law we must keep track of all funds received with any political support.
- We use a miscellaneous spreadsheet that maintains total dollars.
- Word processing primarily.
- Generate databases and use word processing programs extensively to collect and prepare the information.
- Account executives use word processing software to produce press releases, proposals, talking points, and other written documents. Network fax modem allows account executives to send these materials directly to clients or media contacts. Support staff uses customized database programs to track media and legislative contacts as well as information associated with special events. Word processing and customized databases are combined to facilitate targeted mailings.
- Primarily for research to support planning.

(continued)

PRoActive   Continued

- We use computer technology through all facets of our work, from analyzing our historical data for future budgeting, doing backgrounding on clients, prospects, or issues, preparing and implementing plans to conducting, processing, and analyzing opinion/position surveys for internal or client use. From initial presentations to final output, we use computer technology.

12. *What forms of communication technologies/services do you use?*

Equipment	# of Firms	Percentage
Fax machine	21	100%
Modem	21	100%
E-mail	19	90%
Cellular phone	15	71%
Videoconferencing	6	29%

13. *My agency uses communication technology for the following PR tasks:*

	Internal	External	Both	#	Percentage
Media relations	1	4	9	14	67%
Employee communications	8	0	6	14	67%
Industry trade press relations	0	6	6	12	57%
Interoffice communications	10	1	7	18	86%
Client communications	0	1	13	19	90%
Community relations	0	3	3	6	29%
Financial/investor relations	0	4	6	10	48%
Intraoffice communications	7	0	6	13	62%

14. *Communication technologies are used for the following evaluation methods:*

Percentage	# of Firms	Methods
81%	17	Clipping/media mentions
52%	11	Employee productivity/time usage
52%	11	New client leads
52%	11	Profit analysis
48%	10	Billings
43%	9	Positive/neutral media coverage
43%	9	Achieving client goals
43%	9	Stock prices
38%	0	Competition evaluation
33%	8	Media inquiries
19%	7	Sales results
19%	4	Polling
14%	3	Lobbying efforts
10%	2	None

15. *What media services does your agency utilize?*

Services	# of Firms	Percentage
PR Newswire	14	67%
Np/Mgz clipping services	17	81%
AP newswire	12	57%
Video monitoring	12	57%
Businesswire	5	24%
None	1	5%

16. *As a result of using computer technology in your practice of public relations as compared to conventional methods:*

With Computer Technology:	Strongly Agree	Agree	Neutral	Disagree	Strongly Disagree
a) More control over the message	9.5%	52.4%	218%	143%	0.0%
b) More productivity	57.2%	33.3%	9.5%	0.0%	0.0%
c) Management style more participatory	4.8%	23.8%	61.9%	9.5%	0.0%
d) More need for preparedness on deadline	19.0%	28.6%	42.9%	9.5%	0.0%
e) Daily agendas more defined	4.8%	33.3%	42.9%	14.3%	4.8%
f) More of a teamwork approach	4.8%	33.3%	38.1%	23.8%	0.0%
g) Definitions of job roles blurred	0.0%	23.8%	47.6%	28.6%	0.0%
h) More crossover of responsibilities	0.0%	47.61	28.6%	23.8%	0.0%
i) More job stress	4.8%	23.8%	52.4%	14.3%	4.8%
j) More mistakes made	0.0%	9.5%	38.1%	47.6%	4.8%
k) Ability to be more creative	23.8%	57.2%	14.317	4.8%	0.0%
l) Clients expect more for their money	19.0%	33.3%	38.1%	9.5%	0.0%
m) Ability to work with media deadlines	14.3%	38.1%	38.1%	9.5%	0.0%
n) More access to the media	23.8%	52.4%	14.3%	9.5%	0.0%
o) More work done in-house	33.3%	47.6%	9.5%	9.5%	0.0%
p) Ability to handle a crisis more effectively	23.8%	52.4%	19.0%	4.8%	0.0%
q) Work fewer hours	0.0%	0.0%	19.0%	47.6%	33.3%
r) Spend less time working in the office	4.8%	9.5%	23.8%	42.9%	19.0%
s) Need to travel less	0.0%	23.8%	23.8%	52.4%	0.0%
t) Ability to be more proactive	14.3%	47.6%	33.3%	4.8%	0.0%
u) Commitment to ethical use of technology	9.5%	38.1%	42.9%	9.5%	0.0%
v) More concern over data security issues	0.0%	61.9%	33.3%	4.8%	0.0%

(continued)

PRoActive   Continued

17. *Rate the following skills (most important to least important):*

1	Writing	6	Research skills
2	Media relations	7	Management
3	Interpersonal communication skills	8	Public speaking
4	Organization planning	9	Graphic design
5	Computer literacy	10	Desktop publishing

18. *Are new hires expected to be computer-literate?*

Yes   19
No   2

19. *Are current staff members expected to be computer-literate?*

Yes   21
No   0

20. *Were new positions created as a result of computer technology?*

Yes   13
No   8

If yes, what positions?

- MIS positions, of course
- Database administrator, network administrator, and information technology director
- Graphic design dept., database manager, and library researcher
- Network administrator
- CIS coordinator
- Computer support personnel
- Computer technician, and desktop publishing group
- Director MIS
- Perhaps in the future a position will be created
- Macintosh specialist
- Art director, computer manager, and billing clerk
- Part-time staff computer manager

21. *Has computer technology eliminated certain job positions?*

Yes   5
No   16

Positions eliminated:

- Billers
- Secretarial positions no longer necessary—employees use their own computers
- Fewer full-time word processor positions
- Administrative assistants
- Copy secretary

22. *Job responsibilities/Positions merged:*

- Office professionals/secretaries are relegated to more mundane tasks but are also relied upon for some high-end computing tasks such as graphic work and searches.
- Administrators do not need to know so much about graphics now we have the graphic designer. No merging of positions.
- Responsibilities have not changed.
- No.
- Not really.
- We're more self-sufficient; we do all the work ourselves—no need for administrative help.
- Likely—more people are now expected to know and use computer applications.
- Some changes—more on the support side.
- Yes, our presentations department is dispersed to the account coordinators.
- No.
- Most account executives are responsible for producing and editing written materials without assistance from secretaries. With the addition of the art director, most graphics materials needed for clients and for in-house purposes are now handled internally. There is now greater project control and cost-savings. No positions have merged. All employees are expected to accomplish more with their computers.
- The only real change is the adoption of the computer as a tool. Ultimately, productivity is to increase because of this new tool—but creative processes remain the same.
- No.

23. *Training programs:*

- In-house trainer.
- In-house training is done individually as the individual skills, interests, and abilities warrant.
- Both. Cunningham University and $1,500/year for each employee to use on outside training.
- We utilize both sources of training. We have in-house self-tutorial programs in writing with a disk interface. When a new package is introduced, we do have an outside person to help.
- Both—in-house for basic computer skills for our system and outside for senior management.
- Software-specific training by outside consultants.
- In-house training when needed.
- Few; our computer guy isn't a nice guy.
- Both in-house and external—occasional expanded courses, giving deeper instruction on applications.
- Both.
- We have both in-house and outside workshops.
- In-house.
- Plan to do this soon—in-house and outside.
- In-house.
- Most training is handled one-on-one with computer manager. Outside firms provide advanced graphic arts training.
- None.
- We employ a combination of these. For our specialized graphics personnel, outside help is secured. Otherwise, we use in-house training.
- Both.

(continued)

PRoActive   Continued

24. *How often do your employees receive computer training and instruction?*

- When they need it and as we have time.
- Infrequently—as often as they hit a snag and need to learn more to accomplish a task.
- When they start with us, there's basic training. If they need more, we send them out.
- At the time of employment and when something new is introduced.
- Ongoing.
- As needed with new software.
- Once a year or when new software is introduced.
- Almost never; learn as you go.
- Every six months for tune-up or when new software release is used.
- We're just about to dump our current UNIX system for a Windows system. We're in the midst of a great deal of training.
- Continuously, our firm deals only with high-tech computer products.
- Quarterly.
- Occasionally.
- Once, upon hiring.
- Scheduled as needed with individual employees. Graphic arts training about once every six months.
- Minimal.
- Annually.
- At the beginning of their tenure. It should be longer and we should have a refresher course—we don't.

25. *How do you handle security issues such as: securing sensitive/proprietary information, limiting access to information, and dealing with the potential for industrial espionage enabled by the use of communication technologies?*

- Passwords and limited network access.
- Passwords and encrypted data.
- The system administrator assigns all individuals group/departmental access.
- Everyone may sign on using a password but only have access to files they are given privileges to.
- We have a document management system—PC DOC—that secures documents when necessary. We don't have active floppy drives on most PCs—thereby eliminating unauthorized software and data transfers.
- Password access, password updates, secure phone lines. Outside client access to computer system is limited to the bulletin board.
- Network security.
- None.
- Each user is required to have a password that is changed every 60 days. The password cannot be used more than once. It must be a certain length and if you need access to your personal files, you must have the correct password to gain access. An intruder lockout will lock the account if more than three invalid attempts are made to the user's accounts.
- Beginning in our current Unix system, we haven't had problems.
- Everything is security coded.
- Network rights bindery.

- Server-based security.
- Password security as provided by the software and a 24-hour electronic security system as provided by contract with an outside firm.
- Don't use any.
- Not a problem.

26. *What are your primary concerns regarding communication technology?*

   - That expectations will exceed deliverables. That the level of work and commitment new technologies require will reduce productivity. That the technology will change rapidly, making current systems obsolete.
   - That we keep up with the technology.
   - We are so far behind in every aspect. I could not begin to tell you.
   - Security.
   - Data redundancy, software compatibility, archiving and promulgation of inaccurate or outdated information, difficulty of correcting/retrieving inaccurate information once it leaves our shop.
   - Security.
   - User-friendly and accurate.
   - Availability, standardization, costs.
   - Once we spend all this $$ to maximize the system—ROI.
   - Keeping up with all the upgrades.
   - Using technology available to highest and best purpose.
   - Speed and availability.
   - Rate of change and advancements in technology create need to invest in emerging technologies and place ever-increasing pressure on job skills to stay current. Consequently, capital and training budgets are constantly strained.
   - Cost/staff education.
   - Trying to use one end-user tool to communicate internally as well as with clients (e-mail). Other than that, just to keep abreast of features and options available, especially in the fax area.
   - Time, accuracy, and ease of use.

27. *What new technologies are you planning to implement?*

   - Lotus Notes—groupware communications.
   - Greater and wider access within the agency to e-mail (external) services.
   - Desktop videoconferencing. Power PCs for all.
   - Believe it or not—e-mail, centralized faxing.
   - Gateway for e-mail system, broadcast fax, faxing from individual PC with program that keeps track for billing purposes.
   - WAN.
   - Online services.
   - More robust dial-in/dial-out communications for employees—giving them access to information regardless of location.
   - Faxing from desktop, databases, project management, scheduling, document management, press software.
   - Don't know yet.
   - New database.

(continued)

PRoActive   **Continued**

- Internet.
- Ethernet network. Receiving and distributing faxes electronically.
- Document exchange utilities such as Adobe Acrobat.
- Videoconferencing, e-mail, presentations.

28. *In what areas of public relations do you feel that current technologies do not meet your needs? What types of technology would you like to have in your office?*

- Few reliable e-mail connections to editors. Far too many people (currently) do not understand the available technologies. I would like to have: scanner, GIF, CD-ROM, better news servers.
- Compiling media databases accurately and efficiently.
- At this point, we can do all we need to be able to do.
- Media relations database.
- Internet is not reliable—our voice mail is unpredictable.
- More reasonably priced media lists.
- Workgroup software that is easy to implement and use for account executives with the basic technical skills.

29. *What do you feel are the biggest obstacles to technology usage in public relations?*

- Money.
- Money and closed minds.
- Acceptance by clients and media—building management's recognition for the value these services bring.
- A "soft" discipline, more art than science—old "manual typewriter" thinking.
- Keeping up with the progression of technology.
- Stupid people and money.
- Cost, old-school management who is intimidated by new technologies/methods (this could be either agency or client).
- Teaching people how to really use technology. It's here—what do we do with it.
- Ability to learn quickly.
- Training.
- Costs, lack of information on how to easily implement solutions.
- If you get too dependent on technology, each employee has to become more and more of an expert in either computer hardware/software because they are really as intuitive as people say. This detracts from their profession, as either PR associates or graphics personnel. With the aggressive attitude of continual change and improvement coupled with making it "user friendly," the user needs more knowledge and time to use what once was just a tool! A hammer doesn't change, but computer technology and software continue to change. Even faxing is changing.
- It changes so fast; to install and learn a new system becomes obsolete quickly.

*All firms requested a copy of the survey results.

Currently, there are more than 500 word processing packages on the market, varying in degree of complexity and ease of use. Generally, word processing packages can be separated into two categories. On one level are the more expensive, feature-laden programs designed primarily for office and professional use. The complex text-editing capabilities of some of the more advanced word processing programs, such as WordPerfect or Microsoft Word, include reading files into documents, developing style sheets and document templates, and the option of setting up indexes and tables of contents. Less frequent users can choose among lower-cost programs that offer only basic functions. The basic capabilities of inserting characters, words, and sentences; searching and replacing words; moving blocks of text; and formatting text are available in most word processing packages.

As the number of features in word processing packages has grown, they have crossed the line into desktop publishing territory. Desktop publishing packages are usually better than word processing packages at meeting high-level publishing needs, especially when it comes to typesetting and color reproduction. In desktop publishing, high-end quality meets low-end flexibility. Popular programs include QuarkXpress, ClarisWorks, and Pagemaker.

Many magazines and newspapers today rely on desktop publishing software. Businesses use it to produce professional-looking newsletters, reports, and brochures both to improve internal communication and to make a better impression on the outside world. Since publishing in one form or another typically consumes up to 10 percent of a company's gross revenues, desktop publishing has been given a warm welcome by business.

Electronic Spreadsheets.   An electronic spreadsheet allows the user to manipulate numbers the way a word processor manages words. A spreadsheet is created on a computer screen using a matrix of rows and columns to organize business data. Usually, columns indicate periods of time, and rows contain math functions. The intersections or rows and columns are called cells, and each cell holds one piece of data.

Manual spreadsheets have been used as a business tool for centuries, but a spreadsheet can be tedious to prepare; and when there are changes, a considerable amount of work may need to be redone. An electronic spreadsheet is still a spreadsheet, but the computer does the work. Spreadsheets are particularly useful because of their speed in performing complex, interrelated calculations. Users can make cost projections based on one factor, then create another projection in minutes based on different assumptions. The software automatically recalculates the results when a number is changed. This capability lets businesspeople try different combinations of numbers and obtain the results quickly. This ability to ask "What if . . . ?" helps businesspeople make better, faster decisions. Spreadsheets are also useful for inventories, time/resource management, budgets, bookkeeping, forecasts, and any other application where numerical data, once captured, are compared.

Many small and medium-sized public relations firms use accounting firms or continue to do their accounting manually. However, these businesses could easily computerize this function, considering the availability of powerful off-the-shelf accounting software that is geared toward general use in small, medium, or large offices. There are now more than 1,000 spreadsheet and accounting software packages for microcomputers. In addition, spreadsheets provide built-in graphics capabilities that let you change raw numbers into charts for faster interpretation of the data.

Database Management.   Keeping track of records within any office, including a public relations firm, can be made much easier through the use of computers and records management software. Software used for database management handles data in several ways. The software can store data, update them, manipulate them, report them in a variety of views, and print them in as many forms. By the time the data are in the reporting stage, they have become information. A concert promoter, for example, can store and change data about upcoming concert dates, seating, ticket prices, and sales. After this is done, the promoter can use the software to retrieve information, such as the number of tickets sold in each price range or the percentage of tickets sold the day before the concert. Database software can be useful for anyone who must keep track of a large number of facts. Public relations–related uses for database management software include: membership lists, mailing lists, contributions, subscriptions, profiles of contacts, media lists, media events, statistics, survey results, budgets, and bibliographies. There are at present several hundred database-management software packages on the market.

Graphics.   As a general group, graphics hardware and software permit practitioners to create, display, print, and store nontext images using the computer. Aside from this basic definition, the computer graphics field is a free-for-all of digitizers, image processors, drawing and painting packages, computer-aided design and drafting programs, image capture and video display boards, and simple chart- and graph-drawing packages. The most popular and widely available types of graphics software are graphics packages, which can create charts, tables, and graphs commonly used in any business, including the public relations profession.

The many uses for graphics in the public relations industry are evident. The display-quality graphics programs now on the market can be used for publications as well as presentations, hard copy as well as screen images, black-and-white as well as color, and slides as well as printed images. Computer-aided design opens a world of professional quality and cost-effective alternatives to using outside consultants.

Data Communications.   Communications software permits a computer to connect and communicate with other computers, either over common telephone lines or computer cables. A modem is the device used to transfer data between computers over telephone lines.

The modem, short for modulate/demodulate, converts a digital signal to an analog signal—or vice versa—for transmission. There are two primary types of modem software: general-purpose, and service-specific. General-purpose software has dialing directories that can be set up to call online services, bulletin board systems, and many other places. Service-specific software is easier to install because it calls only one place, such as CompuServe, Prodigy, or America Online. Communications software expands the power of a computer by forming a network and working with other computers or even by harnessing the power of a mainframe.

Public Relations and Electronic Media

Since its appearance in the United States nearly a century ago, public relations practice built its foundation on print media. That predominance began to shift in the 1940s when radio and television joined the avenues of communication. Videotape did not appear until the late

1950s; video news releases were uncommon until the 1970s. Interactive videodisc, cable television, and satellite technology were adapted for public relations use in the early 1980s, and multimedia approaches began to surface in the latter part of the decade. The 1990s witnessed a growth in the distribution and usage of VNRs, teleconferencing, and multimedia in the form of CDs and the Internet. The decade served as a crucible for the development of electronic public relations.

"Pushing this electronic evolution is the struggle between online services and the growing glut of 'paper' information," writes researcher Eugene Marlow. This tension is apparent when PR practitioners try to cover all their bases by offering a print version media kit alongside an electronic version that can be downloaded from their Web site.

With electronic media vehicles, some of Walter Lippmann's barriers to communication—geographic, linguistic, and political boundaries—are greatly lessened or eliminated. Time and accessibility have also been dramatically altered. The Internet has moved communication away from one-way toward two-way. This two-way or interactive approach is particularly useful for PR practitioners. Two-way or dialogic communication is compatible with what Grunig and Hunt describe as the ideal two-way symmetrical model of public relations. It is characterized by mutual understanding and respect for the viewpoints of others and it supports truthful disclosure of information. Its aim is understanding rather than persuasion. Never before in the history of the practice of public relations have practitioners had the opportunities for true two-way symmetrical communication that the Internet provides.

Telecommunications: Going Online

Access to worldwide networks is available to anyone with a computer and modem. The potential is there for businesses of all sizes, from the single-person consulting shop to large industrial complexes, to move into the global marketplace. Dial-up network services best address the needs of businesses that don't require the high-speed dedicated resources of Ford, General Motors, and various other industrial giants. Organizations and individuals can dial into a service provider to send and receive electronic mail, or to use tools like Archie, Gopher, Eudora Pro, or the World Wide Web to find specific information on an as-needed basis. Wireless (SpeedChoice) and cable access (@Home) to the Internet are also available and provide nearly instantaneous connection to the world's estimated 2 million Web sites.

Telecommunications play a vital role in the integration of new technologies used in public relations to help meet the challenges of the future. As a medium, telecommunications can help improve effectiveness both by extending reach and efficiency and by shortening the amount of time between the decision to communicate and the execution of the message. In addition, telecommunications methods can increase control over the contents of the message and afford greater capability to measure the effectiveness of the program. Information technology management—the integration of people, information, and technology—is key to business success now and in the future.

The Internet.   Dominating the world of high-speed networking, defining it in terms of sheer size and reach, is the largest, best-known, most used network of all: the Internet.

PRoEthics
Cybercrisis

Situation

"Despite all the excitement created by the Internet, there is an emerging dark side. We are talking about rogue Web sites—sites posted by activists, disgruntled employees, and other anti-corporate types for the purpose of damaging the reputation of the targeted organization."

The Internet is a realm with boundaries yet to be defined, a medium governed by virtually no laws or rules, and a forum that often lacks in good judgment, fairness, and civility. The role of public relations in the Internet Age is undergoing great change. "It is essential that practitioners learn to communicate, develop strategy, and design crisis plans with these rogue sites in mind."

Response/Approach

Here's how a company can prepare for the Internet:

- Surf the Web, join listservs, and linger in newsgroups that talk about your company and its areas of interest.

- Your company should develop a Net crisis strategy and ongoing Internet media plan by researching and assessing the situation.
- Do not ignore or underestimate the problem. It is essential to treat an Internet attack like a true media crisis. You must respond.
- Try and reach the source or individual who is attacking your company on the Internet.
- Tell your side of the story to that source to clear up misunderstandings, misleading information, or inaccuracies.
- Listen. If possible, try to find common ground.
- Be ready to respond immediately, preferably on your own Web page, to the online media, as well as traditional media outlets.
- Lawyers may want to be involved with possible libel cases.

Source: Middleberg, Don. How to avoid a cybercrisis. *Public Relations Tactics.* (1996, November): p. 1, 15.

Emerging in 1968 as a patchwork of computer science departments at seven U.S. universities, it has grown far beyond its humble beginnings. By 2000, it is projected that 200 million people would connect to the Net. Internet services are becoming integrated into the entire corporate value chain, from research and development and manufacturing to the marketing/public relations and customer service divisions.

The ability to find usable information in a timely and efficient fashion is critical to businesses. According to experts at the Second International Harvard Conference on Internet and Society in 1999, the people who use the Internet will ultimately determine the technology it will use and the features it will offer. "We don't make the decisions," said panel member and America Online CEO Steve Case. "Consumers make the decisions." Panelists Marimba CEO Kim Polese and White House technology adviser Ira Magaziner agreed.

Knowing what customers want, where they are located, what they will pay, and who is competing are components in any business plan. Remote collaboration is useful not only in an academic environment but also in the corporate world. By using branch offices and remote facilities around the world, a company can keep information-intensive projects going around the clock and take maximum advantage of its own intellectual resources. In an economy where single-person offices and home-based companies are springing up like mushrooms, the Internet can open up the marketplace and allow small businesses to compete successfully.

Online Information Networks/Databases.   Today, high-tech databases, which put mountains of online information at the fingertips of practitioners, are the research tools of choice at most firms and corporate communications departments. Databases are revolutionizing the way research is conducted. Research, considered by many experts to be the key ingredient to effective client service, is fast becoming a high-tech art form at many public relations firms. Using a variety of online information databases, public relations practitioners can do everything from monitoring breaking news and client press coverage to researching key issues and social trends. Research topics are diverse, ranging from product recalls to recycling to employee communications. Databases also help firms craft new business pitches. It has been said of many users that anything you can imagine can be found online. "Research can only add value," said Karyn Sternberger, manager of information services at Ketchum Public Relation's New York office. "It helps proactive PR firms stay on top of the news. Clients are impressed with the depth and speed of information we can deliver, and many clients are becoming more research savvy in their own operations."

Top executives and information managers agree that knowing what can be extracted from databases, vast electronic libraries of full-text and abstract articles from around the corner or around the world, is the key ingredient to winning the information war. And speed, which databases deliver, is crucial when a firm is looking for time-sensitive breaking news, especially in a crisis, according to Masterton.

In fact, the public relations uses of databases are virtually limitless. Online information can be a priceless asset when a client is on the carpet before Congress or embroiled in such controversies as product liability suits or false advertising charges. The major benefit of databases, of course, is that the gathering of timely information enables a firm and its clients to respond quickly and effectively in any situation.

But a public relations counselor's responsibilities extend beyond a specific client to the whole arena in which that company operates. Enter databases again. "As hard as we try to keep tabs on how our client is doing, it's just as important to monitor what the competition is up to," advises Tom Bartikoski, APR, senior vice president at Minneapolis-based Padilla Speer Beardsley. "We need to know how rivals respond to client initiatives, the financial condition of competitors, even whether they're getting better coverage. A lot of this information comes out of databases." Online research can also help firms win better media coverage by indicating where and how their best efforts should be directed. Databases can spare firms and their clients many hours of work and wasted effort. They can really help prevent practitioners from reinventing the wheel.

However, databases can be used for far more than client support. Many firms also conduct information searches to prospect for new business. Advances in information technology are enhancing efforts by public relations firms to secure new clients. To most public relations firms, obtaining new clients has priority second only to keeping existing clients and serving them well. To be successful in obtaining new clients, a public relations firm must have demonstrated skill, a bit of luck, and knowledge about both the prospective client and the industry and marketplace in which the client participates. The public relations firm must know as much about the prospective client as it can before it attempts to help that prospect with its business problem or situation. To become familiar with a prospective client takes quality information. And this is where the tools of high technology, such as electronic databases, come into play.

Using commercial databases is not necessarily expensive, but an unskilled person doing a search can quickly add up costs. Each database charges for computer time and uses different access protocols, so many public relations executives often prefer limiting access to just a few librarians or researchers who know what they're looking for as well as where and how to find it.

Entrepreneurial firms that might not have the time, money, or personnel to purchase an online information service can "rent" database searches. For instance, for a fee, the Public Relations Society of America (PRSA) Information Center conducts database searches for members on specific subjects and topics.

A researcher may not even need to conduct a search because some databases can be programmed to store relevant data as they come in. Proactive firms willing to pay the extra cost can set up special files with services such as NewsNet and Nexis, so that pertinent articles meeting their specifications are automatically stored for easy retrieval without the time or cost of a conventional search. Lexis, part of the database giant Lexis-Nexis, is the largest legal research database in the United States and is equally information rich to the public relations practitioner.

The public relations professional can also keep abreast of the latest news through online news wires. Several companies, including United Press International, Associated Press, Dow-Jones News Service, and PR Newswire, offer this service. These services provide the latest economic, financial, and political news.

Other services from Nexis, Dow-Jones News/Retrieval, and NewsNet offer the full text of daily newspapers and newsletters. Nexis is one of the best-known full-text databases, containing the full text of articles from about 7,100 news and business publications. The Dow-Jones News/Retrieval Service includes text libraries of about 2,000 newspapers and magazines, financial industry information in addition to quotes and market data.

Some of the more popular databases available in the business arena cover business-oriented media. Examples of bibliographic databases in this area include: ABI/INFORM, Infobank, Management Contents, and Trade and Industry Index.

Demographic and market data are available from a number of online databases, including Advertising and Marketing Intelligence, ADTRACK, SITE II and DORIS, and American Profile, and can be used for preparing political or marketing campaigns.

Other databases are descriptive of industry in general; still others focus on a specific industry. Not only can these databases be used for background information, but industry-specific databases can be used to build mailing lists. Many broad databases also have narrowly focused, specialized files that can greatly enhance client service. DIALOG, for instance, is one of the largest retrievable databases in the world that focuses on science and technology. It also boasts files on food service, technical abstracts, demographics, and the pharmaceutical industry.

The Internet is also an important avenue for practitioners to use to promote or create visibility for their clients as well as related venues via electronic versions of traditional news outlets.

News Web Sites.   A 1998 Pew Research Center study on Internet news readership indicates that the number of Americans reading news on the Internet is growing at an "astonishing" rate. One in five people use the network at least once a week as a supplement to traditional sources of news. The result reflects the Internet's tremendous growth. In 1994, only 4 percent went online for news at least once a week. The number grew to 6 percent in 1996 and then shot to 20 percent two years later. The number of people who "went online" period nearly tripled from 1995 to 1998, rising from 14 percent to 36 percent. The study also reported that people reading news on the Internet are disproportionately younger, better educated, and affluent and place a higher value on getting up-to-date information. The most popular subjects online were science, health, finance, and technology.

Cable.   The Pew Center study also found that cable television's impact on viewership was greater than the Internet's, with 40 percent of Americans regularly watching cable news networks such as CNN, MSNBC, CNBC, or Fox. Cable's audience swelled to 60 percent when specialty programs like the Weather Channel or ESPN, ESPN2 were considered. "Cable's advantage lies in its immediacy," the study concludes. "Americans say they would turn to cable channels first in the event of a big news story, whether it concerned politics, health or sports." George Harmon, newspaper-editorial sequence chair at Northwestern University, was quoted in a CNN Internet news story as describing a "colossal gravitation" toward cable news in the hours after a major story, such as the death of Princess Diana. The same holds true for the Internet: "Site traffic is extremely heavy on the Web when you've got a blockbuster story."

Network News.   Network news programs did not fare well in the study. It found just 38 percent of Americans, mostly older women, describe themselves as regular viewers. The figure is a 22 percent drop from 60 percent in 1993. Television magazines, however, did attract more viewers, especially younger audiences. When traditional network news broadcast viewership is combined with news magazines or morning shows, the audience levels off at 57 percent. It still represents an undeniable erosion.

Newspapers.   Readership of daily newspapers remained "remarkably stable," according to the Pew Center report. It found that Americans continue to rely heavily on their daily paper as a primary source of news. Sixty-eight percent of the study's 3,002 respondents said they read the paper regularly, about the same result as the Pew Center's 1996 finding. The downside is that only 28 percent of people under thirty reported reading a newspaper within 24 hours of when the survey was conducted (April 24 and May 11, 1998) compared with 69 percent of senior citizens. This represents "a far more dramatic generation gap than exists for television news consumption," the study concluded.

Search Engines.   According to the editors of *Wired* magazine in their book *Wired Style,* "Internet search engines are the on-line world's equivalent of the librarian who looks up info in the card index at the public library." They search the Net for information using key words or concepts. Unlike commercial databases, search engines are free as long as you or your firm has Web access. Among them are AltaVista, Excite, HotBot, InfoSeek, Lycos, and Yahoo! There is even a search engine for search engines, among them MetaCrawler is widely used. AOL CEO Steve Case notes that even though the Web will continue to offer more and more content, people will pick the search engines that give them what they want. Successful search engines will accommodate that need.

Electronic Mail.   The communications vehicle with which most people are familiar is electronic mail (e-mail), a staple in offices across the country and around the world. E-mail is the process of sending messages directly from one terminal or computer to another. Or as the authors of *A Quick Guide to the Internet* write, "E-mail is what the United States Postal Service would be if it were perfect: fast, reliable, inexpensive and environmentally safe." Electronic mail is widely used, and its use and value will grow substantially in the future as speedy, targeted communications gain even greater ground in the fight for attention in the average person's in-box and mailbox, notes Affeldt. A practitioner or anyone can send e-mail to multiple sites at the same time; forward mail instantaneously; and send electronic pictures, software, or files.

Other uses are e-mail discussion lists or listservs, Usenet, and IRC. Listservs allow the user to subscribe by e-mail to a topical discussion list. Then everything that other subscribers send on that topic is sent to you automatically via a central computer. The subscribers to this list join the discussion by e-mailing their own comments and responses. Many professional mass communication organizations operate listservs to keep their members up-to-date with the latest news in their fields.

Usenet is a collection of Internet newsgroups. Cavanaugh, Rivard, and Branscomb describe them as "giant worldwide discussion groups, the major difference between them and e-mail discussion lists being that you don't have to subscribe. . . . They operate like a bulletin board in a grocery store where people post messages for the public." You have access to the newsgroup and its messages; however, there is no automatic e-mailing that occurs. In 1997, it was estimated that there were more than 20,000 newsgroups worldwide ranging from scholarly to pornographic.

IRC or Internet Relay Chat is an international array of Internet-connected computers. Known as "live chats" or a "chat room," it is live e-mail forum available twenty-four/seven. What you send appears in real time on all other IRC users' screens. "It's chaotic, like being at a cocktail party and trying to participate in sixteen discussions simultaneously, but it's lively and it's synchronous," explain Cavanaugh, Rivard, and Branscomb. Commercial on-line services such as America Online also allow two users into a "private" chat room where an interview or exchange of information can occur without distraction.

No one knows exactly how many people use e-mail, but Link Resources Corporation, a market research group, estimates there are 11.5 million e-mail users throughout the United

EXHIBIT **2.1**

Stages in the Innovation Process in Organizations

Major activities at each stage in the innovation process

I. Initiation: All of the information gathering, conceptualizing, and planning for the adoption of an innovation, leading up to the decision to adopt.

    1. Agenda Setting: General organizational problems, which may create a perceived need for an innovation, are defined; the environment's search for innovations of potential value to the organization.

    2. Matching: A problem from the organization's agenda is considered together with an innovation, and the fit between them is planned and designed.

II. Implementation: All of the events, actions, and decisions involved in putting an innovation into use.

    1. Redefining/Restructuring: (a) The innovation is modified and reinvented to fit the situation of the particular organization and its perceived problem, and (b) organizational structures directly relevant to the innovation are altered to accommodate the innovation.

    2. Clarifying: The relationship between the innovation and the organization is defined more clearly as the innovation is put into full and regular use.

    3. Routinizing: The innovation eventually loses its separate identity and becomes an element in the organization's ongoing activities.

Source: Adapted from Everett M. Rogers. *Diffusion of Innovation,* 3rd ed. New York: Free Press, 1983, 363.

States. Heavy e-mail users appear better informed than their colleagues, and studies also indicate that employees who join e-mail conferences are generally more likely to participate in the discussions than they would be in face-to-face encounters, writes Baig.

    This approach to communicating is a powerful and cost-effective tool for public relations professionals because of its speed and because it can be combined with mailing lists to accurately reach a targeted audience worldwide. Mass mailings can be easily targeted and there are no additional postage costs. The advantages and applications of electronic mail for public relations can be seen in all areas, including investor relations, community relations, employee relations, government relations, and crisis management.

World Wide Web

The Web was conceived in March 1989 by Tim Berners-Lee of CERN (the European Laboratory for Particle Physics) who proposed a way to distribute and receive information globally via the Internet in the form of specially coded or hypertext documents and pictures. Hypertext allows users to view other documents via a link and then return to the original document or location. The landscape of electronic communication was further altered when in February 1993 students at the University of Illinois developed the first known browser, Mosaic, which allowed the user to access the Web, then read and retrieve documents from

WWW servers. In addition, information could be downloaded or uploaded from many forums. No longer was the Internet exclusive to the members of a small academic or governmental circle. Rather, anyone with the required equipment was inclusive to the Net, and browser software became the first step in its democratization. Today there is a variety of software to let users travel the Web. Brand names include HotJava, Netscape Navigator, and Microsoft Explorer.

Hypertext has given way to hypermedia that includes audio, video, animation, and graphical elements. HTML, or Hypertext Markup Language, and a range of Web design software provide an open door to literally the world for corporations as well as private citizens via their Web sites. A Web site, as *Wired* magazine notes, "is any collection of pages that live on the Web." The pages are accessed at an "address" through a main title or contents page called a "frontdoor." For communications purposes, Web site names should be selected carefully and can go far in helping a client establish an Internet presence. The domain is also a point not to gloss over. Three-letter top-level domains for Internet addresses in the United States are .net for a computer network, .com for a commercial organization, .org for miscellaneous organizations, .mil for the military, .gov for government, and .edu for educational institutions. More domains are expected to increase the possible servers, using their names and addresses. Addresses outside the United States use a two-letter country abbreviation such as ca for Canada, jp for Japan, au for Australia, or nl for the Netherlands.

As Cavanaugh, Rivard, and Branscomb explain, "World Wide Web sites give the ability to provide visibility for their clients. Instead of trying to gain access to the existing media, the Internet has become the medium that has the potential to deliver for a PR practitioner's clients almost unlimited access and visibility with total control of the message." Its effective use has the ability to finely target an audience and communicate with it directly, thereby eliminating the traditional gatekeeping function of the mass media.

Until the mid-1990s, broadcasting through television or radio was one-way communication. NBC began experimenting with the medium in a big way during the 1996 Olympic Games in Atlanta. NBC maintained an active Web site providing information about sporting events and biographies of competitors. Today, all networks and many local TV and radio stations maintain Web sites. Hit television shows and even movies regularly promote their Web addresses during the credits or in print or broadcast ads. There are even fans devoted to favorite TV shows who create and maintain Web sites offering their own plot lines, episode guides, summaries, photo galleries, and critiques. Many rival the official sites in their depth, design, links, and coverage. The movie industry also has capitalized on this direct link to film afficionados. For example, in 1999, New Line Cinema signed a multimillion-dollar contract with AOL that will give its films a major promotional push to 2001.

Web sites are "pure polyglot: part publishing, part broadcasting, part narrowcasting, part casting for profits," write *Wired* editors. "They involve real-time interaction, HTML links, place-ness, and a sense of community. They are dynamic, not static." They should be timely, comprehensive, easy to navigate, and easy to use. These observations should be carefully considered when a practitioner recommends creating a Web presence for a client. Web sites that are not maintained and infrequently updated can harm rather than enhance a client's reputation or image. Kent and Taylor provide five strategies for communication professionals to assess two-way communication with Internet publics. The presence or absence of these principles is indicative of the extent to which an organization is effectively capitalizing on the potential of the Web. Kent and Taylor's five principles are

- The dialogic loop
- Usefulness of information
- Generation of return visits
- Ease of the interface
- Rule of the conservation of visitors

The loop refers to the need to provide feedback to the public. It is pointless to post e-mail addresses to which your client fails to respond. The response must also be timely and professional. Response and content together constitute the major bulk of a successful loop that is essential to building relationships.

Kent and Taylor maintain that all Web sites should concentrate on providing information of general value to all publics, regardless of whether a site is industry specific or user specific. Although content should be the impetus that drives the engine of an effective Web site, many rely on eye-catching graphics that lack substantive data. The structure of the information is important because sites should offer information of consistent value to the publics

---

PRoActive
Web sites

With the increasing use of Web sites to disseminate information, this article focuses on what must be done to keep a Web site continually impressive. Just having a Web site isn't good enough. What needs to happen?

- View content as a marketing tool.
  "The purpose of corporate Web sites is fundamentally marketing and sales. Visitors reading a particular article are self targeted, and companies have an unprecedented opportunity to create links to marketing material." Old Web sites can do damage by portraying an unconcerned image.

- Commit to a content program.
  "On the Internet, content must be tended to on a monthly, weekly, or even daily basis. Companies must be prepared with tools and techniques that take advantage of the Web's interactive nature: e-mail notices to visitors about new features, listserv opportunities, and sophisticated company-supplied search engines."

- Provide systems for easy content management.
  "Content must be readily and easily available online in a private and secure area to everyone. A properly designed content management system helps with the multi-headed approval processes in major corporations as well."

- Determine how to get it accomplished.
  "The key question is, who will be responsible?" Will it be an internal job or something that a company searches for outside?

Source: David E. Gumpert. "Freshening the Web Site." *The Public Relations Strategist,* 3 (Fall 1997): 42–44.

they serve. As Elmer notes, a Web site that is a well-organized information extension of an organization engenders positive attitudes in the public.

Return visits to a Web site are critical for media organizations, as they prefer to be regarded as a credible source of information. Sites that feature changing issues, special forums, and experts to answer questions and interact with the online public will be more likely to spark return visits.

In terms of accessibility, no dialog will occur if a site is inaccessible. Kent and Taylor say graphics that take a significant amount of loading time are less effective attention grabbers than well-typeset pages. Web sites should not be overwhelmed by gratuitous special effects that ultimately prove to be a distraction.

Site design should be aimed at slightly below average equipment. Kent and Taylor suggest allowing users to choose between a basic version of the site and a supercharged version with all the bells and whistles. In this way, the public can interact with an organization on its own terms. A site that serves only the technologically privileged may leave particular publics with a negative image of an organization.

The rule of conservation concerns links that can lead visitors off site. Visitors select a particular site for what the site offers and not to shop around. Links that lead visitors astray are self-defeating in that surfers may never return to the original site. Advertising links are particularly egregious and sponsored advertising often entices visitors away. Sites weighed down with ads may drive a visitor away. If the goal of the Web site is to provide information, then ideally advertising should be avoided or strategically placed to reduce distractions.

Dialogic or two-way communication is ideally suited as a concept to guide relationship building on the Internet and to maximize the Web's potential for significant communication. But this means little if individuals practicing public relations are unskilled in working in the medium or are unaware of how to appeal to the Internet's diverse audience.

People: The Adoption of Technology

All of the hardware, software, and telecommunications services are useless unless people adopt these technologies. Technophobia runs rampant in the business arena with many companies falling behind in the marketplace simply because they lack the determination to become techno-savvy. Public relations practitioners are no exception. People as well as organizations go through a process of adopting and adapting to technological innovations. Before these new technological tools can be of use, they first must be accepted and integrated into the work environment.

The Diffusion of Innovations

According to Rogers, "The main elements in the diffusion of new ideas are: an innovation, which is communicated through certain channels, over time, among members of a social system." An innovation is an idea, practice, or object perceived as new by an individual. The characteristics of an innovation, as perceived by the members of a social system, determine its rate of adoption. Five attributes of innovations are relative advantage, compatibility, complexity, trialability, and observability.

Relative advantage is the degree to which an innovation is perceived as better than the idea it supersedes. The degree of relative advantage may be measured in economic terms, but social-prestige factors, convenience, and satisfaction are also often important components. It does not matter so much whether an innovation has a great deal of objective advantage; what does matter is whether an individual perceives the innovation as advantageous. The greater the perceived relative advantage of an innovation, the more rapid is its rate of adoption, Rogers notes.

Compatibility is the degree to which an innovation is perceived as being consistent with the existing values, past experiences, and known needs of potential adopters. An idea that is not compatible with the prevalent values and norms of a social system will not be adopted as rapidly as an innovation that is compatible. The adoption of an incompatible innovation/technology often requires the prior adoption of a new value system.

Complexity is the degree to which an innovation is perceived as difficult to understand and use. Some innovations are readily understood; others, such as new technological equipment, are more complicated and will be adopted more slowly. In general, new ideas that are simpler to understand will be adopted more rapidly than innovations that require the adopter to develop new skills and understandings.

Trialability is the degree to which an innovation may be experimented with on a limited basis. New ideas that can be tried on the installment plan will generally be adopted more quickly than innovations that are not divisible. An innovation that is trialable represents less uncertainty to the individual who is considering it for adoption, as it is possible to learn by doing.

Observability is the degree to which the results of an innovation are visible to others. The easier it is for individuals to see the results of an innovation, the more likely they are to adopt it. Such visibility stimulates peer discussion of a new idea, as friends and associates of an adopter ask him or her for innovation or evaluation information about it. Rogers notes that some consumer innovations such as home computers are relatively less observable and thus may diffuse more slowly. In general, innovations that are perceived by receivers as having greater relative advantage, compatibility, less complexity, trialability, and observability will be adopted more rapidly than other innovations.

How Technology Changes Work

Technology is dramatically changing the way both individuals and organizations work. By providing timely access to data, computers let businesspeople spend less time checking and rechecking data and more time getting work done. This inspires informed decision making and improves overall productivity.

Information technology is fundamentally changing the practice of public relations. As competition increases, good people are not enough; substantial year-in and year-out investments in technology and redesign work processes are increasingly necessary to compete successfully.

Since the installation of technology at the public relations firm of Manning, Selvage, & Lee, the success rate in obtaining new clients has risen to about 60 percent from 30 percent prior to installation. Lonnie Unger stated, "While our creative talents and professional personnel clearly contribute to the winning of new accounts, the account people, nevertheless,

EXHIBIT **2.2**

Electronic PR Forecast

Eugene Marlow, in his book *Electronic Public Relations,* offers a ten-point consensus of what public relations professionals predict will happen in the twenty-first century in regard to the impact of technologies:

- Electronic media will annihilate the concept of a mass audience.
- Electronic PR will continue to expand exponentially.
- Demand for VNRs will grow.
- There will be increased interactive media usage by the public relations industry.

- Use of paper will decrease.
- Newspapers and magazines will adopt electronic versions.
- Journalists may bypass the PR practitioner as information buffer.
- There will be an increase in public relations consultants and consulting firms.
- PR practitioners will come from diverse backgrounds and professions.
- Public relations will remain a business of relationships.

---

are learning more about a potential client's business and are working better and faster because of the high-technology tools, all to the benefit of our current and future clients."

Experts in process reengineering estimate that professional service firms should be able to maintain quality and improve productivity by about 6 percent each year. Whether that's true of public relations or not, it's now possible to arm a single practitioner with tools to do jobs that used to require a small department, using technology support for document creation, media contact, research, internal and external communication, project management, and much more. As the experts predicted, there are fewer people producing more quality work.

Technology has also streamlined the public relations office. New positions include database administrators, information technology directors, network administrators, desktop publishing and graphic design staff, and general computer-support personnel. Many secretarial and administrative assistant positions are no longer necessary now that public relations practitioners have their own computers. Computers have provided practitioners with more control, allowing them to produce and edit written materials and create graphics in-house. In addition, databases are used to conduct research, monitor breaking news and client press coverage, research new clients for business pitches, prospect for new business, keep track of key issues and social trends, monitor client competition, and help win better media coverage by indicating how and where efforts should be directed.

The adoption of technology in the public relations office has also led to a concern about security. Most firms use simple passwords to limit access to data. At the Evans Group (the thirtieth-ranked firm), the practitioner who responded to Gorman's survey stated:

> Each user is required to have a password that is changed every 60 days. The password cannot be used more than once. It must be a certain length and if you need access to your personal files, you must have the correct password to gain access. An intruder lockout will lock the account if more than three invalid attempts are made to the user's accounts.

Summary

Public relations is a field that has traditionally favored the personal touch in communications. Most public relations executives describe themselves as "people-oriented," "nuts and bolts" individuals with little experience using advanced telecommunications technology. In past literature, practitioners have voiced concerns that in the drive to automate the process, some of the personal touches will be sacrificed. Computer technology is not intended to do that. In fact, one founder of a high-tech company believes "public relations is helping invent the industry itself." Because of the degree of change in high-tech firms, public relations is enormously important. "Unlike other forms of communications, public relations can turn on a dime," explains Digital Island CEO Ron Higgins. "PR is part of Digital Island's DNA."

QUESTIONS

1. What are the five strategies Kent and Taylor suggest to assess two-way communication with Internet publics?

2. Discuss three technologies used by PR practitioners.

3. What does Marlow say PR practitioners predict will happen in the future in regard to technology usage?

4. In what ways can technology change the way PR practitioners work?

READINGS

R. Bobbitt (1995). "An Internet Primer for Public Relations." *Public Relations Quarterly* 40 (3): 27–32.

Michael T. Cavanaugh, Joseph D Rivard, and H. Eric Branscomb. *Quick Guide to the Internet.* Boston: Allyn and Bacon, 1997.

M. L. Kent and M. Taylor. "Building Dislogic Relationships through the World Wide Web." *Public Relations Review* 24, no. 3 (1998): 321–334.

Eugene Marlow. *Electronic Public Relations.* Belmont, CA: Wadsworth Publishing Company, 1996.

M. Morris and C. Ogan. "The Internet as Mass Medium." *Journal of Communication* 46 (1): 39–50 1196.

Everett M. Rogers. *Diffusion of Innovations.* New York: The Free Press, 1983.

USWeb and Rick E. Bruner. *Net Results: Web Marketing That Works.* Indianapolis, IN: Hayden Books, 1998.

Constance Hale (ed.) *Wired Style: Principles of English Usage in the Digital Age.* San Francisco: Hard-Wired, 1996.

Fraser Seitel. The Practice of Public Relations (5th ed). New York: Macmillan, 1992.

"The Future of Public Relations Is On the Internet." *The Public Relations Strategist.* vol. 5, no. 1 (Spring 1999); 7–10.

DEFINITIONS

With the rapidly advancing state of technology, new terms and computer jargon are added to the language on a frequent basis. In order to succeed in today's workplace, public relations practitioners must keep their techno-knowledge current. The following definitions are provided as a framework to further the understanding and know-how of those who must provided as a framework to further the understanding and know-how of those who must survive and thrive in a computer-literate world.

adoption: A decision to make full use of an innovation as the best course of action available.

communication: A process in which participants create and share information with one another in order to reach a mutual understanding.

communication technology (information technology): Encompasses all electronic technologies including hardware, software, and online services.

computer: A machine that accepts data (input) and processes them into useful information (output).

computer literacy: The awareness of, knowledge of, and capacity to interact with computers.

database: A vast electronic library of full-text and abstract articles from around the corner or around the world; a collection of interrelated files stored together with minimum redundancy.

desktop publishing (electronic publishing):   The use of a personal computer, special software, and a laser printer to produce high-quality documents that combine text and graphics.

electronic mail (e-mail):   Refers to messages sent or received through bulletin boards and online services, as well as office networks and the Internet.

facsimile (fax) technology: The use of computer technology to send digitized graphics, charts, and text from one fax machine to another.

Gopher: A menu-based system for exploring Internet resources.

graphical user interface (GUI):   An image-based interface in which the user sends directions to the operating system by selecting icons from a menu or manipulating icons on the screen by using a pointing device such as a mouse. Windows and Macintosh use this format.

integrated software: All-in-one software with several applications, usually including a simple modem program.

Internet: A worldwide public communications network that provides file transfer, remote login, electronic mail, news, and other services as well as access to information, people, and other resources.

multimedia: Documents that include different kinds of data—for example, plain text, audio and video, text in several different languages, or plain text and a spreadsheet.

network: A computer system that uses communications equipment to connect two or more computers and their resources.

online services (information utilities):   Commercial consumer-oriented communications systems; a place that can be called with a modem that charges subscription fees or hourly rates for files, fellowship, and games, plus shopping, news, sports, weather, and other information. CompuServe, America Online, Prodigy, Netscape Navigator, and Microsoft Explorer are the primary online services.

telecommunications: The union of communications and computers.

word processing: Computer-based writing, editing, styling, storing, and printing of text.

World Wide Web (WWW):   A hypertext-based system for finding and accessing Internet resources.

3 Ethical and Legal Concerns

Doing What's Right

CHAPTER OUTLINE

Ethical Principles

Philosophers

Decision-Making Models

Legal Considerations

Publicity and Propaganda

CHAPTER OBJECTIVES

When you have completed this chapter, you should be able to:

- Know what is meant by ethics
- Determine your ethical orientation
- Know how to use models to aid decision making
- Understand how laws may affect the way a practitioner communicates
- Distinguish the differences between the legitimate and illegitimate persuader

If persuasion techniques are used in our message gathering and dissemination, then ethical and legal concerns will emerge. One question a public relations practitioner must ask is: Are my persuasion methods legitimate or illegitimate, ethical or unethical? And there are other possibilities: Are my tactics unethical but legal? Is there a point when publicity can turn into propaganda? Am I applying my ethics or my boss's ethics? Before any of these questions can be answered, it's necessary for the individual practitioner to develop and explore personal ethical conduct.

According to researcher Cornelius Pratt, "Ethics is the essence of maintaining effective relationships in public relations. Yet, study after study has called into question the ethics (or morality) of . . . practitioners." Pratt's study of PRSA members found that "beliefs of top managers are perceived as more ethical than those of both practitioners and peers." In a study by Larry Judd, none of the respondents gave high marks to the honesty and ethical standards of practitioners: Fifty-five percent selected the CEO as the most credible source of information while only 5 percent chose a PR officer.

Pearson writes that "Public relations practice is situated at precisely that point where competing interests collide. . . . Serving client and public interests simultaneously is the seemingly impossible mission of the public relations practitioner." This impossible mission is what Gollner calls a "crowding in" of external issues on organizational decision making. He describes a "shrinking world in which the mutual dependence among . . . institutions (systems) is increasing rapidly." A result of these tensions is incompatible values. Noted researcher Scott Cutlip asserts that there is a fundamental ethical dilemma facing practitioners: "how to maintain credibility . . . how to represent the client, yet stay separate and independent to tell the truth."

The situation is then ripe for public relations to step in as the agent to resolve the resulting conflicts. However, there is a problem. Ryan and Martinson suggest that there is no objective standard for ethical decision making: "If public relations has adopted any underlying principle, it is possibly the subjectivism (or individual relativism) theory that each individual must establish his or her own moral baselines." Wright also argues that individual ethics may determine public relations practice. Shamir, Reed, and Connell's findings support the stance that "a strong predictor of professional ethical standards is the degree of reported personal ethics."

How then can practitioners develop their own code of conduct? "Ethics education leads the list of suggestions," Pratt writes.

Ethical Principles

Doctors take the Hippocratic oath to heal and do no harm, witnesses swear to "tell the truth and nothing but the truth," police officers promise to render aid, and Native Americans ask others to walk a mile in another man's moccasins. Each of these actions has a basis in ethics; each seeks to explain differing points of view, some with greater clarity than others.

"Contemporary professional ethics revolves around these questions: What duties do I have, and to whom do I owe them? What values are reflected by the duties I've assumed?" write Patterson and Wilkins.

The concept of ethics originated with the Greeks, who defined it as the study of what is good for the individual and society. Epicurus said, "Ethics deals with things to be sought and things to be avoided, with ways of life and with *telos* [the chief good or aim]." Today, ethics asks us to make rational choices based on principles that help us arrive at decisions and actions that are morally justifiable. When the choice is made, the individual must also be able to explain the ethical decision to others. "Ethics is less about the conflict between right and wrong and more about the conflict between equally compelling (or equally unattractive) values and the subsequent choices that must be made between them," Patterson and Wilkins affirm.

Philosophers

Aristotle

Aristotle taught in the fourth century B.C. that individuals should seek virtue for its own sake. He required that individuals take responsibility for their actions because they possess free choice. This means that "ethical behavior might require adhering to a personal interpretation of what is right or good, even if that means going against the flow of current thought in society," writes Conrad Fink. Aristotle's system is also known as virtue ethics. Patterson and Wilkins write: "[T]he way to behave ethically [in the Aristotelian sense] is that (1) you must know what you are doing; (2) you must select the act for its own sake and (3) the act itself must spring from a firm and unchanging character." This boils down to the approach that happiness, or "flourishing" as some scholars term it, means using practical reason for ultimate human good. Commonly, this concept is reduced to a "golden mean" whereby virtue lies between two extremes. For Aristotle, ethics was a reflection of man's contributions to the good of society. This contribution also required the individual to sacrifice in order to better humanity as a whole, be it in time or happiness lost.

Hobbes

Thomas Hobbes delved into mankind's psychological motivations and viewed fear and selfishness as prime motivators of conduct. Writing in the 1600s, he believed that people—not rulers, governments, and, to update his examples, corporations—possess true power.

Milton

In the same era, John Milton developed his "open marketplace of ideas" concept with its "self-righting process," which presumably would allow the informed audience to decide the truth of an issue. In *Areopagitica,* he writes, "Let all with something to say be free to express themselves. The true and the sound will survive, the false and unsound will be vanquished." This dictum may have been true in the past before digital technology made it impossible to distinguish the truth from a lie. Seeing, or hearing for that matter, is no longer believing.

Hume and Mill

David Hume injected a scientific approach into ethics studies with the introduction of empiricism. This concept says that knowledge equals experience and verification if it is derived from experimentation or observation. He argued that usefulness or "utility" is the correct measure for any ethical standard. He dismissed the notion that good can be discovered through reason. A century later, John Stuart Mill expanded this theme, saying that ethics meant creating the greatest happiness for the greatest number of people. To Mill, the outcome or consequence of an action was of prime importance.

PRoSpeak
Public Relations and the Law

The First Amendment to the Constitution declares: "Congress shall make no law . . . abridging freedom of speech, or of the press." With no constitutional protection of free speech and free press, public relations would be impossible in the United States.

On the other hand, the constitutional guarantee of freedom of expression makes no distinction between ordinary individuals and professional communicators, including public relations practitioners. As the Supreme Court of the United States ruled in 1991: "Generally applicable laws do not offend the First Amendment simply because their enforcement against the press has incidental effects on its ability to gather and report the news."

The Supreme Court's interpretation of the First Amendment on the general applicability of laws and regulation to any type of expression explains why PR practitioners should be concerned with various laws affecting their profession. In *Public Relations Law* (1969), the 882-page seminal book on the relations between the law and public relations, author Morton J. Simon has stated: "Public relations is a 'horizontal' function. It is, therefore, subject to a broad spectrum of seemingly unassociated legal regimens."

As for a growing need for an understanding of public relations law, Frank Walsh has argued in *Public Relations and the Law* (1988): "Knowledge of public relations law places the practitioner in a better position to service his/her individual organization or clients. Knowledge of public relations law also places the practitioner in a position to better serve the entire profession. If an individual practitioner suffers the personal and financial hardships of legal actions, the profession suffers right along with him or her."

More recently, Professors Greg Lisby (Georgia State), Maureen Rubin (California State-Northridge), Louise Hermanson (South Alabama), and Jane Bick (Georgia State), criticizing traditional media law textbooks for ignoring public relations as a deserving topic, have proposed that mass communication law courses in colleges and universities

Kyu Ho Youm, Professor
Walter Cronkite School of Journalism
*   & Telecommunication*
Arizona State University

should include a public relations perspective. They have observed:

> In their professional lives, print, broadcast, and public relations students will work together on a daily basis in a symbiotic—at times, however, antagonistic—relationship. Thus, it is wise for all journalism/mass communication students to become familiar with the legal concerns and responsibilities of their future colleagues and adversaries.

What are the areas of law that demand more than a casual attention from PR practitioners? A safe rule of thumb based on the First Amendment jurisprudence is that PR practitioners should err on the side of caution rather than of wild guess about the seemingly ever-changing law. As Walsh aptly notes, "Like any other specialized area of the law, public relations law will seldom offer black-and-white answers. Rather, public relations law exists in the grey area of legislative actions and court interpretations."

Libel law is a case in point. Indeed, PR practitioners must recognize that libel poses "perhaps the most complex and confusing rules for everyday tools of the profession," according to Walsh. This is hardly surprising in that "there is a great deal of the law of defamation that makes no sense." Factual inaccuracy is not protected by the First Amendment, while expression of opinion is. The thorny question is how to make a neat separation between fact and opinion under libel law.

Copyright is another important area of law that applies directly and frequently to public relations. When do PR practitioners use information from sources without violating the Copyright Act and when do they turn to the Copyright Act for protection of their own work outside the "fair use" doctrine? This and related questions most likely will challenge PR practitioners to be closely acquainted with the evolving law.

From the perspective of public relations law, confidentiality promises with the news media is a positive development in recent years. Since 1991, when the Supreme Court rejected the news media's First Amendment argument for a right to "burn the sources," the case law has strongly indicated that PR practitioners should expect their confidentiality agreements with the media to be protected as a contractual obligation under law.

Advertising, which is a close cousin to public relations, is more extensively protected by the First Amendment now than in the past. Particularly noteworthy is the fact that the constitutional rationale behind the growing protection of advertising since the mid-1970s is anchored to the people's "right to know" by way of the free exchange of information. It should be emphasized, however, that the First Amendment contours on commercial expression are still not as wide as those on non-commercial expression.

Corporate and financial law is considered "the most difficult" area by PR practitioners. But the critical roles of the Securities and Exchange Commission (SEC), the Federal Trade Commission (FTC), and other government agencies in the operations of numerous corporate and financial establishments require the practitioners to understand the complex statutory and administrative regulations.

Other subjects of public relations law, such as contracts and liability, deserve more than a commonsense knowledge. While PR practitioners are not often involved directly in contracts, employee contract, photo release, and photo agreement can become a fertile ground for creating potential legal problems for the practitioners. Ted Baron, president of a New York public relations firm, advises: "In a field where increased reliance, responsibility, and trust are being placed by companies on public relations counsel, there must be increased awareness of the need for means of effectively deterring breaches of your clients' interests—if not your own."

Kant

Immanuel Kant is known for his "categorical imperative" or the premise that choices should be arrived at through reason and have the power to be applied to all societies at all times. This approach is duty-based, either strict (not to murder, not to lie) or meritorious (to aid others, to show gratitude). To Kant, an individual's intent was the point on which ethics turns, not the result of the action.

Rawls

Political philosopher John Rawls's theory of distributive justice says that justice should be considered equal to fairness. To achieve this goal, Rawls said every individual must take an "original position" behind a "veil of ignorance." This means that rational people would willingly put aside their awareness of social and political status in order to be free of bias. Behind this "veil," persons would be able to consult their conscience and analyze a range of views to arrive at a reasoned choice. Two values emerge from this exercise—liberty of all is valued and weaker parties are protected. By balancing these individual liberties while protecting the weak, a considered moral judgment or "reflective equilibrium" results.

Royce

Josiah Royce was an American theologian who, in the mold of Aristotle and Kant, believed that there could be a single overriding principle guiding ethical conduct. To this turn-of-the-century Harvard educator, the principle was loyalty. Royce defined loyalty as a social act: "The willing and practical and thoroughgoing devotion of a person to a cause." In 1908, Royce wrote: "My theory is that the whole moral law is implicitly bound up in one precept: 'Be loyal.' " However, this approach is not without its problems, specifically how can one distinguish among competing loyalties—to an employer, a discipline, and a philosophy? Royce offered a two-part test to determine whether a cause was worthy of support. First, a worthy cause would engage an individual's interest; and second, it would encourage and enhance the loyalties of others. This allows people to reject unethical causes and depends upon a spirit of community and democratic cooperation.

Ross

Modern-day philosopher William David Ross asserts that, unlike Kant or Mill or Royce, there is more than a solitary ethical value. Ross proposes six competing duties that he calls the Pluralistic Theory of Value whose force is based upon personal nature: fidelity, gratitude, justice, beneficence, self-improvement, and not to harm. To Ross, these values are equal if the circumstances of the choice are equal. Patterson and Wilkins suggest two additions to the list: veracity, or "the duty to tell the truth," and nurture, "the duty to help others achieve some measure of self-worth and achievement." This approach is particularly useful to the public relations practitioner who must balance competing loyalties and roles.

Decision-Making Models

Bok

Sissela Bok writes that unfortunately there is a casual approach of professionals to ethics that those who must cope with the consequences of deception are oblivious to. "For them, to be given false information about important choices in their lives is to be rendered powerless. For them, their very autonomy may be at stake." She also has little faith in codes and writings on professional ethics because "existing codes say little about when deception is and is not justified." Bok believes that "we must at the very least accept as an initial premise Aristotle's view that lying is 'mean and culpable' and that truthful statements are preferable to lies in the absence of special considerations. This premise gives an initial negative weight to lies."

It's clear that Bok's goal is to stress the positive value of telling the truth, or veracity. It is equally apparent that the principle is the basis for trust between individuals, and among groups and audiences. This principle, then, has special significance for the public relations practitioner in that trust is the bedrock of credibility.

Bok offers a framework for making ethical decisions based upon the following premise: "the concept of publicity with the view of justification in ethics as being directed to reasonable persons." Bok borrows the concept of publicity from John Rawls, who believed that a moral principle must be capable of public statement and defense. Justification is suggested by Ludwig Wittgenstein, who observes that "justification consists in appealing to something independent." Blending these ideas, Bok offers what she calls a "workable test for looking at concrete moral choice."

These steps or levels of justification are: conscience, peer consultation, and the test of publicity. The first level is appealing to one's conscience or inner judge. This soul-searching is needed for the most basic of moral choices. The second level goes beyond one's own personal analysis to ask others what they think. These "others" may include friends, family, or experts either living or dead.

Bok says this step "can bring objectivity, sometimes wisdom, to moral choices and lead to the demise of many an ill-conceived scheme." In the third level of public justification, the audience is broadened to include a sample of reasonable individuals with divergent points of view. The greater the impact of the decision, the more consultation is required.

Potter

Harvard theologian Ralph Potter developed a decision-making model that allows for values and loyalties to be examined in addition to facts and philosophies. The four steps of the so-called Potter Box should be taken in order, beginning with understanding the facts. The second step asks you to be honest about what you truly value. In this case, however, value takes on the meaning of what you are willing to sacrifice, for example, truth or privacy. In the third step, you are directed to apply a range of philosophical principles from Aristotle's Golden Mean to Ross's Plurality of Values. The final step asks you to articulate your loyalties and to determine if they conflict. This process forces you to think about short-term and long-term consequences.

By making use of these models, ethical decision making may have a better chance to emerge (see Exhibit 3.1). "Thinking about ethics won't make many . . . choices easier, but, with practice, your ethical decision making can become more consistent. Ethics will become not something you have, but something you do," conclude Patterson and Wilkins.

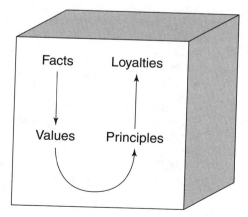

FIGURE 3.1   The Four Steps of the Potter Box

EXHIBIT **3.1**

Ethical Types

In examining our pluses or minuses, it may be useful to try to describe at what point we currently find ourselves along the ethics continuum.

Absolutist
To the ethical absolutist, there is one code of conduct that is eternal and that applies to everyone. Actions are categorized as right or wrong, regardless of any shifting opinions or circumstances.

Relativist
The relativist ties morality to the feeling that no individual can judge another's ethics; to do so indicates bias. To this individual, no one action is superior to another because rules of conduct are different across cultures.

Objectivist
The objectivist advocates absolute ethics. These standards are objective because they are "separate" from the person and are based on standards other than opinions.

Subjectivist
This individual sees ethics as the preference of a person. This believer holds that the mental state of persons determines their moral judgment.

Attitudinal
This type of subjectivism means that if you are in agreement with another's beliefs, then this defines appropriate conduct.

Consequential
This type of objectivism holds that the goodness or harm of an action can be determined only by its consequence or effect on others.

Deontological
To this individual, the merit of action itself, not the consequence, is the basis for ethical decision making.

Teleological
This is similar to consequence theory in that what really matters morally are good and bad consequences.

Hedonist
The rightness or wrongness of an action is dependent upon the pleasure or displeasure it produces.

Egoist
According to Jaksa and Pritchard, "The egoist view is that one should seek to maximize good consequences and minimize bad consequences for oneself."

Altruist
This utilitarian approach holds that this individual attempts to promote the greatest good for the greatest number of individuals.

Legalistic Ethics
This is an absolutist system whose roots are in tradition or a religious moral code. Morality is defined by the majority of the members of the society in which this is in place. This is also referred to as consensus ethics because individuals are ethical to the extent that they adhere to the code.

Antinomian Ethics
In Hegelian terms, it is the antithesis of the legalistic stance. Antinomians decry all rules. They seek no guide other than their instincts or feelings at any given moment. Although they consider themselves humanists, in reality they are closer to anarchists. Lowenstein and Merrill write, "This ethical (or nonethical) system might simply be referred to as 'whim ethics.' "

Situation Ethics
This is a rational compromise between legalistic and antinomian ethics. Decision making begins in traditional ethical approaches but departs from rules when it is necessary to do so. These individuals examine a situation, then think before detouring around an ethical principle. They do not act on instinct alone. According to the conclusions of one researcher who examined "ethical factors," American and Canadian PR practitioners were strong on social responsibility and financial morality factors, but socioeconomic factors suggested more compromising ethics, "ignoring absolute ethics in favor of situational ethics."

Source: Adapted from Ralph L. Lowenstein and John C. Merrill. *Macromedia: Mission, Message and Morality.* New York: Longman, 1990.

Legal Considerations

Ethics is a branch of philosophy that has to do with self-legislation and self-enforcement. It is personally determined and personally enforced. Although law, according to ethicist John Merrill, "quite often stems from the ethical values of a society at a certain time, law is something that is socially determined and socially enforced." The need to know how client and practitioner can be affected by these socially determined factors is as compelling as the need for ethical decision making.

According to researcher Marian Huttenstine, "public relations itself continues to have its functional roots in commercial speech, advertising, traditional speech and the press. As a result, the law that applies to this field is a blend of statutory and case law as it has evolved in all those areas."

The First Amendment provides that "Congress shall make no law . . . abridging the freedom of speech, or of the press." In 1976, the U.S. Supreme Court in *Virginia State Board of Pharmacy v. Virginia Citizens Consumer Council* stated that commercial speech, or a message of a promotional nature, is worthy of First Amendment protection, but not without restrictions on time, place, and manner of the communication. This means that commercial speech can be regulated by the government to ensure truthfulness. This being the case, it is wise to examine the range of statutes that may aid or impinge upon the practitioner's activities on behalf of a client.

Freedom of Information Act (FoIA)

The FoIA can act as an important research tool for PR practitioners to gather information from government files about their competitors. FoIA covers the Departments of State, Justice, Defense, Commerce, Treasury, Education, Energy, and Health and Human Services. Any individual may request information under the Freedom of Information Act, 5 U.S.C. 552, as long as it is not exempt. Exemptions include data or documents about financial institutions, oil and gas wells, personnel information, trade secrets, national security, and law enforcement investigations. Studies show that the majority of requests for access to government files are from corporate offices; media usage is about 5 percent. After a request is made in writing, the law requires that the agency reply within ten business days.

Broadcasting

Up until 1987, this Federal Communications Commission (FCC) policy allowed access to the airwaves to offer contrasting points of view on controversial issues. With its demise, and the death of the Personal Attack Rule, practitioners lost their leverage in providing their clients a forum to reach large audiences. The only element that survived is the Equal Time Rule. This is because the rule is part of the 1934 Communications Act and can be struck down only by an act of Congress. The rule allows opposing candidates equal time on the air. What usually occurs is that rather than offering candidates time to state their platforms, stations will avoid any mention of the candidate so that no information is disseminated. In 1980, the FCC also struck down licensing criteria that required stations to air public service announcements (PSAs). Although stations continue to air PSAs, this is strictly an option.

The change opened the door for the emergence of Web sites and home pages that carry, in some cases, unverifiable information on private and public individuals and issues.

Libel

This occurs when an individual's reputation is damaged either by publishing or broadcasting a story that subjects the person to public ridicule, hatred, or scorn. To be actionable, the defamation must meet five conditions: publication or communicating information to a third party, identification, statements used that are capable of harming one's reputation, proof the statements are false, and proof of fault. It is also important to remember that anyone who repeats the defamation, such as a newspaper that may have prepared a story from a release, is also liable.

Invasion of Privacy

There are four torts or wrongful acts that can be committed against a person or his or her property in the area of privacy. They are intrusion into the solitude of another, false light, public disclosure of private information, and appropriation.

Intrusion.   Intrusion refers to physical invasion or electronic eavesdropping; an example of this may be monitoring and taping telephone calls. In some states, it is a criminal offense to tape conversations unless both parties consent. Federal law allows conversations to be taped as long as one party consents. The exception occurs if the conversation is intended to be broadcast; then both parties must agree to it, and a beep must sound at regular intervals. Since state laws vary widely, when in doubt, ask permission to record and get the consent on tape.

False Light.   This tort involves creating a false impression of a person or an event. It is not necessarily defamatory but may simply be an exaggeration. This situation may occur when a photograph is wrongly positioned near a headline that is referring to another individual or story. Practitioners should be mindful of this when designing collateral materials for clients or coordinating publication of a newsletter or in-house magazine.

Public Disclosure of Private Information.   This violation of another's privacy involves disseminating information of an embarrassing nature that is not of public concern. This invasion violates standards of "common decency" perceived by individuals of "ordinary sensibilities."

Appropriation.   This unlawful act refers to using an individual's name or likeness without permission for commercial gain. To avoid this occurring even unintentionally, practitioners should regularly use consent release forms. Although they do not afford total protection, they do demonstrate intent.

Financial Communication

For those companies that sell stock, the Securities and Exchange Commission (SEC) requires that each organization engage in "timely disclosure" of information that would affect the price or sale of shares and that the information provided to interested parties is not

PRoEthics

Confusing Situation with "Situational Ethics"

"Public relations practitioners genuinely interested in behaving in an ethical manner must bring some theoretical construct to their decision-making process. That is not to say, it must be emphasized, that an advance degree in moral philosophy is a prerequisite to ethical behavior in public relations."

This article aims "to demonstrate why PR practitioners need to understand that it is essential that they consider the situation in ethics—even if one rejects most vigorously the practice of situational ethics."

One solution might be "for the practitioner to confirm the facts as released while declining to provide any additional information. One must not, however, jump from that position to one that allows that all information should be kept secret and that, in a democratic society, the affairs of public institutions are none of the public's business.

"The key, from an ethical perspective, is that the practitioner not attempt to make an exception to himself or herself. The practitioner must communicate that information he or she would insist that others communicate under these particular circumstances. In other words, in considering circumstances, one must apply the same rules—principles—to himself or herself that he or she would apply to others.

"If the act itself is bad—lying, for example, to someone who is entitled to the truth—the action itself must be judged bad; circumstances do not change that reality. Similarly, a practitioner whose motivation is to deceive the public, even though his or her language might not qualify as a lie in a literal sense, also engages in unethical behavior."

Source: Adapted from David L. Martinson. "Public Relations Practitioners Must Not Confuse Consideration of the Situation with 'Situational Ethics.'" *Public Relations Quarterly* 42 (Winter 1997–1998): 39–43.

false or misleading. If these provisions are violated, the action may amount to insider trading, which is punishable by imprisonment, fines, or both. To protect themselves, public relations firms now include a "hold harmless" clause in their contracts. This states that the firm and its practitioners will regard what the client tells them as truthful.

Added to these areas are what Huttenstine calls "painfully 'in' words in the arena of public relations." These include duty, detrimental reliance, vicarious liability, and copyright and fair use.

Duty. Duty refers to a legally enforceable obligation to conform to a particular standard of conduct. Does this mean a practitioner owes a duty to a client? This duty question has arisen in many cases involving communications law, particularly in the "Soldier of Fortune" case. In this instance, an individual may place a classified ad in a magazine describing his or her special skills (i.e., weapons specialist, pilot, or ex-Marine). Someone else then hires the person to break the law. Following a criminal case, the publication rather than the advertiser is sued for damages. Why? Because the publication either knew or should have known that the person placing the ad offered to perform illegal acts.

Even with cases to the contrary stating that no duty exists to screen such advertisements, the legal climate has changed. The Court of Appeals, reviewing Federal Trade Commission (FTC) action, found that in the case of *American Home Products Corporation v.*

Johnson and Johnson, "An advertising agency is liable for deceptive advertising along with the advertiser when the agency was an active participant in the preparation of the ad and knew or had reason to know that it was false or deceptive." Huttenstine writes that "knew or should have known . . . echoes the definition of duty. It takes no great stretch to apply that reasoning to public relations practitioners." She recommends using the FTC's three-part test to decide if the facts presented are reliable and if an obligation exists on the part of a practitioner to investigate claims:

- There must be a representation, omission, or practice that is likely to mislead the reader/listener.
- The act, practice, or message must be considered from the perspective of the reader/listener who is acting reasonably.
- The representation, omission, practice, or message must be material.

Detrimental Reliance.   When a source reveals information under the promise of confidentiality, the courts also play a role. According to Huttenstine, "Detrimental reliance develops when one relies upon a promise or information in deciding to do or not do something and is then injured when that promise or information is broken or faulty." Examples of this in a public relations sense abound from touting airline safety records to specialized medical care. If the content of the messages conveyed is called into question, the most often cited legal action is detrimental reliance.

Vicarious Liability.   According to *Black's Law Dictionary,* vicarious liability means that one party is held responsible for the acts of another due to the relationship that exists between them. The account executive, photographer, artist, even part-time worker or freelancer may create liability for an agency if privacy is invaded.

Copyright and Fair Use.   Copyright protects the tangible expression or fixed form of one's work, not an idea or a concept. Mediums of expression may include books, newspapers, newsletters, magazines, corporate publications, and pictorial and graphic works. Under Article 1 §8 of the Constitution, a copyright holder has exclusive rights to reproduce the work; prepare derivative works; distribute copies to the public by sale, rental, lease, or lending; perform the work publicly; or display the copyrighted work. Although protection of a copyright does not turn on its registration with the Library of Congress, without it the copyright is nearly impossible to enforce. If works are "created for hire," then the employer holds the copyright. However, in the absence of a written agreement, rights usually reside with the individual who created the work. In 1989, the Supreme Court found that when not stated otherwise, freelancers own the copyright to their material. This may be of particular importance in public relations if freelancers create and produce a proposal for a client, then prevent your firm from using it.

There are instances when use of copyrighted material is allowed even without the permission of the owner. The term to describe such instances is fair use. Factors considered in deciding fair use include the purpose (commercial or noncommercial), nature of the material, quantity of the portion used, and the effect of the use on the market value of the copyrighted work. Educational, critical, and research uses are protected under the fair use provision. When in doubt, secure permission from the copyright holder and cite it in the work.

Technological advances, such as high-speed and color copiers, low-cost scanners, instant photography, and audio/video recording, have brought copyright concerns to the forefront. It is important to remember when dealing with the Internet that when you operate a Web site, you are a publisher and subject to the same copyright protection guidelines as other forms of copying, that is, permission is required. Permission is also required to use protected material on Web sites and home pages and to link to Web sites. The permission notice should be clearly stated.

General copyright guidelines include:

- Materials first published after 1978 are protected for the life of the author plus fifty years.
- After 1976, unpublished works are protected.
- Works published prior to March 1, 1989, are required to indicate copyright ©.
- Most government documents are unprotected.

PRoEthics
The Internet

Internet communication is protected by the First Amendment, and the courts have so far endorsed a broad interpretation when it comes to Web sites. A federal court described the Net as a "unique and wholly new medium of worldwide human communication," when it struck down a key provision of the Computer Decency Act of 1996, the first Congressional attempt to regulate content. The judicial hands-off approach leaves users to rely on self-regulation to protect themselves and the medium. *Forbes* columnist Francis Fukuyama believes the practice of business on the Internet comes down to one thing: trust. Trust begins with predictable value-based behavior: ethics.

To date, there have been many breaches. Unscrupulous Internet users have raised concerns about fraud, disinformation, and even death threats. When a Federal Trade Commission sampled medical Web sites in 1997, investigators found hundreds of false or deceptive advertising claims in just a few hours, according to Reuters News Service. A site established by Internet access provider America Online prompted a defamation suit that same year when a White House official demanded $30 million in damages after an AOL subcontractor posted rumors about his private life on a gossip page. In California, a criminal defense attorney subpoenaed information from a site that solicited opinions about an ongoing murder trial. The lawyer claims the survey damaged his client's chance for a fair hearing.

Professor Debra Johnson writes that information technology "may make behavior in an electronic network morally different from other behavior." She argues that the reach of Internet communication is greater and therefore potentially more harmful and that the difficulty of verifying the online identity of communicators creates unique problems of integrity.

If the government cannot censor Net communication, it can pull the plug on access technology. The end result would be the same—the loss of a valuable communications tool. Perhaps an Internet code of ethics with teeth may be in the offing.

Publicity and Propaganda

For the sake of retaining personal and professional credibility, the public relations practitioner must be a legitimate persuader. What differentiates legitimate from illegitimate? Intent. A legitimate persuader seeks to inform in a balanced and fact-oriented fashion. This practitioner does not make use of the techniques of the propagandist—generalities, unfair association, faulty analogies, straw man, ad hominem (attacking the person rather than the argument), name calling, card stacking, or bandwagon. The legitimate persuader is characterized by a desire to retain an audience's trust, to refrain from indulging in what Merrill calls "the dishonest treatment of information" in the form of distortion or exaggeration. He or she also avoids stereotyping, using opinion as fact, emphasizing the negative, begging the question, employing tokenism (using small or insignificant gestures instead of an adequate, responsible effort), and using intentional ambiguity.

"A main strategical technique is a constant concern with passionate rhetoric and advocacy," writes ethicist Merrill. "The propagandist has little or no use for dispassionate argument, trying to avoid open discussion and questions ... their main technique is the avoidance of rational dialogue." By this description, it's clear why many practitioners could mistakenly confuse their techniques in the name of a desired outcome or achieving a campaign goal.

Merrill suggests an acronym that captures the essence of illegitimate persuasion or propaganda, which may keep practitioners from tumbling over the edge. Propaganda is PASID: Persuasive, Action-oriented, Selfish, Intentional, and Devious.

Propaganda is planned. So are the tactics in a public relations campaign. As practitioners, the goal is to remember where we are going and to give voice to those activities in an ethical way. It is far too easy to step over the bounds of legitimate persuasion into the murky arena of manipulation to achieve an objective. The end cannot justify the means for a public relations professional if credibility is to remain intact.

Summary

PR is defined by its credibility. That credibility can only be maintained if practitioners are well informed as to how to make decisions they can explain and defend. Ethics creates special problems for the practitioner because of the dual nature of the role. Bivins notes that "The key difference between the roles of advocate and counselor is the degree of autonomy allowed to each. . . . With autonomy comes an expectation of objectivity. . . . However, for the advocate, autonomy is not particularly valued or desired. In fact, . . . a more desirable trait is loyalty." Seib and Fitzpatrick explain that PR professionals "promote mutual understanding and peaceful coexistence among individuals and institutions. They serve as a vital link in the communications process, making the remote proximate and demystifying the arcane."

This chapter outlines the broad types and approaches to ethical considerations as well as offering models of ethical decision making. It also discusses society's method of making enforceable decisions—the legal system, specifically, those laws that affect public relations: copyright, invasion of privacy, libel, and confidentiality.

QUESTIONS

1. What is meant by Aristotle's "Golden Mean"?

2. What are Bok's levels of justification?

3. Explain how the Potter Box works.

4. Under what conditions could a public relations practitioner be protected under the rule of confidentiality?

5. What are the techniques of an illegitimate persuader?

READINGS

Karen Breslau. "A Capital Cyber Clash." *Newsweek* (October 20, 1997): 130, 63.

Glen T. Cameron and Patricia A. Curtin. "An Expert Systems Approach for PR Campaigns Research." *Journalism Educator* 47, no. 2 (Summer 1992): 12–18.

Robert Cialdini. "Persuasion Principles." *Public Relations Journal* 41, no. 10 (October 1985): 12–16.

Erik L. Collins and Robert J. Cornet. "Public Relations and Libel Law." *Public Relations Review* 16, no. 4 (Winter 1990): 36–47.

Meryl Davids. "Believe Me." *Public Relations Journal* 43, no. 10 (October 1987): 16–43.

Francis Fukuyama. "Trust Still Counts in a Virtual World." *Forbes,* ASAP supplement (December 2, 1996): 33, 69.

Internet Activities Board. Ethics and the Internet [online]. (November 1997). Available: ftp://ds.internic.net/rfc/rfc1087.txt.

Bruce H. Joffe. "Law, Ethics and Public Relations Writers." *Public Relations Journal* 45, no. 7 (July 1989): 38–40.

Debra Johnson. "Ethics Online." *Communications of the ACM* 40 (January 1997): 60–65.

L. Perdue. Web ethics [online]. November 1997. Available: www.webethics.com.

Reuters News Service. "Internet Sweep Finds False Health Advertisements." November 5, 1997. New York, NY: Reuters News Service.

Philip Seib and Kathy Fitzpatrick. *Public Relations Ethics.* Fort Worth, TX: Harcourt Brace and Company, 1995.

Don Sneed, Tim Wulfemeyer, and Harry W. Stonecipher. "Public Relations News Releases and Libel: Extending First Amendment Protections." *Public Relations Review* 17, no. 2 (Summer 1991): 131–144.

4

Campaign Components

Links in the Communication Chain

CHAPTER OBJECTIVES

When you have completed this chapter, you should be able to:

- Learn how to write effective goal/objective statements
- Know how the MBO approach complements PR
- Understand the role of campaign team members
- Recognize budgetary categories

Regardless of the nature and intent of a particular campaign, there are certain campaign components that comprise every public relations effort. Just as every automobile has a steering wheel, every communications campaign should have the "planning" component.

The components that make up a public relations campaign are relatively finite and are most always utilized in some meaningful order. While the degree and intensity of usage of any given component may vary from campaign to campaign, they are for the most part interrelated and cannot be left out of the campaign planning process.

For example, an aging domestic product introduced in a foreign market that is not familiar with either its name or its application might require a disproportionate amount of research by the communications planning team. Yet once the research findings are complete and verified, the actual execution of the campaign may be quite swift and straightforward.

It All Begins (and Ends) with Research

Investigation, data collection, verification, exploration, or situational analysis—it all begins (and ends) with research.

Actually research is the one campaign component, from a practical standpoint, that could be left out of the campaign process. The only problem is that the on-time completion of a smooth-running campaign would demonstrate very little. The client will invariably—and rightfully—ask what was verifiably accomplished on their behalf.

Without research and evaluation, it is nearly impossible to ascertain what a campaign does accomplish. It may create strong weekend foot traffic or produce several newspaper stories, but what does all of that translate into and does it satisfy the objectives of the campaign? Without research, only guessing will produce an answer.

Norman R. Nager and T. Harrell Allen state that "Research is more than common sense, as valuable as that may be. Common-sense judgments are sometimes correct, but not always. The public relations profession needs some strategy that reduces the error in its recommendations."

There are many different types of research: primary and secondary, formal and informal, qualitative and quantitative. Which type of research and the methodology or design applications that a campaign manager chooses depend on both the campaign objectives and the budget.

For example, with the desire for achieving primary, qualitative information, the researcher has numerous options for data collection. There are scientific surveys, probability samplings, tests to measure results, computer-assisted analysis, content analysis, media tracking models, unobtrusive measures, and futures research techniques.

The selection of a research methodology is less significant than the result it provides and how the findings may direct a campaign. "Research is a major tool of the practitioner, but research reports themselves are not the purpose of the work," remind Nager and Truitt. "That purpose is the strategy, the policy, the major campaign that derives from the knowledge research provides."

The Planning Process

If research can be considered the "compass" for the campaign expedition, then planning is surely the road map. And, as with most explorations, both are tools that are quite helpful in reaching the desired destination.

Planning is without question the most critical component in any campaign. The only reason it isn't the first official step in the campaign process is that research often provides an informational backdrop for the planning process. The data derived from almost any type of research allows for more realistic goal setting and accurate strategy development, including the establishment of timetables.

Simply put, planning brings meaning to a campaign. Without it, it is anyone's guess as to where a campaign will lead and what it will produce. "Communication for the sake of communicating is superfluous. Communication for the achievement of organizational objectives is imperative. That's important to remember because communicators sometimes get so carried away with the arts-and-crafts nature of communication activity that they forget the very management-centered nature of the communication function," states practitioner Thomas A. Ruddell.

The reference to "management" should be broadly interpreted to mean the authoritative body that requested the campaign, desires the realization of its objectives and, because of the aforementioned, is willing to provide the resources necessary to fund the effort.

Management, or the client, is central to the issue of planning as it is usually at this important step that a campaign is either launched or tabled. The campaign plan promotes understanding and agreement between the PR manager and the client. It provides information, forms hypotheses, establishes goals, makes recommendations, provides timetables and budgets, and offers objective evaluation—all of the things that make clients comfortable enough to approve the budget and agree that the campaign should now begin.

Goals and Objectives

There is some disagreement as to the meaning of the terms "goal" and "objective." Are they the same thing? If not, why are they used so interchangeably? Ruddell provides a practical and meaningful analysis: "A goal is a clear statement of intent to solve a significant problem or achieve a significant result within a specific time frame. An objective is one of the action steps through which a goal is to be accomplished."

This perspective suggests that the goals are eminent and the objectives are secondary and play an assistance role. The definition of these terms is important only as it helps the campaign planning team communicate clearly, both with themselves and with the client to which they hope to "sell" their program ideas. In his definition, Ruddell also seems to be suggesting that a goal should produce a measurable result within a given period of time. This thinking is fair, if not mandatory, in justifying any campaign and the resources it requires.

Seitel offers another interpretation: "An organization's goals must define what its public relations goals will be, and the only good goals are ones that can be measured. Public relations objectives and the strategies that flow from them, just like those in other business areas, must be results-oriented."

As for goals, Seitel says any good one will stand up to these five questions:

1. Do they clearly describe the end result expected?
2. Are they understandable to everyone in the organization (for example, the PR agency and the client firm)?
3. Do they list a firm completion date?
4. Are they realistic, attainable, and measurable?
5. Are they consistent with management's objectives?

The answers to these questions are essential to maintaining credibility within the corporate structure. After all, every supervisor or department head is going to want to know, "Is my public relations manager effective, and are his or her programs really making a difference?"

According to Cutlip, Center, and Broom, "objectives spell out the key results that must be achieved with each public to reach the program goal." In practice, they create focus, provide guidance and motivation, and specify outcome criteria. Objectives, if they are clear and in writing, can keep the team and their program on track.

Cutlip, Center, and Broom say objectives are most useful if they follow a pattern:

- Begin with "to" followed by a verb describing the direction to the intended outcome.
- Specify the outcome.
- State the magnitude of change or level to be maintained in measurable terms.
- Set the target date when the outcome will be achieved.

It is also useful to pair a goal with its objective(s) so the planning component can clearly relate how the activity contributes to the outcome. These program objectives would cover the life of the project or campaign and follow a timetable, depending upon the duration of the program. For example, if the campaign is one year, objectives might be written to reflect what is to be accomplished each month or what action might be taken after research indicates an objective has been met as the program matures. Often, an organization's management may number the goals and their corresponding objectives to avoid drift (for example, Goal 2 would carry Objectives 2a through 2j).

Cutlip, Center, and Broom offer an example of a program goal and two of its several objectives. It's clear that the more precise the objective is, the better the chances of achieving it.

- Goal. "To reduce the number of delivery drivers seriously injured or killed while driving on the job from a five-year average of five per year to no more than two in the next fiscal year."

- Objective. "To increase, within six weeks after starting the program, the percentage of drivers from 8 percent to at least 90 percent who are aware that in a typical year, four company delivery drivers are seriously injured and one is killed while driving on the job."

- Objective. "To increase, within two months after starting the program, the percentage of drivers from 5 percent to at least 80 percent who know that 55 percent of all fatalities and 65 percent of all injuries from vehicle crashes could be prevented if seat belts were used properly."

Management by objective (MBO), a mainstay in most organizations, can provide public relations professionals with a powerful source of feedback. Introduced by Peter Drucker in 1954, MBO can tie public relations results to management's predetermined objectives. Even though procedures for implementing MBO programs differ, most programs share these points:

- Specification of the organization's goals with objective measures of the organization's performance
- Conferences between a superior and a subordinate to agree on achievable goals
- Agreement between the superior and the subordinate on objectives consistent with the organization's goals

- Periodic reviews by the superior and the subordinate to assess progress toward achieving the goals

"Again," says Seitel, "the key is to tie public relations goals to the goals of the organization and then to manage progress toward achieving those goals. The goals themselves should be clearly defined and specific, practical and attainable, and measurable."

Assembling the Campaign Team

Perhaps nowhere does the adage "Two heads are better than one" apply more appropriately than in public relations campaign planning.

Seldom is a campaign created, much less implemented, by a single individual. Instead, there are usually two or more professionals who comprise the public relations campaign team, and the result of their collective work almost always translates into a superior effort.

Of course, the larger the corporation or PR agency, the larger the campaign team is likely to be. For example, it is not unusual for Fortune 500 companies to employ several hundred communications professionals in a single corporate headquarters with many others scattered throughout their regional offices. Similarly, some PR agencies, such as Hill & Knowlton and Burson Marsteller, have hundreds of counselors and account executives in one location, and they may assign dozens of them to a single client account if their billings can justify the manpower.

The obvious question in such a scenario is, "Who's in charge?" At the very least, the client will want to know, and it is simply good management to let everyone involved in a campaign project know whom they can look to for leadership.

Directing most public relations efforts is a campaign manager or project leader, who is responsible for everybody as well as everything that transpires during the campaign. Like a quarterback in football or the basketball team's point guard, this seasoned individual leads the communications team throughout the campaign. He or she provides the practical experience, professional knowledge, and, sometimes most importantly, the inspirational leadership that are necessary to motivate the campaign team toward accomplishment. And every team leader has an assistant—accomplished, trained, and every bit as capable—just in case the field general happens to call in sick.

In the larger team format, specialization is typical. There may be a campaign leader with several program or function coordinators who are responsible for such areas as news materials, media relations, special event planning, and employee relations. Some teams are so diversified that there are individuals who do nothing but write speeches for the CEO or handle the spouse programs. Needless to say, both of these functions, if overlooked, could loom as the most important of the public relations campaign.

In smaller companies or agencies, one or more individuals will normally handle all of these responsibilities. That is how the term jack-of-all-trades was coined; it is also how thousands upon thousands of some of the best practitioners are regarded. The career development formula is simple: Learn to do everything and if you do it well, you'll soon be managing others to do the same.

Program and Message Planning

With the campaign team in place and the goals clearly stated, it then becomes time to develop the campaign programs, including message strategies intended for the various audience segments.

"The conceptualization of messages," according to Robert E. Simmons, "should not be viewed entirely, or even primarily, as a creative activity. Creativity is a process that takes content specified by the MBO and makes it more effective through imaginative execution." In other words, creativity, simply for the sake of pretty pictures and catchy headlines, is a waste of energy. The creative thoughts must be applied against the backdrop of reality . . . against the reality of what the client is demanding. What are the campaign goals, and how might strategic marketing and creative, persuasive messages lend themselves to a successful outcome?

According to Simmons, achieving message arousal, and the awareness that goes along with it, is one of the toughest challenges facing the campaign manager. This "message impact" is necessary in order for a campaign to break through what Simmons refers to as "communication clutter." Encountering approximately 3,400 messages each day, consumers are "overwhelmed by the potential information-processing demand and thereby are engaging in selective exposure."

Advertising industry guru David Ogilvy suggests that "magic words" such as new, free, save, and win in headlines or slogans greatly improve the chance of attracting attention to the content that follows. That premise supports the idea that "rewards" can motivate audience members to become more willing to be exposed to a message.

Of course there is less control of the content of public relations messages than there is with advertising campaigns. It is almost impossible to control how the media will characterize a topic, no matter what is said about that particular subject in the neatly prepared media kit. However, there are numerous opportunities with collateral materials in which a campaign manager is in a position to control the message content, if prepared to do so. The key is to know what to say, how to say it, and when to say it.

The other factor that greatly influences the effectiveness of one's campaign messages is continuity between message and medium. Will those consumers who see and hear the basic message come to understand and trust it because it is being consistently portrayed throughout the campaign?

"The different messages in a communication campaign should be recognized as part of the same effort, whether the format is print, radio, television, brochures, or direct mail. A 'building' effect, which improves memory and learning, is accomplished through message continuity devices," writes Simmons.

These "message continuity devices" might be a centralized theme such as "It's the real thing," "Because you care to give the very best," or "Just do it!" Other such devices in collateral materials could be graphic treatments like logos, symbols, colors, and distinctive typefaces. Finally, the music or customized jingles, distinctive voices (who could mistake the familiar sound of Paul Harvey's booming voice?), and famous individuals who either serve as spokespersons in print and broadcast ads or make event appearances can bring familiarity and continuity to an integrated communications campaign.

Creating a Budget

If, as previously suggested, the steering wheel might be the symbol for the campaign's planning component, then surely the budget is analogous to the fuel tank. Similarly, the more gasoline or dollars in the tank, the further the automobile or communications campaign will go.

There are two primary budgetary categories that comprise almost all expenses associated with a traditional public relations campaign. There are the human resources, or people time, and the hard costs, or out-of-pocket expenses, that are normally incurred in the course of planning and executing a program or campaign.

The latter is actually a bit easier to predict, assuming good planning. Once all aspects of a campaign have been approved by the client, they can be put out to bid and qualified. The list of such hard costs might include everything from printing to catering to research. Normally, such expenses carry a 10 to 20 percent markup (17.65 percent is an industry standard), which represents the commission earned by the agency or department and is meant to cover basic administrative costs.

Harnessing the cost of those human resources expended in a campaign is a bit more difficult. Most calculations for "people time" are made by the hour and are based on a scale of hourly professional fees (normally anywhere from $75 to $200 per hour). What can be tricky is estimating up front—clients don't want surprises along the way—how many total hours the campaign will require to complete. More and more corporations and outside clients are requesting fixed project budgets prior to approving the campaign work. Unless previously agreed, overruns become the expense of the PR department or agency and erode against project profit. Little wonder then that budget calculations and estimating are critically important components of any campaign.

Monitoring budgets, especially in a large organization, can be more difficult and time-consuming than preparing the original budget. Whether a budget is several hundred dollars or in the millions, the only real way to monitor such expense activity is to produce and review monthly budget updates. That way, problem areas can be detected early and corrected before mounting costs become a major problem.

Much has been said throughout this text about building confidence and credibility with clients, be they corporate colleagues or outside customers. Nothing, except an effective campaign result, will do more toward building this professional respect and esteem than keeping a campaign on budget.

Campaign Evaluation

The public relations campaigns with the most integrity are those that begin and end with research. Clearly, no other campaign component brings more meaning or measurement to the public relations effort than what is derived from research. Though simply acknowledged here as a key component, it will be explored in depth in another chapter.

"Research should be applied in public relations work both at the initial stage, prior to planning a campaign, and at the final stage to evaluate a program's effectiveness," states Seitel. "Early research helps to determine the current situation, prevalent attitudes, and difficulties that the program is up against. Later research examines the program's success, along with what else still needs to be done. Research at both points in the process is critical."

Research will assist the campaign manager in answering the tough, inevitable questions that most clients will be asking, such as "Where was I?" "Where am I now?" and "How did I get there?" Without formal or informal research, it is just a matter of guesswork.

Newsom, Scott, and Van Slyke Turk summarize the importance of research this way: "Using research, then, helps the PR practitioner to anticipate problems, to evaluate ongoing problems, to pretest the effectiveness of certain tools, to profile a public and its attitudes, to accumulate information about effective use of media, and to evaluate completed programs and campaigns."

Put that way, how could any serious counselor or client indulge in the public relations campaign process without it?

Summary

Like ingredients to bake bread, each campaign component is necessary in developing a public relations program. Leave out a component, and the end result is markedly different.

No one campaign component is more important than another. Rather, it is the order and the quality of their execution that are key. Like dominos, each campaign step follows a logical order and pushes the process along toward successful completion.

However, public relations is a dynamic process, and seldom are its programs implemented in a laboratory-like setting. The environment is ever-changing; so the campaign manager must also be flexible in adapting to the circumstances and challenges that arise.

QUESTIONS

1. Cite three examples of a campaign component and briefly explain each.

2. How do goals and objectives differ? Which supports which?

3. Define MBO. What is its relevance to the public relations practice?

4. Give a couple of examples of memory devices and explain how they help promote increased understanding of the campaign messages.

5. What is the difference between primary and secondary research?

READINGS

Scott M. Cutlip, Allen H. Center, and Glen M. Broom. *Effective Public Relations* (7th ed.). Englewood Cliffs, NJ: Prentice Hall, 1994.

Norman R. Nager and T. Harrell Allen. *Public Relations Management by Objectives.* (7th ed.). New York: Longman Publishing, 1984.

Norman R. Nager and Richard H. Truitt. *Strategic Public Relations Counseling.* New York: Longman Publishing, 1987.

Doug Newsom, Alan Scott, and Judy Van Slyke Turk. *This Is PR: The Realities of Public Relations,* 5th ed. Belmont, CA: Wadsworth Publishing Company, 1993.

Carol Reuss and Donn Silvis. *Inside Organizational Communications.* New York: Longman Publishing,
1985.

Fraser P. Seitel. *The Practice of Public Relations, 5th ed.*
Columbus, OH: Merrill Publishing Company,
1992.

Robert E. Simmons. *Communication Campaign Management: A Systems Approach.* New York: Longman
Publishing, 1990.

DEFINITION

management by objectives (MBO):   As originated by Peter Drucker in 1954, management by objectives
is the concept of directing an organization or program based upon mutually agreed objectives and
measuring the eventual program outcome against those same standards so as to objectively measure
the success of the programming.

5 Research and Theories

Navigating the Journey

CHAPTER OUTLINE

Sources of Knowing

Quantitative and Qualitative Research

Public Relations Research

Public Relations Theories and Models

Communication Theories

Persuasion

Motivation

Practitioners' Use of Research

CHAPTER OBJECTIVES

When you have completed this chapter, you should be able to:

- Understand the importance of research in public relations
- Learn the steps in the research process
- Become acquainted with the types of research available
- Understand how credibility may help or hinder messages

It has been variously defined as doing your homework, fact finding, and getting your bearings. It's needed most but at times least practiced. It's research.

Lindenmann's survey of top practitioners "found that research is talked about more than it is practiced in public relations." Why? Time, money, and "apprehension about the complex process of survey research" top the list. Scholars Fleisher and Mahaffy believe that PR professionals, with their inclination for creativity and dependence on words and language, have a deep-seated fear of numbers and contend conducting research will involve complicated statistical processes. However, if public relations is to grow in esteem and value to an organization, research is one of the best ways to prove to management that it contributes to strategic areas as well as to the bottom line.

Newsom and Carrell define research as "digging, thinking, verifying and analyzing. It is the act of deciding between the probable and the improbable, the true and the false, the likely and the doubtful, the acceptable and the unacceptable, and the right and the wrong." In this light, research clearly is desirable in all public relations situations.

Sources of Knowing

How do we know what we know? Sources of our understanding stem from personal experience, tradition, authority, peers and public opinion, and scientific inquiry.

Personal Experience

Our personal experience tells us much of what we know about our environment. We think for ourselves and make decisions. Much of the knowledge and wisdom passed down from generation to generation is the fruit of experience. Ary, Jacobs, and Razavieh write that "the ability to learn from experience is generally considered a prime characteristic of intelligent behavior." However, no two individuals experience a situation in exactly the same way.

Tradition

This category refers to bits of wisdom "everyone knows." It asks, "How has this been done in the past?" The answer then serves as a guide for our actions. Babbie writes, "we give up finding out for ourselves in favor of accepting what has always been believed." However, some traditions have later been rejected, such as the belief that eating red meat makes you strong.

Authority

If we cannot determine an answer through personal experience or tradition, we tend to look to experts for truth. In the past, these authority figures may have included a chief, ruler, or high priest. Today, these individuals would be doctors, lawyers, clergy, or political leaders. Kerlinger writes, "life could not go on without the method of authority," which is "the method of established belief." Much of what we know has its roots in authority.

Peers and Public Opinion

According to Babbie, "Much of what we 'know' is a function of what everyone around us seems to 'know.' Peer groups have a special conforming pressure that's wielded among friends and close acquaintances." On the more impersonal side, public opinion can also be a source of knowledge. Rayfield, Acharya, Pincus, and Silvis define it as "the prevailing view of some public on a given subject." Wilcox and Nolte caution that "Public opinion is not just mass opinion. It is the sum of individual opinions on a subject that affects them. . . . Someone must call for action and the action must be possible." Cutlip, Center, and Broom write that "Most scholars agree that public opinion represents a consensus, which emerges over time, from all expressed views that cluster around an issue in debate, and that this consensus exercises power."

Scientific Inquiry

What is scientific research? American philosopher Charles Peirce calls the "method of science" a series of small independent, objective steps that lead to the truth. Its major difference from the other methods of knowing is that it is self-correcting. That is, there are built-in checks in the process. As Peirce explains, "it is necessary that a method should be found by which our beliefs may be determined by nothing human, but by some external permanency such as the method of science." Kerlinger defines the scientific approach as "a systematic, controlled, empirical and critical investigation of hypothetical propositions about the presumed relations among natural phenomena."

Wimmer and Dominick simplify this definition by offering a series of clarifying statements. Scientific research is:

- Public—It depends on information that is either published or freely available to other researchers.

- Objective—This step attempts to eliminate the idiosyncrasies or biases of researchers. Facts are the basis of results, not the interpretation of facts.

- Empirical—This step ensures that information is measurable or can be counted. This is necessary to develop dependable results or, as Peirce writes, "such that the ultimate conclusion of every man shall be the same."

- Systematic and cumulative—In order to derive useful information from our investigations, it is not necessary to start from scratch. In fact, most researchers examine whatever previous studies or results may shed some light on their own questions. This helps researchers to establish order and consistency, to check their results against others, and to develop explanations or theories for why people behave as they do or why situations occur.

- Predictive—Wimmer and Dominick explain that "Science is concerned with relating the present to the future . . . one reason why scientists strive to develop theories is that they are useful in predicting behavior."

Quantitative and Qualitative Research

Scientific research can take one of two forms: quantitative or qualitative. Both types are scientific and systematic; both offer reliability and validity. The first step for both is the recognition or definition of a problem or, as John Dewey describes it, "a felt difficulty or obstacle." This general subject is then narrowed to specific questions or hypotheses. As basic as it seems, asking the right question or questions is one of the most difficult stages of the research process. The next step is to determine a theory that aids in explaining why something is occurring or not occurring. It also provides a way to verify results and can stimulate new knowledge about a topic. The design of the research plan varies, depending on the items or variables to be explored and the "goodness of fit" between the research question and the method that is most useful in answering it. After the design (for example, a mail survey) is put into action, data are collected. The data are then analyzed and interpreted so that conclusions can be drawn. Analysis may take the form of a computer program to "crunch" numbers, or it may be more sensitive to a different approach, such as a case study.

Both quantitative and qualitative research follow specific procedures (see Figure 5.1):

- Statement or definition of the problem
- Review of prior related research studies
- Research design
- Data gathering
- Data analysis
- Interpretations
- Conclusions

However, there are some important differences. Since each approach is based on different assumptions, Exhibit 5.1 offers a checklist of the distinctions associated with each.

Quantitative Research

This requires that the data or information one gathers can be measured in some way and generally uses numbers to communicate results, which (according to Daft and Lengel) can make this the least "information rich" medium in conveying accurate assessments. The phrases associated with the approach are experimental, hard data, and statistical. Key concepts include hypotheses, significance, and replication. Its goals are to test theories, establish facts, show relationships between variables via statistical tests, and prediction. Its design is highly structured, formal, specific, with a sample to be studied drawn from a population that is large. Some designs feature control groups; all use random selection of subjects. The relationship

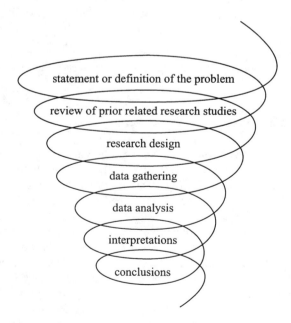

FIGURE 5.1   Research Steps

EXHIBIT **5.1**

Characteristics of Qualitative and Quantitative Research

Phrases Associated with Approach

Qualitative

- ethnographic
- fieldwork
- soft data
- symbolic interaction
- inner perspective
- naturalistic
- ethnomethodological
- descriptive

- participant observation
- phenomenological
- Chicago school
- documentary
- life history
- case study
- ecological

Quantitative

- experimental
- hard data
- outer perspective
- empirical

- positivist
- social facts
- statistical

Key Concepts

Qualitative

- meaning
- commonsense understanding
- bracketing
- definition of situation
- everyday life

- understanding
- process
- negotiated order
- for all practical purposes
- social construction

Quantitative

- variable
- operationalize
- reliability
- hypothesis

- validity
- statistically significant
- replication

Names Associated with Approach

Qualitative

- Max Weber
- Charles Horton Cooley
- Harold Garfinkel
- Margaret Mead
- Anselm Strauss
- Eleanor Leacock
- Howard S. Becker
- Raymond Rist
- Estelle Fuchs

- Herbert Blumer
- W. I. Thomas
- Everett Hughes
- Erving Goffman
- Harry Wolcott
- Rosalie Wax
- George Herbert Mead
- Barney Glaser
- Hugh Mehan

Quantitative

- Emile Durkheim
- Lee Cronbach
- L. Guttman
- Gene Glass
- Robert Travers
- Robert Bales

- Fred Kerlinger
- Edward Thorndike
- Fred McDonald
- David Krathwohl
- Donald Campbell
- Peter Rossi

Theoretical Affiliation

Qualitative

- symbolic interaction
- ethnomethodology

- phenomenology
- culture
- idealism

Quantitative

- structural functionalism
- realism, positivism

- behavioralism
- logical empiricism
- systems theory

(continued)

EXHIBIT **5.1**   Continued

Academic Affiliation

	Qualitative		*Quantitative*
■ sociology	■ anthropology	■ psychology	■ sociology
■ history		■ economics	■ political science

Goals

	Qualitative		*Quantitative*
■ develop sensitizing concepts	■ grounded theory	■ theory testing	■ show relationships between variables
■ describe multiple realities	■ develop understanding	■ establish the facts	■ prediction
		■ statistical description	

Design

	Qualitative		*Quantitative*
■ evolving, flexible, general	■ design is a hunch as to how you might proceed	■ structured, predetermined, formal, specific	■ design is a detailed plan of operation

Written Research Proposals

	Qualitative		*Quantitative*
■ brief	■ often written after some data have been collected; reviewed	■ extensive	■ thorough review of substantive literature
■ speculative		■ detailed and specific in focus	■ written prior to data collection
■ suggests areas to research which may be relevant	■ not extensive in substantive literature	■ detailed and specific in procedures	■ hypotheses stated
	■ general statement of approach		

Data

	Qualitative		*Quantitative*
■ descriptive	■ people's own words	■ measurable	■ operationalized variables
■ personal documents	■ official documents and other artifacts	■ quantifiable coding	■ statistical
■ field notes	■ counts, measures		
■ photographs			

Sample

	Qualitative		*Quantitative*
■ small	■ theoretical sampling	■ large	■ random selection
■ nonrepresentative		■ stratified	■ control for extraneous variables
		■ control groups	
		■ precise	

Techniques or Methods

Qualitative

- observation
- reviewing various documents and artifacts
- participant observation
- open-ended interviewing

Quantitative

- experiments
- survey research
- structured interviewing
- quasi-experiments
- structured observation
- data sets

Relationships with Subjects

Qualitative

- empathy
- emphasis on trust
- egalitarian
- intense contact
- subject as friend

Quantitative

- circumscribed
- short term
- stay detached
- distant
- subject-researcher

Instruments and Tools

Qualitative

- tape recorder
- transcriber
- the researcher is often the only instrument

Quantitative

- inventories
- questionnaires
- indexes
- computers
- scales
- test scores
- statistics

Data Analysis

Qualitative

- ongoing
- models, themes, concepts
- inductive
- analytical induction
- constant comparative method

Quantitative

- deductive
- occurs at conclusion of data collection

Problems in Using Approach

Qualitative

- time-consuming
- data reduction difficult
- reliability
- procedures not standardized
- difficult studying large populations

Quantitative

- controlling other variables
- reificaton
- obtrusiveness
- validity

Source: Adapted from Robert C. Bogdan and Sari Knopp Biklen. *Qualitative Research in Education.* Boston, MA: Allyn and Bacon, 1982.

between the research and the subject is distant and detached so their interaction will not contaminate data. The data analysis is deductive and occurs at the end of the data-gathering step.
Types of techniques used include:

- Surveys
- Experiments

- Structured interviewing
- Quasi-experiments
- Ex post facto
- Structured observation
- Content analysis
- Semantic differential

Qualitative Research

This type of research describes or analyzes data without the use of statistical analyses; however, results can be expressed with numbers. Phrases associated with qualitative research include fieldwork, naturalistic, descriptive, documentary, case study, symbolic interaction, and participant observation. It seeks to generate understanding, meaning, and social construction; it describes multiple realities that spring from what Glaser and Strauss call "grounded theory." Bogdan and Biklen describe this process as "a funnel: things are open at the beginning (top), and more directed and specific at the bottom." Its design is flexible, continually evolving. The data are descriptive and may include personal or organizational documents, field notes, photographs, and subjects' own words. The sample is purposely small and nonrepresentative. The relationship with subjects is one of empathy and trust, with intense contact. This is done so that the researcher can assess the context of a situation and can interpret the setting more accurately. The qualitative investigator assumes nothing is trivial. Data analysis is inductive and compares models, themes, and concepts.

The most common forms include:

- Legal research
- Historical research
- Case studies
- Focus groups
- In-depth interviewing

Limitations

Limitations in using the quantitative approach include controlling for unrecognized variables, obtrusiveness, and validity. Qualitative research is time-consuming, its procedures are not standardized, and there is difficulty in both studying large groups and reducing the data gathered to a usable form. Its results can only be generalized to the specific group under study, unlike quantitative methods that can be used to reach conclusions about larger populations because the sample is representative. Even though some researchers would support the power and superiority of the quantitative approach for its objectivity and lack of preconceived ideas, Poincaré disagrees: "It is often said that experiments should be made without preconceived ideas. That is impossible. Not only would it make every experiment fruitless, but even if we wished to do so, it could not be done." Some investigators have combined components of both quantitative and qualitative approaches, for example, by conducting open-ended interviews first before designing questionnaires.

PRoSpeak
Research in Public Relations Campaigns

No topics in public relations practice attract more interest than research and evaluation. Research is simply the controlled, objective, and systematic gathering of information for the purposes of describing and understanding public relations situations and interventions. Evaluation combines research findings with judgment, past experience, and values to determine the worth of public relations efforts. In most campaigns, research is the feedback mechanism that makes public relations two-way.

Few practitioners, however, studied applied research methods as part of their professional education. But lack of knowledge and skill are not the biggest problems. Most dangerous of all reasons for not using research to plan, monitor, and evaluate public relations is the claim that public relations campaigns deal with "intangibles not amenable to research and measurement." Imagine an exchange with an MBA-trained client or line manager in which the practitioner uses the "intangible" claim:

"What do you mean by 'intangible?'"

"I mean that public relations deals with things that can't be measured or counted."

"Why should I pay you for something that can't be measured or counted?"

"Because every organization needs public relations, and I am an expert."

"Good points. Here's your money."

"Where? I don't see any money!"

"Of course not, it can't be counted. It's what you call 'intangible.'"

As strange as that sounds, many—if not most—public relations campaigns are conceived, conducted, and concluded without real research input. The most common approach is to use no research at all. The next most frequent approach is to use what are loosely called "informal methods"—often meaning that somebody ran a focus group or did some intercept interviews at a meeting or trade show, or worse, casually and carelessly talked with a few people and accumulated some press clippings. And because so many clients and

Glen M. Broom, Ph.D.
Professor and Chair,
Department of Journalism
San Diego State University

bosses now demand accountability and ask for evidence of having "moved the needle" or "made the numbers change," the "evaluation-only" approach is also common. All miss the point and real value of using research in public relations campaigns.

First of all, research increases your understanding of the problem. You design the campaign based on the diagnosis of the problem situation. Research helps you identify the forces working for and against you—inside and outside the organization. It helps you identify from among all the various stakeholder groups the target publics essential to achieving the campaign goal. Armed with the foundation of information gathered by your research, you are able to write specific and measurable objectives for each of the publics. After the research helps you identify target publics and establish the objectives for each, it also gives you the detailed understanding necessary for developing campaign action and communication strategy.

Second, research monitors the program as it is being implemented and records how closely it conforms to the campaign plan. The "formative" uses include documenting what happened, and making adjustments and mid-course corrections. Not only must you track campaign effort and output, but you must develop a detailed understanding of what

(continued)

PRoSpeak   Continued

happened in order to later evaluate the campaign and make improvements for the next campaign.

Third, research provides feedback for assessing campaign effects. Unless you can document campaign impact, you will not be able to assess campaign success or failure. You will also have difficulty evaluating the relative worth of your campaign vis-à-vis campaign costs. Measures include the intended outcomes specified in campaign objectives, as well as the criterion stated in the overall goal. Campaigns typically attempt to change what people know, how people feel, and what people do. The campaign goal provides the summative measure of what will happen if all or most of the outcomes stated in the objectives are achieved. The research findings at this stage not only answer client and management demands for evidence, they also provide the information needed to improve future campaign efforts.

Research elevates public relations work from its relatively safe haven as an artistic endeavor and makes it part of an organization's management system. For those who aspire to having a seat at the management table, knowing how to do, interpret, and use research is an imperative.

It should come as no surprise that when I am asked, "When do you recommend doing research in public relations campaigns?" my response is, "Before, during, and after the campaign." You can't wait until midway or after the campaign. Research is not an "add on." In fact, it is safe to say that effective campaigns and effective research are inseparable. Research provides the structure and procedures for gathering, storing, retrieving, and applying information for making decisions before, during, and after the program. In short, research is the basis for the management information system that makes public relations a management function, as well as a managed function. What is the alternative?

Public Relations Research

Most research in public relations is either basic—related to building public relations theory—or applied—designed to solve problems. Karlberg makes a further distinction between instrumental and critical research. Instrumental refers to pragmatic research and is concerned with micro-level questions and techniques. Critical research is concerned with theorizing the broader implications, or the macro-level effects of PR in society. Thus far, instrumental research has been the dominant form in public relations.

Much of the published research on public relations has been conducted by those in academia, according to Pavlick's studies in 1987 and supported by Pasadeos, Renfro, and Hanily in 1999. "Public relations is still in its youth as a scholarly discipline . . . characterized by a greater presence of didactic works (textbooks) than older disciplines that . . . rely on original research. . . . Public relations . . . draws a lot of its inspiration from practice, which is more likely to be explained in textbooks than in journal articles," the trio concludes. Pavlick's review of public relations literature, published in the 1980s, indicates that 80 percent of the authors are associated with universities. Theoretical research was virtually nonexistent in the private sector during the same period, according to professors Ryan and Martinson.

Pavlick wrote that scientific research in public relations should illuminate the process of public relations, that is, what will and will not work. Brody and Stone assert that the primary concerns of PR research should involve human attitudes, opinions, and perceptions. But Karlberg believes critical research should raise important questions about PR's social implications. For example, as Heath notes, some scholars criticize corporate practitioners for conveying pointless communication and cluttering already choked channels with more light and noise and attempting to influence public perceptions on behalf of nebulous self-interests. Pearson states that another criticism arises from the notion that universal ethical principles, such as truth and fairness, do not exist within the practice of PR.

Applied research involves two main subthemes: strategic and evaluation. Strategic research is used in campaign or program development and is situational and problem-oriented. Evaluation research is conducted to determine a program's effectiveness. It can be summative—determining if goals and objectives were met—or formative—a tool to improve future efforts. Flay and Cook identify six types of questions with which summative research concerns itself: audience, implementation, effectiveness, impacts, cost, and causality. Atkin and Freimuth explain that formative research provides data and perspectives to improve messages during the course of a campaign.

According to Lerbinger, there are four major categories of research as it relates to public relations:

- Environmental monitoring programs
- Public relations audits
- Communication audits
- Social audits

Wimmer and Dominick suggest that a fifth category be added to the list: evaluation research.

Environmental Monitoring Program

Environmental monitoring occurs when practitioners scan the landscape to identify trends that may affect an organization. The two-phase program sounds an "early warning" to recognize emerging issues. Wimmer and Dominick suggest that this "often takes the form of a systematic content analysis of publications likely to herald new developments." The publications could include journals or trade magazines. This first step might also assemble a panel of community leaders or influentials who are surveyed on a regular basis to learn what ideas or trends they believe are significant. Phase two may monitor public opinion using either a panel whose members remain the same and who are quizzed over time or a cross-sectional poll in which a random sample is surveyed once.

Public Relations Audit

Simon describes this intensive study of internal and external audience relationships as a "research tool used specifically to describe, measure and assess an organization's public relations activities and to provide guidelines for future public relations programming." The goal of the study, Wimmer and Dominick explain, is to measure an organization's standing "in the eyes of its employees, and . . . with regard to the opinions of customers, stockholders, community leaders." It is an attempt to take the pulse of the health of an organization's entire public relations program and its interaction with its stakeholders.

This open-system rationale means "it engages in interchanges with the environment. . . . This interchange is an essential factor underlying the system's viability," writes Buckley. In the initial step, an organization's important audiences are identified via personal interviews or a content analysis of external communications. The next stage is to rate how these segments regard the organization. Rating scales or semantic differentials are often used to develop a profile.

PRoActive
Applying Research Methods

Because accountability is coming to the forefront of the field, research in public relations is now impacting the evaluation process. "As public relations practitioners earn degrees in the profession, the question of how, why, where and what research should be taught is debated by practitioners and educators." This article reported the results of a 1995 study of 400 public relations practitioners.

Findings
- Of the practitioners surveyed, 51% said they learned to conduct or produce research themselves on the job.
- Of those surveyed, 46% learned to use research on the job.
- The 12% who had five or fewer years of experience were exposed to undergraduate public relations programs addressed in a public relations research course.
- Of those surveyed, 13% learned to conduct research in their undergraduate education
- Of those surveyed, 21% learned to use research information from undergraduate instruction.
- Practitioners who did use research said it helped in planning, implementing, and evaluating their work.
- Practitioners who did not use research cited lack of money, time, and people as their main limitations.
- Of those surveyed, 12% of practitioners conducted focus groups, 11% used mail surveys and market research, and 10% used telephone surveys.
- The majority of practitioners said they spent less than 25% of their time on research.

Recommendations
What educators can do:

- Become more involved in general mass communication or speech communication courses that currently provide research education for public relations students.
- Design teaching units that address the application of research to PR practice.
- Offer PR research opportunities in all PR classes.
- Offer continuing professional education for current practitioners through seminars, sharing research, and other types of learning situations.
- Involve practitioners in providing real-life projects for students.

What practitioners can do:

- Invite more educators to participate in internships and other sabbatical-type learning opportunities to keep abreast of what is happening in the profession.
- Bring research concerns to educators for their evaluation. Educators generally possess a range of research skills and often have access to graduate students and computer centers that can help in conducting research projects.
- Volunteer to provide hands-on practice opportunities for PR students in courses that range from principles to campaigns.
- Take an active role in PR student activities, especially in PRSA chapters, by serving as professional advisers.

Source: Adapted from Barbara DeSanto. "Public Relations Practitioners and Research: Relating Their Experience to Practitioners." *Southwestern Mass Communication Journal* 13 (1998): 67–75.

Communications Audit

This audit focuses upon the internal and external channels of communication used by an organization. The techniques used are readership surveys of publications, content analyses of external media, and readability studies of materials that are distributed inside and outside the organization.

With regard to internal communications audits, research has shown an apparent relationship between the communications climate within an organization and employee loyalty, commitment, and job satisfaction. Several studies indicate that employee publications and the "grapevine" are most frequently cited by employees as the "most used" mediums to receive organizational information. The employees' immediate supervisor is, almost without exception, identified as the employees' "most preferred" communication source.

Social Audit

This type of audit focuses on social performance, in other words, how responsible the organization is to society. "The audit provides feedback on such company-sponsored social action programs as minority hiring, environmental cleanup, and employee safety," Wimmer and Dominick explain.

Evaluation Research

Rossi and Freeman suggest two levels and attendant questions at each stage of the evaluation process:

- Planning—What is the extent of the target problem? How do the costs relate to the benefits?
- Implementation—Is the program reaching the target audience?

Rayfield et al. suggest that, for the most part, public relations practitioners use four types of research to ask questions and get answers:

- Experiments—Questions, answers, and observation take place in a controlled setting.
- Field research—A practitioner/researcher can observe people in a natural setting.
- Unobtrusive research—This category includes library and database searches, files, client information, and consulting experts.
- Surveys—Data are collected by means of a questionnaire, either mail or telephone, or in-depth interviewing.

According to Hendrix, the survey is the most widely used method to gauge the opinions, needs, and expectations of internal and external public relations audiences. The primary types are mail and telephone surveys. To be successful, each must pay particular attention to how the questions or statements are constructed, as well as why and to whom the questions are asked. Dillman writes that success is also based upon the structure of the question.

Four types of questions can be identified:

1. Open-ended—Respondents are free to create their own answer.
2. Close-ended with ordered choices—Single-dimension answers are provided for selection.

3. Close-ended with unordered answer choices—"Answer choices are provided, but no single dimension underlines them," Dillman explains.
4. Partially close-ended—Choices are provided, or respondents can create their own.

Before a survey is finalized, it is important to pretest the instrument to discover defects; otherwise, the results will be of limited value. Dillman suggests that pretesting should be conducted more than once, "searching for people who represent each major segment of the population."

Other important concepts in survey research are population, sample size, and response or return rate. A population is a group or class of objects, subjects, or units. Rayfield et al. write that a population "consists of all of the people the researcher is interested in studying." However, it is seldom feasible that a study could include every member of a population. Sampling allows the researcher to infer characteristics of a population by focusing on an appropriate sample size. Generally, the larger the sample, the more closely it will resemble the population as a whole. In addition, the larger the sample is, the smaller the chance for error.

Obviously, the more completed surveys one can collect the better; in fact, it is necessary for a study's response rate to be statistically significant. The results of Dillman's Total Design method studies conclude that "response rates to mail questionnaires are usually lower than those obtained by either of the interview methods [telephone or face-to-face]."

Public Relations Theories and Models

Botan and Hazelton point out that "there has been little of public relations research that is theory driven. However, there is an apparent, increasing commitment to theory-driven research." Perhaps this avoidance is because, as James Grunig writes, "few [theorists] have developed unique theories of public relations." In the past, public relations has borrowed heavily from communication and other social science theories. He proposes a "symmetrical view" that regards the "purpose of public relations as managing conflict and promoting understanding."

He arrives at this "original theory of public relations" from several research traditions, which suggest a two-way model including coorientation, systems theory, interest-group liberalism, and conflict resolution. These presuppositions include:

- Communication leads to understanding—The purpose of communication is to generate understanding.
- Holism—The whole is greater than the sum of its parts.
- Interdependence—Although organizations are bounded, they continue to penetrate their boundaries and environments.
- Open systems—Systems freely exchange information.
- Moving equilibrium—Each system moves toward balance. "In the symmetrical approach to public relations, cooperative and mutual adjustment are preferred to control and adaptation."

To these concepts, Grunig adds the following ideas, reminiscent of MacGregor's Theory Y assumptions:

- Equality—"People should be treated as equals . . . regardless of education or background."
- Autonomy—"Autonomy maximizes employee satisfaction."
- Innovation—"New ideas and flexible thinking should be stressed."
- Decentralization of management—"Managers should coordinate rather than dictate." This also increases autonomy, innovation, and satisfaction.
- Responsibility—"People and organizations must be concerned with the consequences of their behaviors on others."
- Conflict resolution—Resolution should be achieved through negotiation, communication, and compromise.
- Interest-group liberalism—Boyte describes this as groups of citizens who "champion interests of ordinary people against unresponsive government and corporate structures."

Grunig and Hunt also developed three other theoretical models of public relations, based on the flow of communication between an organization and its publics, its direction, and its potential for influence. These models are:

- One-way asymmetrical (press agentry/publicity)
- One-way symmetrical (public information)
- Two-way asymmetrical (scientific persuasion)

Grunig explains these models as representing the "values, goals and behaviors held or used by organizations when they practice public relations.

"Press agentry/publicity describes propagandistic public relations that seeks media attention in almost any possible way. The public information model characterizes public relations as practiced by 'journalists-in-residence' who disseminate what is generally accurate information about the organization but do not volunteer negative information."

"The press agentry/publicity and public information models . . . stress . . . outgoing information from the organization . . . and the relative absence of feedback," explain Gaudino, Fritsch, and Haynes.

Grunig's two-way asymmetrical model allows for a two-way flow of communication, which uses social sciences and data on audiences to design a persuasive campaign. This has been termed "scientific persuasion" as opposed to the two-way symmetrical model whose goal is mutual understanding between an organization and its publics. This approach approximates what Cutlip, Center, and Broom as well as Simon have termed "social responsibility." Grunig argues that "the two-way symmetrical model is a more moral and ethical approach to public relations . . . it is also a more effective model in practice."

Dozier, Grunig, and Grunig also note that the press agentry and public information models emphasize "the flow of information outward from an organization. . . . Communicators using these models do not serve as channels of information from public back into management decision making." The two-way asymmetrical model is more sophisticated because the communicator gathers information used in management decision making; "communicators develop messages that are most likely to persuade publics to behave as the organization wants." However, the two-way symmetrical model is clearly superior among the models Dozier, Grunig, and Grunig explore. This model uses knowledge and understanding of publics to manage conflict and promote mutual benefit. It places the communicator in a somewhat paradoxical situation as "advocates of the organization's interests in negotiations with key publics but also advocates of the publics' interests in discussions with the organization's strategic planners and decision makers."

To practice either of the two-way models, communicators need expertise in strategic research, defined as reliable information that is systematically collected about large and small publics that affect the organization. This differs from tactical research, which is the ability to gather information in order to generate or distribute messages. Tactical research can be problematic in that, as Dozier, Grunig, and Grunig note, it is process-oriented, and chief executives rarely settle for a process that does not contribute to the bottom line.

Research to date has provided evidence that the two-way symmetrical model makes organizations more effective; however, many organizations still practice the other models with heavy overtones of manipulation. Kelly put Grunig's four models to the test in a national survey of fund-raising practitioners. She found that the press agentry model was practiced most often. However, in a survey of public relations programs among PRSA members, Deatherage and Hazleton found mixed support for Grunig's theory. Their investigation revealed that the two-way symmetrical model was a significant predictor of perceived PR effectiveness, but they suggest that press agentry and persuasion are not necessarily asymmetrical; in fact, they may prove to be symmetrical, depending on the motives of the practitioners.

Sociological Concepts

In her work, Marcia Prior-Miller explores four sociological perspectives that may enrich public relations for their focus on organization theory. They are symbolic interactionism, exchange theory, conflict theory, and structural-functional theory.

Symbolic Interactionism.   Symbolic interactionism says that reality is what people think it is; they construct it through their interaction and derive meaning through their symbols. This continual process of redefining reality means that organizations must come to see themselves, in part, as others see them. The term, coined by Herbert Blumer in 1937, assumes that human experience (and for that matter, organizational culture) is mediated by interpretation. The concept depends on what W. I. Thomas calls the "definition of the situation," which suggests that individuals examine and "define" situations before they act and that these definitions actually create reality.

Exchange Theory.   As Prior-Miller explains, "people form and sustain relationships when they believe the rewards from those relationships will be greater than the costs." This theory may be useful in examining how decision making is negotiated in relation to the extent to which the organization values its public relations functions. Sullivan, Dozier, and

PRoEthics
Worldviews

"The assumption that asymmetrical and symmetrical worldviews influence the selection of public relations models and consequently the effectiveness of public relations is central to Grunig's (1989, 1992) theory of public relations excellence." Worldview is defined as "assumptions that practitioners . . . have about such things as morality, ethics, human nature, religion, politics, free enterprise, or gender." If, as a practitioner, you adhere to an asymmetrical worldview, you are supposed to influence publics in ways that will benefit your organization. Symmetrical worldview practitioners should have "mutual understanding as a primary goal for public relations."

This research randomly sampled 500 members of the Public Relations Society of America; 145 individuals responded. This was the first attempt at measuring symmetrical and asymmetrical worldviews while assessing the relation between the worldviews, examining the four models of public relations, and public relations effectiveness. (The four models include press agentry, public information, and a two-way symmetrical and asymmetrical worldview).

Findings
Support for Grunig's belief that the theory of public relations excellence is a normative theory (that is, it doesn't describe or predict what people actually do but rather what people should do): "Respondents who scored higher on the symmetrical worldview measure, lower on the asymmetrical worldview measure, and used the two-way symmetrical model of public relations were more successful."

Questions still remain as to why and under what circumstances an organization will change its attachment to worldviews as well as hold a simultaneous belief in competing theories and practices.

Source: Adapted from Christina P. Deatherage and Vincent Hazleton. "Effects of Organizational Worldviews on the Practice of Public Relations: A Test of the Theory of Public Relations Excellence." *Journal of Public Relations Research* 10 (1998): 57–71.

Hellweg's study indicated that even years of experience did not translate into practitioners moving up in the organization or into higher-paying roles. This notion translates, writes Prior-Miller, into some propositions:

- The more often hiring organizations find they are able to retain highly experienced practitioners at low salaries and hierarchically low positions, the more likely they are to continue offering low salaries.

- The more often hiring organizations have received feedback in the past that indicates practitioners will apply for and accept placement in positions without greater rewards, the more likely they are to continue to offer low salaries and hierarchically low positions to experienced individuals.

- The greater profit hiring organizations receive as a result of their actions, the more likely they are to continue to perform the action.

- The greater the dependency of practitioners on hiring organizations for job tenure, the greater the hiring organizations' power over practitioners, and the less power practitioners have to require higher pay for their skill and knowledge.

Conflict Theory.   This theory assumes that organizations are the result or product of conflict from their members or ranks. Conflict is then inevitable because of competing goals, as well as the values of the organization and the individuals who comprise it. This approach runs counter to the idea that consensus is the natural order.

Structural-Functional Theory.   This asserts that society and its structures or organizations are more than the sum of their parts. The position public relations holds within an organization might be the basis for its strength or weakness, or whether its activities are recognized and rewarded.

- The more integrated practitioners are in the organizational network, the greater the practitioners' rewards.
- The higher the position of public relations is in the organizational structure, the greater the practitioners' rewards.
- The greater the professional qualifications that are required of the practitioner, the greater are the rewards.

Communication Theories

Communication offers other ways of looking at the world that often assist practitioners in orienting their thinking and research. These theories focus on how a message moves from a sender through the media to the receiver. However, this does not necessarily mean that just because the ideas are conveyed, acceptance and action will result.

Two-Step-Flow Theory

Step one assumes that opinion leaders are informed by the media on issues; they then analyze and interpret the data. In step two, these leaders disseminate the information to the public. This vertical and horizontal process was first noted by Lazarsfeld, Berelson, and Gaudet in a study of the 1940 presidential race. They wrote, "it became clear that certain people in every stratum of a community serve relay roles in the mass communication of election information and influence."

Multistep-Flow Theory

This explanation of how ideas are adopted holds that there are opinion leaders on an array of topics, such as education or politics, with varying degrees of influence on other opinion leaders and the public at large.

Opinion-Group Theory

In this scenario, opinion leaders play important roles in the formation of public opinion, but their major influence is in galvanizing opinion. According to Wilcox and Nolte, "The group is centered on an opinion leader—a person who is listened to by the others—although he or she may not be identified or recognized as such. This leader is the one who gets information from outside and comments on it to the group." Scott explains that this leader may possess formal or informal power. Formally, the power is derived from authority or a position held. Informally, the people themselves may confer power upon an individual.

European public relations practitioner Bill Mallinson suggests that "what public relations theory does exist has been borrowed to a large extent from communications theory." He identifies what he believes are useful constructs to integrate theory and practice:

- Gerald Miller's Two Ps in a Pod: Based on the work of social psychology, he believes "that effective, ethically defensible persuasion and effective, ethically defensible public relations are virtually synonymous."

- The Pragmatic Approach: Based on general systems theory, "people are considered as objects who create patterns of behavior." To Mallinson, a practitioner could use this concept by tailoring campaign messages to elicit certain types of behavior from its target audiences, thereby increasing the likelihood of success. This approach "can enable the practitioner to assess the likelihood of different types of behavior when planning a corporate campaign, provided that he or she is aware of external—and also unpredictable—factors that also affect behavior."

- The Psychological Box: This perspective sets out to show that the brain creates communication. It views human behavior as the result of stimuli, organs, and responses. It "is relevant for the public relations practitioner in that it should help to make him or her sufficiently responsive to individuals or groups to study their characteristics and both tailor the message and choose the appropriate medium for sending a message."

- The Interactionist Outlook: This "promotes the idea that communication creates the self, since it is viewed as a series of social symbols to which people relate. As such, the symbol assumes a special importance, since it is the crucial link that causes people to communicate with each other." This concept demonstrates the value of considering another person's or group's point of view, in light of one's own.

- The Dramatist Factor: With Erving Goffman as the primary modern proponent, the dramatist approach works under the premise "that we are all social actors on the stage of life, and that one of our chief concerns is how best to present our self to the public at large." Front-stage behavior is outside appearance. Backstage behavior is how people react in situations where they are not being watched or do not have to worry about people judging their behavior.

"Connected to the idea of the individual's relationship towards a group, and sometimes towards another individual, 'mystification' can form an important aspect of the dramatist's behavior. It consists mainly of keeping the right amount of detachment so as to intrigue and mystify others," according to Mallinson.

Another aspect of this perspective on communication is "derisory collusion," a situation where two parties know information that a third or fourth party is not privy to, and therefore the act of communication is altered. "The dramatist factor in communication teaches many a lesson for the public relations practitioner. . . . An understanding of its basic tenets can be of considerable help at meetings, whether between two people or groups: it can help to judge when, and how, to go through the motion, when to get down to brass tacks and how to recognize the hidden agenda that often exists, and then whether to openly ignore it, create the impression of being unaware of it, having secretly recognized it, or even create the impression of creating an impression, and last but not least, when and how to address it."

Persuasion

It's "the process of preparing and delivering messages, through verbal and non-verbal symbols, to individuals or groups in order to alter, strengthen or maintain attitudes, beliefs, values or behaviors," say Woodward and Denton. Merrill cautions that it is "hard to run from. . . . It is subtle; it is complex . . . persuasive symbols trigger already existing predilections, and our biases are further strengthened. Often times, we are persuaded, not by overtly persuasive techniques, but by neutrally presented information."

Newsom and Carrell write that persuasion can be viewed in one of three ways or perhaps a combination of "a learning process," "a power process," and "an emotional process."

Cutlip, Center, and Broom add that an individual's actions can be influenced in one of four ways: purchase, patronage, pressure, or persuasion. "In public relations, persuasion is used. The basic objective of programs is either to change or to neutralize hostile opinions, to crystallize unformed or latent opinions in your favor, or to conserve favorable opinions."

Each of these views is based upon the needs and benefits of an audience or public. Wilcox and Nolte describe this pairing as "self-interest" or a condition in which each member of the target audience asks, "What's in it for me?" Abraham Maslow's hierarchy of needs (see Figure 5.2) is often cited in discussions of what fuels public action, both group and individual. These needs are:

- Physiological needs
- Safety needs
- Social needs
- Ego needs
- Self-fulfillment needs

Wilcox and Nolte argue that most public relations activities concern themselves with the lower-level needs and tend to downplay or avoid higher-level needs because they are more abstract. However, research indicates that it is becoming important to meet these needs in order for organizations to create environments in which employees are appreciated and held in high esteem. This engenders loyalty and may make the difference between success and failure of a corporation, particularly if crises occur.

More than twenty years ago, Otto Lerbinger described five "designs" of persuasion. He termed them stimulus-response, cognitive, motivational, social, and personality. The first is based on association, such as in the classic case of Pavlov's dogs that were conditioned to respond to a tuning fork. This simplistic approach is inappropriate to fit the needs of a complex issue but may be useful in situations in which a practitioner wishes to link a client with a program or concept, as in Ford's "Quality Is Job 1" program.

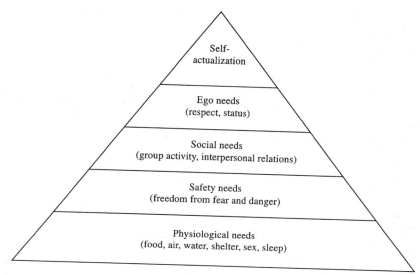

FIGURE 5.2   Maslow's Hierarchy of Needs

The cognitive model assumes that individuals are capable of drawing the correct conclusion if presented with sufficient information. Its weakness is that it does not take into account the motivations of the audience and therefore undercuts its ability to persuade. Motivational models expand the envelope of persuasion by seeking to fulfill the emotional needs of a target public, as in the case of Maslow's hierarchy. Social design of persuasion is related to the motivational model in that it is dynamic and includes social status and group norms leading to the most acceptable patterns of behavior. Newsom and Carrell point out "that if you are trying to persuade across major regional, ethnic or national boundaries, the same message is unlikely to be appropriate in every case. You'll have to prepare separate messages based on different social influences." In terms of personality, Janis warns that even if a practitioner's messages are aimed at large groups, it is still necessary to recognize that it is composed of a range of individual personality types. There is no monolithic group.

William McGuire identified what he asserts are the steps in the persuasion process. His matrix cites twelve output or "response steps" not unlike those outlined in Everett Rogers's diffusion theory. Rogers's process lists five steps through which individuals acquire new ideas: awareness, interest, trial, evaluation, and adoption. McGuire expands this to include exposure to the message, attending, liking the message, comprehending, skill acquisition, yielding, memory storage, information search and retrieval, deciding on the basis of retrieval, behaving in accord with decision, reinforcement of desired acts, and postbehavioral consolidating. "The successive response substeps [are] required if the communication [message] is to be effective," McGuire contends. The social psychologist suggests that they are also "useful checklists for constructing and evaluating a communication campaign."

Each approach focuses on the main thrusts of all communication, namely, the source, message, channel, receiver, and destination (see Figure 5.3). McGuire terms them "input factors" or "persuasive message options that can be manipulated."

INPUT: Independent Variables (Communication) / OUTPUT: Dependent Variables (Response Steps Mediating Persuasion)	SOURCE	MESSAGE	CHANNEL	RECEIVER	DESTINATION
1. Exposure to the communication					
2. Attending to it					
3. Comprehending it (learning what)					
4. Yielding to it (attitude change)					
5. Deciding on basis of retrieval					
6. Behaving in accord with decision					

FIGURE 5.3   The Communication/Persuasion Model as an Input/Output Matrix

Adapted from William J. McGuire. *Theoretical Foundations of Compaigns in Public Communication Campaigns,* 2nd ed. Ronald E. Rice and Charles K. Atkin (Eds.). Newbury Park, CA: Sage (1989).

Grunig proposes another way of deriving meaning from the persuasion process by offering a situational perspective. This involves the concepts of problem recognition, constraint recognition, referent criterion, involvement, information seeking, and information processing. These steps complement McGuire's and Lerbinger's schemas but also reflect the belief that important issues will generate greater involvement on the part of individuals because they become stakeholders, that these stakeholders will deliberately seek information to fulfill their needs, and that some of the data gathered will be unplanned. In Grunig's words, "how a person perceives a situation explains whether he will communicate about a situation, how he will communicate and whether he will have an attitude relevant to the situation."

In the discussion of persuasion and public relations, a term emerges that is vital for both—credibility. It could mean, and has meant, a person or entity worthy of belief, of good character or truthfulness. A credible source then would exhibit good sense, character, and objectivity, thereby heightening credibility. However, researchers such as Carl Hovland point out that some people forget their first impression of a source but remember a general point of view they conveyed. This is known as the "sleeper effect." Hovland writes that "the increased persuasion produced by a high credibility source disappears. Similarly, the decreased persuasion produced by a low credibility source vanishes."

Motivation

Pace defines "need" as "something that is essential, indispensable, or inevitable to fill a condition." It can also be used "to refer to the lack of something." Maslow's approach to the needs and goals as the driving force of behavior turns on his belief that only unsatisfied needs move people to act on a goal. Others have built upon and continue to critique and refine this theory.

ERG Theory

Alderfer's theory condenses Maslow's five categories of need into three: existence (physiological needs), relatedness (needs for relationships), and growth (need to achieve potential). This refinement of Maslow's system recognizes that even though existence needs may go unsatisfied, other categories may also play a part in directing behavior. Alderfer, unlike Maslow, also argues that satisfied needs may continue as an overriding influence in decision making.

Motivator-Hygiene Theory

Herzberg contends that two sets of factors influence employee motivation in organizations: job satisfaction (motivators) and job dissatisfaction (maintenance or hygiene). Motivators may include recognition, responsibility, or personal growth; maintenance or hygiene factors refer to pay, job security, and policies.

Expectancy Theory

Vroom's theory highlights choices rather than needs and offers three assumptions:

1. If I behave in a certain way, I can expect certain rewards. Vroom calls this outcome expectancy.
2. Every outcome has value or valence.
3. If I decide to work hard, my efforts will achieve specific goals. This is termed effort expectancy.

Practitioners' Use of Research

In *Precision Public Relations,* Harry O'Neill wrote in 1988 that "Research is becoming a vital tool for public relations because the days of intuition and gut feelings are over. No longer is the public relations professional allowed to assume . . . that a particular effort had the desired effect. Management wants facts to justify public relations activities and proof of their efficacy." That same year, Daniel J. Edelman wrote that measurement is clearly one of the greatest needs of the PR program, with Patrick Jackson, editor of *pr reporter* and past president of PRSA, echoing that the most potent word in the practice of PR is "evidence," and research provides that evidence.

A decade later, that "evidence" remains elusive for some practitioners even though CEOs monitor communication and decision making and hold executives accountable for their strategies and programs, according to Lawrence Foster, writing in *The Public Relations*

Strategist. In their book *Using Research in Public Relations,* Glen Broom and David Dozier identify five major approaches to research in program management. They are:

1. The no research approach
2. The informal research approach
3. The media event approach
4. The evaluation only approach
5. The scientific management approach

No Research

In the no research approach, there is often no input from an organization's environment, or publics, into the organization. Research is not used in either the planning or evaluation of programs or of specific activities. Practitioners in this type of approach are often "out of the loop" of information and decision making. They then must explain or defend management decisions or actions in which they had no say.

Informal Research

The informal research approach may include conducting focus groups, then using the results to conduct an entire PR campaign. This type of information gathering is much of what passes for research in PR.

Media Event

The media event focus is conducted solely to generate attention and news coverage. Broom and Dozier cite an example of a survey on attitudes toward organ transplants conducted for the American Association of Critical Care Nurses. The commissioned survey cost a few thousand dollars yet generated enormous national publicity.

Evaluation Only

Evaluation only research tracks the implementation of a program and assesses its effect. This approach is not regarded by management as essential for planning a program and limits its potential usefulness.

Scientific Management

The scientific management approach, suggested by Frederick Taylor, is at the core of PR management. In this type, "research is done to define the problem situation for the purpose of planning a public relations program. . . . Second, research is done to monitor . . . performance accountability and for strategic adjustment. . . . Third, research is done to measure program impact or effectiveness with respect to goals and objectives. . . . Research adds a layer of complexity to the practice of PR and elevates its function from its relatively safe haven to an artistic endeavor," Broom and Dozier note. This reference to artistic endeavor is, in fact, a partial definition for the characteristics of strategic planning.

For Karlberg, the future of public relations research will hinge on a symmetrical approach that will require a reevaluation of accepted premises and well-established research traditions. There exists a need for new forms of interdisciplinary collaboration that are creative. And ultimately, there is a need for effective strategies to make results of research broadly available to the general public.

Summary

Doing our homework, examining our critical thinking, posing questions, and answering them accurately are the goals of public relations practitioners. An understanding of research, theories, persuasion, and motivation can help us achieve these tasks, in both internal and external settings. As Cutlip, Center, and Broom write, "Even though it will not answer all the questions or sway all decisions, methodical systematic research is the foundation of effective public relations." The exercise may take a variety of forms, from monitoring trends and examining our messages and policies to measuring our organization's social responsibility and evaluating campaigns. Whatever the form, its value to the profession is in creating an atmosphere of discipline in our approach to counseling clients. This will become easier to accomplish in future public relations campaigns if the use of artificial intelligence software programs, called expert systems, proliferate.

QUESTIONS

1. What are the sources of knowledge?

2. What are the characteristics of quantitative and qualitative research approaches?

3. How could a practitioner use each in a public relations setting?

4. Explain how Grunig's two-way symmetrical model works.

5. What is a theory?

READINGS

Robert C. Bogdan and Sari Knopp Biklen. *Qualitative Research in Education*. Boston, MA: Allyn and Bacon, 1982.

Carl H. Botan and Vincent Hazelton, Jr., eds. *Public Relations Theory*. Hillsdale, NJ: Lawrence Erlbaum Associates, 1989.

Lawrence Foster. "10 CEOs send a Message to Public Relations." *Public Relations Strategist 1,* no. 1 (Spring 1995), 4.

Robert L. Heath. "A Public Relations Research and Education: Agendas for the 1990s." *Public Relations Review* 17, no. 2 (Summer 1991): 185–194.

Michael Karlberg. "Remembering the Public in Public Relations Research: From Theoretical to Operational Symmetry." *Journal of Public Relations Research* 8 (1996): 263–278.

Bill Mallinson. *Public Lies and Private Truths: An Anatomy of Public Relations*. London, England: Cassell, 1996.

R. Wayne Pace. *Organizational Communication*. Englewood Cliffs, NJ: Prentice-Hall, 1983.

Roger D. Wimmer and Joseph Dominick. *Mass Media Research*. Belmont, CA: Wadsworth Publishing Company, 1991.

Gary C. Woodward and Robert E. Denton, Jr. *Persuasion and Influence in American Life*. Prospect Heights, IL: Waveland Press, 1988.

DEFINITIONS

paradigm: Ritzer describes this as a loose collection of logically held together assumptions, concepts, or propositions that orient thinking and research.

population: Kerlinger defines it as "all members of any well-defined class of people, events or objects."

qualitative: Data analysis is not numerical in nature; it concerns itself with descriptive paradigms and context.

quantitative: Analysis involves statistical measures and tests of significance, with results generalizable to a population.

sample: A group or selection of the total population that a researcher desires to investigate.

theory: A proposition that tries to explain the observed facts related to a specific problem.

6 Strategic Planning

Beginning with a Road Map and Compass

CHAPTER OUTLINE

Organization Environments
Strategic Planning
Long-Range Planning
Power and Influence

Budgeting
Strategic PR Planning
Target Audiences

CHAPTER OBJECTIVES

When you have completed this chapter, you should be able to:

- Understand the characteristics of rational, natural, and open systems
- Discern the differences between strategic planning and long-range planning
- Identify types of power
- Compare budgeting strategies
- Understand the components of successful strategic public relations
- Recognize promotional message approaches and appeals

"Like research, planning in public relations is essential not only to know where a particular campaign is headed, but also to win the support of top management," writes Fraser Seitel, then director of public affairs for the Chase Manhattan Bank. Understanding the planning, managing, and budgeting process may help practitioners to "transcend the boundaries of their own craft and analyze and understand the needs and strategies of their operating and support units" to "gain a place at strategy sessions," write practitioner Robert W. Kinead and educator Dena

Winokur. "Within the . . . profession, the ability to influence strategic planning varies widely. Some practitioners get involved in developing game plans at the highest corporate level, while others simply implement communications moves once a strategy is set by others."

Editor and publisher Paul Holmes writes in *Inside PR: The Magazine of Reputation Management* that many public relations professionals who become part of senior management "will need to look at their role in an entirely different light. They must get away from the notion that public relations is about press agentry, or publicity, or managing the media. They must see public relations as a policy-shaping discipline." He calls for a practice whose roots are anchored in behavioral science and counseling.

Grunig and Hunt suggest that PR managers perform what organizational theorists call a boundary role. That is, they function on the edge of an organization, with one foot firmly planted inside the organization and the other outside, a liaison or facilitator between internal and external publics. If this balancing function is accurate, what must this individual know in order to earn a place at the strategy table?

Seitel says that these corporate linesmen must "consider the relationship of the organization to its environment . . . work within organizational confines to develop innovative solutions to organizational problems . . . must think strategically . . . be willing to measure their results . . . using management by objectives (MBO), management by objectives and results (MOR), and program evaluation and research technique (PERT)." In addition, Grunig and Hunt caution that these practitioners must also be knowledgeable and comfortable with the elements of their organization. These include functions, structure, processes, and feedback.

Organization Environments

It is appropriate then to begin our discussion of these issues by providing an organizational perspective of the types of environments in which organizations live and the components that must be present for practitioners to find their way in complex situations.

Parsons writes that "the development of organizations is the principal mechanism by which . . . it is possible to get things done to achieve goals beyond the individual." Scott places these "mechanisms" into three major categories: rational, natural, and open systems.

A rational system is defined as "an organization that is collectively oriented to the pursuit of relatively specific goals and exhibiting a relatively highly formalized social structure." The Scientific Management Approach fits into this category. It seeks to scientifically analyze tasks performed by individual workers "in order to discover those procedures that would produce the maximum output with the minimum input of energies and resources."

Frederick Taylor believed the adoption of the approach would usher in a new era of industrial peace because the interests of labor and management would be compatible. Taylor felt that "there could be no disputes about how hard one should work or the pay one should receive for labor." However, workers resisted time study procedures in the attempt to standardize every aspect of their performance and rejected incentives.

A natural system proposes that "an organization is a collectivity whose participants are little affected by the formal structure or official goals but who share a common interest in the survival of the system and who engage in collective activities, informally structured, to secure this end." This category is represented by Parsons's social system model or the AGIL model.

All social systems are confronted by four basic system problems: adaptation, goal attainment, integration, and latency or pattern maintenance. The schema is applied to society as a whole.

Parsons places stress on the importance of the organization-environment relationship, "the organization being viewed as a subsystem within a more comprehensive social unit, and the environment seen as more a stabilizing element sustaining and legitimizing the organization."

Certainly from a public relations perspective, we can see the importance of monitoring the needs of the environment and the needs of its inhabitants—more specifically, employees. If an institution fails to adapt and to attain goals, pathologies may arise. An example of this organizational illness would occur if the organization expends most of its resources and energy to maintain itself rather than achieving specified goals. Alienation, internally and externally, could occur and ultimately doom the organization's survival.

An open system is "an organization as a coalition of shifting interest groups that develop goals by negotiation; the structure of the coalition, its activities, and its outcomes are strongly influenced by environmental factors." The systems design approach characterizes the open system. It is "a source of ideas to improve the design of the organization—determine proper workflows, control systems." It seeks to change and improve the organization as viewed from a managerial perspective, not simply to describe and understand them.

This system also incorporates a school of thought known as interorganizational analysis. This dual-pronged view offers two ways of involvement with the environment that may be useful to PR practitioners. The first, population ecology, is based on Darwin's survival of the fittest concept. It states that the environment chooses which organization will survive. It is a passive response to external forces. The second, political economy, stresses the process of adaptation to the environment and is decidedly active in relation to outside forces. This last form is most like the situation public relations should find itself in. As Perrow writes, an open system is characterized by "dissolved boundaries divided by the organization and its environment." Among the various flows of elements, the flow of information is most critical. "The gathering, transmission, storage and retrieval of information are among the most fateful activities of an organization." From a public relations perspective, the ability to organize information for immediate use is vital. It makes it possible to "get things done," as Parsons points out, and "to achieve goals beyond the reach of the individual."

Strategic Planning

These systems all require planning, but most aligned with public relations is the open system, which requires a constant scanning of the environment, internally and externally, now and in the future. One concept that allows practitioners to develop schemas for how to handle tomorrow is strategic planning. This approach should not be confused with another oft-used approach—long-range planning. The two are different, yet many people use the terms synonymously or combine the processes entirely, as did one organization with its "long-range strategic planning" approach.

Strategic planning is a process of assessing what you have and where you want to go. It focuses on developing a good fit between an organization's activities and the demands of the environment around it. It looks at the big picture in short time frames, seeks goals that

PRoSpeak

Strategy Is Everything

The reason is simple. Strategy answers that most vital question in every campaign, "Why are we doing this?"

Planning a strategy is the essential first step in any public relations campaign. The biggest mistake practitioners and their clients or employers make is to plunge into tactical activities without a guiding strategy. It is better to have a sound strategy with weak tactical follow-through than a misdirected strategy with strong follow-through . . . because the latter may be taking you rapidly in the wrong direction!

One common problem is keeping straight on the difference between strategy and tactics. An easy way to accomplish this is to use simple-minded strategic planning, which asks four questions:

- Where are we now?
- How did we get here?
- Where do we want to be?
- How will we get there?

The answers constitute a strategy. The details of activities, messages, and media that will be employed to carry out the strategy are the tactics.

Patrick Jackson
President
Jackson, Jackson & Wegner

Steps in the strategic planning process:

1. Campaign strategy must be preceded by a general strategy of public relations, namely, what type of outcomes do you expect a public relations campaign to deliver? In almost every case the answer must be to motivate, reinforce, or modify behavior. Goals such as "to communicate," "to influence opinion," or "to alter attitudes" are half-steps at best. As a CEO of GM once put it, "I don't care whether people love our cars. What I want to know is, Are they buying them?" GM can only pay its bills when cars are bought, not admired or talked about. Short of that, nothing matters.

2. Whose behavior must we influence to meet campaign goals? For years practitioners used mass communications to "blanket" everyone of possible interest. Then research showed that such mass audiences were fictitious—that in fact on every topic there are many interest groups, and no one appeal or

message touches all their concerns or approaches to the subject. Today successful campaigns target the very specific groups that are able and likely to be ready to act in ways that will meet the objective —whether that be making a purchase, supporting a public policy measure, voting for a candidate, or attending an event. Auto dealers provide a handy example of the targeting strategy: From auto registration records they gather the names of those whose cars are four years old or older. Who is more likely to be needing a new car soon?

3. How will we motivate the target groups to action? Groups of people do not suddenly decide to behave in certain ways, out of the blue. Sociologists say that a select number of opinion shapers drive the decision-making process—opinion leaders. A central strategy question is to determine who the opinion leaders are in the target groups, and what will motivate them to join our cause. Finding answers is one of the most vital uses of research in public relations. Automakers would therefore target mechanics, gas station owners, car buffs, and others whose opinions about cars would carry the power of expertise.

4. Will the target groups need to progress through certain intermediate behaviors before they're ready to adopt the ultimate desired behavior?

For instance, if someone asks you to buy a new car, it's highly unlikely you'll immediately say yes. That ultimate behavior will need to be preceded by a visit to the showroom, a test drive, comparative shopping, and other prepurchase behaviors. Sound strategy for a campaign to sell autos, therefore, might well be to motivate target publics to undertake one of these intermediate behaviors rather than risk turning them away by asking for the ultimate behavior at the start.

Within each of these planning steps there are many nuances and usually several options. Research is a major factor in strategic planning because it is often the only guide to choosing among options. The bon mot is true: "All sound public relations begins with research."

Two elements define most successful campaigns:

1. The willingness of those carrying them out to devote the time and energy, at the beginning, to devising a guiding strategy
2. Then sticking to it—rather than being distracted by opponents' actions, occasional criticism or bad press, or just plain cold feet

Sometimes strategies must be altered, of course—but our firm's experience of forty years in designing strategies strongly suggests that in 90 percent of cases, pushing ahead and disregarding the distractions is, at that stage, the preferable strategy.

---

can be accomplished, wants to make critical decisions wisely, tends to operate in an open system as opposed to a closed one, and attempts to cope with a turbulent, changing environment based on more qualitative data such as opinions and intuition. Strategic planning is an art rather than a science and is future-oriented. It is a process (not a plan), which is fluid and flexible, taking the history of the organization into consideration in the belief that the past has an effect on an organization's future.

There are five main categories of strategic planning:

1. Mission
2. Current condition of your organization
3. Market analysis, scanning the environment
4. Where you want to go
5. What you must do to get there

This planning must be conducted at the top. It should be concerned with doing the right thing, not necessarily what's expedient. Effectiveness of the process is much more important than efficiency, and the planning must take into account what the organization does well, known as a core competency, and should decide what to concentrate on.

Long-Range Planning

Conversely, long-range planning is typically used in longer time frames (usually five years), formulates an inflexible blueprint as to how to approach the environment, and focuses on quantitative data. It is also characterized by a gap between planners at the top and planners at an operational level. Other disadvantages are that frequent turnover of executives may disrupt the planning process, budgets are not realistically linked to plans, and crises, complex goals, or short-term decisions cannot be accommodated. It almost never takes an organization's saga, or history, into account and may find that it is out of touch with its publics.

Power and Influence

Power can be described as the ability of "A" to make "B" act in a way that "B" would not otherwise do. Emerson suggests that "It would appear that the power to control or influence the other resides in control over the things he values. . . . In short, power resides implicitly in the other's dependency." The source of power may spring from expertise, experience, numbers, communications networks, or resources, both human and financial. It may reside in a position, such as president, or in a person, as with a charismatic leader. It may also be derived from reputation or organizational membership, such as a professional association. It can also be formal or informal. Oftentimes, influential employees with no formal authority may be responsible for the success of a project if their opinions are valued by coworkers. Symbols of power in the workplace may include a designated parking space, use of the most up-to-date computer and software, an office with a view, or a spacious work area.

Types of Power

- Lester Thurow's "Zero-Sum Society" reasons that an increase in power of one individual results in a corresponding decrease of another. This may manifest itself in a struggle between a chairman of the board and a CEO.
- Synergy refers to the sum total of power greater than 100 percent. It also assumes that power can accumulate.
- In pyramidal power, influence resides in a power elite who can control across issues and across time, as in the White House versus Congress.
- Pluralistic power can be described as a series of small power pyramids in which influence is not transferable.

Other concepts that are helpful in an examination of power are authority, force, and leadership. To Weber, authority equals power (resources) plus legitimacy (position). Force would be achieved when power is combined with illegitimacy of position, as in a dictator. True leadership is a result of power plus legitimacy plus respect. Cutlip, Center, and Broom refer to these steps as the Four Ps: pressure (coercion), patronage, purchase, and persuasion.

It is persuasion that is the desired form of power or influence that public relations utilizes. Its strength is in its potential for securing impartial third-party endorsement. This feature, in effect, strengthens the message crafted and directed to a public or publics. Even in an era in which Web sites and home pages dominate the landscape, thereby making the public relations content more controlled than ever, care must still be taken in disseminating messages.

Budgeting

Planning may include controlling a budget. This can be regarded as the degree to which one activity is emphasized over another. The two major orientations in budgeting are Wildavsky's stance that it is first and foremost a political process ("all budgeting is political"), and Schick's belief that budgeting is a rational process and can be improved upon technically. Wildavsky explains that setting goals is highly political and that most important decisions are already made prior to any rational process. Scott affirms this position with "who controls the budget has the power."

According to Seitel, "Budgeting in public relations is, by definition, somewhat arbitrary." Tucker suggests that the success of budgeting is in "estimating the extent of resources . . . and estimating the cost and availability of those resources."

Cutlip, Center, and Broom agree that "there is as much art and artistry in public relations budgeting as there is science" but offer three guidelines:

1. Know the cost of what you propose to buy.
2. Relate the budget to specific results.
3. Use computer software to manage the program.

Since budgeting may require the skills of many specialists to estimate costs, providing a budget narrative, or explanation as to why you are spending what, can ease the process. "In the final analysis, practitioners must have realistic budgets . . . and must be able to link costs to performance and outcomes," write Cutlip, Center, and Broom.

Types of Budgeting Approaches

Wildavsky defines a budget as "a document containing words and figures that proposes expenditures for certain items and purchases." The approaches are many and varied.

Incremental/Decremental. The oldest and easiest to construct, it is based on last year's budget plus or minus line items. It distributes funds appropriately rather than proportionally and represents a balance of power where the squeaky wheel gets the grease. It causes the least conflict but disregards goals and activities and does not take the future into consideration.

Formula. This type uses a base figure, then adds a specified percentage. It is simple to use and seems logical and objective, but it discourages innovation and new programs.

Planning, Programming, and Budgeting System (PPBS). This focuses on both input and output, the past and the present. It forces participants to state explicit objectives, features multiyear funding, estimates resources needed, estimates benefits, supplies alternative ways to meet goals, then evaluates and revises the process. On its face, it is a reasonable approach, but Aaron Wildavsky cites its failure to define clear goals and quantify them. A single activity may also serve more than one goal.

Zero-Based. Pyhrr formulated this approach, which can best be described as microeconomic. Then Georgia governor Jimmy Carter used the system, which stands in marked contrast to PPBS. This type justifies every activity from zero. It features discrete decision packages, which consist of a purpose, objectives, consequences, and performance. These packages are prioritized and then forwarded to top management. The shortcomings of this approach are that it takes an enormous amount of effort and paperwork, people tend not to read the packages, and it is difficult to determine which packages are more important than others.

Performance.   Resources are allocated according to the performance of tasks. It attempts to improve efficiency and quality and is useful to determine accountability. The downside is that it is subjective, political, and difficult to measure.

Line Item.   Every expenditure is listed and approved, line by line. Once the budget is approved, the managers/administrators of the budget are seldom allowed to deviate from the line items. Even the president of an organization, or of the United States for that matter, has no authority to transfer funds between broad functional categories.

Quota.   An organizational unit is allocated a specific amount; then its managers must plan how to use it without exceeding it.

Program.   This form of systems analysis focuses on outputs, that is, goals, objectives, and end products. Evaluation is based on a cost-effectiveness analysis as a means of achieving goals.

Planning and Management Techniques
Related to Budgeting

The best way for public relations to accrue more meaning to an organization is to be able to measure its results. One way to accomplish this is to adopt techniques that are specifically designed for that purpose. The following offer a range of tools the practitioner may employ to quantify the value of the function. They are also helpful in assessing the type of organizational environment in which practitioners may find themselves. Identifying the type of budget and the assumptions leadership makes about its organization, its culture, and its employees will inform the planning of the public relations specialist.

Management by Objectives (MBO).   In this scheme, a subordinate and a superior mutually establish objectives, usually in a one-year time frame, for the subordinate to accomplish. Evaluation is based on the fulfillment of the agreed-upon tasks.

Management Information System (MIS).   The history of decisions, goals, and budgeting is stored in a computer database. The data can then be manipulated to conduct simulations and make projections as to the impact of decisions. This process aids in developing contingency plans.

Program Evaluation and Research Technique (PERT).   This breaks a project into its component parts or activities; then an estimate is made as to the time it takes to perform each activity, identify which items are critical major activities, and target key personnel. It also uses graphic representations to identify subactivities in terms of specific target dates, and it treats uncertainty by including probability estimates of meeting dates and offers contingency plans for a range of possible outcomes.

Delphi Technique.   This technique queries individuals about goals and objectives using a mailed questionnaire. The results are summarized, prioritized, then returned to respondents for revision several times. Its goal is to minimize a biasing effect of dominant individuals by arriving at opinion consensus and synthesis without face-to-face contact. This presumably prevents one of the perils of Janis's groupthink phenomenon.

Nominal Group Technique (NGT).   To achieve consensus, this technique relies upon face-to-face meetings at which goals are presented one at a time and written down, with no discussion. When all goals have been recorded in some format, then discussion begins, one item at a time. Each participant ranks the goals privately; then the results are mathematically pooled. This committee format reduces distractions and extraneous discussion.

Theory X/Theory Y.   Douglas McGregor proposed two theories he terms Theory X and Theory Y. The Theory X proponent believes that people dislike work and must be forced to produce, and that the average person seeks security but avoids responsibility. Theory Y supports the position that people like work, they exercise self-direction and control, their satisfaction of ego and self-realization are their ultimate goals, and they seek responsibility.

Theory Z.   William Ouchi and his colleagues coined the term to reflect the Japanese management-labor relationship. This theory encompasses seven key characteristics:

1. Long-term employment
2. Slow evaluation and promotion
3. Moderately specialized careers
4. Consensual decision making
5. Individual responsibility
6. Informal control using explicit measures
7. Holistic concern for the employee

TQM and Knowledge Management.   Inspired by Demming's work in the 1950s, this enterprise-wide management process seeks to ensure that quality is continually improved from the perspective of the external customer. This concept should result in a culture that integrates strategy with work processes and moves the focus away from competition and cost toward cooperation and value for both internal and external publics. However, according to James Quella, vice chairman of Mercer Management Consulting, total quality management fails to examine the differences in customers; it doesn't adequately identify future competitors or market segments in order to produce products in time to do something about them. Quella is a proponent of knowledge management—the idea that knowledge as well as the ability to have and control it—will result in individuals at all levels of the organization possessing the information they need to make good decisions.

Seitel points out that public relations can apply these approaches by setting goals that are in step with their organization, then making progress toward achieving them.

Strategic PR Planning

According to Thomas Harrison, writing in *Nonprofit World,* "At the heart of this type of [strategic] public relations is management by objectives and not the old school's 'PR by press release' . . . the plan must be flexible enough to allow for new creative ideas or unanticipated opportunities within the established organizational objectives." Broom and Dozier write that strategic planning "sets the organization's direction proactively, avoiding 'drift' and routine repetition of activities."

Cutlip, Center, and Broom portray strategic planning as a four-step cyclical process:

1. Defining the problem
2. Planning and programming
3. Taking action and communicating
4. Evaluating the program

Marston's R-A-C-E model is also used in the planning process by many practitioners:

R = research
A = action/planning
C = communication
E = evaluation

Harrison outlines the crucial steps for an effective strategic PR plan:

- Perform a situational analysis
- Define your PR objectives
- Identify target audiences
- Specify key or core messages
- Target media
- Pinpoint strategies
- Select tactics or program elements
- Choose a staff
- Prepare a staff
- Create a timetable
- Activate the plan
- Measure results

A situational analysis is normally the result of information gathering, using both quantitative and qualitative forms. This problem statement reflects an examination of the overall organizational and marketing goals. "The situation analysis represents the unabridged edition of the problem definition, as it contains all the information and data collected about the internal and external environments," write Broom and Dozier.

The goals set forth may take many forms. Goals may be categorized as

- Social: This deals with a desired outcome in relation to society, such as an assessment of society, individual development, transmission of values, provision of leadership, or improvement of standard of living and quality of life.
- Output: This refers to the organization's relationship to the clientele the institution serves as opposed to society as a whole.
- System: This at times takes precedence over other goals. It revolves around an organization's sustaining itself: its survival, expansion, or contraction.
- Product: This refers to the goods and services produced.
- Derived: This focuses on the politics of an organization and its desired outcomes involving community service or investment policies.

Goals generally are perceived as the top priority within an organization because they provide a sense of direction. However, there is always the danger that goals may become displaced. In this condition, an organization becomes more interested in maintaining itself than reaching its goals. An example of this in a university setting might be lowering admission standards or offering offbeat classes to attract paying students. Goal succession can also take place. This process occurs when an organization changes its emphasis from one area to another. Again in an educational arena, this may occur if a university decides to place a higher importance on teaching as opposed to research. Goals may also be manifest (out in the open) or latent (unspoken or not formally expressed). They are also seen by many publics as the degree of control an organization may wield over people.

Goals give an organization and a public relations program a direction, the ultimate desired outcome. "Objectives describe specific results to be achieved by a specified date for each of the well-defined target publics," write Broom and Dozier. "If written properly and based on an accurate assessment of the problem situation, public relations objectives make you a results-oriented manager."

Target Audiences

Target audiences or publics are identified in the context of their link to your organization, program, or event. They may be defined in terms of geographics, demographics, or psychographics: Geographics refers to a geographic boundary or region; demographics refers to statistical data available about groups, such as age, sex, income, or education level; psychographics has been called lifestyle analysis and classifies individuals as to their interests, that is, "what they think, how they behave and what they think about," explain Newsom and Carrell. Current techniques have become increasingly sophisticated so that it is possible to continually narrow audiences through means of tracking what they buy and focusing on products and services designed for their needs and interests.

Wilbur Schramm designed a model to illustrate two factors, source and receiver, in a communications process. However, as practitioners develop objectives for promotional messages, you will focus upon the receiver, message, medium, and target public(s). Noise, "a term to describe all possible obstacles that can keep a message from getting through clearly," as Moriarty explains, is the major problem in communicating effectively. It may take the form of language, word selection, channel clutter, technical difficulties, or psychological barriers such as fatigue or anger.

Although seen as advertising techniques, there are a few concepts that may help to formulate a message strategy in public relations. Applied broadly, they may provide an appropriate framework for a range of clients, products, or services. William Bernbach, of the ad agency Doyle Dane Bernbach, stresses that a promotional message is important, but it is not enough. "You have to startle people into an immediate awareness . . . in such a way they will never forget it," he believes. "What's the use of saying all the right things . . . if nobody's going to read them?" He cautions that to be effective, messages must be conveyed with "freshness, originality and imagination."

In 1961, Leo Burnett offered his philosophy that every subject, product, or service contains "inherent drama." This natural news angle is "the art of establishing new and meaningful relationships between previously unrelated things in a manner that is relevant, believable and in good taste, but which somehow presents the product in a fresh, new light."

Rosser Reeves, at one time chairman of Ted Bates & Company, is credited with one of the most enduring approaches—the "Unique Selling Proposition" or USP. Originated in the

1940s, this technique features three parts that must be present for positive results to occur. As Book and Schick explain each promotional message must "make a proposition to the consumer. . . . The proposition must be one that the competition either cannot or does not offer. . . . The proposition must be so strong that it can move the mass millions . . . pull over new customers to your product."

David Ogilvy, of Ogilvy & Mather, insisted that individual messages must contribute to a long-term marketing program based on what he called "brand image." He emphasized content over form and advised practitioners: "Build sharply defined personalities [for clients] and stick to those personalities. . . . It is the total personality of a brand rather than any trivial product difference which decides its ultimate position in the market," according to Book and Schick.

Jack Trout is known for his concept of "positioning." He suggests that there is too much "marketing noise" in our society. He explains that "the mind is the battleground" in that it is constantly sorting through competing messages. "Like a memory bank, the mind has a slot or 'position' for each bit of information it has chosen to retain. . . . It filters out everything else." This means that to win a favorable impression among publics, it is necessary to "dislodge" a widespread support or somehow relate your client to the leader's position.

Appropriate appeals are also integral to communicating effectively. Moriarty explains that an appeal takes "the basic human need and translates it into a motivational structure." It has the power to "arouse innate or latent desire."

Exhibit 6.1 offers a list of basic appeals. This concept is derived from Maslow's hierarchy of needs and later updates by psychologist Melvin Hattwick. Hattwick identifies eight areas critical in promotional communication because "they are easily aroused, they are strong, and they are practically universal." They are:

- Food and drink
- Comfort
- Freedom from fear and danger
- To be superior
- Companionship of the opposite sex
- Welfare of loved ones
- Social approval
- To live longer

Moriarty says, "The goal of creative strategy is to identify the one appeal that is the strongest and that will trigger . . . action." According to Strauss and Howe's research, the generational characteristics of the target audience also play a major role in message selection and success. They recommend examining how generations were raised, what events they witnessed, and what social mission they were given as they matured.

Messages can also be tailored to audience segments via a variety of communication channels. These channels are typically defined as controlled and uncontrolled media. Hendrix explains that "controlled media . . . involves communication about the client that is paid for by the client." On the other hand, "uncontrolled media involves the communication of news about the client or organization to the mass media and to specialized media outlets. The objective . . . is favorable news coverage of the client's actions and events." Exhibits 6.2 and 6.3 provide the types of channels a practitioner may select to convey messages. These medi-

EXHIBIT **6.1**

Possible Appeals in Promotional Messages

- Acquisition: Money, possessions
- Affiliation and belonging
- Aspiration: Achievement, accomplishment
- Comfort
- Convenience: Saving time or effort
- Economy: Saving money
- Egoism: Recognition, approval, pride, status
- Emotion
- Fear: Safety or embarrassment
- Family: Affection, protection
- Love and sex
- Nostalgia

- Humor: Joy, laughter
- Poignancy
- Relief
- Sorrow: Grief, suffering
- Health
- Respect: Role models
- Luxury
- Mental stimulation: Curiosity or challenge
- Pleasure: Amusement, entertainment
- Sensory stimulation: Touch, taste, smell, sound

Source: Sandra Moriarty. *Creative Advertising Theory and Practice.* Englewood Cliffs, NJ: Prentice-Hall, 1986.

ums continue to expand, especially with new technological applications such as electronic mail and computer database networks that make it possible, for example, for authors to answer readers' questions via their computer keyboard.

Stanton points out that "there are variations in organizational structure of worldwide operations of major public relations firms." However, Manning, Selvage, and Lee support the view that certain patterns have become evident:

- Public relations operations in each country should be run by nationals of that country.
- A regional manager and close coordination of units on a regional basis are important.
- Equity relationships offer two-way benefits.
- A balance must be maintained between global and regional business plans and strategies.
- Local requirements must be factored into public relations programs and their execution.
- Doing business around the world is more complex than ever.

Karen MacLeod, of Kellogg USA, also supports this multifaceted approach and suggests that companies "plan centrally and execute locally."

Raymond L. Kotcher, of Ketchum Public Relations Worldwide, writes that successful public relations practiced outside U.S. borders "requires a physical presence in the area." As regards Latin America, he notes that "you can't just translate a news release and pass it along from one country to the next." You would have to account for differences in language, local media expertise, cultural differences, and political and economic climates. "It requires a capacity for coordinated communications." He cites a case in which one of Ketchum's clients was constructing a large pipeline project in Peru. "The operation had to address the concerns of the indigenous peoples and some two dozen international special interest groups, who carefully monitored our every move."

EXHIBIT **6.2**
Controlled Media

Print Methods
- House publications
- Brochures, information pieces
- Handbooks, manuals, books
- Letters, bulletins, memos, faxes
- Bulletin boards, posters, flyers
- Information racks
- External periodicals
- Annual reports
- Commemorative stamps
- Exhibits and displays
- Mobile libraries, bookmobiles
- Mobile displays
- Attitude or information surveys
- Suggestion boxes, systems
- Pay, billing, or mailing inserts
- Written reports
- Training kits, aids, manuals
- Consumer information kits
- Legislative information kits
- Teacher kits, student games
- Window displays

Audiovisual Methods
- Institutional films
- Slide shows
- Filmstrips
- Opaque projectors, flannel boards, easel pad presentations
- Transparencies for overhead projectors
- Telephone calls, phone banks, on-hold recorded messages
- Multimedia exhibits and displays
- Audiotapes and cassettes
- Videotapes and cassettes
- Visual and multimedia window displays

- Oral presentations with visuals
- Multimedia training aids
- Specially equipped vans, trains, buses, boats, airplanes, blimps

Interpersonal Methods
- Formal speeches, lectures, seminars
- Roundtable conferences
- Panel discussions
- Oral testimony
- Employee counseling
- Legal, medical, miscellaneous counseling
- Committee meetings
- Staff meetings
- Demonstrations
- Speakers' bureaus (recruiting and training speakers, speech preparation, clearance, subjects, speakers' guide, engagements and bookings, visual aids, follow-up correspondence)
- Training programs
- Interviews
- Social gatherings
- Face-to-face reports

Electronic Methods
- Teleconferencing
- Interactive videodisks
- Electronic news releases
- Electronic faxes
- E-mail
- Online systems
- Electronic postings
- Chat rooms
- Listservs
- Web sites
- Home pages

Sources: Adapted from Jerry Henrix. *Public Relations Cases,* 2nd ed. Belmont, CA: Wadworth Publishing Company, 1992 and Eugene Marlow. *Electronic Public Relations.* Belmont, CA: Wadsworth Publishing Company, 1996.

EXHIBIT **6.3**

Uncontrolled Media

- News releases (print and video)
- Feature stories
- Photographs with cutlines (captions) or photo opportunities
- News conferences
- Media kits
- Radio/TV public service announcements (PSAs) (nonprofit organizations only)
- Interviews
- Print media
- Broadcast media
- Personal appearances on broadcast media
- News tapes for radio
- News slides and films for TV
- Special programs for radio and TV

- Recorded telephone news capsules and updates from an institution
- Informing and influencing editors, broadcast news and public service directors, columnists, and reporters (phone calls, tip sheets, newsletters with story leads, media advisories)
- Business feature articles
- Financial publicity
- Product publicity
- Pictorial publicity
- Background editorial material (backgrounders and fact sheets)
- Letters to the editor
- Op-ed pieces

Sources: Adapted from Jerry Henrix. *Public Relations Cases,* 2nd ed. Belmont, CA: Wadsworth Publishing Company, 1992 and Eugene Marlow. *Electronic Public Relations.* Belmont, CA: Wadsworth Publishing Company, 1996.

As the world becomes more interdependent, a more appropriate strategic response to a turbulent and ever-changing environment may occur—collaboration. Head-to-head-competition may become less and less appealing as a means to interact with publics and get messages across (see Exhibit 6.4). Bloland writes that "recognition of interdependence attenuates the urge toward competition, since vying with one another not only may produce an unpredictable and undesirable array of winners and losers but may threaten the stability of the whole community" in a rapidly changing environment.

Collaboration engenders greater mutual trust among members, which, in turn, generates more collaboration. Through collaborations, coping skills can be learned from other organizations. "Collaboration changes interdependence from a dangerous, system-threatening, competitive liability to a positive, system-strengthening, cooperative asset," Bloland asserts.

Warren Bennis wrote in 1967 that "Integration, distribution of power, collaboration, adaptation and revitalization" are the future's "major human problems. . . . How organizations cope with and manage these tasks will undoubtedly determine the viability and growth of the enterprise." His "organization of the future" trains for change, offers counseling, develops new incentives for socialization, building collaborative, problems-solving teams, and developing "supra-organizational goals and commitments." All these tasks are highly compatible with the role of public relations now and in the twenty-first century.

E X H I B I T **6.5**

Planning Models and Characteristics

- Formal-rational: A bureaucratic approach with a formal mission and goal-centered problem solving, it assumes everyone has some value. Its advantages include high visibility, continuity, reduced politics, and reduced conflict. Its disadvantage is that the process is not objective, as the model assumes.

- Organizational development: As human relations model with emphasis on individuals, it is consensus-centered and uses collaborative effort. It always features an evaluation step, focuses on informal and internal relations, and increases open communication. Groups are viewed as a "human system," learning and problem solving are desirable, and individuals are allowed to grow. Its advantages are that it motivates people and eases change. However, it is extremely time-consuming and requires a change agent.

- Technocratic/empirical: Rational, planning techniques are quantifiable and goal-centered, and simulations for predicting events or variables are used; trend analysis, forecasting, and procedural and tactical expertise are required, and computer skills are a must. This type emphasizes precision and analysis as well as requiring a large database; it does not account for any nonrational dimension of planning.

- Philosophical synthesis: This approach asks the meaning of knowledge. It is consumer-oriented and exercises logic, reason, and debate; it requires intellectual expertise, commitment to ideals, and an elite community. This intensive strategy gets everyone involved, when it works. However, there is no specific program and it is time-consuming.

- Political advocacy: Adaptive and rational, it is priority-oriented; it uses negotiation and compromise, coalition formation, advocacy and analysis, and an interest-group emphasis and representation. Its advantages are that it is practical, is politically realistic, and may produce change. However, an organization may easily lose direction or deal with issues in a piecemeal fashion; there may be the emergence of one dominant group.

- Coordinated anarchy: This is characterized by decentralization with loosely linked components/departments; each unit does its own planning and can be described as environmental in that it reacts to its current milieu. Spontaneity is its primary advantage, in addition to autonomy and flexibility for each unit. The major disadvantage is that departments within an organization are interdependent and therefore in need of a range of substantial resources.

- Radical and antiplanning: This form lets the marketplace direct its future. It supports the view that planning is socialistic and negative and that it is better to muddle through. Its disadvantages are obvious, with the major potential result of the demise of your organization.

Summary

The global environment is increasingly a complex, interdependent place characterized by change. This change leads to uncertainty because of the constant need to find new ways to adapt. Complexity fosters confusion, and interdependence engenders vulnerability. The solution would appear to be collaboration: a strategic public and private relationship between or among an array of interests.

Organizations use strategic planning both to look ahead and to try to control their relationships with their environments. There are several planning and budget scenarios whose value to the organization a manager may quantify. However, as Thomas Peters and Robert Waterman warn, "The problem is that planning becomes an end in itself." If this occurs, a corporation, and certainly a public relations department or firm, may set itself on a dead-end road. Seitel concludes that "No matter how important planning may be, public relations is assessed principally in terms of its action, performance, and practice."

QUESTIONS

1. What type of system does public relations operate within?

2. Contrast strategic planning and long-range planning.

3. What is synergy, and how does it apply to public relations?

4. Is budgeting a political process?

5. Describe three different budgeting processes.

6. Describe the promotional message philosophies of Reeves, Trout, and Ogilvy.

READINGS

Barry R. Armandi, John J. Barbera, and Harold W. Berkman. *Organizational Behavior: Classical and Contemporary Readings.* Dubuque, IA: Kendall/Hunt Publishing Company, 1982.

Warren Bennis. "Organizations of the Future." *Personnel Administrator* 9 (1967): 238–247.

Harland Bloland. "Collaboration, Information, Uncertainty: The Washington Higher Education Community." (1986). Unpublished paper.

Albert C. Book and C. Dennis Schick. *Fundamentals of Copy and Layout.* Chicago: Crain Books, 1984.

James E. Grunig and Todd Hunt. *Managing Public Relations.* New York: Holt, Rinehart and Winston, 1984.

Melvin Hattwick. *How to Use Psychology for Better Advertising.* Englewood Cliffs, NJ: Prentice-Hall, 1980.

Jerry A. Hendrix. *Public Relations Cases,* 2nd ed. Belmont, CA: Wadsworth Publishing Company, 1992.

Douglas McGregor. *The Human Side of Enterprise.* New York: McGraw-Hill, 1960.

Sandra E. Moriarty. *Creative Advertising Theory and Practice.* Englewood Cliffs, NJ: Prentice-Hall, 1986.

David Ogilvy. *Confessions of an Advertising Man.* New York: Dell, 1964.

William Ouchi and Alfred M. Jaeger. "Type Z Organization: Stability in the Midst of Mobility." *Academy of Management Review* 3 (April 1978): 305–314.

Charles Perrow. *Organizational Analysis: A Sociological View.* Belmont, CA: Wadsworth Publishing Company, 1970.

Rosser Reeves. *Reality in Advertising.* New York: Knopf, 1963.

Wilbur Schramm and Donald F. Roberts, eds. *The Process and Effects of Mass Communication.* Urbana: University of Illinois Press, 1971.

W. Richard Scott. *Organizations: Rational, Natural, and Open Systems.* Englewood Cliffs, NJ: Prentice-Hall, 1981.

William Strauss and Neil Howe. *Generations: The History of America's Future, 1584 to 2069.* New York: William Morrow and Company, 1991.

Jack Trout and Al Ries. "The Positioning Era." *Advertising Age* (April 24, May 1, 8, 1972).

DEFINITIONS

budget: A document containing words and figures that proposes expenditures for certain items and purchases.

goal: A statement that provides an organization or a public relations program with a direction and an ultimate outcome.

natural system: An organization whose participants are little affected by the formal structure or official goals but who share a common interest in the survival of the system and who engage in collective activities, informally structured, to secure this end.

objective: A statement that describes specific results to be achieved by a specific date for specific publics.

open system: An organization as a coalition of shifting interest groups that develop goals by negotiation; the structure of the coalition, its activities, and its outcomes are strongly influenced by environmental factors.

persuasion: The desired form of power or influence that public relations utilizes.

power: The ability of "A" to make "B" act in a way that "B" would not otherwise do.

rational system: An organization that is collectively oriented to the pursuit of relatively specific goals and exhibiting a relatively highly formalized social structure.

7 Setting Objectives and Creating the Plan

Getting from Here to There . . . on Time

CHAPTER OUTLINE

Determining the Need for a Campaign
The Multistep Process of Campaign Planning

CHAPTER OBJECTIVES

When you have completed this chapter, you should be able to:

- Develop a problem statement
- Set objectives to solve the problem
- Recognize budget-conscious research techniques
- Understand the difference between strategy and tactic

The campaign plan is a blueprint that guides all public relations activity toward the accomplishment of predetermined goals. Just as a construction foreman wouldn't pick up a hammer and start building without consulting a blueprint, so the public relations practitioner should not move forward on a campaign without a plan.

One obstacle to developing a campaign plan is the time required to develop it correctly. Too many practitioners simply "fly by the seat of their pants," depending upon prior experience and gut feelings to complete public relations tasks. The unfortunate reality of public relations is that many practitioners use the tools—news releases, special events, or community involvement—in reaction to specific situations with scant consideration of strategy. Some succeed in spite of themselves in the short run, but a career built on reactionary public relations cannot stand the test of time.

Knowing that a public relations campaign is needed and actually committing the plan to paper are two entirely different things. For the beginning public relations practitioner, moving from assignment to completion may be daunting.

Determining the Need for a Campaign

How does the public relations professional determine that a campaign is needed? Most commonly, the need for a campaign is an outgrowth of some manner of an organizational problem, situation, or opportunity. Perhaps the organization is new and providing a new service, is forced to issue a product recall, or has discovered a new use for its oldest and most successful product.

Each of these situations requires a public relations campaign to solve the problem or take advantage of the opportunity. And each problem/opportunity was discovered via some level of situation analysis. A situation analysis program at its most basic level requires that public relations professionals meet regularly with the various departments within an organization to determine their direction and what effect the situation will have on the organization as a whole. They must also study trade publications and professional journals about the industry in which the company operates, read media coverage on the organization, and review customer feedback. Any public relations practitioner can build these steps into an effective situation analysis program.

A more comprehensive situation analysis program might include formal survey research; regular reviews of pending legislation that may affect the industry; a competitive analysis; networking with key community and business leaders, to stay informed of local changes; and reviews of media coverage on competitors and the industry as a whole. It is likely that this broad situation analysis program would require the addition of staff members.

Regardless of the level at which situation analysis is conducted, the steps will help identify potential problems that may require a public relations campaign to avoid or mitigate the effects on the organization. Newsom and Scott state that "the most valuable public relations activity is that planned to prevent problems or at least solve them while they are small." Another benefit of situation analysis is that it provides a justification for the public relations campaign plan, which must be submitted to upper management for approval. This common frame of reference is often helpful in gaining the cooperation of management, a necessity for the public relations professional.

The natural outgrowth of all this research is a clear and accurate understanding by all parties of what the organization needs in order to address the problem it faces.

The Multistep Process of Campaign Planning

Planning is actually a process of specific steps, and as Cutlip, Center, and Broom explain, it can make something happen or prevent something from happening. Developing a public relations campaign to address an organizational need takes place in five stages: Develop a problem statement, set objectives that solve the problem, define strategies to achieve the objectives, outline tactics to be employed, and establish a means to evaluate the campaign.

Develop a Problem Statement

What is the specific problem faced by the organization? What need was identified through the situation analysis? Write it in the form of a statement and refer to it throughout the campaign planning process. The problem statement will provide a focus for each of the remaining steps. Every action taken should be a step toward solving the problem.

Set Objectives That Solve the Problem

Objectives could also be termed "solution statements." They are the things that need to be accomplished in order to solve the identified problem and provide the overriding mission to be accomplished by the remaining elements of the plan.

Guidelines for Setting Objectives. First, campaign objectives must be consistent with both organizational and departmental objectives. This ensures that the campaign will benefit the organization and increases the chance that upper management will support the campaign. Second, objectives should be realistic, taking into consideration the human and financial resources available, asking, What is attainable? Third, objectives should specifically state what is to be accomplished. The statements should center on either an attitudinal change or a behavioral change in one or more segments of the organization's public. Finally, objectives should be measurable. Deborah Hauss believes that measurement of campaign results is fast becoming a necessity if public relations planners are to remain competitive: "To set measurable objectives, many practitioners are now strongly suggesting the inclusion of research as part of a campaign's overall strategy from the outset."

Planning a campaign without following these generally accepted guidelines to set objectives is no smarter than throwing nails and boards into the air and hoping they fall into the shape of a house.

Most public relations experts agree: Research steps should be built into campaign objectives. A pretest/posttest is necessary to determine whether a campaign was successful. The required research may be narrow or broad, depending largely upon the time, budget, and expertise of the practitioner.

But research need not be incredibly expensive to provide the information needed (see Exhibit 7.1). Hauss polled practitioners across the country to devise a list of budget-conscious research techniques.

Define Strategies to Achieve the Objectives

The first step in defining strategies is to segment and prioritize publics. Who must alter their attitude or behavior for the goals to be accomplished? For mass campaigns, it is easy to simply call upon the nebulous "general public," but many public relations professionals claim that the American market is so segmented that the general public no longer exists. Try to narrow it down by identifying the demographics (who they are) and psychographics (what they are like) of the organization's consumer base.

One way to do this without spending a great deal of money on formal research is to rely on research already conducted for you. Call the sales department of the local television stations, and give them the basic demographics of your consumer base—age and gender.

EXHIBIT **7.1**

Research Techniques for the Low-Budget Campaign

- Implement small, statistically correct "mini-surveys."
- Include an 800/888 number in communications to capture responses and code sales leads.
- Identify a specific department in the return address on all press releases, and track the number of callers per release.
- Use a database search to find/confirm media pickups.
- Track number of "hits" on the Web site.
- Collect and analyze e-mails.

- Conduct online surveys.
- Send a survey along with a thank-you note to all customers resulting from a major campaign.
- Develop and collect response cards.
- Use graduate students from the local college/university to conduct surveys.
- Implement intercept surveys at the place of business and offer some small incentive for participation.
- Conduct focus group/roundtable sessions with customers and/or industry leaders.

Find out what programs are most popular among that group and watch them, not for the programming but for the advertisements that appear within the programs. What are the messages and themes? Can any of them be tailored to your campaign? Similar research can be conducted with radio stations and magazines, which tend to have narrowly targeted formats.

If the objectives are specific, it will be fairly easy to identify the appropriate publics. Do the goals require a need for employees to change their attitude about the corporate benefits package? Then an internal communications campaign is necessary. If the goals include increased sales, then the company's customer base is the obvious primary public, but vendors and salespeople may be key publics as well. Create a list of every single group that is even remotely implied by the objectives, and list them in order of priority. Are there any who are so obscure that they can be removed? Which group is going to require the most attention? Which has the greatest impact upon the results of the campaign? The answers to these questions should help in prioritizing the list.

The next step in defining campaign strategies is to find out everything possible about these targeted publics. What do they think? What do they read and watch? Whom do they admire? Use the basics of persuasion theory (see Chapter 5) to craft a message that is consistent with campaign objectives and appropriate to each public.

Outline Specific Tactics (Procedures) to be Employed

The campaign objectives identify the desired response; the strategies define who is to respond and what message will draw the appropriate response. Tactics pinpoint the communication channels in a series of precise steps that will breathe life into the campaign.

Because the campaign planning process generally takes place over several days or weeks, it is always a good practice to review objectives again before continuing to ensure that all programming is consistent with the mission defined at the start. At this point, it would also be appropriate to determine if there are other departments within the organization that will be affected by or should contribute to the campaign.

PRoActive

America West Arena Fifth Anniversary Marketing Communications Proposal

Background

The America West Arena opened June 6, 1992, with a flurry of events, which quickly established it as the Southwest's premier entertainment venue. Through the expertise and commitment of its management and staff, that reputation has grown. As home of the Phoenix Suns, the Arena has enjoyed worldwide media attention.

As the America West Arena approaches its fifth anniversary, we wish to develop a marketing communications campaign that strengthens the Arena's reputation and brings even greater positive attention to the benefits it brings to the community. Why? Because people who are familiar with the Arena are more likely to consider visiting it—despite their possible concerns about coming downtown. In addition, a positive corporate reputation and visibility in the media improve future potential for lucrative corporate partnerships. Finally, the debut of the Bank One Ballpark in 1998, and it is important to strengthen the image of the America West Arena so that the community understands that the Ballpark's way was paved by the successful operation of the Arena.

Objectives

What do we wish this campaign to accomplish? How will success be measured? These questions are answered by establishing campaign objectives, the foundation of any marketing communications campaign. It is essential that all parties agree on these objectives, and that every program idea is tested against them to ensure that limited dollars are spent wisely.

1. Build community awareness that the America West Arena is celebrating its fifth anniversary.
2. Establish the Arena's position as a good corporate citizen.
3. Build awareness among promoters, agents, and managers that the America West Arena is celebrating its fifth anniversary.

Strategies

Strategies answer the question, "How will we accomplish the campaign objectives?" They are the method by which the objectives will be reached. Below each objective is a list of corresponding strategies and potential programming.

Objective 1:   Build community awareness that the America West Arena is celebrating its fifth anniversary.

A) Create media and sponsor partnerships to carry the anniversary message to a widespread Valley audience.

- Work with America West Airlines to create a special section in their in-flight magazine commemorating the Arena's anniversary.
- Work with America West Airlines to create an incentive program for travelers coming to Arizona during the fifth anniversary celebration (i.e., if your copy of the AWA in-flight special section is autographed, receive free tickets to an AWA event or have travelers show their AWA ticket stub to receive a discount at the Arena).
- Pitch the *Arizona Republic* on a special business section communicating the message of how AWA has driven the improved downtown Phoenix economy.
- Work with the *Arizona Republic* to create a promotion, either in the special section or on their Web site.
- Create a "public service announcement" and/or documentary that tells the story of the Arena's impact on the economy; use time-lapsed photography and testimonials to demonstrate what Phoenix was before the Arena and the incredible changes brought about by the facility. Use on Phoenix Channel 11, in the Arena, and on Fox (all have appropriate outlets for this, even though the Arena is not a charity).

(continued)

PRoActive   Continued

B) Create an event to commemorate the Arena's anniversary.
- Plan and execute a special event, which will gain positive media attention for the Arena.
- Potential events include an exclusive concert with a big-name entertainer or an open house with proceeds designated for charity, especially a downtown project (clean up an area or assist a nearby school).
- Another event idea is a re-creation of "Family Circus Sunday" with children's activities on the concourse, continuous entertainment, building tours (including locker room), and door prizes.
- Any birthday party for the Arena should include a giant cake, balloons, music, etc.
- Create a media event by placing five large prop candles on top of the Arena for the summer.
- Decorate the building with new garage banners.
- Work with Barclay Communications to hold a movie premiere at the Arena; stage it like a Hollywood premiere with red carpet, celebrities arriving in limos, dinner on the concourse, etc.

C) Develop advertising and promotions.
- Create a one-time print ad for the *Arizona Republic*.
- Reformat the ad for use in any available advertising panels in the Arena.
- If budget allows, create a radio campaign.
- If budget is not available, work with stations to create a promotion (i.e., every time they play a song from an artist who has played at the Arena, we get a mention and they give away something such as commemorative item, ticket voucher, T-shirt).
- Another promotional option is to develop a contest in which winners receive tickets to their top five concert events over the next year.
- Depending upon how the numbers fall, create a ten-millionth customer celebration with ample media coverage.

- Use the occasion of the anniversary to launch a frequent customer program. A "Welcome Guest" card would be punched at each non-sports event; after guests attend five paid events, they would receive a sixth event free or discounted.
- Create a promotion in which a giant ice sculpture of the Arena's fifth anniversary logo sits on the plaza and visitors guess what time it melts completely. The winner receives cash ($5,000) or event tickets.

D) Use established in-house communications vehicles to carry the anniversary story.
- Create a commemorative lapel pin or patch and give to all Arena employees.
- Host a management-served breakfast for Arena employees to thank them for their service; honor those employees who have been here all five years.
- Write article(s) for *BackTalk*.
- Create a fifth anniversary logo to display on matrix boards, advertising, and other printed materials; create stickers or a stamp that would be affixed to all outgoing mail.
- Develop a *Fastbreak* special section.
- Include an anniversary celebration and promotion on the Arena's Web site.
- Because the Arizona Rattlers were the first sports team to play in the Arena, develop an anniversary celebration as part of the game operations at one Rattler's game.

Objective 2:   Establish the Arena's position as a good corporate citizen.

A) Develop a corporate giving program.
- Establish a budget and create a system for responding to the many donation requests the Arena receives.
- Encourage staff members from all areas of the Arena to serve a term on a committee that reviews requests and makes donations.

B) Develop a community-giving promotion to commemorate the anniversary.
- Commit five cents from every ticket sold to an entertainment (nonsports) event during the

Arena's fifth anniversary year, or another set period of time, to fund five local charities—"Take 5."

- Hold a news conference with the charity representatives to announce the program.
- Send out regular news releases with updates on how the money is being used by the charities.
- Create publicity opportunities at the charity sites (i.e., TV cameras at an inner-city Boys and Girls Club).
- Take a five-day window and allow Arena employees to give time to a charitable cause (like Labor of Love); generate news coverage of the service events.

Objective 3: Build awareness among promoters, agents, and managers that the America West Arena is celebrating its fifth anniversary.

A) Create a trade print ad.
- Create a one-time print ad for selected trade publications.

B) Communicate with appropriate industry contacts.
- Send a letter to those who have brought an event to the AWA, thanking them for their business.
- Research and select an appropriate commemorative item to send to key industry contacts (i.e., silver coin, framed for display).

Anniversary Proposal and Plan
Fifth Anniversary Campaign
November 1997–February 1998

I. **Ten-Millionth Customer Promotion**
Wednesday, Nov. 12
America West Arena

II. **Five-Year Birthday Celebration**
Sunday, Dec. 28
America West Arena

III. **Web Site News Conference**
Tuesday, Jan. 6
America West Arena

IV. **America West Arena Web Site Promotion**
Jan. 12–Feb. 9
World Wide Web

V. **AWA Web Site Promotion Winner Prize Drawing**
Sunday, Jan. 18
America West Arena

Ten-Millionth Customer Celebration
America West Arena Kickoff Event
Fifth Anniversary Promotion I

Date: Wednesday, Nov. 12

Location: NW doors off of Arena plaza at approximately 6:10 P.M. before the Phoenix Suns take on the Milwaukee Bucks at 7 P.M.

Description: Similar to that of the Publisher's Clearing House Prize Patrol, we will stage a big celebration as soon as the "Ten-Millionth Customer" walks through the door. The winner will be drenched in fanfare including balloons and confetti falling from the ceiling; background music; the Gorilla; a photo with Jerry Colangelo and Bob Machen; upgraded seats for that game; autographed Suns, Rattlers, and Coyotes merchandise; and a Team Shop goodie bag.

We will also single out the winner with some type of recognition during the game through a PA announcement and/or a time-out break introduction to the crowd.

Publicity: An advisory will go out on Monday, Nov. 10, to make media aware of the Ten-Millionth Customer celebration. During follow-up calls we'll tip off the media with a time frame to ensure live coverage during their 6 P.M. newscast.

Five Year Birthday Celebration
America West Arena
Fifth Anniversary Promotion II

Date: 6 P.M. on Sunday, Dec. 28

Location: America West Arena Plaza

Description: We will hold a birthday party on the Plaza for the Arena and all children who either are

(continued)

PRoActive   Continued

already five or will be five by June of 1998. Everyone will gather on the Plaza, sing happy birthday, and make a wish as the Suns Gorilla jumps out of a huge cake. Basha's has already agreed to donate several sheet cakes so that everyone will be able to celebrate with birthday cake.

Additionally, we will have a register-to-win contest for a pair of tickets to see the Harlem Globetrotters on Saturday, Jan. 17.

Publicity: A release/advisory will go out on Friday, Dec. 26. Follow-up calls will be made Saturday, Dec. 27. This promotion has the potential to be a fantastic photo opportunity and will also serve as a vehicle to promote the upcoming Web site promotion to be launched in January.

Additionally, we can add this on the Arena Monthly Calendar of Events, Dec. Marquee, and in Arena PA announcements at events leading up to the date.

Web Site News Conference
America West Arena
Fifth Anniversary Promotion III

Date: Tuesday, Jan. 6

Description: We will hold a news conference to release the upcoming Web site promotion. A demonstration of the Web site contest, via the Arena Web site, will help the media to better understand what the contest entails.

At that time we will distribute media materials outlining the contest, including the upcoming prize drawing on Jan. 18.

Promotion: We will send the print, radio, and TV media a teaser gift with an advisory attached on Friday, Jan. 2, inviting them to attend the news conference. The teaser gift will be a bottle of champagne with the Arena's Fifth Anniversary logo on the label, a helium balloon, and a media advisory. Follow-up calls will be made on Monday, Jan. 5.

For radio stations, in addition to the champagne, we will give Fifth Anniversary T-shirts to give away on-air to promote our contest.

Web Site Scavenger Hunt Contest
America West Arena
Fifth Anniversary Promotion IV

Dates: Jan. 12–Feb. 9

Description: On Jan. 12 the Arena will kick off its Fifth Year Anniversary Scavenger Hunt on the Arena Web site, www.americawestarena.com.

For people wishing to participate in the scavenger hunt but who do not have computer access:

a) A complete printout of the Arena Web site will be available at the America West Arena Box Office.

b) We also hope to have a computer store involved. Its staff will be at all Arena events promoting our Web site scavenger hunt, and participants will also be able to go to a store location to participate in the hunt.

The scavenger hunt will consist of five questions. The answers can be found within the pages of the Web site. The five questions will cover the five different chapters of the Arena's Web site.

Questions:

1) What prize was won for the Coca-Cola Concert Connection, for the Tina Turner concert?

   Answer: Limousine ride, dinner for two, and tickets to the concert

2) What event is happening at the America West Arena on Valentine's Day of 1998?

   Answer: KOOL Rock 'N' Roll Oldies

3) What phone number would you call if you needed further information on discounted tickets to upcoming America West Arena events?

   Answer: (602) 379-7878

4) Alvan Adams is currently employed with the America West Arena; what is his official title? (Shortcut—use the site map to help you find America West Arena Staff)

   Answer: Vice President and Assistant General Manager

5) What are the five teams that play at America West Arena?

Answer: Phoenix Suns, Arizona Rattlers, Phoenix Coyotes, Phoenix Mercury, and Arizona Sandsharks

All participants who correctly finish the scavenger hunt will be entered into a drawing for one of five grand prizes. The prizes will be gifts from major building sponsors.

Potential Prizes:

- One-year car lease from Dodge and/or Toyota
- $5,000 CD with Bank of America
- Road trip to an away Suns game for winner and five (5) friends; trip includes airfare, tickets to the game, and hotel
- $5,000 computer equipment gift certificate at computer store
- Pair of framed gold tickets to all Coca-Cola Concert Connections for one year

Publicity: In addition to the news conference on Jan. 6, another release will be faxed on Friday, Jan. 9. The scavenger hunt will be promoted through several radio station promotions, *Get Out, The Rep,* e-mail letter to all past Web site entries, Suns TV and radio drop-ins, and PA announcements at other Arena events including the anniversary promotions leading up to this one.

AWA Web Site Promotion Winner Prize Drawing
America West Arena
Fifth Anniversary Promotion V

Date: Sunday, Feb. 18

Description: All five scavenger hunt winners will receive a pair of tickets on Feb. 18 when the Suns take on the Los Angeles Lakers. At halftime, winners will go to center court where they will choose different doors and turn keys or do some other kind of "stunt" to choose one of the five grand prizes.

Prizes will be awarded by a sponsor representative (giving additional exposure) and Jerry Colangelo and Bob Machen if they are available.

Publicity: A news release specific to this promotion will go out on Monday, Feb. 9, listing the winners' names and details of the prize giveaway at AWA. An additional news release will be faxed Monday, Feb. 16, encouraging media to attend the prize drawing at halftime.

Conclusion

We look forward to reviewing these ideas with you. Because it is unlikely that all of these programs could be implemented, we will need to prioritize the projects to ensure that the Arena receives maximum benefit. Finally, a budget must be established for any desired programming.

Next, identify all the possible ways to reach the targeted public. This can be accomplished by brainstorming among the campaign team members. If other departments are involved, it is a good idea to include a representative from those areas. Sometimes individuals from outside the organization (such as clients or a special-interest group) should be included if they have a strong interest in the campaign.

Brainstorming.   This group problem-solving technique to generate ideas was developed by Alex Osborn, president of BBDO, in the 1930s. "[It] uses the brain power of a number of people to intensify divergent thinking and increase the number of available ideas," explains Moriarty.

Brainstorming should be a fun process in which the participants feel free to be creative and maybe even a little crazy. Get away from the office if there are distractions. Serve refreshments. Select one person as the moderator and another as the recorder; a marker board or flip chart is helpful to keep ideas in front of everyone. Start by clarifying the strategies, and then let all participants offer their ideas for accomplishing them.

Six Golden Rules for Brainstorming

1. Get comfortable—loosen the ties and kick off the shoes.
2. No idea is a bad idea, so no criticism is permitted.
3. It is perfectly acceptable to borrow someone else's idea and build on it.
4. Go for quantity—ideas can be judged at a later date.
5. Everyone must participate.
6. Think big.

If the ideas slow down or dry up altogether during brainstorming, what Osborn refers to as "cramps of creativity," take a break. Obstacles to creativity may be criticism, lack of flexibility in thinking, giving up too soon, or the fear of feeling foolish. Moriarty adds that an "overdependence on strategy and research findings" may also inhibit brainstorming. When the group returns, the moderator can toss out some words related to the message or the target public, and the group can free-associate, building ideas from there. Other places to inspire ideas are holiday calendars, history timelines, listings of media outlets, and even general-interest magazines. This process has generated many unique and effective public relations tactics and should provide a multitude of ways to communicate with the targeted audience.

From the list of ideas generated during brainstorming, the campaign planner should select the appropriate options based on adherence to the objectives, budget, and overall feasibility. It is likely that multiple tactics will be used in combination in order to achieve the campaign's objectives.

The following is a list of tactics that might be used in a public relations campaign:

- Create and distribute press materials
- Host a news conference
- Write letters to the editor
- Organize a community coalition
- Develop a speakers' bureau
- Host a special event
- Create a contest
- Develop and distribute a newsletter
- Hire a lobbyist
- Create a brochure
- Research and write a crisis communications plan
- Host a meeting
- Participate in a trade show
- Work with a sponsor to create a sales promotion
- Conduct a media training seminar
- Enter a corporate recognition program
- Sponsor a community program
- Host a media roundtable discussion

This list is certainly not exhaustive; the possibilities are bounded only by the practitioner's creativity and resources.

Following the selection of specific tactics, an action plan, which outlines the specific steps (including who is responsible for the tasks and the deadline dates), should be written for each communication program. A budget number can then be assigned to each element. Finally, the plan may be executed—the actual communication takes place.

Establish a Means for Evaluating the Campaign

If measurable objectives were set in the beginning of the planning process, then there is a means for measuring the effectiveness of the campaign. Budgets will always be tight and many managers are cautious. The resources committed to a public relations campaign must be justified.

Media clips are just not enough; by themselves, clips are a primitive way of evaluating a campaign. As a second step, develop a content analysis for the clips. What message was defined in the campaign strategies? Did that message appear in any of the news coverage? On a scale of 1 to 10, how closely did the article reflect the intended message? Were the facts correct? How many people saw/read the message? What was the cost per impression? All of these methods can enhance the usefulness of the media clips.

If the objectives were sales-oriented, how many inquiries were generated by the campaign? How many sales? Does this represent an increase over the previous year? Did market share increase? If pretests were conducted, the posttest should now be completed.

Once these results are collected, they should be codified into a report for management. This report should review the campaign objectives and clearly indicate how they were met or why they were not accomplished. A summary should indicate which elements of the campaign should be employed again and which should be eliminated. This type of reporting will be helpful in planning future campaigns.

The following case study is a synopsis of the PRSA Silver Anvil award-winning community relations program conducted by the Maryland Stadium Authority with Trahan, Burden & Charles, Inc. (TBC).

CASE STUDY   Campaign Outline: "Route, Route, Route for the Home Team"

Situation Analysis
Oriole Park at Camden Yards, the new home of the Baltimore Orioles baseball team, opened in April 1992. Impact studies showed that without use of public transportation by fans, commuters, and other residents, the city's downtown community and interstate highway system would be affected by major traffic congestion and parking problems. During the past thirty-eight years, less than 2 percent of the fans traveling to the team's former stadium had used public transportation. They had to change their habits.

Problem Statement
There is traffic congestion and not enough parking for fans at Camden Yards.

(continued)

Objectives
- To educate the public about transportation options (an attitudinal change)
- To seek cooperation in using these transportation services and alternative driving routes (a behavioral change)

Strategies
The theme "Route, Route, Route for the Home Team" was developed, based on the popular baseball song.

Tactics
To keep costs down, TBC identified media partners, businesses, and others willing to donate or trade time and space. An aggressive media relations effort included a kickoff event, editorial board meetings, radio/sports show interviews, presentations to community groups, a television public service announcement, and transit signage.

Evaluation
Use of public transportation by Orioles fans exceeded preset goals by more than 25 percent.

Summary

Planning a public relations campaign is an arduous task, but the benefits of preparedness, accountability, and the ability to prove results are the payoff for the time spent in planning. A commitment to this process requires the public relations practitioner to be a visionary, a cheerleader, a diplomat, and a counselor.

As public relations takes on an increasing role in corporate strategy, campaign planning has become a highly valued skill. The 1990s have seen public relations finally begin to take its place in the corporate boardrooms; some public relations professionals are even taking their place behind the president's desk. As this knowledge of and appreciation for the role that public relations plays in the organization increases, so will the expectations. By thinking and acting strategically, public relations professionals will find themselves included when strategy is determined. By planning, evaluating, and proving results, the public relations campaign will not only be a viable tool within the organization—it will be valued as well.

QUESTIONS

1. What is a situation analysis, and what benefit does it generate in setting campaign objectives?

2. Cite two guidelines that are useful to campaign planners as they work to set objectives.

3. What are the "Six Golden Rules for Brainstorming"?

4. Cite three research tactics discussed in the chapter and briefly explain each one.

5. What is the difference between a strategy and a tactic? Give an example of each.

READINGS

Deborah Hauss. "Measuring the Impact of Public Relations." *Public Relations Journal* (February 1993): 15.

———. "Readers Share Research Secrets." *Public Relations Journal* (February 1993): 18.

Doug Newsom and Alan Scott. *This Is PR: The Realities of Public Relations.* Belmont, CA: Wadsworth Publishing Company, 1981.

"Silver Anvil Winners Focus on Crucial Issues." *Public Relations Journal* (June 1993): 15–16.

DEFINITION

situation analysis: A program for researching the atmosphere in which an organization exists so as to identify issues, trends, problems, or opportunities that affect the organization.

8 Internal vs. External Executions

Bringing the Bull's-Eye into Focus

CHAPTER OUTLINE

Types of Internal Audiences

Types of External Audiences

How Audiences Influence Strategy and Techniques

CHAPTER OBJECTIVES

When you have completed this chapter, you should be able to:

- Understand the information needs of internal and external audiences
- Apply two-way communication techniques
- Compare guidelines to actual case studies

Much will be said throughout this textbook about efficient execution and targeted reach of a desired audience segment. Neither goal is possible without first knowing exactly with whom you wish to share your message and where they spend their waking hours. In other words, who comprises the target audience, and how can you best reach them?

Internal and external audiences can be quite different, although defining either category may prove difficult. Definitions have less to do with demographics and more to do with locale. In fact, the same audience segment for a given campaign may qualify for both the internal and the external audience category—quite possibly all in the same day.

For example, a local school board may wish to share new guidelines for student/ teacher ratios and decide that they want to reach both educators and parents with their important message on the same day. The teachers, or internal audience, are told first via a faculty meeting. Yet these teachers may also have children and thereby become the parental or external audience that receives an informational letter upon arriving home.

Audience makeup is ever-changing, and there is a likelihood that the same individual spans both audiences in the same day as a consequence of the same campaign. What might be different are the channels of communication used in reaching these people internally versus externally. A more typical campaign effort, however, would be the desire to reach multiple audiences with different messages, thus necessitating custom channels of communication with equally distinctive information. That is what makes campaign planning and execution challenging.

Types of Internal Audiences

Generally speaking, internal audiences are more easily defined and readily accessible. They tend to be both homogeneous and captive.

Without question, employees constitute the largest and most fertile internal audience that can be targeted by public relations strategists. Well-informed employees go a long way toward both improved productivity and quick networking of information in an organization.

From an International Association of Business Communicators Conference Board study involving 281 firms nationwide, Kathryn Troy summarizes the respondents' desire that "Today's top corporate managers expect communicators not only to inform employees and help bolster morale but also to craft messages that will influence employee behavior." The implication is clear: Public relations practitioners are being given the opportunity to lend their communications skills to the ever-important role of management, which further validates their credibility, if not their contribution.

PRoActive

Something in the Air at FedEx

During the 1998 holiday season, FedEx reported that about 6,000 employees rallied in support of the company during an imminent pilot strike. Cameras from all the local television stations were on hand to capture the event, which was held between the company's corporate office in Memphis and its main hub at Memphis International Airport. In this location, the rally was in plain view of the pilots who were threatening the strike.

In addition to choosing a key rally location, event participants were given credit for developing the slogan, "Absolutely, Positively, Whatever It Takes," and for getting a local advertising agency to donate banners that displayed the slogan. Rally supporters then used the FedEx Web site to spread details about the event.

As is the case with many internal PR plans, members of the FedEx PR department denied they were involved with the rally. Perhaps FedEx workers were able to stage such a well-organized event without the help of professionals. Or, as many PR professionals suspect, perhaps the event was actually given a jump start with a well-executed public relations and in-house communications plan.

But regardless of who initiated the event, the company received positive publicity from the rally. Now, the PR team at FedEx has the opportunity to create a campaign that builds upon the loyalty and positive messages of the event. In December 1998, the pilots at FedEx dropped their strike threat rather than risk losing jobs, and their union reached a tentative agreement on the company's first labor contract.

Employees aren't the lone internal audience. Corporations and even nonprofit associations almost always have a board of directors or advisers and consultants. As these people become vested with authority and control of an organization, they too must be considered a priority in the flow of communication.

Other internal audiences might include the families of employees (who are most readily reached through other members of their household), corporate "alumni" or former employees, and, to some extent, corporate investors. Obviously, these latter categories are not immediately internal audiences, yet they are relatively captive.

Types of External Audiences

For every internal audience, there are at least two external segments. By the very nature of how business is conducted, an organization is usually more interested in its external constituents. Some or all of the following audiences will likely be of special interest to public relations managers at some time during their careers.

■ Customers no doubt head the list of audiences most often sought by the public relations manager. After all, this audience segment represents a company's lifeline; without customers, there would be no company. Therefore, customers are an audience that should be contemplated and respected by all.

■ Suppliers and vendors are other critical publics; their trust in a firm customer will determine how that organization fares when problems arise. Will products continue to be delivered to an ailing or beleaguered company? What of a merger or hostile takeover? How do these inevitable transactions strain or change long-standing working relationships?

■ Industry relations are also quite important and yet many times are overlooked by communicators. The reality of these relationships is that an organization cannot go far if it doesn't at least have the understanding and respect of its peers. An example here would be a trade association such as the Public Relations Society of America.

■ Media as a collective group certainly comprise a most important audience. Particularly significant are the print and broadcast journalists, who serve dual roles as their own external audience as well as the gatekeepers of information reaching many other audiences. Knowledge, experience, and patience are real assets in dealing with this sophisticated audience.

■ Government at any level constitutes another external public that should be addressed from time to time. Rare is the organization that goes totally unlegislated, and a strategic communications campaign can be the difference in its public standing and the level of regulation experienced. While lobbyists have traditionally handled this role, more often the PR practitioner, if qualified, will be asked to also assist.

■ The general public makes up a real audience, although quite large and more difficult to cover. Technically speaking, this group includes everyone within a given geographic area. It is less frequent that a campaign sets out to reach every man, woman, and child in a community, city, state, or nation, but when that mass awareness is desired, it requires intense application of every campaign component and the use of almost all communication channels.

PRoEthics

The United States vs. Lt. Kelly Flinn

Problem

On May 22, 1997, Secretary of the Air Force Sheila E. Widnall approved First Lieutenant Kelly Flinn's request for resignation in lieu of court martial. But the story was not in the granting of this request—which would send the service's first female B-52 pilot back into the civilian sector with a general discharge—but the troubled path that led her, and the Air Force, to this settlement.

Situational Analysis

Charges were preferred against Lt. Kelly Flinn on January 28, 1997, after a three-month investigation regarding two unprofessional relationships, one with an enlisted member and one with the husband of an enlisted woman stationed with Flinn at Minot Air Force Base, North Dakota. Charges included making a false official statement and disobeying a direct order, stemming from her relationship with the married man and her attempt to cover it up.

The Uniform Code of Military Justice prohibits lying, disobeying a direct order, fraternization, and (in cases where it is prejudicial to good order and discipline) adultery. The current chief of staff of the Air Force is renowned for his accountability policy.

The information had already been released to the public. There is a tendency for the media to be suspicious of the military, and coverage is not always balanced. In the past, the Air Force has suffered court losses in the area of fraternization when civilian lawyers have successfully argued that its culture has eroded. Lt. Flinn has a significant status as the service's first female B-52 pilot and has been honored for her achievements during her three and a half years on active duty.

Planning

Goal

- To maintain the integrity of the Air Force disciplinary process

Objective

- With due process, try Lt. Flinn on the preferred charges; through a decision by her peers, let the record show how her actions violated the Uniform Code of Military Justice.

Target Audiences

- Members of the U.S. Air Force and their families
- Elected officials who have the ability to enact legislation regarding the military
- Appointed officials who have the ability to implement policy changes in the military
- The general public who supports the military not only with taxpayer money but also with recruits
- The media reporting on the issue

Action

Strategies

- Take the high road.
- Release general information about the military justice system and the Uniform Code of Military Justice.
- Respect Lt. Flinn's right to privacy.
- Protect information as part of the ongoing legal action against a member.
- Centralize the response; channel all queries to the Pentagon.

Tactics

- Release statistics about the number of court martials with adultery charges broken down by sex.
- Allow the media to cover the trial.

Implementation

- Response to queries when permissible
- Repetition of key messages at all levels

Communication

Message Content

- Personal relationships between Air Force members become matters of command concern when they adversely affect morale or discipline or are otherwise detrimental to mission accomplishment.

(continued)

PRoEthics   Continued

- Air Force standards are gender-neutral and are applied evenly and equitably.
- This is not a case about adultery; it is a case of making a false official statement and disobeying a direct order.
- The tools of the military trade are deadly; their nature requires military personnel to be held to higher standards to ensure proper conduct in carrying out their important mission.

Core Themes
- Air Force standards are universally known, unilaterally applied, and nonselectively enforced.
- Integrity is the bedrock of Air Force values; it requires devotion to honesty and truthfulness.

Evaluation

Feedback
- Perform content analysis of media coverage.
- Monitor Web site activity.
- Monitor content of Congressional statements.

- Monitor content of e-mails sent to the Pentagon.
- Monitor the decision of a court martial or Secretary Widnall regarding discharge.

Program Adjustment—Short-Term
- Adjust messages accordingly to counter opposing messages.
- When the issue is no longer pending, release all available information and correct the record.

Program Adjustment—Long-term
- Redefine the public affairs role in high-visibility cases.
- Create information sources to explain the legal system and the Uniform Code of Military Justice.
- Include nonconventional scenarios in public affairs planning.
- Enhance information across the field to increase the magnitude of lessons learned.

- "Splinter" or specialty external audiences that relate to a particular organization and its goals or its agenda are virtually endless. In the previous situation, it might be unwed mothers, dental hygienists, hot-air balloonists, or the clergy. Depending on the intent of a particular campaign, these audiences might become further defined by targeting Asian unwed mothers, male hygienists, balloon pilots, east of the Mississippi and Protestant-only clergy. As a general rule, the more tightly defined the audience segment, the easier it is to reach.

How Audiences Influence Strategy and Techniques

Never does a sport better symbolize the communications process (at least the one-way variety) than archery. Archers spend most of their time zeroing in on a target, carefully positioning themselves for the best opportunity to hit the bull's-eye. Then, and only then, do they let an arrow fly toward its intended destination.

It stands to reason then that wherever an audience resides, that is where one must go in order to reach it. In other words, the audience doesn't come to the message; the message must reach the audience. Ideally it does so at a place and time when that audience is most predisposed to receive it.

Unlike simple target practice, the communicator must also be sensitive to timing. When will an audience—in reality, a group of individuals who don't view themselves as part of a homogeneous group—be most predisposed to hearing, understanding, and retaining a message? Is it in the morning while dressing for work or during the afternoon while driving home? How about after dinner while watching television or reading the newspaper? Perhaps it's while they're on the way to church, or en route to the airport as they leave for vacation.

These are strictly timing considerations, and they represent important options to the strategic communicator. It may or may not seem fair that public relations professionals must be concerned with the idiosyncrasies of their target audience. However, when the issue of effectiveness is at stake, it becomes the absolute responsibility of communicators to do whatever it takes to reach and influence the marketplace on behalf of their campaign objectives. Said another way, no one will ever hang the target in front of the oncoming arrow; that is why the archer, as well as the campaign strategist, will be forever regarded for precision.

The following case studies represent public relations campaigns that were directed to an internal audience, an external audience, or both. These campaign overviews will demonstrate how strategies and techniques differ, depending on the type of audience being reached (internal or external) and the nature of the goal.

As has been previously suggested, the larger the audience to be reached, the more diverse the programming becomes. These case studies demonstrate a parallel between increasing audience size and an expanding number of messages and communication channels.

CASE STUDY   MeraBank: Where the Employees Became the Champions

MeraBank, formerly a savings and loan institution in Phoenix, Arizona, decided to launch a new advertising campaign to reposition itself among the young urban professional market.

The theme line of the television campaign was "First Thing in the Morning" and was meant to suggest that the best bankers were those who awoke before the competition and were ready to answer the bell of the Eastern stock markets.

Artigue and Associates was hired by the bank's marketing department to coordinate the announcement of the campaign and its objectives, as well as how the employees could participate in a corresponding sales/incentive promotion. At the time, employee morale was sagging and internal communication was poor.

Numerous brainstorming sessions by the agency's account team led to an internal employee relations campaign that played off the Barcelona Olympics. The bank's "First Thing" slant led to a breakfast event and eventually a promotional tie-in with General Mills and its famous "Breakfast of Champions" slogan. It was decided that each bank branch manager would conduct early-morning staff meetings over breakfast and give employees a sneak preview of the new TV ads. At these same sessions, the managers introduced a sales incentive program that was flavored with a sports theme. In fact, one of the prizes was the winning department's picture printed on a real box of Wheaties cereal.

Promotional details aside, the key to the success of this campaign was the targeting and penetration of several internal audiences, or subaudiences. This meant utilizing MeraBank's existing channels of communication, from the traditional (employee newsletter) to the unconventional (the company grapevine). It was felt that employees would respond favorably to the "Champions" programming if they only knew about it and understood it.

The introduction of the program began with paycheck envelope stuffers that contained background information about the program and teasers about the upcoming "Breakfast of Champions." Similar information began to appear in the employee newsletter and on bulletin board posters. After

(continued)

department heads were apprised by senior management of the upcoming advertising campaign and corresponding sales promotion, their weekly staff meeting agendas covered what was coming, and why. It wasn't long before a positive change in employee attitude and their growing interest were noticeable. They were, in fact, responding to what Daft and Lengel call "information-rich" face-to-face communication and the pride of knowing something significant about their organization before it is public.

As Richard G. Charlton reminds corporate communicators, "Employees need and want to know what is expected of them . . . if an employee is not informed and loyal, and does not exercise initiative and good judgment, the company may sustain immense damage before problems are spotted and corrected." And as MeraBank executives discovered in their campaign, enlightened employees will work harder to produce an improved bottom line. They simply must be shown the way.

After every bank branch in Arizona had held their breakfast meetings, they were grouped into larger divisions or "teams" that would compete against one another for new customer accounts and gains in deposits. Branches were decorated by their employees with a sports theme, and customers were encouraged via banners and lapel pins to inquire about this corporate Olympiad. Sales results were tabulated and circulated among the divisional team leaders on a weekly basis. There was constant monitoring by the agency and corporate account executives as to the level of understanding, motivation, and participation. Certain program modifications were made as necessary. For example, a twenty-four-hour hotline was added for employees when it was discovered that there were too many questions about the ad campaign that couldn't be answered by branch managers. The CEO was utilized in this prerecorded Q&A situation, which seemed to bring him and the staff line employees closer together.

The results of this ninety-day campaign were impressive. At all levels of the bank, employees showed both high understanding and support of the new marketing direction. This knowledge carried over into enthusiasm, which then translated into improved customer service. Ultimately, this all led to the kind of sales results that senior management had hoped would transpire.

Even after the "Champions" program was completed, certain communications programming remained in place as this captive homogeneous audience proved to be hungry for more information about their organization and how it compared to other financial institutions.

The paycheck stuffers evolved into a regular employee newsletter. Regular branch staff meetings began to crop up and continued to take place. Even senior management began to get out into the branches and meet with employees on a more regular basis. As a result of the awards given to the several winning branches, a permanent employee recognition program was established and implemented. In essence, the execution of this internal campaign was so well received that its target audience demanded permanency of the two-way communications that it fostered.

CASE STUDY **One Million Guests Who Got "The Pointe"**

It took The Pointe Resort at Squaw Peak in Phoenix just a few years to reach a major milestone: The welcoming of its one-millionth guest. In anticipation of that milestone, the marketing staff decided that they would share the impressive news with the local Phoenix marketplace. Again, Artigue and Associates was retained to help draft the campaign plan and coordinate its execution.

The client goals were varied, but each was quite specific. First, the internal audience of some 3,000 employees were to be made aware of this corporate achievement, thereby congratulating them on their dedication and commitment. Second, the local media (and to a lesser extent, the trade

ONE IN A MILLION – THAT'S THE POINTE!

Six years and countless awards later, The Pointe is honored to soon be celebrating the arrival of its one millionth guest. While many of these guests have no doubt been out-of-town visitors and convention goers, it is quite clear that the success of Pointe Resorts is due to the citizens in our community.

Since 1976, an overwhelming response from Phoenicians has chartered our course: that of unequalled success and explosive growth in the Valley. As a Phoenix-owned, Phoenix-managed resort company, it is only proper that we find ourselves catering to the

particular needs of the Valley. In doing so, we have earned the title of "Arizona's Own Resort," and for that, we are indeed quite proud!

Some time this August, our millionth guest will walk through the door. He or she will receive special V.I.P. treatment, including an all expenses-paid one week vacation and other luxury gifts. While only one person can become our official "Millionth Guest," the management and staff of Pointe Resorts would like all Phoenicians to know how much we appreciate your patronage and continued support.

Phoenix – you're one in a million!

The Pointe®
at Squaw Peak

7677 North 16th Street · Phoenix, Arizona 85020 · (602) 997-2626

FIGURE 8.1   The Pointe Resort Ad

press) were to be informed of this milestone, and news and feature coverage were to be cultivated. Finally, sales opportunities, linked to the publicity generated, were to be created by encouraging the traveling public to stay at the resort and possibly become the actual one-millionth guest and win the corresponding prize package.

Because of the high level of awareness desired by the client, it was decided that this promotional campaign would be executed to both its internal and external constituents simultaneously. So, just as media kits were prepared and released to the local beat reporters, feature writers, and national trade press, numerous internal communication channels (newsletters, paycheck stuffers, bulletin board posters, and even a pep rally) were used to reach the employees. The theme on all the materials was "1,000,000 Guests Can't Be Wrong . . . Have You Gotten The Pointe?" An advertising campaign was then created to reach the local and regional market, encouraging travel to any one of the three Pointe resorts during the special promotional period.

What is important to note with this campaign is the degree of control, or lack thereof, that the campaign manager had over the various audience segments. Working from the inside (employees) and moving outward (general public), control of the message decreases. The media are relied upon to tell the story about the resort's milestone, but it is not likely that it will be the complete story or that it will include anything having to do with the promotional prize package for the lucky one-millionth guest. That is where the advertising plays an important and costly role.

(continued)

CASE STUDY   **Continued**

And cost is the other significant factor to be considered by the PR manager when attempting to reach multiple audiences with a similar campaign message. The basic rule of thumb is that it will greatly increase as the target for the message moves outward. This is generally the case whether advertising expenditures are involved or not. The fact is that external audiences are less easily defined and many times more mobile, which necessitates a greater number of impressions to make a message stick.

The Pointe campaign is a good example. In that case, the external audience was all of Phoenix, with some emphasis on middle- and upper-income households. Only after repeated news stories (many of which were generated by on-site special events), an advertising campaign (see Figure 8.1), and direct mail to selected ZIP codes was there any notion that something special was about to happen at The Pointe at Squaw Peak. The employees, on the other hand, were extremely aware of the pending milestone and the corresponding sales promotion, although only a fraction of the campaign budget was spent to reach them.

The final result of this internal/external campaign was success. Employees were energized with pride, which spilled over to what the guests called "superb service." The local and regional markets became adequately informed of the milestone and, more importantly to the client, motivated to stay at the resort to take their chances in winning the prize package. Room reservations nearly doubled compared to the same time period in previous years. The eventual winner of the one-millionth guest prize package was an unsuspecting family of four who were visiting Phoenix for the first time to spend their week's vacation away from the Indiana cold. So much for local reach!

CASE STUDY   **RTC vs. Keating: Landmark Battle Sets Stage for Multifaceted Campaign**

In the fall of 1989, a confrontation that had been brewing in Phoenix for some time finally came to a head. It involved local developer, financier, and resort owner Charles Keating, Jr., and his nemesis of several years, the Resolution Trust Corporation (RTC). At the center of this particular struggle was ownership and control of the ultra-posh Phoenician Resort, which was originally developed by Keating.

Keating had already forfeited his 55 percent ownership in the resort property to the RTC but would remain in day-to-day control of the hotel until his Kuwaiti partners exercised the right to join forces with their newfound governmental partner and oust Keating (something the RTC had been pushing for). The Kuwaitis elected to do so just before Thanksgiving. That was the easy part; the difficulty would come in actually removing the reluctant Keating from the $300 million mountainside resort without damage or loss to the property or real inconvenience to the guests.

Though a small army of lawyers, accountants, security officials, and consultants were hired to effect the change in management, the internal and external communications for such an undertaking were almost overlooked. It was the final week of planning before Evans/Artigue Public Relations was retained by the RTC/Kuwaiti ownership to navigate them through these most interesting waters—a hostile takeover of a 610-room resort hotel in the middle of the night.

Few communications campaigns could pose as many challenges in reaching multiple audiences with very different messages as the midnight takeover of the Phoenician resort. There were at least thirteen distinct audiences, which included retained employees, terminated employees, on-property guests, suppliers/vendors, local industry representatives, government officials, travel

Message Action Plan—The Phoenician Resort Takeover
Implementation Beginning November 16, 2 A.M.

Audience	Primary Message – 1st 24 hrs	Secondary Message – 24-72 hrs	Ongoing Comm.	Phone Call	Fax/Mailgram	Face-to-Face	Letters	News Conf.	Meetings	Advertising	Bulletin Board Materials	Invoice or Paycheck Stuffer	Responsibility	Exact Timing
Staff Employees	■		■			■			■		■	■	General Manager	Graveyard shift (3 am) Day shift (8 am)
Mgt. Employees	■		■	■		■			■			■	General Manager	7:30 am
In-House Guests	■						■						Resident Manager and Concierge	All day
Convention & Visitors Bureau		■	■		■		■		■				General Manager and PR Agency	11/17
AZ Office of Tourism		■	■		■		■		■				General Manager and PR Agency	11/18
Local Media	■		■					■					PR Agency	Immediately following takeover
National Media	■		■					■					PR Agency	Week of event
Local Government	■		■		■		■		■				General Manager and PR Agency	Following week
National Government		■	■	■	■		■						RTC and PR Agency	Month of event
Travel Agents	■		■	■	■		■		■	■			Sales Manager	Immediately
Meeting Planners	■		■	■	■		■		■	■			Sales Manager	Immediately
Vendors/Suppliers		■	■	■	■		■		■				Director of Purchasing	Week of event
Key Customers		■	■	■	■		■			■			Sales Staff	Immediately, ongoing
Incentive Houses	■		■	■	■		■		■				Sales Manager	November and December
Industry Analysts		■	■	■	■		■						RTC and PR Agency	November
Board of Directors	■		■	■	■	■			■				General Manager	Ongoing
Resolution Trust Corp.	■		■			■			■				General Manager	Ongoing

FIGURE 8.2 Message Action Plan Utilized by the Campaign Team to Communicate with Both Internal and External Audiences

(continued)

agents/agencies, airlines, corporate customers (meeting planners), competitors, local media, trade media, and, of course, the national media. There were actually a dozen other subgroups that by necessity, as "retained employees," had to be segregated into management, staff, English-speaking versus foreign language–speaking, and so forth. Other examples of audience segmentation were state versus federal politicians and print versus broadcast media. Even though planning is always essential to a communications campaign, it becomes even more so in a multiple-message, multiple-audience campaign. Such was the case here. Strategic planning and precise execution were the mandatory ingredients to communicating clearly and credibly with vast numbers of important constituents. At stake was the future of the resort hotel.

A message action plan (MAP) was critical in delineating audiences and shaping their corresponding messages. The MAP shown in Figure 8.2 portrays such audience/message/medium relationships in detail and underscores the need for keen organization on the part of the campaign manager. Without the use of such a planning tool, one runs the risk of sending the wrong message to an intended audience, which in some cases is worse than that constituency receiving no message at all. What is necessary in a multidimensional campaign such as this one is what Ron Actis, then of General Motors, calls a "synchronous communications process." This process would ideally get "the right message to the right audience at the right time with the right medium . . . all the while with progress measured on a continuous basis."

Timing becomes the other critical factor, particularly in a problematic campaign such as this one. For example, if travel agents had not been assured of the stability of the hotel before getting bombarded by their customers about pending reservations, they could have hurt rather than helped preserve the reputation and viability of the hotel. In many instances, when a message is received is as important as how it is received.

This is why most of the internal communications in this campaign were designed to take place face-to-face. One of the first official acts of the new general manager was to address more than a thousand employees in the hotel ballroom where he explained what had happened and why. Written information was then disseminated, and an intense question/answer session took place. These kinds of hands-on communications opportunities are usually available in reaching an internal audience; in almost all circumstances, they should be seized.

A short summary of what became an intense week-long campaign, and eventually a ninety-day maintenance effort, is difficult here. Suffice it to say that the many diverse audiences all received their messages in a timely and direct fashion. Because there was a single source for the dissemination of this important information, there was minimal confusion as well as good campaign continuity. The internal execution of this campaign went so smoothly that on-property guests (the hotel was full) didn't know that anything significant had taken place in the middle of the night.

It would have been risky, if not dangerous, to have had the internal and external executions handled by separate parties. That usually invites misplaced or ill-timed communications strategies. Instead, a single conference room or "Command Center" was set up and became the heartbeat for all communications. Any inquiry, whether it was from media, staff, or guests, was directed to the communications center. Even outside callers were transferred by operators to the Evans/Artigue staff for answers to their questions.

The net result of this intense, multifaceted campaign was the glare of national and even international media attention: For at least a seventy-two-hour period following the RTC takeover of the resort, Keating's dismissal made headlines everywhere (see Figure 8.3). Yet with all the exposure, the hotel continued to function smoothly; there was no interruption of business or loss of important guest reservations.

FIGURE 8.3   A Sampling of the Local and National Headlines That Made the Phoenician Takeover Sensational

Summary

Internal communications campaigns are the most manageable, external campaigns are more difficult, and the combination of the two (for any given purpose) is the most challenging of all. The fact is that the serious public relations practitioner will have ample opportunity to deal with each of these three types of campaigns and must be prepared to handle all they demand.

Planning is key to any campaign execution. Without it, there is little or no chance for campaign managers to reach their target audiences with messages that are understandable and timely. Planning simply means knowing what needs to be said, to whom, and when. The channels through which the information is transmitted are not always obvious, yet they should be examined and agreed upon, based on effectiveness, efficiency, and cost. Finally, it is most important to note that there are no absolutes in campaign planning. A campaign might begin as internal and, due to the evolution of issues, grow to become a full-fledged external campaign.

The campaign manager not only must be ready to handle such surprises but should have anticipated them in the first place—which brings everything back to planning. Anticipation, preparation, programming—these are the key ingredients to any strategic communications campaign, whether it be for an organization, a state, or a nation.

QUESTIONS

1. For most corporations, what is their largest internal audience? What are some of the basic methods of reaching this constituency?

2. Name three audience types that are associated with internal and external campaigns.

3. Select one of the case studies profiled in this chapter and discuss its inherent campaign components.

4. What are the advantages of a MAP?

5. What is the single most important component of any communications campaign?

READINGS

Richard G. Charlton. "The Decade of the Employee." *Public Relations Journal* (January 1990): 36.

Richard L. Daft and Robert H. Lengel. "Information Richness: A New Approach to Managerial Behavior and Organizational Design." In *Research in Organizational Behavior.* JAI Press: 6, 191–233.

Patrick J. McKeand. "GM Division Builds a Classic System to Share Internal Information." *Public Relations Journal* (November 1990): 24.

9 The Product Campaign

Helping Make the Cash Register Ring

CHAPTER OUTLINE

Public Relations Becomes a Marketing Partner

Public Relations in the Marketing World

New Product Rollouts vs. Maintenance and Growth

Product Campaigns Create Special Considerations

CHAPTER OBJECTIVES

When you have completed this chapter, you should be able to:

- Understand what is meant by marketing PR
- Recognize the importance of integrated communications
- Define benchmarking and its steps

No other public relations effort will take the practitioner further into the realm of marketing than the product campaign. Inherent in its objectives is the expectation of selling a product or service, thereby increasing market share and ensuring that the manufacturing process can go on.

Of course it doesn't always work that way. The road is littered with product failures, campaign situations where this went wrong or that didn't go quite right, or maybe even both.

In one study, Chicago consulting firm Kuczmarski & Associates examined the success rates for 11,000 new products launched by seventy-seven manufacturing, service, and consumer products companies. Barely half the products, or just 56 percent, were even being sold only five years later.

Another study conducted by Booz Allen & Hamilton Inc. revealed that 46 percent of all new product development costs go to failures, which curiously is up from that figure three decades ago.

The debate rages, although it goes unsolved, as to why so many sophisticated companies have difficulty getting consumer products to market and then keeping them there. Is it product integrity—a natural void between what is promised and what is delivered? Or does it have to do with unnecessary products that are simply not in demand?

Yorum Wind, a professor of marketing at Wharton School of Business, has yet another theory: "If companies can improve their effectiveness at launching new products, they could double their bottom line. It's one of the few areas left with the greatest potential for improvement."

If, as Wind suggests, it's a marketing dilemma that plagues new product introductions, then public relations professionals can stand up and be counted as valuable members of the new product marketing team. After all, if it isn't just a matter of more money and muscle that ensures the successful introduction of a product; it may simply require more marketing style and clarity. Public relations can and should be able to address the sometimes sensitive association between corporation and customer, while bringing about valuable synergy between traditional marketing programs and the lesser understood public relations strategies and tactics.

Public Relations Becomes a Marketing Partner

Enter marketing public relations (MPR), a distinct discipline that has recently been added to numerous Fortune 500 marketing departments for the purpose of separating the array of PR functions and their intended audiences. For example, corporate public relations (CPR) is a term that has been coined to encompass all those nonsales-oriented PR activities designed to reach noncommercial audiences (i.e., employees, shareholders, or suppliers).

Thomas L. Harris reminds all practitioners, regardless on which side of the PR fence they reside on, that the need for cooperation between CPR and MPR is essential. "Public relations will have to abandon its intellectual pretensions and its disdain of the marketing function, and marketers will have to become increasingly aware of how the social, political and economic environment affects consumers and the opinion-makers who influence attitudes toward companies and their products. This synergy cannot be achieved if marketing and public relations are seen as rivals rather than allies."

Already such notable companies as Proctor & Gamble and General Motors have moved to integrate their marketing communications programs; many others are following their lead. The goal is to combine the potential of both marketing persuasions so as to maximize the positive impact when bringing product to market. Harris says, "The impact of MPR today on the sale of products from Trivial Pursuit to the Ford Taurus, from Diet Coke to Disney World, shows that product publicity is no longer a hit-or-miss proposition. It is now a strategic tool of MPR, which is an integral element of the marketing communications plan."

PRoSpeak
Marketing Public Relations

Marketing public relations emerged in the late 1980s as both the largest and fastest-growing segment of the public relations industry. About 80 percent of all dollars spent for public relations services in the United States today is allocated to marketing support activities. Those PR practitioners who specialize in corporate image development, government affairs, environmental PR, investor relations, or other niche segments must be satisfied with munching on the remainder of the pie.

Once called "publicity," marketing public relations has also earned a much higher level of respect. Budgets are not "what's left over from advertising," and PR people today, more often than not, play a key strategic role in shaping the messages for the entire marketing program for the companies they serve. In fact, not infrequently, marketing public relations executives have a big say in the way the business strategy of the company is positioned to its audiences as well.

In 1989, *Adweek,* a prominent advertising trade magazine, raised the profile of our profession by commenting, "Managing the news, and creating an ambient mood around a product, has become a strategic imperative, not a marketing afterthought."

The reason, of course, is that business has begun to recognize the critical role marketing public relations plays in managing the way key publics view not only a company's products or services but the company as well as the chief executive.

In 1985, Harold Burson, reflecting on the evolution of public relations over his career with author Norm Nager, California State University, Fullerton, said, "At first, the decision was already made by the executive, and he'd call the public relations person and ask, 'How do I say this?' (PR) was at that time largely a press function. In the era of the 1960s, the executive asked not only 'How?' but also 'What do I say?' That's gone on for a long time. In the 1980s, the public relations counselor was being asked more and more, 'What do I do?'"

Burson's comments represent a tremendous escalation in the role of public relations, especially

Sue Bohle, APR
President
The Bohle Company
Los Angeles, California

marketing public relations, where we literally walk our clients through the process of an interview that not only can sell their product but also can make their career.

But having marketing public relations recognized for its importance and having more companies want it do not make it any easier to deliver, especially if your standards are high.

Gone is the day when a well-written product press release could be mass mailed to the nation's newspapers, recording terrific clips. A good idea is still a good idea, but there are just so many more of them, and the competition for space devoted to products and services is stiff.

Gone, too, is the notion that anyone could possibly have the "contacts" to regularly or even, upon request, deliver a major project feature in the publication of choice. Editors change positions, magazines and newspapers change formats, accounts turn over, and in-house responsibilities get merged out of existence. Today, a practitioner has to understand the medium with which he's dealing.

(continued)

PRoSpeak   Continued

Since we can't "read the magazine" for every editor with whom we deal, we have to learn to know the fundamentals of the medium and be quick studies of current issues.

And what about press conferences? At one time, press conferences were the principal way of delivering all marketing news. Today, they are all but obsolete. Editors want their own hour with the spokesperson, and they are too busy to traipse across town or away from the trade show to get the product and marketing information they expect you to deliver in the press kit.

Good phone salesmanship has emerged as one of the important tools of marketing PR. Clients can't afford to send us out on the road as much. We rarely "do lunch" with editors. After the pitch letter goes out, it's up to us to manage the phone sell. Everyone in my agency role-plays for the first year on the job.

A few marketing courses are helpful, if you want to do well in the field. We pay the full cost of all professional development or university courses in writing, PR, or marketing. After all, our marketing public relations programs look more and more like something right out of an MBA course. We have to talk the language of tomorrow's managers.

And then there must be internal controls—a rigorous set of quality standards and an editing process that passes each piece of paper by several managers before the pitch, product announcement release, article, or speech makes it out the door.

Emerging is a focus on making everything in marketing public relations "right" before you send the pitch or make the first call. In fact, at The Bohle Company, we've begun referring to something as small as a product pitch letter as "strategic." At the risk of overusing an important word, we discuss our strategy for positioning a story, our strategy for determining which media will most likely be interested, the best strategy for approaching the editor, the right day and the right time to call, and so on. Each detail is honed.

The challenge for those executives who have chosen marketing public relations as a career will be to continue to grow, and to alter and improve methods of practice, as the field becomes even more sophisticated. With more than twenty years under my belt, I'm just trying to stay even with all those bright young journalism and public relations graduates who've chosen to join our firm and help make it grow. The next decade will be interesting.

Clearly, the push is toward integrated marketing communications (IMC), another buzzword that is pervading the ranks of marketing departments everywhere. It is a sophisticated term for a simple approach—working together as a team. As corporate CEOs come to understand the principle of this one-stop planning/implementation/evaluation process, they will not only request it, it will become a mandate.

As William D. Novelli categorizes the trend, "IMC is clearly in the best interests of the client. There is no question about it. The synergy that results from genuine integration can help clients two ways: Cost savings in terms of marketing dollars . . . and a gain in effectiveness from the concentration of power that results from advertising, PR, promotion, direct marketing and salesmanship all firing together."

Said another way, Kenneth Wylie reports that "marketers are pushing promotion agencies to find the shortest possible distance between product and customer. With all this intermingling taking place, the industry lexicon is gaining nuance. Integrated marketing and promotional marketing better define the work of the more progressive sales promotion agencies of today's market."

CASE STUDY   IMC Takes a Bite Out of Potato Chip Market for Frito-Lay

"Doritos Day," or D-Day as it came to be known, was a big event for Tracy-Locke Promotional and Regional Marketing and its client, Frito-Lay. After all, in a single day more than 13,000 employees across the country had given away 6 million bags of new Nacho Cheese Doritos in what must be regarded as the largest one-day sampling program ever.

This one-day event, which was planned and carried out in just sixty days, generated more than $6 million in incremental sales alone. With the company's employees acting as the key component, the campaign was designed to introduce the reformulated Doritos flavor, stimulate consumer trial, secure shelf displays at the retail level, and energize the staff.

Each and every one of these objectives were realized. Besides the multimillion-dollar increase in new sales, Frito-Lay realized a 14 percent increase in secondary retail displays, a 5 share-point gain in dollar volume, and a coupon redemption rate of 35 percent to 40 percent.

The bottom line to this phenomenally successful case history is the combining of marketing energies that are normally employed alone. Separately, product trials or merchandise displays are not significant, but utilized in conjunction with one another, and with the involvement of a large and enthusiastic employee base, they form the backbone of a strong IMC campaign.

CASE STUDY   IMC Helps Gillette Cut to the Quick in Reaching 27 Million People

Another huge product campaign success that employed the principles of integrated marketing was Gillette's nineteen-country launch of its SensorExcel razor. As the result of a carefully orchestrated public relations effort that was part of a $100 million marketing campaign, more than 27 million people were introduced to Gillette's newest product in just three days. The integrated marketing plan involved New York–based Porter Novelli from the outset; it was charged with developing and coordinating a global communications strategy.

Although the mechanics for making the SensorExcel announcement differed from country to country, the message strategies were constant and the timing of the announcement was simultaneous. "The world really is one marketplace from a communications standpoint. While the strategies and messages are global, the public relations has to be local," points out John Darman, business director for new products, Gillette North Atlantic Group (GNAG). They also must be integrated with one another, regardless of the differences in customs and language that are encountered when spanning several continents. Gillette's marketing team, in close association with a worldwide network of marketing partners, clearly demonstrated that size and distance between marketplaces are no excuse for the absence of an IMC approach.

Gillette followed up on its success with the introduction of MACH3 in April 1998. The roll-out began two months before the product was available in stores. "It was one of those rare instances where you see the true impact of PR, since advertising didn't start until August," says Adele Myers, account supervisor at Porter Novelli, New York. Thousands of razors, targeted to become the flagship of the company's blade business, were sent to well-known figures in entertainment, sports, and politics.

A $300 million marketing campaign supported the effort, as well as a significant presence on the Internet for the first time and an online news bureau for media only. The site offered media

(continued)

materials and visuals for downloading. A press conference staged simultaneously in the United States, Canada, and Western Europe created momentum. Gillette sent teaser cards to 300 TV talk shows, news anchors, weathermen, and radio deejays in all major markets. The teasers challenged males, the target audience, to go to work unshaven. If they did, Gillette would give them a gift—a kit with the MACH3, gel, towel, mirror, and publicity materials.

The results? One week after it was on store shelves, MACH3 was the best-selling razor for the time period. Impressive, but what is truly significant, according to Adam Leyland of *PR Week*, is that "PR got a far larger slice of the budget than would have been the case ten or even five years ago and proved its worth many times over."

Public Relations in the Marketing World

After examining the cost efficiencies of public relations and the credibility factor inherent in product editorial coverage versus advertising, as Aaron D. Cushman points out, "CEOs and marketing VPs are really listening. Meanwhile, savvy marketers hungry for intelligent alternatives to advertising are finding their answer in public relations—but in public relations as practiced by experienced, marketing-oriented practitioners."

Little wonder that public relations has finally seemed to arrive in elite marketing circles. Well-documented effectiveness on a consistent basis has earned PR programming a solid reputation among advertising and marketing executives alike. Add to that the fact that escalating media costs and declining program audiences have combined to confound the most able brand managers.

According to Alan Miller, president of Chicago sales promotion agency Flair, the integration of PR and promotion is being driven by the clients. "Clients don't care where good ideas come from," he says, "but they want marketing programs that move brand and add value."

Edelman/New York general manager George Drucker summarizes the clients' demand for integrated and effective marketing this way: "They want PR that moves product off shelves."

Surveys indicate that public relations is being increasingly adopted by marketers as a proven means to bring a product or service into the mass market. Even more than a decade ago, a study of seventy CEOs of major companies, conducted by the International Association of Business Communicators, ranked public relations "slightly higher" than advertising in terms of return on investment. In a separate survey, marketing executives indicated they no longer rely "solely" on advertising, emphasizing that "it is vital to have alternative marketing tools."

Clearly public relations has become one of the prime alternatives. In fact, PR can outperform advertising, according to Daniel J. Edelman, chairman of Daniel J. Edelman, Inc., given the right product or service and the right circumstances. He lists four specific instances in which public relations can play a more effective role than advertising:

1. When there is a revolutionary breakthrough product that can make "news"
2. When industry regulations limit or preclude the use of television advertising for a product

3. When the media environment is negative and needs to be turned around quickly
4. When the company is new or small and there is little money available for advertising

The practical result of public relations' popularity has been the restructuring of corporate marketing departments in almost every industry. No longer is the public relations department comprised of a couple of entry-level employees tucked away in an office next to the mail room. Rather, they are corporate managers who sit on the executive committee and report to the vice president of marketing. This phenomenon varies from industry to industry but is especially evident in the financial, medical, electronics, and consumer products arenas.

On the agency side of the field, the emergence of public relations as a respected marketing component saw the acquisition of numerous national and international PR firms by their counterparts, national and international advertising agencies. There was a rush by ad agencies to quickly acquire and integrate PR services into their arsenal of marketing services so as to stave off client criticism and the possibility of losing business.

This discussion, however, is not about a footrace between two complementary marketing persuasions. Clearly, what is best for the advertising and public relations professions, as well as for the clients that pay for these services, is teamwork through integration.

The popularity of public relations is good news for that profession, but its practice and programs will never replace the important role that traditional advertising plays. Instead, public relations can and should become comfortable lining up, side by side, with the advertising profession and partnering in both the privilege and responsibility of bringing products to the marketplace.

New Product Rollouts vs. Maintenance and Growth

Without question, the strategies, tactics, and timing involved in bringing a new product to market vary greatly from those utilized in cultivating the growth of an existing or mature product. Each campaign requires an equal amount of ingenuity, planning, and precision, yet the approaches could be as different as day and night.

For example, in the aforementioned Gillette case study, an aggressive and well-planned publicity blitz, backed by the reputation and resources available to a Fortune 500 company, provided ample opportunity to reach tens of millions of consumers in a matter of days.

But how might a leading, yet aging brand approach the same objective of reaching millions through an integrated marketing program? In the case of the Kellogg Company, it was through a marketing partnership of their quality brands and an extremely creative cross-promotion.

CASE STUDY   **Corporate Costars and Cross Promotion**

In a 1993 *Advertising Age* front-page story, a headline shouted, "NBC and Kellogg Co-Star." The article went on to explain the extraordinary alliance created between these two marketing giants. The public relations–oriented promotion involved stars of five NBC hit sitcoms appearing on Kellogg's cereal boxes, matching specific cereal eaters with television shows they are most likely to

(continued)

watch. At the time, the marketing campaign was thought to be the largest ever between a network and a marketer.

According to the *Advertising Age* story, Kellogg kicked off the integrated marketing program with in-store displays in 30,000 supermarkets that touted a watch-and-win contest tied to the premieres of ten new NBC prime-time series. The contest awarded 100 free trips, valued at $10,000 each, to any destination in yet another tie-in with an airline and hotel chain.

The joint-venture promotion was a classic example of two plus two equaling five! One need only listen to the brimming enthusiasm of the participating brand managers. "The contest is designed to create some media-mania," said Alan Cohen, NBC's senior vice president of marketing. He estimated that the cereal boxes alone would generate almost 1 billion impressions for the network shows. "We think of them as 100,000 mini-billboards in the most uncluttered environment—people's homes."

Countered Carlos Gutierrez, executive vice president of sales and marketing at Kellogg USA, "We were looking for an event promotion with strong consumer appeal for our products that would create excitement among the [media] trade."

It did that and much more.

Product Campaigns Create Special Considerations

Because the intricacies of campaign planning are outlined in Campaign Components and Strategic Planning, they will not be repeated here. Only those nuances unique to product marketing, and their relationship with public relations programming, will be explored.

Such PR programs as highly regulated product marketing, product recalls, cross-brand promotion, national/international product shows, event marketing, infomercials, and benchmarking are among those situations or opportunities in which public relations should take a lead role.

It must be reiterated that integration is the key to involving public relations (or for that matter, any sales or promotional function) in the marketing process. Planning and integration, though seemingly basic, are the steps so often forgotten by campaign managers, even those within the same department or company. Once a product has been introduced or a problem has arisen, attempts to involve the resources of public relations will most likely be too late.

Marketing/communications expert Michael O. Niederquell presents the benefits of interjecting PR strategies in the marketing mix this way, leaving little question as to when the process should begin: "It is at the front end, during the planning, when public relations must be plugged in if it is to succeed in performing functions we are all familiar with." He outlines those functions as follows:

- Softening the marketplace, predisposing consumers to accept advertising and promotional messages
- Building credibility and nurturing public sentiment for the company and its services, products, and brands
- Extending the impact and reach of marketing programs
- Delivering cost-effective, often inexpensive support to external marketing budgets

PRoEthics
Keeping Secrets

The tobacco industry has demonstrated unethical tactics to keep trade secrets secret. We live in an age where the public wants to know information and some corporations want to keep information. "And since public relations at tobacco companies seems to have utterly failed in any role of protecting the public interest, public relations practitioners, too, might examine their roles in organizational practices of confidentiality and secrecy."

Private information is divided into two categories:

- Entrusted information, collected from others (personal information provided by individuals, such as job applicants or clients seeking services)
- Originated information, generated by the organization itself (knowledge protected by patents and copyrights and the realm of non-public information known as trade secrets, industrial processes, lists of customers, market data, and proposals)

The "stakeholder theory" and the principles of PR argue that "corporate management has a positive duty to pursue the interests of the broad range of stakeholders, or publics, not just stockholders." There should be guiding principles for corporations dealing with secret information:

- A corporation has an ethical obligation not to keep secret from stakeholders that information which is necessary for them to make decisions concerning the harm or benefit the corporation has on their well-being.
- A corporation has an ethical obligation to provide decisional stakeholders with corporate information that is essential to their decisions about the specific relationships they have to the corporation.
- The ethics of corporate secrecy and confidentiality must be based on understanding the personal autonomy of individuals and on the ethical principle of respect for that autonomy.

Decisional stakeholders are defined in this article as those who "make specific decisions that establish a formal, definable relationship to the corporations—stockholders, employees, customers or vendors. The Federal Securities and Exchange Commission requires the disclosure of material information, the timely release of information, and the prohibition of insider trading."

Societal stakeholders are defined in this article as "individuals or groups who are impacted by the corporation, not because of any decisions on their own part but through the decisions of the organization." Communities and the neighbors of corporate facilities are examples.

Source: Adapted from Thomas A. Schick and Ida C. Schick. "The Ethics of Keeping Corporate Secrets." *Public Relations Strategist* 4 (Summer 1998): 29–32.

"To the marketer, public relations should be viewed as the thread that holds the marketing communication bundle together. Public relations can weave the singular marketing message that may begin with a new product rollout speech by the CEO extending down to the copy on the side of the packaging," adds Niederquell.

Highly Regulated Product Marketing.   That notion is especially relevant as it relates to highly regulated industries such as health care. Large pharmaceutical companies that have invested millions of dollars in new products have much at stake and many times look to the PR manager or counselor to develop those strategic introductory messages that are persuasive enough to be effective but delicate enough to keep the FDA happy. That governmental agency has had growing concerns that too many PR tactics have been aimed at the end user of medicines or medical devices, rather than at the recommending physicians.

Regardless, a survey of nearly 200 pharmaceutical executives by the New York City–based PR firm Wang Associates documented that both usage and spending of PR dollars were up and would continue to rise. Survey highlights, as summarized by Marilyn L. Castaldi, include the finding that 40 percent of pharmaceutical executives feel marketing PR is underused despite the fact that they reported spending upwards of 25 percent of their total marketing budget on public relations programming.

Why the popularity in an industry noted for being appropriately conservative? Because, as a survey respondent suggested, "public relations can develop the integrity and trust that are essential if pharmaceutical companies are to maintain a good rapport with their publics."

What must be remembered by the PR strategist, and practiced with diligence, is the sensitive balance between marketing zeal for a product and ethical responsibility to an unknowing public. For example, although it may be most appropriate for selling cars, the use of a celebrity spokesperson to introduce and promote drugs may not be in the best interest of the practitioner's client.

Product Recalls. Another problematic application of public relations involves the use of its communications strategies in the product recall process, or what some industry observers have suggested is "marketing in reverse motion." After General Motors introduced its Saturn automobiles, it found itself recalling almost all that had been sold so that a short-circuiting wire that caused fires could be replaced—not a positive situation for any automaker, particularly one attempting to carve a niche with a new brand line.

PRoActive

Falling Arches

Situation

"McDonald's is in trouble. Sales are down, new products are failing, marketing and advertising aren't working, analysts are wary, consumers are confused, and franchise owners are angry." What went wrong?

- Complacency—success can mask potential problems or growing areas of concern.
- Corporate ego—no one thinks as an individual.

- Shaken confidence—new products have not equaled guaranteed success as in years past.
- Loss in public trust—lawsuits have affected the way the public perceives the company.

Response/Approach

Outsiders believe that McDonald's should take some time to get itself in order and commit to an organized plan of attack. Another suggestion involves "doing research to find out what the company's customers, franchises, analysts, and press are thinking."

Source: Adapted from Steve Crescenzo. "Trouble under the Golden Arches: An American Icon's PR Crisis." *Public Relations Tactics,* (September 1997): 1, 14, 26.

According to Ray Serafin, in an industry article titled "Saturn Recall a Plus for Saturn," the young company turned the biggest problem in its brief history into "a public relations bonanza." Although the recall would be both costly ($8 to $35 million) and time-consuming, Saturn's marketing, advertising, and public relations executives had developed programs that actually reinforced their strategic position as the "friendliest, best-liked car company in the United States." Only because of a cohesive marketing team approach was there the idea-becomes-reality concept of creating a TV commercial in which a Saturn rep flew to Alaska to fix a recalled car. The spot was part of Saturn's advertising campaign with the theme: "A different kind of company. A different kind of car."

Cross-Brand Promotions. Cross-brand promotions, particularly when utilized for the introduction of a new product or brand, are a classic example of advertising and PR commingling to the benefit of marketing managers and their sales goals. In effect, the campaign strategist is bringing together two quality brand names and creating an even more compelling reason for the consumer to "step up to the plate" and purchase a product(s).

CASE STUDY **Coffee Maker Brews Potent Product Launch**

Millstone Coffee, a Seattle-based specialty coffee maker, took the concept of cross-promotion to an extreme when it actually named one of its new coffee blends after a local sports team, the NFL Seattle Seahawks. "Seahawks' Choice" capitalized on the popularity of the local football team and helped create instant and high-level visibility for the new brand.

Supporting the advertising campaign that helped launch the new product, the PR agency swung into high gear and developed several community activities that would attract corresponding publicity for the brand. For instance, research turned up the purported originators of the "wave," and they were extensively interviewed on local radio and TV about the sports phenomenon they had created. Meanwhile, billboards popped up around town depicting the crowd wave and asking, "Wave if you love Seahawks' Choice." More publicity for the brand and Millstone ensued when the company made the decision to donate a portion of every Seahawks' Choice purchase to a local charity.

CASE STUDY **Banking on Suns and Diamondbacks**

Breaking all Arizona banking sales records was the cross-promotional campaign labeled "Suns Banking." This was another instance of a company making a positive association with a professional sports team for the benefit of its new brand.

In this marketing joint venture, Bank of America and the NBA Phoenix Suns teamed up to attract new checking account and passbook customers to the bank, which had just entered the Arizona marketplace (see Figure 9.1).

In a substantial newspaper advertising campaign, Suns Banking was introduced statewide, and basketball fans learned that they could have personal checks that carried the Suns' colors and logo. Anyone signing up for the flashy checking account would receive a Phoenix Suns twenty-fifth anniversary videotape. These videos had been created by the team for another purpose but were

(continued)

DON'T LEAVE HOME PLATE WITHOUT THEM.

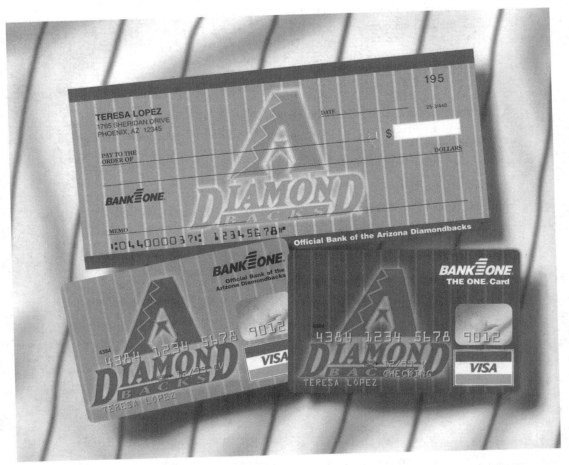

Which is the best way to express your love for the Diamondbacks? (A) Tattoo your back with a picture of Matt Williams.

(B) Get Bank One Diamondbacks Banking — checks, credit card and THE ONE® Card. Plus our nifty limited edition baseball cap.

We suggest trying (B) first. Visit Bank One, the official bank of the Arizona Diamondbacks. Or call **1·888·4·DBACKS.**

To One.

FIGURE 9.1   Product Advertising and Corresponding Collateral Materials That Helped Launch "Diamond Backs" and "Suns"

SIGN UP FOR SUNS BANKING™ NOW, AND IT COULD BE YOUR TICKET TO THE PLAYOFFS

Right now, when you open a Suns Banking checking account at Bank of America, you could win two tickets to a Phoenix Suns' home playoff game. This is your chance to witness the monster slams of Sir Charles and wicked outside shooting of Danny Ainge live at the America West Arena. We'll hold a separate drawing for tickets to each home game, so there's plenty of chances to win!

Only Suns Banking at Bank of America will get you a free custom Suns checkbook cover when you order Suns logo checks, and now the chance to win playoff tickets.

Don't miss your chance to see the Suns in the playoffs. Visit your local branch or call 1–800–THE–BofA to sign up for Suns Banking today.

BANKING ON AMERICA

FIGURE 9.1   Continued

This Saturday only, open a checking account at Bank of America and we'll pay your monthly service charges for one year.

Plus we'll throw in a free order of Phoenix Suns checks. A free Suns checkbook cover. And a free Phoenix Suns 25th Anniversary highlight video. All part of our exclusive Suns Banking package.

So lace up your sneakers and hurry to the nearest Bank of America branch or call 1–800–THE–BofA this Saturday to take advantage of this slam dunk offer.

BANKING ON AMERICA

All branches open Saturday 9am–2pm
Full-service Smitty's branches open 8am–9pm

FIGURE 9.1   Continued

made available to the bank in an exclusive arrangement so that they could use them as a Suns Banking premium. The $19.95 video made a fantastic giveaway and became a strong marketing incentive in the program.

The cross-promotion was supported with English and Spanish collateral materials and strong point-of-purchase visuals in the branches, in multimedia advertising, and of course in the arena where the basketball team played. Several publicity and promotional campaigns on radio also worked to support this integrated communications program. Suns Banking resulted in several reorders of the videotape, an extended advertising campaign, and a sales goal that was shattered like a backboard. A similar campaign was launched in 1998, in the Arizona Diamondbacks debut year as an expansion team of major league baseball, with similarly striking results.

National/International Product Shows.   Many times the campaign objective is not reaching the end consumer but rather convincing third-party "opinion leaders." Such is the case with national and international product shows or exhibits.

The automobile industry is perhaps most visible when it comes to product introductory campaigns. Most major metropolitan cities across America play host to annual car shows, where consumers and journalists alike flock to the glitzy rollouts to see what Detroit intends for the coming year. What the beat writers say about certain makes and models has much to do with that brand's ultimate success in the marketplace.

What the PR manager does to influence the media is largely dependent on his or her planning and program preparation. Are the appropriate trade and consumer media in attendance, and do they have proper news materials to "allow" them to write a favorable story? Are the ranking management executives and/or engineers from the automakers available for interviews? What about preshow visits to the assembly plant, test drives, and access to third-party testimonials?

The point is that much can and should happen before a new car rolls out into the dealer showroom. The same publicity campaign strategies apply to most new product introductions, whether they be medical devices, home appliances, or recreational products. But as Ilyssa Levins reminds publicists, "There are thousands of clever PR tactics that can be employed to publicize your product, but if they don't relate to the brand's marketing strategy, they won't affect the bottom line." Once again, planning and preparation are key.

Event Marketing.   Special events have always been a staple in public relations programming, but only recently have they gained the popularity they now enjoy in marketing circles. Perhaps that has to do with coining the term "event marketing," which has replaced the special event designation and which gives the practice a more serious tone—it's the same thing, only now the marketing department can embrace the concept.

A classic example of event marketing on a national scale was Lever Brothers "Singin' in the Shower" events that took place in thirty cities one summer. Designed to bring awareness to all of

(continued)

Lever's soap brands as well as their corporate name, not-so-shy contestants actually took showers in public places—like New York's Grand Central Terminal—while singing their original songs, which of course included the Lever soap names. Between the involvement of demographically correct radio stations in each market, corresponding point-of-purchase displays in 12,000 supermarkets (the sales force was involved in the promotional concept six months in advance), and lots of broad, national exposure surrounding the "Singing' in the Shower" finals at Hollywood's Universal Studios, Lever Brothers was more than just a little bit pleased. There were on-site drawings to send two people from each city to the Hollywood finale.

"We got millions of impressions just from the people stopping at these events. This raised awareness for all brands: Dove, Shield, Lifeboy, and Lux," boasts Tony Rigione, senior promotion development manager for the company.

Was this just a lucky hunch that worked, something that only comes along once in a great while? Not likely. Even though there were lots of creativity and hard work that went into producing this successful grassroots event, it utilized the basic principles so necessary for event marketing of a product: advance planning, involvement of the sales force, solid media support on the local level, concept originality, involvement of joint-venture partners, advertising support and tie-in, terrific media appeal (good TV visuals), in-store coordination with strong point-of-purchase displays, and of course extensive public relations support. These principles can and should apply in any special event that has as its objective product sales.

Infomercials.   Nowhere is the objective of selling more pronounced than with one of the newest marketing/communications approaches: infomercials. These two-minute "spots" to half-hour television "programs" are a combination of traditional advertising and talk-show promotion that brings a persuasive message to the viewer.

The appeal and effectiveness of infomercials resulted in a multibillion-dollar industry. More significantly, the medium helps advertising and public relations professionals in ways never before imagined. The National Infomercial Marketing Association had projected that, by 1995, this medium would help generate sales of $1.8 billion. The industry exceeded that projection and, after two name changes, is now the Electronic Retailing Association, serving the worldwide interests of infomercial marketers, TV shopping companies, multimedia marketing, and short-form direct-response marketers. The Washington, D.C.-based trade association reports its total retail sales in 1999 at $2.56 trillion, with electronic retailing sales equaling $75 billion and infomercials and TV shopping weighing in at $8.6 billion.

In most cases, the infomercial is meant to sell a product or service—either immediately through direct response or later when the consumer sees the product on the store shelf or needs the service and makes the connection with what was learned from these long-running commercials. However, savvy public relations people are also beginning to use the infomercial format as a means of bringing their news or feature stories to life. It could be the introduction of a new product via demonstration or the positioning of an issue or political candidate through meaningful questions and answers, but in either case, the lengthier format provides the time necessary to inform and persuade, as their Web site counterparts are doing.

As with every other communications program or strategy that might be utilized, infomercials and a Web presence must be integrated into the marketing campaign and supported by the more traditional advertising and PR campaign programs. Like spokes in a wheel, each communications channel combines to bring strength and continuity to the forward progress of the marketing campaign.

Benchmarking.   Finally we come to the issue of benchmarking. As is always the case, evaluation through objective measurement is a critical factor in substantiating any marketing effort. Where did one begin, and how much ground was covered through the campaign process? Were the goals accomplished? Based on what criteria?

Benchmarking is a term for the practice of research and evaluation. Webster's dictionary defines benchmark as "a point of reference from which measurements may be made; something that serves as a standard by which others may be measured." Clearly the term is important and relevant to the communications planning process.

According to Robert C. Camp of Xerox, the company that is generally credited with bringing benchmarking to business, there are five generic phases of the benchmarking process: planning, analysis, integration, action, and maturity (see Figure 9.2). Each of these steps is intended to help the campaign manager bring clarity, direction, and measurement to a campaign.

Benchmarking

Planning	1. Identify what is to be benchmarked 2. Identify comparative companies 3. Determine data collection method and collect data
Analysis	4. Determine current performance gap 5. Project future performance level
Integration	6. Communicate benchmark findings and gain acceptance 7. Establish functional goals
Action	8. Develop action plans 9. Implement specifications and monitor process 10. Recalibrate benchmarks
Maturity	• Leadership position attained • Practices fully integrated into processes

Source: Robert C. Camp. *Benchmarking: The Search for Industry Best Practices that Lead to Superior Performance.* Milwaukee, WI: Quality Press, 1994.

FIGURE 9.2   How Xerox Benchmarks: 10 Steps to Measuring Campaign Success

"Build evaluations into everything you do," says Nancy Goldberg, associate director of the Center for Corporate Community Relations at Boston College. "Know your program, its strengths and weaknesses. Know the companies you compare yourself to and be clear about why you've selected them. Know what you're looking for and what makes them the best."

There are four distinct applications of benchmarking—internal, competitive, noncompetitive, and generic—and each gives the public relations professional an opportunity to assess a campaign using several different measuring sticks. For example, internal benchmarking would draw comparisons only with other similar communications processes within a company, while the competitive application would measure one industry campaign against that of a similar competitor. Clearly this benchmarking application brings the issue of relativity into the evaluation process.

Xerox CEO David Kearns summarizes benchmarking best: "It is the continuous process of measuring products, services, and practices against the toughest competitors or those companies recognized as industry leaders." It is in Kearns's final category, that of communications practices, where benchmarking will become a valuable tool for the campaign manager into the twenty-first century.

Summary

While public relations purists will express some disdain about the prospect of being lumped into the broader marketing category, there are certain advantages to being invited to the party. There is the issue of professional respectability, the opportunity for larger program budgets, and the chance to become involved in more meaningful corporate assignments, which can translate into visibility, growth, and reward.

Beyond gains for the person or the profession, there is a more important reason for public relations and marketing to come together: the benefit of the client or company they serve. It is to create the synergy that has been discussed throughout this chapter by integrating the various campaign planning and implementation processes.

"Marketing needs public relations to interpret the world beyond demographics and psychographics . . . to help it understand internal as well as external audiences and how to deal with society's gatekeepers as well as shopkeepers," state Ehling, White, and Grunig, all public relations advocates. "Public relations should play a vital role in determining not only what companies say but also what they do. . . . Public relations possesses a priceless ingredient essential in any effective marketing program today—its ability to lend credibility to the product message."

Are public relations professionals ready to assume this important role alongside their marketing partners, thereby taking their place in corporate boardrooms across America? The answer is an individual one, and for those who answer in the affirmative, the future is quite promising.

QUESTIONS

1. What is MPR, and how does its focus differ from the more mainstream practice of public relations?

2. What are some of the reasons that public relations has gained in stature and importance within the marketing arena?

3. Cite two or three instances in which PR can play a more effective role in product marketing than its counterpart, advertising.

4. What are some of the marketing advantages derived from cross-brand promotion?

5. Define benchmarking and explain its value to the public relations process.

READINGS

Kate Fitzgerald. "NBA Stars Go to Walls for Dutch Boy Paint." *Advertising Age* (April 19, 1993): 33.

"Foreign Ads Go Farther with Public Relations." *International Advertiser.* 13 (December 1986): 30–31.

Deborah Hauss. "Let's Do Launch." *PR Week* (January 25, 1999): 16–17.

Carole M. Howard and Wilma Mathews. "Global Marketing: Stop, Look and Listen." *Public Relations Quarterly* 31, no. 1 (1986): 10–11.

Marcia Katz and Ken Rabin. "Prescription for New Product Introductions." *Public Relations Quarterly* 38, no. 1 (1993): 12–14.

Ray Serafin. "Saturn recall a plus—for Saturn." *Advertising Age.* (August 16, 1993): 4.

Heather Schoeny. "Koala Springs International's Product Recall." *Public Relations Quarterly* 36, no. 4 (1992): 25–26.

Susan Schaefer Vandervoort. "Public Relations, Store Tie-Ins Launch 'Green' Cosmetics Line." *Public Relations Journal* 47, no. 4 (1991): 24–26.

Robert C. Weaver. "Ten Basics of Industrial Product Publicity." *Public Relations Quarterly* 36, no. 1 (1991): 39.

DEFINITIONS

cross-brand promotion: A sales promotion involving two or more product brands that borrows from both the consumer goodwill for these products and their combined marketing resources through creative and unusual marketing tactics.

marketing public relations (MPR): A specialized practice of public relations that concentrates its programming focus exclusively on the customer and potential customer audiences. MPR professionals, though perhaps once part of the corporate or public affairs department, are now reporting to the head of marketing and are supporting sales objectives.

10 The Issues Campaign

Managing Molehills Before They Become Mountains

CHAPTER OBJECTIVES

When you have completed this chapter, you should be able to:

- Know what is meant by issues management
- Identify the life cycle of an issue
- Apply concepts in a case study problem
- Understand how activist groups help shape an issue

An issues campaign is like none other in the practice of public relations. The approach, strategies, and techniques used in managing such campaigns are founded in the best combination of offensive and defensive communications tactics, which is to say, PR strategists or "issues managers" (as they are commonly referred to) must show themselves to be well-rounded players who can play both offense and defense.

Sports metaphors aside, issues management is very much about competition; conflict almost seems inherent. After all, there are at least two sides to any issue, and seldom do they ever come together in agreement. The playing field can be the hometown zoning board or the floor of the United Nations, yet almost always the spectators—the public and their opinions—deliver the final verdict on any given issue.

Often it is the issues manager who decides how and where the contest will be waged, who will participate, and what the game plan will be. Issues managers can and should attempt to control the tempo of the contest, if not the score itself. It is an opportunity, if not the responsibility, of the issues manager to be squarely involved in the public discussion.

It has long been argued whether an issue can actually be managed. Senior counselor and campaign strategist Patrick Jackson prefers to describe the process as "issues anticipation." Semantics aside, this lofty public relations responsibility sets out to manipulate, if not set, public policy and law. It is from that eventual outcome that people are asked to conduct their lives.

One of the more meaningful definitions of this evolving public relations function is put forth by Brad Hainsworth and Max Meng in their comprehensive study of a corporate approach to issues management practices. It states: "Issues management, then, can be best understood as an action-oriented management function that seeks to identify potential or emerging issues (legislative, regulatory, political, or social) that may impact the organization, and then mobilizes and coordinates organizational resources to strategically influence the development of those issues. The ultimate goal of issues management should be to shape public policy to the benefit of the organization."

From that definition flow several guidelines from which the serious issues campaign manager may draw. First, identification of an issue as it is emerging is important, and frequently critical. Second, the outcome of an issue can be influenced by the proper amount of carefully planned and well-timed communication strategies. Finally, as with so many public relations functions, management's active involvement in the entire issues management process is absolutely necessary.

Triggering the issues management cycle, according to Laurie Wilson, is accurate information. Without it, the strategist can only guess. "Preceding the identification of an issue and permeating the entire process should be research. Research activity must be an ongoing function, which serves to continually gather general and specific information not only about issues and public opinion but about a number of other situation-specific phenomena including social norms, cultural orientations, governmental and societal structure, and physical and geographical characteristics."

Wilson's assessment suggests that it is an ever-changing environment, and only through ongoing and timely research can the issues manager realistically hope to identify and shape the issues. In practical terms, what may have initially been a citywide issue could, over a period of time, evolve to the extent that only the east side of town may now care. Only research will reveal such shifting attitudes and, more importantly, why the changes are taking place.

Realistically, an issues manager will anticipate potential or emerging issues through the availability of good secondary research. It is not likely, even in large PR agencies or corporations, that ongoing primary research will be available to ferret out every trend or special-interest group activity. Rather, staying current with one's daily and weekly newspapers, various national business magazines (for example, *Time, Newsweek,* or *U.S. News & World Report*), local television newscasts, news/talk radio programs, and in particular relevant trade or industry periodicals will produce an intelligent understanding of current affairs.

Issues Management as a Public Relations Function

In 1977, W. Howard Chase coined the term issue management. Designated as the "new science" of public relations, it consisted of a new and different communications response to those who disapproved of business activities. Some experts now call the science issues management, while others refer to it as issue management, but the objectives are the same: "To introduce and validate a breakthrough in management design and practice in order to manage corporate public policy issues at least as well or better than the traditional management of profit-center operations." The result, according to Chase, will lead to fundamental revisions of costly, inefficient, and divisive practices of traditional hierarchical management.

One of the earliest research projects conducted to determine the definition and key functions of issues management was implemented by Brown. By studying public affairs practitioners and corporate executives, Brown concludes that the functions of issues management must occur continuously and be focused on the task of benefiting the company via management.

Case studies attempting to assess the status of issues management in corporate settings have been conducted throughout the last decade. Post conducted a landmark study by identifying the critical decision of integrating a public affairs perspective into corporate planning and management as a means of the company's adjusting to its external audiences. Surveys were sent to 400 public affairs personnel. The return rate was 40 percent; 75 percent of those respondents said they assist in the issue identification, monitoring, and analysis processes. More importantly, perhaps, is that 64 percent of the respondents said they provide issues information to the strategic planning group, and 61 percent of the respondents review their organization's strategic plans to determine whether they are sensitive to social and political trends.

Fox surveyed ninety corporate public relations practitioners to determine how the professionals perceive issues management. He concludes that the respondents do not see issues management as a separate function of public relations but as one of the job duties typically performed by a practitioner.

Six years after Chase introduced the concept, Ehling and Hesse conducted a telephone survey of 120 public relations practitioners randomly selected from the Public Relations Society of America's directory. The questionnaire asked respondents their awareness of issues management, their exposure to issues management, their perception of issues management as a "new tool," their perception of issues management methodology, and their perception of issues management as an exclusive public relations tool. The researchers found that only 18 percent of those surveyed expressed high awareness of issues management, 40 percent had little awareness, and 42 percent had none; 55 percent had little or no exposure to issues management, and even though the respondents admitted to little awareness, 48 percent said issues management was not a "new tool." Among those who said they were aware of issues management, 85 percent indicated that issues management was not a tool used exclusively by public relations practitioners.

Following the Ehling and Hesse study, Wartick and Rude focused on the question of who should be practicing issues management. The sample was drawn from eight corporate staffs. The subjects were selected based on their approaches and experiences with issues management. The primary issue manager was chosen from each company, depending on that person's contribution to issues management and leadership in the field. Based on the extensive interviews, the researchers conclude: "In some companies, issues management functions as a highly visible, externally oriented, separate and distinguishable corporate activity. In others, issues management functions as a lower-profile, internally oriented, problem-related process within established corporate departments."

Hainsworth and Meng surveyed twenty-five of the largest publicly traded corporations in the United States. The findings suggest a general agreement that issues management "included identifying potential issues, forming strategies to effectively influence those issues, making recommendations to senior management, developing a corporate position on each issue, and monitoring each issue."

The studies mentioned made great strides in issues management research. However, they failed to define the function. Heath and Cousino state that only when there is a consensus on the definition of issues management can an accurate assessment be made regarding how well and comprehensively public relations practitioners are performing issues management.

In 1985, Chase and an associate outlined five steps (see Exhibit 10.1) to identify and manage issues systematically:

1. Issue identification
2. Issue analysis
3. Issue change strategies
4. Issue action programs
5. Evaluation of results

EXHIBIT **10.1**

Issue Management

The five steps of public policy management, as identified by Chase as well as Heath and Cousino are:

1. Issue identification: Recognizing trends that may become specific issues that might help or hinder a business. Identification may be made by, but is not limited to, the chief executive officer (CEO), senior executives, middle management, other employees, key publics, community leaders, or the media.
2. Issue analysis: Prioritizing an issue by using qualitative and quantitative research, utilizing such methods as leadership surveys, media content analysis, public opinion surveys, and legislative trend analysis.
3. Issue change strategies: Management's methods of dealing with change. They may be reactive, adaptive, or proactive. A reactive strategy defines an attempt by the organization to postpone public decisions with tactical maneuvers. An adaptive strategy implies an openness to change and relies on planning as a tool to anticipate change. A proactive strategy attempts to shape the direction of public policy decisions by determining the issue, acting upon it, and timing the change.
4. Issue action programs: Technological (e.g., recycling centers) or social and behavioral (e.g., scholarship fund) programs that are organized and coordinated by public relations management with financial, human, communication, and testing resources.
5. Evaluation of results: Review of the real versus intended program results in written form.

According to Chase, the primary goal or objective of the "issue identification" step is to place initial priorities on emerging issues. Heath and Cousino add four functions required for successful issues management from their exhaustive review of public relations texts:

1. Involvement of public policy experts in strategic business planning and management
2. Issue communication
3. Issue monitoring and analysis
4. Efforts to meet changing standards of corporate social responsibility

They said the four functions are equally important and that any company failing to perform all of them is not engaging in issues management.

When Is an Issue an Issue?

Before further examining the intricate management of issues, it seems prudent to define what an issue is. After all, if you can't see it, how can you deal with it? Or said another way, if the CEO doesn't seem to care, then why should anyone else?

Not quite so simply, an issue may be an issue when someone, nearly anyone, forms an opinion on something or someone and decides to take a stand. Of course we all have opinions about nearly everything in our lives, but it is only when we become vigilant that an issue begins to take shape. That attitude, opinion, or belief, when acted upon, becomes the fuel that sets things into motion. Then, it is only a matter of time.

PRoEthics

Dr. Death

Situation

Dr. Jack Kevorkian, a retired Michigan pathologist, has been called "Dr. Death" by the media because he has a history of assisting with suicides. The William Beaumont Hospital-Royal Oak has been the deposit site for many of the victims.

Response/Approach

At first, the hospital management did nothing, saying that it was simply a receptacle. None of the patients had an affiliation with the hospital. "Patient confidentiality prevented hospital staff from releasing the name of the deceased, but if reporters called with a name, often obtained from Kevorkian's lawyers, they would confirm it." After several bodies had arrived, the PR tactics changed. "We began to talk more publicly about how this was an inappropriate thing.

"Early on in the Kevorkian news cycle, Hospice of Michigan drafted a position statement criticizing his work and advocating pain management, patient comfort, counseling for patients and family members, and other aspects of the hospice program. Administrators and volunteers continue to send letters to editors and write opinion pieces."

Source: Adapted from Sandra A. Svoboda. "Dealing with Dr. Death: The PR Dilemmas Created by Jack Kevorkian." *Public Relations Tactics* (May 1998): 1, 18.

Meng has analyzed the life cycle of the typical issue and has broken the developmental process into five stages. As portrayed in Figure 10.1, these stages are shaped by both duration (or time elapsed) and pressure exerted on an organization by outside agents. As time unfolds and pressure increases, a given situation will progress through some or all of its life cycle.

Stage 1: Potential Issue.   This stage, according to Meng, consists of a defined phenomenon that has the potential to become an issue of concern to the organization. A trend can be referred to as a potential issue. Ideas prompting potential organizational change can also be referred to as potential issues. These types of ideas have not yet captured public attention, even though some experts or publics may already be aware of them.

Stage 2: Emerging Issue.   At this stage, there is a gradual increase in the level of pressure on the organization to accept the issue. The increase is mainly due to the activities of a public pushing the issue. During this phase, a public continually tries to legitimize the issue and gather support from various influencers and other publics to strengthen public acceptance of the issue.

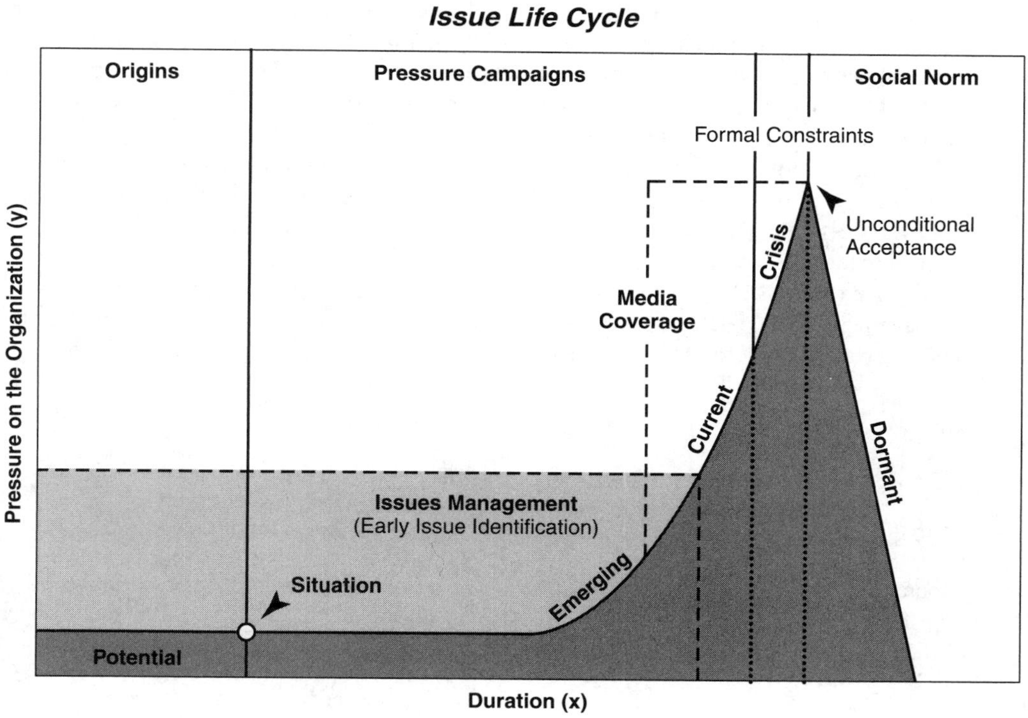

Issue Life Cycle

FIGURE 10.1   Issue Life Cycle

Copyright 1992 March. Reprinted by permission of *Public Relations Journal,* published by the Public Relations Society of America, New York, NY.

Stage 3: Current Issue.   The issue at this stage has matured, displaying its full potential impact upon the organization. A current issue is generally enduring, becomes quite pervasive, and increases in intensity. At this point the public at large, influential individuals, and other publics recognize the importance of the issue and place pressure on governmental bodies and agencies to introduce formal constraints to deter or change the behavior of the organization or industry.

Stage 4: Crisis Issue.   According to Meng, the issue has finally reached a formal institution that has the authority to impose formal constraints in an attempt to resolve it. At this stage, the organization's options have decreased; however, it must set a policy in response to the crisis.

Through formal constraints, the issue is unconditionally imposed upon the organization or industry. Basically, it has no other alternative but to accept the issue by deterring or changing its behavior.

Stage 5: Dormant Issue.   When an issue follows the full course of its life, it eventually reaches the height of pressure required to force the organization to accept it unconditionally. The issue at this point becomes a norm within the organization and in society.

In some cases, suggests Meng, an issue will not reach the height of pressure required to be forced upon the organization. It might never have secured the support required to force action. Some organizations may choose to accept a limited degree of change in their behavior in hopes of appeasing their influencers, or to avoid the issue being imposed upon them through formal constraints. Furthermore, some organizations may choose to try to intervene in the issue's evolution during its early stages to prevent unconditional acceptance.

In these situations, an issue should never be considered settled. The organization may often believe it has stopped the issue's evolution or that the issue is "resolved," but an issue is never "solved" once and for all. At some point in the future, another individual or public may initiate the issue's rebirth.

From Meng's analysis of an issue and its five-stage life cycle, one point is clear: Issues management as a proactive responsibility of the public relations practitioner is neither by choice nor as time permits. It is a mandatory function for most every organization, particu-

---

E X H I B I T 10.2
Identifying Issues

Robert Moore, Ph.D., lists seven different procedures for identifying issues:

1. Designation by the chief executive officer
2. Informal discussions among senior executives
3. Selection by a staff unit for senior management consideration and refinement
4. Structured polling of senior executives
5. Identification by division or profit-center managers
6. Formal exploratory planning beyond the typical limits of corporate strategic planning
7. Scanning by staff volunteers of a wide variety of publications

larly those that hope to control their own destinies. The alternative will be public policy, regulation, and control of one's organization fashioned by persons outside that organization who hold largely opposing agendas.

The watchwords of the serious issues manager are: anticipate, react, plan, negotiate, compromise, execute, manage, analyze, and evaluate; then, in all likelihood, be prepared to repeat them again and again.

CASE STUDY   Philip Morris

Since the advent of television, and the mass awareness and educational opportunities that it has created, any consumer who is literate understands (if not fears) the health dangers of cigarette smoking.

Anyone charged with public relations responsibilities on behalf of the major cigarette manufacturers must live with the ongoing issue of antismoking campaigns by various activist groups and governmental agencies. Opposition is a constant; controversy lingers.

One corporate posture could be to simply ignore the antismoking groups. After all, no amount of dialogue with activists as zealous as these would likely change their opinions about smoking. And to wage a heated public debate about the unproven claims linking cigarette smoking and cancer would be as risky as it would be costly. The best strategy, then, would seem to be to continue employing Washington lobbyists in hopes of stemming the tide against increased regulation of the industry.

That's not how the public relations strategists and issues managers at Philip Morris USA see things. Rather, they prefer to be proactive by demonstrating a responsible corporate stance on this issue—one that acknowledges the obvious concerns that the public has about smoking while maintaining their basic corporate belief that adults deserve the individual right to enjoy cigarettes, if they so choose.

"Tobacco: Helping Youth Say No" is an informational booklet prepared by this cigarette giant and made available free of charge to parents who would like to help their children resist peer pressure to smoke by communicating on the subject. The booklet is presented in full-page, national ads under the seemingly contradictory headline, "Philip Morris Doesn't Want Kids to Smoke."

The body copy in the ads reiterates the company's position that "we don't want children and teenagers to smoke." Further, Philip Morris reminds readers that it has a long-standing commitment to work within the tobacco industry to strengthen the marketing code and state legislation, making it tougher for youth to purchase cigarettes. The company goes so far as to credit itself with "Working with retailers for strict compliance with state laws prohibiting sales of cigarettes to minors."

Within a single but quite volatile product industry, this is a good example of an excellent issues campaign. It seems driven by a strategy to confront the issue head-on with substantive information that smoking opponents are forced to acknowledge as at least reasonable.

The time and money invested by Philip Morris to create the parents' booklet, not to mention the costs associated with a national advertising campaign, can only enhance its responsible smoking stance. In 1999, Philip Morris USA debuted a second national campaign as parts of its Youth Smoking Prevention Program. TV spots feature the Surgeon General Warning and the slogan "Think. Don't Smoke." that encourages teens to deflect peer pressure. This proactive informational approach, coupled with the company's ongoing governmental affairs effort on the state and federal level, is a no-nonsense, multifaceted program by Philip Morris to maintain market share and consumer confidence.

C A S E   S T U D Y   **America West Arena and the ADA**

Another good illustration of issues management in motion is the programming by the management and PR staff of the America West Arena in Phoenix, Arizona. Although not as comprehensive or as far-reaching as the aforementioned case study, this campaign demonstrates how foresight, planning, and the desire to reach consensus helped prevent costly and potentially embarrassing problems later. It also later served as a guide for policies and progress at BankOne Ballpark, home of Major League Baseball's Arizona Diamondbacks.

In the early stages of the design and construction of the America West Arena, the public relations department's issues tracking system revealed a rising trend of concern to the facility—accessibility for the disabled. Communications with the U.S. Justice Department convinced them that the then upcoming Americans with Disabilities Act (ADA) would require the Arena to carefully plan for dealing with this special-interest group.

Several Phoenix city officials reported that local activists in the disabilities community would be looking for a high-profile test case for the ADA and that the Arena would be a likely target. A survey of other NBA teams revealed that no major facility was doing anything about this issue beyond simply complying with current city codes; most had never heard of the ADA. Interviews and meetings with key members of the city's disabilities community revealed that no local sports or entertainment facilities were giving credence to the ADA movement. This solidified Arena management's decision to be at the forefront on this issue.

Objectives for this long-term campaign were:

- To eliminate the potential for lawsuits by making the America West Arena fully accessible both in the physical facility and through policy
- To establish the Arena's reputation among the disabilities community
- To generate mass awareness of the Arena's accessibility

To accomplish these objectives, primary publics were identified as the disabilities community and city officials; a secondary audience would be the general public. The first element of the plan was to establish the America West Arena Operations Committee on Disability Concerns (OCDC). With the assistance of local disabilities assistance groups, the Arena established a nine-member committee of both disabled and able-bodied representatives who had expertise in disabilities and/or Arena operations. The purpose of this committee, as stated in the bylaws written by the members themselves, was to research potential policies on Arena accessibility and make recommendations to Arena management.

The OCDC members spent more than a year researching policies and fine-tuning recommendations for Arena parking, employee training, ticketing, sight lines, and grievance procedures. With very few changes, the Arena accepted and implemented each of these policies. For example, all the food service areas within the Arena installed picture menus for the speech-impaired and braille menus for the blind. Additionally, all counters were constructed at three feet for wheelchair access. An assistive listening device was purchased for the hearing-impaired to use at no charge. TDD lines were installed at several public phone banks and in the Arena ticket office.

In order to let the disabilities community know about the Arena's progressive policies on accessibility, a brochure on Arena access was produced (see Figure 10.2); alternative formats such as large print, braille, and cassette tape were provided. Based on the committee's recommendation, the brochure was distributed through disabilities advocacy organizations, at Arena ticket outlets, and by mail. Additionally, an accessibility hotline was established so that a guest could get answers to questions not addressed in the brochure.

A publicity campaign targeting both the disabilities media and the mass media was planned as well. Editors of publications that target various disabilities were contacted about stories and

FIGURE 10.2   America West Arena BankOne Ballpark Brochures

offered tours of the building. Interviews were scheduled with disabled members of the committee. The primary message was that the Arena is fully accessible and is willing to receive input from members of the community. Mainstream media received the message next, using the same strategy. Whenever possible, disabled members of the committee were used as spokespersons on this issue to establish the Arena's credibility.

Finally, an open house for the disabled was held in conjunction with the Arena's grand opening celebration. The event featured information, tours, entertainment, and refreshments—a casual setting for those with limited mobility to become familiar with the Arena at a nonbusy time. It would

(continued)

also allow them to get information on the Arena's accessible features and see the wheelchair sections for themselves.

As the OCDC became more proficient in anticipating the needs and desires of its constituents, several opportunities arose that the Arena chose to pursue. For example, the Phoenix Suns practice court was offered as a practice and game site for the Samaritan Wheelchair Suns (basketball team) as well as a local wheelchair rugby team. The Arena was also made available at no charge for the annual Disabilities Expo hosted by a local rehabilitation center. Finally, the Arena and Phoenix Suns hosted a "Disabilities Awareness Night" at a basketball game. All these elements served to expose new members of the community to the Arena and its accessibility policies. These proactive steps served to prove to the disabilities community that the Arena's commitment could be trusted.

Despite the Arena's best efforts, some activists in the community continued to criticize the Arena through the media. Because these complaints were based on opinion and not on fact of compliance with the ADA, the Arena was not obligated to respond. However, in the name of good community relations, the Arena hosted a meeting with the complainants to evaluate the perceived problems. As a result, some of the changes were agreed to, based on an overall objective to become an accessibility showcase and to win the long-term approval of this special-interest group. With the exception of certain activists, the community has reacted favorably to the Arena's efforts.

During the first year in the new facility, a survey of 100 disabled Arena guests revealed a superior rating in virtually all areas of operation. Arena management agreed that the OCDC should remain as a standing committee so that future situations involving this special-interest group could be addressed in a timely manner.

CASE STUDY   **Dow Corning**

Now, an example of a not-so-successful issues campaign, or, as a *Public Relations Quarterly* article authored by a group of Michigan State University students was headlined, "A Public Relations Nightmare: Dow Corning Offers Too Little, Too Late."

In this case study, student authors Rumptz, Leland, McFaul, and Solinski and their professor Cornelius B. Pratt tell the sobering story of the Dow Corning Corporation and its mishandling of the national breast implant scare of 1992. It centered around concerns by the Food and Drug Administration that silicon-based implants could be dangerous as they sometimes leaked silicone into the body. Doctors have linked silicone leakage to breast cancer.

Although this episode is about crisis communications and Corning's seeming lack of desire to deal with its publics in an open manner, it also sheds light on its management of the emerging issue.

Breast implants were first introduced by Corning in the early 1960s. An issues management strategy should have been devised at the outset. What might the health risks be? How could ongoing research be used to monitor the eventuality of those risks? Would a product recall ever be necessary, and what of those women who needed leaking implants removed? Most importantly with regard to the company's credibility, how would a finely tuned communications plan bring together the relevant constituents that would no doubt demand answers to their many questions? As Pratt and his students aptly point out, "An informed response to long-range ramifications is a crucial ingredient of issues management."

Rampant public concern of both physicians and their patients, fueled by the media, prompted the FDA in January 1992 to issue a moratorium on silicone breast implants, pending further research and the availability of more compelling evidence on the association between the usage of the implant and auto-immune disease. The problem didn't end there.

By 1995, approximately 170,000 women filed claims that they had become ill due to ruptured implants. At that point, Dow Corning Corporation sought Chapter 11 bankruptcy protection. Three years later, the corporation agreed to a plan that would pay $3.2 billion to claimants from a trust that will operate over the next sixteen years; the agreement allows Dow Corning to exit bankruptcy and places a cap on the damages that can be awarded individually from the trust. Plaintiffs are also allowed to pursue individual claims. Despite the settlement, Dow Corning continues to maintain that its implants do not cause the broad assortment of health problems blamed on them, such as lupus and immune system disorders.

The Issues Management Campaign

The issues management campaign or process is not unlike other, more traditional public relations campaigns. The components are much the same: research, planning, implementation, and evaluation. It is the purpose of an issues campaign that sets it apart. Most PR campaigns are designed with some intent for promotion of a specified product or service. An issues campaign, by its very nature, is more concerned with protection and preservation of an organization's general welfare or standing within its sphere of operation.

As indicated, issues must be identified early on. Once into the "current stage," as Meng defines it, an organization will have lost some control over the outcome of its issue. And, as was the case in the Dow Corning example, unattended issues can quickly progress into the "crisis stage" and rage out of control.

But identifying an issue before it appears on the front page of the newspaper is easier said than done. Are PR professionals really expected to become Dick Tracy–like just so they can stay ahead of zealous special-interest groups? What are the realistic components of such a process, and how do they fit into the framework of a practitioner's typical workweek?

- Read all that is available regarding your organization or industry, particularly from leading industry journals and major metropolitan newspapers. Creating a reading network among colleagues will allow for professional dialogue and the exchange of news stories and commentaries. Internet chat rooms and listservs are also helpful.

- Periodically talk with industry experts or opinion leaders to discuss their views about trends and emerging issues. Most will be willing to share their opinions and, in return, will become supportive allies. These individuals could range from politicians to heads of regulatory agencies.

- Budget for selected local and out-of-town conferences or seminars related to a subject or industry. Attendance will foster the regional or national networking possibilities as well as provide knowledge of the more timely industry trends.

- If possible, hire a lobbyist to monitor public affairs on behalf of your organization. This could pay for itself with the return of valuable industry intelligence.

■ Subscribe to a news clipping service that can provide prerequested subject matter from news stories that air on radio and television or that run in newspapers and magazines.

■ Interface with the leaders of those special-interest groups that affect your industry. For example, if you are employed by a large paper manufacturer, you might target the Sierra Club or the National Audubon Society in order to learn what their concerns really are.

Techniques in Managing the Issues Campaign

Although there is no perfect formula for the management of a given issue, certain techniques or applications stand to reason. Every situation is a bit different. Even the same topical issue may require an altered approach as the environment, and thus the attitude and temperament of those involved, changes. However, there are certain managerial techniques that deserve consideration by the issues manager.

To borrow from that famous Boy Scout motto, "Be prepared!" It is almost impossible to overprepare for the potential issues related to a specific industry. The wise counselor will role-play every conceivable scenario imaginable: For example, an automaker might plan for issues ranging from air bag safety regulations to rising fuel costs; health-care professionals might be thinking about insurance regulations; and hoteliers should consider how the passage of certain state laws could adversely affect room occupancy (witness what Colorado experienced after its state legislature passed a law limiting the scope of gay rights).

No amount of premeditation of the issues will help if the public affairs staff does not have the understanding and support of their management team to deal with those same issues. This support should begin with the CEO and continue through the board or executive committee. It will only happen if the PR staff encourages and coaxes management involvement.

Related to management involvement is an organization's consent that dialogue be established with the media. What are the media's thoughts or concerns regarding your particular industry? Do they understand and trust your company's role on a given issue? If not, the responsibility for providing more access to journalists falls to the issues manager.

Equally important is the promotion of regular public debate. Too often, organizations build barriers to dialogue within their marketplace rather than fostering two-way communication. Speakers bureaus, public forums, newsletters, and neighborhood roundtables are but a few examples of how an organization and its constituents can be linked together.

Not all publics will be friendly, much less fair—especially those special-interest groups that are on the opposite side of an issue. But once again, establishing dialogue is critical for learning of potential issues and curbing them before they become full-blown problems. The best advice here is to simply learn to listen.

When disputes do arise, be willing to settle them quickly and fairly. Long are the lists of people or organizations that have further complicated their lives because they weren't willing to listen, communicate, compromise, and build bridges to fill a void of disagreement or misunderstanding. Sometimes being right isn't enough; being understood or accepted is what will keep the picket signs off your property.

Akin to the goal of building consensus is the need to sometimes involve a third party. These outsiders might be a certain industry expert, media management, or perhaps an individual from elsewhere in your company. This fresh perspective and objectivity might be the difference in arbitrating difficult issues.

Knowledge of both state and federal laws affecting your industry, and the likely issues surrounding it, are central to staying ahead of an issue. As laws change, so does what an organization must do to prepare for a difficult issue. Because it is unrealistic to expect a PR person to also be a full-time public affairs manager, the employment of a paid lobbyist might make sense.

Practitioners must be ready to develop new and positive programming that addresses the inherent conflict of an issue. In other words, dealing with issues cannot be done with smoke and mirrors. Rather, a strategy and corresponding program(s) must demonstrate an organization's position on an issue. The parents'/children's informational booklet from Philip Morris is a good example of targeted, creative programming.

Don't always assume that it is the opponent's position that must change. One's own views, beliefs, or policies may need to be examined and ultimately altered. If that is what it will take to confront and resolve an issue, then so be it. Sometimes issue resolution is best if it comes from within.

Communication Tools Available to the Issues Manager

More than with any other public relations campaign, an issues campaign demands that the communication of key messages be precise and timely. This requirement puts a premium on the communication channels that are available to the campaign leader. Even though every situation calls for its own strategic approach, it is likely that a combination of channels will be used in order to achieve the clarity, frequency, and persuasiveness of a message surrounding an issue.

Without question, the daily newspaper is the channel of most controversy used by opposing sides of an issue. Whether a huge metropolitan daily or an urban, weekly tabloid, this medium has the ability to follow an issue in exacting detail, no matter the length or complexity of debate.

From hard news accounts on page one (or any section of the newspaper) to columnists sharing their personal views to opinion page editorials to wide-ranging commentary in the letters to the editor section, newspapers can and do breathe life into an issue. The question, then, is how the issues manager will utilize these communication channels—these public forums for debate—in order to influence public opinion about an issue important to the organization.

If newspapers provide the unrelenting, detailed coverage of a public issue, then the electronic media can be regarded as a spontaneous and powerful information tool for the issues manager. Radio and particularly television provide timely information on an issue through ongoing spot coverage, sometimes redirecting how an emerging issue unfolds and ultimately where it lays dormant.

An extreme example of how network television both helped create an issue (almost overnight) and then fueled it into heated national controversy is CBS's coverage of the state of Arizona's vote on a 1990 proposition that would have allowed for a Martin Luther King, Jr., civil rights state-paid holiday. When CBS Sports reported the possibility of Arizona's

PRoSpeak
A View from the Newsroom

I'm sitting in a paneled conference room with a notepad on my lap. Next to me are other members of my newspaper's editorial board. Across the polished table sits a group of business or political leaders. The subject could be the federal budget deficit, a corporation's controversial proposal to build a toxic waste facility or an Indian tribe's plan for a gambling casino. Frequently, the meeting is followed by another session with representatives of the other side of the issue.

While our staff members are great people who are kind to children and small animals, these meetings aren't fun for the guests. The purpose is to hear the guest's position, examine the facts and the logic and seek answers to all of the logical questions readers would have. It need not be impolite, but it can be grueling. It can also be embarrassing, as when a freshman congressman complained that our editorial was wrong on a piece of legislation, then demonstrated that he didn't even know the specifics of the bill he supported.

One element that all meetings share in common is timeliness. By the time an issue comes to the editorial board, it either has or is about to erupt as a public issue. Only on rare occasions do we sit down and chat with guests about issues that will bloom years later. A lot of time is devoted to these sessions, considering that the board may field only three or four people on average for such a session. But we're not the reason people come to us; it's our readership, which is in the many hundreds of thousands every day. These readers don't take orders from us, but they do read our pages, and when we say something that makes sense to them, it can have a powerful effect on the views.

These editorial board meetings are part of the routine that experts follow when their objective is to influence public opinion. There are other steps necessary as well, such as hitting the television stations for time on their local interview programs, providing speakers for service club programs, staging community forums, furnishing op-ed commentaries for newspapers, talking to reporters, or visiting electronic media programs. They're all part of the job of influencing public opinion.

Paul Schatt
Associate Editor,
The Arizona Republic

I don't buy the myth of the genius public relations person who can sell the public on anything with slick manipulation; the public, and opponents, usually expose pretenders or those who stray from the truth. But intelligent, skillful public relations practitioners can wield real influence in shaping public opinion, through their thoughtful analysis of the real core issues involved in a client's campaign. They can do their best work simply by calling to the attention of media people the background and the best understanding of the facts. Candor is a great asset, as is command of the facts.

When it comes to an editorial board meeting, facts and information are key; we don't set aside too much time for slide shows or other fancy presentations. We want a principal person involved in the issue to tell us what we ought to know, and answer our questions.

The aim in these editorial board sessions is to find the truth and determine the best policy for our newspaper. The opportunity for the guest is to focus the issues and frame the public debate. In fact, one of the most important opportunities for them is to frame the key questions that should be answered by the decision-makers.

Public affairs professionals know that he who can determine which questions are raised has a strong advantage. The same piece of legislation can be seen as a way to close a loophole that allowed special interests to escape taxes, or as an outrageous tax increase that will hurt millions of hard-working citizens.

Editorial page editors know that their editorials aren't likely to be the key to deciding how the public votes on an issue. But the issues raised in competently written editorials will affect how the public thinks about the issues and, perhaps, the questions people seek to answer before they decide. In that sense, we're in the same sort of business that public affairs professionals are, although with far different roles. The connection isn't always understood by journalists or public relations professionals.

The relations between journalists and public relations professionals sometimes are adversarial; they shouldn't be, any more than they should be adoring. They both have important jobs to do, and their roles are different but not the issue, being fair to various sides of the controversy. The public relations professional must answer all logical questions that arise within his area of responsibility. That is reactive. On the proactive score, what are the points that haven't been raised? What is the alternative story line that should be explored? Is there important background being overlooked or over-simplified by the opposition?

In my view, there's no reason for antagonism, particularly if both sides understand their roles. The editorial board may grill the representative of a company fighting for a controversial rezoning application . . . but it shouldn't ever become a personal argument; it's part of the job for each side. We should respect the public relations professional who does a competent job, regardless of our affection for the point of view being supported.

No public relations practitioner can invent an issue if the facts don't back it up. No public relations practitioner can head off a national debate over a pressing issue that has been thrust into the public mind through a dramatic news event—try to prevent debate over mine safety after a major accident. But a hard-working, intelligent public relations professional can have an impact on public opinion by making the very best case that the facts will support. And that's what the job requires.

---

losing hosting the 1993 Super Bowl (a politically sensitive National Football League might reconsider if the vote failed) on the eve of the statewide election, voters were outraged by the appearance of the threat. Subsequently, as research later revealed, more than 60,000 citizens switched positions and voted against the holiday, stating that they would not be "bullied into a decision" due to political or economic pressures.

If ever there was a case of the media creating and then influencing an issue, this was it. The Arizona/CBS/NFL episode was accidental, but it clearly demonstrates how dominant a medium can be as a communications tool utilized to influence a mass audience.

News talk radio is another extremely important channel for the issues manager, if only because it allows for comprehensive discussion of an issue, and usually with opportunity for immediate response from the listening audience. Radio's call-in format allows for questions and answers, which can facilitate better understanding of an issue. Radio can also provide for both sides to be heard simultaneously, thus decreasing the rampant rhetoric usually found in a heated issues campaign.

Nonmedia channels provide smaller audiences but can make up in targeting and message control what they lack in reach. Everything from newsletters and white paper series to informational brochures and direct-mail campaigns can be regarded as legitimate opportunities to reach, inform, and ultimately influence public(s). Even simplistic approaches as basic as telephoning constituents (although this is usually accomplished through sophisticated phone banks), sending e-mails, or holding neighborhood meetings can provide a means to communicate with a targeted audience.

There is also the larger domain known as issues advertising campaigns. What has heretofore been outlined are those information channels that the issues manager might consider utilizing with traditional publicity tactics. But what of using these same media or channels through paid, controlled-message circumstances? In larger corporations where the stakes are much higher, this is done all the time.

Fortune 500 companies can regularly be seen advertising more than just their products. In full-page advertisements, they push their causes and the positions that may ultimately support their products or services (see Figure 10.3).

Yet, issues advertising has come under fire for the same reason public relations professionals use this approach—its effectiveness. On one side of the argument are the advertisers that tout First Amendment rights in magnifying their voice before tens and hundreds of thousands of readers or listeners. Opponents, however, say no one side of an issue should have unfair advantage to access simply because they can afford it.

Bert R. Briller, manager of creative services at the Television Information Office of the National Association of Broadcasters, puts it this way: "Television networks reject advocacy spots to avoid the so-called deep pockets pitfall. The agenda of public discussion, they feel, should not be set by those who have the greatest financial assets and can therefore afford to pay for commercials."

PRoActive
Politics and Web Campaigns

Among all its other uses, the Internet has made it possible to revolutionize the PR aspect of politics. Although it's far from changing the way campaigns are won and lost, the importance of using the World Wide Web as a political PR tactic is growing.

Some of the most obvious advantages of digital PR are that it allows for a more personal side of campaigning; it's cheaper than radio, television, or direct mail; and more and more people are going online every day.

PR practitioners and politicians alike are starting to see the value in hitting the Web, and they are using it in various ways. For example, Republican Bob Dole mentioned his Web site on many occasions during his 1996 presidential campaign. Jesse "The Mind" Ventura used the Internet to wrestle his way to the governor's office in Minnesota in 1998. His campaign team gathered e-mail addresses at conferences and used them to target possible voters to gain their support. However, using this type of contact can backfire if not done correctly. A mass distribution of mail can annoy many voters who might consider it electronic "junk mail."

Step-by-step on the campaign trail, candidates have also used the Internet to stir the pot and point out issues. For example, Washington State congressional candidate Brian Baird created a Web site called "missedvotes.com" to point out the occasions his opponent missed votes in the state senate. He promoted the site by referring to it in his speeches and literature. Other candidates are simply spending money on banner ads, which advertise their personal campaign sites.

In March, 1999, publisher Steve Forbes, promising a "new information campaign," became the first person to announce his candidacy for President on the Internet via a taped address on his Web site, www.Forbes2000.com. He intends to use his Web site for virtual fireside chats with online voters.

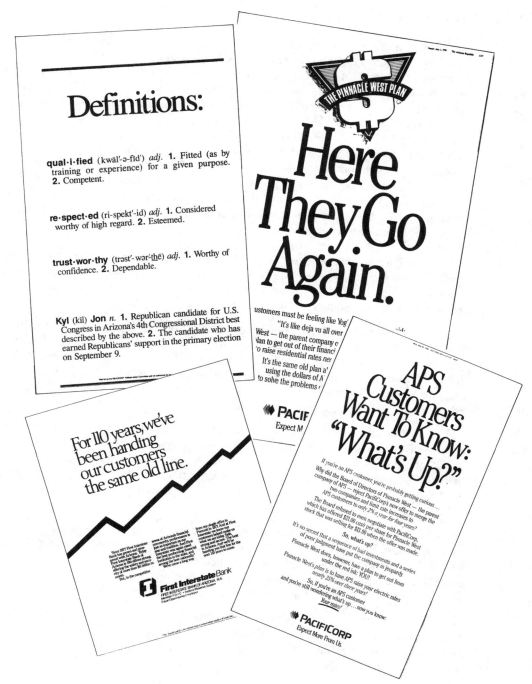

FIGURE 10.3   Issues Advertising Has Grown in Popularity due to Its Effectiveness

Dealing with Activist Groups

In the simplest of terms, an activist can be defined as anyone who feels so strongly about something that they actually attempt to do something about it. That qualifies thousands upon thousands of people in America as consumer activists—which of course makes the issues manager's job even more challenging. It is one thing to keep track of established organizations that represent specific causes (the American Medical Association, the Environmental Protection Agency, or the National Rifle Association), and still another to anticipate what newly formed splinter groups might do on any given day. These "third-party" activist groups, however difficult to sometimes reach or work with, must be considered a more accurate barometer of what the public is thinking. If properly cultivated, these self-appointed opinion leaders will, in fact, point the issues manager to the potential and emerging issues of the day.

Mary Ann Pires, a New York–based counselor specializing in public affairs, lays out a seven-point checklist on how to reach out to activist groups and participate with them in shaping the issues they help create.

1. Learn how to work with activist groups. There is a small body of knowledge developing, and talking to colleagues who have worked with such groups can easily speed the education process. Attending workshops or seminars on this public affairs specialty will also assist serious counselors in doing their homework.

2. Work with a consultant. Unlike more conventional lobbying and public relations activities, success in this field requires relationship building with nontraditional constituencies. Moreover, its objective is public policy support for your organization. Working initially with consultants who specialize in third-party group relations is the best way to get a program under way because they have in-depth knowledge of the territory and have established relationships of trust with these groups.

3. Build the program on your own if you cannot bring external resources to bear. Have a good sense of the universe of third-party groups before you start. Study them; try to match your target groups to your organization, for prospecting purposes, based on a potential mutuality of interest, not just the client's or organization's needs. A bona fide stake for the third parties in your particular issue is the only basis upon which an organization can hope to build support.

4. Be honest. As programs are implemented with outreach to various groups, such traits as found in the Scout Handbook will give most valuable direction. Pires emphasizes that such traits as honesty (about intentions and objectives), modesty (being careful not to over-promise), discretion (in respecting confidences), and respect (for the contact's position, accountability, and available time) are essential in this work.

5. Establish realistic goals. Sensible time frames about the work that is being done are most important. (Think in terms of years, not weeks—you can always be surprised.) At the same time, avoid struggling with senior management about their expectations by identifying interim payouts on the client's or company's investment.

6. Agree on specific agendas. Look for a variety of possible cooperative projects that make sense. Loaning corporate in-kind services (printing, meeting facilities, and access to computers) to a third-party group and sponsoring attendance for one of their leaders at a professional development conference are both examples of services that cost an agency or corporation relatively little but that are extremely valuable to these groups.

7. Consider an outright grant. An unrestricted grant (a cash amount not restricted to specific uses) is the most sorely needed—and most appreciated—thing that can be done for a third-party activist group. This should be considered only if a foundation of trust is present. But understand: As the check is sent, it guarantees nothing. Consumer and public interest groups are not for sale.

Summary

Perhaps the most intriguing assignment any public relations, public affairs, or issues manager will ever face is the reality of an emerging issue that was not entirely anticipated. Even if planned for, it poses the ultimate challenge.

Even though an issue may confront by a surprise attack, it ultimately takes on most of the familiar characteristics outlined in this chapter. After all, no matter what the industry, locale, or timetable, people are much the same everywhere and will react to an organization's behavior or response in much the same predictable way.

All of which is to say, certain principles do, and always will, apply. Treat the so-called enemy as the human beings they are. Try to understand their attitudes, opinions, and values; more importantly, attempt to address them in the programming that is developed. Come to understand the principles of compromise and apply them generously. Finally, realize that once an issue has entered the realm of public domain, it will not and should not go away until it is adequately resolved to the satisfaction of all concerned. In other words, corporate America—even nonprofit America—has a social responsibility to conduct themselves with an acute sensitivity if they expect to benefit from the support of the general marketplace and thrive well into the future.

As issues management scholar Wilson so succinctly states, "No other approach (than social responsibility) will provide the specific societal and cultural understanding to effectively reconcile the public agenda with long-range corporate goals."

QUESTIONS

1. Define issues management and explain the two or three most important components of this public relations function.

2. Name the five stages of an issue, according to Meng, and briefly describe what each stage looks like to the issues manager.

3. Why do some senior counselors suggest that issues management is a misnomer, and that it is not actually possible to perform such a function?

4. How does research play a role in the issues campaign process? What are the shortcomings of such a campaign without the research component?

5. Cite several techniques for managing an issues campaign as outlined in the chapter.

6. Why have issues advertising campaigns come under fire by network television? Is their criticism justified? Why or why not?

7. Explain the difference between an "institutional" and a "third-party" activist group.

READINGS

Bert R. Briller. "The Issue of Issue Ads." *Public Relations Journal* (October 1986): 30–43.

Thomas Ferraro. "Forbes Announces Presidential Bid on New Web Site." Reuters. March 16, 1999. www.foxnews.com

Brad E. Hainsworth. "The Distribution of Advantages and Disadvantages." *Public Relations Review* (Spring 1990): 83–89.

Max Meng. "Issue Life Cycle Has Five Stages." *Public Relations Journal* (March 1992): 23.

Philip Morris USA. "Tobacco: Helping Youth Say No." [booklet]. P.O. Box 41130, Washington, DC 20018.

Mary Ann Pires. "Working with Activist Groups." *Public Relations Journal* (April 1989): 30–32.

Mark T. Rumptz, Robb A. Leland, Sheila A. McFaul, Renee M. Solinski, and Cornelius B. Pratt. "A Public Relations Nightmare: Dow Corning Offers Too Little, Too Late." *Public Relations Quarterly* (Summer 1992): 30–32.

Laurie J. Wilson. "Corporate Issues Management: An International View." *Public Relations Review* (Spring 1990): 40–51.

DEFINITIONS

activist: One or more individuals, or a group of like-thinking individuals, who attempt to influence public policy or political agendas through their active and sometimes aggressive involvement in a particular issue. The power that activists wield is the clout bestowed upon them by a trusting public and sympathetic media.

issue: When someone forms an opinion on something or someone and decides to take a stand.

norm: When an issue follows the full course of its life, it eventually reaches the height of pressure required to force the organization to accept it unconditionally.

trend: A potential issue or idea prompting potential organizational changes.

11 The Information Campaign

Does Smokey Bear Practice Safe Sex?

CHAPTER OBJECTIVES

When you have completed this chapter, you should be able to:

- Know when an information campaign is needed
- Identify key elements
- Apply concepts in successful case studies

This is your brain.
This is your brain on drugs.
Any questions?

If those three sentences convey the image of an egg sizzling in a frying pan, then you already know something about public information campaigns. The popular frying pan spot, developed by the Ad Council and the Partnership for a Drug Free America, is one of the most memorable in the public information genre.

There are, of course, a host of others. Remember:

"Buckle Up for Safety, Buckle Up."
"You Could Learn a Lot from a Dummy."
"Every Litter Bit Hurts."
"Be Smart. Don't Start!"
"You Are What You Eat."
"Safe Sex."
"Take a Bite Out of Crime."

Or the granddaddy of them all:

"Only You Can Prevent Forest Fires."

Those slogans have one thing in common: They're the clever tag lines or core themes of well-known public information campaigns aimed at changing social behavior for the good of humanity, the environment, or the individual.

Does Memorable Work?

Interestingly enough, there is considerable debate in academic and research circles regarding whether being memorable is the same as being effective. Some of the campaigns mentioned above, even Smokey Bear, have earned poor marks from some researchers for placing style over substance. That accusation harkens back to controversial ads introducing the Infinity line of automobiles. The multimillion-dollar campaign was launched with television spots showing beautiful environmental scenes—but no cars. Comedian Jay Leno put it best when he joked that the cars were selling okay, "but sales of rocks and trees have skyrocketed!"

Similarly, is Smokey Bear preventing forest fires, or selling millions of dollars of stuffed animals and licensing logos? Is the frying egg getting kids off drugs or giving them something cool to laugh at while they're stoned? The jury has been out on these questions for decades.

Setting Parameters

Before we evaluate the possible effect of these and other public information campaigns, it is important to define just what a public information campaign is—and should be. A good definition can be found in *Public Communication Campaigns*. Ronald E. Rice and Charles K. Atkin define it this way:

> Most of us have frequently viewed television public service announcements, heard radio spots, seen posters, read magazine ads, conversed with community volunteers, called hot-

lines or received pamphlets about topics such as planning our families, conserving our energy, reducing our alcohol or cigarette consumption, saving our forests and registering to vote. These are some of the elements of public communication campaigns, which are purposive attempts to inform, persuade, or motivate behavior changes in a relatively well-defined and large audience, generally for noncommercial benefits to the individuals and/or society at large, typically within a given time period, by means of organized communication activities involving mass media and often complemented by interpersonal support.

If that's a bit weighty, let's simplify. Public information campaigns are efforts to: (a) get people to stop doing bad things that diminish society (i.e., smoking, drinking, doing drugs, trashing the countryside, and eating high-fat foods), and/or (b) get people to start doing good things (i.e., using seat belts or condoms, eating more fruit and vegetables, and staying in school).

Seems easy enough. Just get the good message out in a positive, interesting manner that leaves an impact, right? Not necessarily. Consider the seat belt campaign of the last three decades.

Buckle Up

Car crashes are, and have been for decades, the leading cause of death among people between the ages of one and thirty-four. We've all heard the comparisons. More people die on America's roads in one year, 60,000, than died in the entire Vietnam War. A big part of the problem was and is drivers' continued aversion to the lifesaving protective straps. Although the government estimates that 55 percent of all deaths, and 65 percent of all auto accident injuries, could have been prevented by seat belts and shoulder straps, adults and children still must be reminded or, in some states, fined before they'll use them.

What we have is a behavioral problem, one so entrenched that it provides the ironic twist of a classic joke. "Why is it," a popular comedian asks, "that people refuse to use seat belts in cars where they can save their lives, yet everyone is forced to use them on airliners, where they don't make any difference at all?"

Why indeed? Over the years, various private and governmental agencies have tried to modify this attitude through an onslaught of laws and public information campaigns. Some have worked, while others have had no effect. E. Scott Geller of Virginia Polytechnic Institute studied the seat belt public service campaigns and determined that some of the most obvious images used to goad the public into buckling up are precisely the ones that fail. Professor Geller says the early scare tactic campaign showing, rather graphically, what happens when you don't use seat belts missed the mark:

> The anxiety elicited by the vivid portrayal of the disfiguring consequence of a vehicle crash can interfere with the viewer's attention and retention, or cause viewers to avoid this unpleasant sight in subsequent TV spots after the first part of the scene is shown. Consequently, many viewers may have missed the end of these spots, which demonstrated the problem's solution [i.e., using safety belts].
>
> Rather than using such fear appeals, communication campaigns to promote safety belt use should adopt the principles of social learning theory . . . and illustrate through

behavioral modeling the comfort and convenience of using a safety belt, or how safety belt users would not be hurt in a crash. The most natural way to depict behavioral modeling of safety belt use on TV is not during a public service announcement, but during actual TV programs and movies. . . . Most of the entertainment shows on TV do not show safety belt use.

What Professor Geller is saying is that if James Bond and Tom Cruise aren't buckling up, no one else will.

In 1984, crash dummies Vince and Larry injected humor into the "buckle up" message with more success than initial campaigns. The "You Could Learn a Lot from a Dummy" proved popular with audiences and aired for more than fifteen years before the campaign matured and was retired in 1999.

Incorporating It into the Story

In a similar light, the producers of the "Freestyle" television program designed distinct public information messages into their stories and plots. The program itself was an overt effort to change mores and attitudes in children regarding such issues as sexism and sex-role stereotyping.

Robert LaRose, a telecommunications professor, was part of the "Freestyle" evaluation team. He describes the PBS program's ambition as "a concerted effort to extend the successful Sesame Street model of purposive television for children to the 'affective domain' of beliefs, attitudes and behavior. The goal of the series was to reduce sex-role stereotyping effects on children's preoccupational activities and perceptions of adult work and family roles."

Crime Dog

One campaign that continues to be well received is canine pal McGruff the Crime Dog. Started in 1979 as a method of alerting people to basic crime prevention tips, the campaign was built around McGruff, a cartoon dog drawn like a 1940s police detective. PR campaign experts Garrett J. O'Keefe and Kathleen Reid explain:

> The 'Take a Bite Out of Crime' campaign was . . . initiated under the sponsorship of the Crime Prevention Coalition, a group of government, private and not-for-profit agencies, with the major media components of the program produced by the Advertising Council. Major objectives included generating a greater sense of individual responsibility among citizens for reducing crime; encouraging citizens to take collective preventive actions, as well as to work more closely with law enforcement agencies; and enhancing crime prevention programs at local, state and national levels.
>
> The Ad Council's volunteer agency for the campaign, Dancer Fitzgerald Sample, designed the media materials around an animated trench-coated dog, McGruff, who called on citizens to help 'take a bite out of crime' by making their homes more secure, by taking more precautions when outdoors, and by working together with their neighbors in neighborhood/block watch programs.
>
> Importantly, the highly publicized national media campaign was supplemented by a full range of locally promoted supplemental activities across the country by law enforcement agencies, community groups and businesses. The first media messages were disseminated via television, radio, newspapers, magazines, billboards, and posters in late 1979.

Hundreds of thousands of supplemental brochures and related materials containing more specific information also were distributed.

Learning from the mistakes made by the "Buckle Up for Safety" campaign, the McGruff effort downplayed the most fearsome aspects of crime and instead emphasized the more positive prevention tactics. Minus the scare tactics, the campaign worked. O'Keefe and Reid found "particularly strong evidence of behavioral change" resulting from the public information effort:

> The campaign-exposed group reported significantly greater activity in nearly all behaviors specifically advocated by the PSAs [public service announcements], with no such changes found for non-advocated behaviors. These findings held when potentially confounding variables (e.g., exposure to other crime-related media stimuli and direct victimization experience) were controlled for.

Not to be overlooked, a major component of the campaign's success was that the public simply took to the appealing McGruff character and remembered what he had to say. In 1991, researchers again attempted to gauge the impact of the National Crime Prevention Council's campaign and found the following:

- Awareness of McGruff reached 88 percent among crime prevention practitioners and 80 percent among the general public.
- Of the respondents, 86 percent said they paid attention to the antiviolence ads.
- Nearly one-third said they learned from the ads, and one-fifth said they acted on what they had learned.

Smoking Smokey

For all their success, the McGruff creators were by no means pioneers in the animal symbol game. One of the most successful, if not the most successful, public information campaigns of all time was developed around another character—Smokey Bear.

Eugene F. McNamara, Troy Kurth, and Donald Hansen offer an interesting history of this character-driven public information campaign:

> This campaign began in 1942 as part of the wartime response to potential wildfires caused by enemy bombing, and to the shortage of firefighter personnel. The newly formed Wartime Advertising Council created a media campaign kit: The first poster's message was 'Careless Matches Aid the Axis (Germany, Italy, Japan)—Prevent Forest Fires.' The idea of using a bear as the symbol of forest fire prevention was conceived by representatives of the Foote, Cone and Belding advertising agency and the Forest Service. The 1944 Smoky Bear poster was produced by Walt Disney; the 1945 poster has Smokey in dungarees and a ranger's hat, pouring water on a campfire, with the message, 'Smokey Says—Care Will Prevent 9 Out of 10 Forest Fires.' The slogan, 'Remember, Only You Can Prevent Forest Fires' was developed by Foote, Cone and Belding in 1947. The symbol of Smokey Bear became so well known that it was legally protected by Congress in 1952, and it provides yearly royalties for the Smokey Bear campaign.
>
> The Ad Council and its supporters continue to work in cooperation with the Forest Service on the Smokey Bear Campaign. During the 1970s, about $50 million was allocated

annually to the Smokey Bear campaign. In 1979 alone, over $1 million worth of materials were produced and distributed, involving mailings to thousands of television and radio stations (representing four billion electronic media impressions), and messages placed for free (estimated at a total commercial value of over $55 million) in thousands of newspapers and magazines, along with numerous billboards.

So we know Smokey's a big winner in the public awareness sweepstakes. And the big bear's an even bigger winner in the endorsement arena. But is Smokey doing the job as hired—stopping forest fires? McNamara, Kurth, and Hansen give a resounding yes. "Acreage lost through wildfires has dropped substantially from the 30 million per year before the program began in 1942 to less than 5 million. Gross cost-benefit figures for the Smokey Bear campaign are encouraging: The estimated resource savings over the first 30 years of the Smokey Bear campaign amount to $17 billion, yet the annual program budget is half a million dollars, not including Ad Council donations." A public awareness survey conducted in 1976 showed a near-universal 98 percent aided-recall awareness of Smokey Bear. The 1990s saw Smokey graduate to his own Web site at www.smokeybear.com where he will no doubt continue to be an effective communications tool.

The trio of researchers credit Smokey as an "engaging and a fairly credible source used consistently as a symbol of the fire prevention concept. The extremely large exposure through multiple media outlets, made possible by the Ad Council's continuing support, has provided far greater coverage for a longer period of time than for any other PSA-based campaign. The original slogan—'Only You Can Prevent Forest Fires'—attempts to involve the audience member personally and especially relevant because of the large percentage of fires caused by humans."

However, all isn't perfect in the forest, even with Smokey on duty. The researchers warn that Smokey's incredible popularity may now be working against the campaign. The creative minds behind this super-successful information campaign can applaud themselves—but they can't succumb to the temptation to ease up.

"As suburbanites expand their residential areas into the countryside, and as more people visit forest areas every year, they bring with them urban habits and minimal knowledge about forest conditions that contribute to the large number of preventable wildfires."

Crying in the Rain of Garbage

While Smokey is, for the most part, an unqualified success, another popular public information campaign—the one that has the single, most memorable image in PSA history—was given mixed reviews by academics from its debut.

Robert B. Cialdini takes us through the "Every Litter Bit Hurts" campaign: "The classic public service announcement against littering begins with a short of a majestic-looking American Indian paddling his canoe up a river that carries the scum and trash of various forms of industrial and individual pollution. After coming ashore near the littered side of a highway, the Indian watches as a bag of garbage is thrown, splattering and spreading along the road, from the window of a passing car. The camera pans up from the refuse at his feet to the Indian's face, where a tear is running down his cheek, and the slogan appears: 'People Start Pollution, People Can Stop It.' According to the Keep America Beautiful organization, this PSA is the single most memorable and effective message ever sent to the American public against litter and pollution; everyone they talk to about littering recalls the ad."

Cialdini concedes the "memorable" part. It's in the critical "effective" area that things start getting sticky. "Despite the fame and recognition value of this spot, it may contain aspects that may be less than optimal and perhaps even counterproductive in their impact upon viewers' littering behavior. In addition to the laudable (and conceivably effective) recommendation in the ad urging viewers to stop littering, there is an underlying theme, as well, that a lot of people do litter: Debris floats on the river and lies at the roadside, trash is tossed from automobiles, and we are told that 'people start pollution.' . . . In the process of communicating that littering is contrary to prescriptive norms, then, the PSA also may have communicated the undercutting message that littering is consistent with popular norms."

What Cialdini's referring to is the "movie theater syndrome." People tend to litter in areas that are already trashed, adding their own signature to a previously existing mess. This is why, much to movie theater owners' endless chagrin, people feel culturally comfortable with dropping their greasy popcorn, gooey Milk Duds, and sticky soft drinks on movie theater floors when they wouldn't dare exhibit the same antisocial behavior at the local opera house or symphony.

Similarly, a park that is kept sparkling clean moves people to find the trash bins, while a park where the maintenance is less diligent merely encourages more trash. Therefore, researchers say the classic Native American crying PSA would have been even more effective if the passing car had dumped the garbage into a clean environment.

"Our data suggest that even classic PSAs may contain unintended elements that could undermine optimal effectiveness, and formative research should be conducted before expensive PSA production to detect and help eliminate such unfavorable elements," according to Cialdini.

In fact, the Ad Council assesses this impact by measuring response to the ads before and after their release. Front-end research, such as copy testing and focus groups, is conducted by the volunteer advertising agency before creating the campaign. In addition to the tabulation of 800-number calls and anecdotal data to gauge effectiveness, as of 1999, the Council has increased research assistance and funding to uncover more precise information about the effects of its messages. What can be said is that "PSAs are an effective means of communication and education. Even if the message is used alone or is unwelcome and intrusive, the PSAs increase awareness, reinforce positive beliefs, intensify personal concern and move people to action," according to statements on its Web site, www.adcouncil.org/body_research_impact.html. The Council points out that the longer its ads run, the greater effect they have on the audience.

Staying Alive

Public health issues are common ground for public information campaigns for obvious reasons. Year after year, six to eight leading causes of death on the Surgeon General's annual hit list are caused by preventable behavioral problems. Most of these are the downside of smoking, drinking, and bad diets.

Such behavior-caused societal problems, in turn, produce fertile ground for public information campaigns aimed at changing the way people act. Tens of millions of dollars have been funneled into efforts to gently persuade the public to: eat better foods to avoid cardiovascular disease; stop smoking in order to dodge a growing list of savage cancers; use condoms or practice abstinence to combat AIDS; and avoid alcohol when driving.

These campaigns, for the most part, have been successful in getting at least some people to change their behavior and live longer, healthier lives. Researchers have found that death rates and astronomical medical expenses associated with the specific behavioral-caused diseases have decreased by varying degrees following aggressive public information campaigns.

Sadly, however, a still startling number of people simply ignore the campaigns and cling to their deadly, addictive vices. This is not so much a failure of the public information campaign as it is the impossible task of overcoming entrenched habits and other psychological factors. In these cases, it's doubtful that cuddly bears, tearful Native Americans, Bogie-like crime dogs, catchy slogans, or anything else could stop someone from, say, puffing on a cigarette. If increasingly alarming warnings printed on cigarette packages and the smokers' own hacking coughs and wrinkled faces haven't done the trick, a clever public information campaign certainly won't.

Safe Sex

The AIDS awareness campaign, another effort aimed at changing hazardous but well-entrenched behavior, has come under particular scrutiny. This is partly because of its plague-like consequences, and partly because of its politically charged history. The scrutiny, in turn, provides us with numerous studies to judge the campaign's high and low points.

"A key lesson from medical history is that preventing disease is usually less costly and more effective than treating and curing disease," says researcher Kathleen K. Reardon in one such study:

> However, as with forest fire prevention or environmental protection, most people are hesitant to commit their time, resources and energy to crises that seem remote. With regard to health, this attitude has always been problematic. However, current high rates of drug abuse, adolescent pregnancy, alcoholism, and the threat of AIDS render such complacency a serious threat to the well-being of individuals and society.
>
> Persuasion theory and research have much to offer a journey into the jungle of diseases for which cure is an insufficient or unachieved answer. For example, consider campaigns to combat alcoholism. What works with one age group does not necessarily work with another. . . . The case of AIDS is similar in this regard. There is no single underlying cause for the continued spread of AIDS. Hence there is no single means of prevention. Alcoholism and AIDS require multimethod and multichannel interventions guided by prior theory and research in a variety of disciplines, of which communication is an important one. With AIDS, there is an even greater urgency to discover factors that produce high-risk behavior. After all, there is no cure for AIDS at this time; there is only prevention. The answer lies in the development of persuasive interventions for use via both mass media and interpersonal communications channels.

Reardon determined that it's critical to educate children about AIDS as early as possible because children traditionally have little concern for health matters. "Nothing jeopardizes or undermines attempts to prevent adolescent AIDS more than the absence of a sense of responsibility for one's own health. It is difficult for youngsters suddenly to become concerned about their health at the age of 14 or 15. Concern for health must start at a much earlier age." In particular, this early concern must be based on a set of health values derived from parents and teachers. "Research indicates that peer groups are [also] valuable resources in health interventions, especially when the focus is on teenage sexual and contraceptive behaviors, smoking and alcohol use."

This finding was not lost on the creators of a tobacco prevention campaign aimed at youth. In 1995, the Arizona Department of Health Services awarded a media contract to Phoenix-based Riester Corporation to develop public relations, advertising, and marketing campaigns aimed at adolescents and pregnant women, with emphasis on both general and Hispanic audiences. The campaign execution focused on peers using the slogan as their self-expressed attitude towards tobacco. The adolescent campaign slogan "Tobacco. Tumor Causing, Teeth Staining, Smelly, Puking Habit" generated national and international interest, with more than thirty-five states and the health ministry of Japan requesting information.

After conducting initial research with sixty youths ages eight to seventeen, preadolescents and teens were interviewed and observed in focus groups and in one-on-one sessions. The communication team learned some important lessons from doing their homework. The messages should:

- Be delivered by peers
- Contain intense graphic scenes, humor, and grossness
- Use a situational approach, not lectures, that demonstrate changing social norms
- Affect them now, not years from now, i.e., social acceptance, sports achievement

Clearly, the underlying theme was that to be successful, Riester had to create messages that appealed to kids, not adults. The paid media campaign used sixty-second and thirty-second television ads in both English and Spanish placed during appropriate shows with youth appeal—"Beverly Hills 90210," "Friends," "MTV Top 20," "Home Improvement," and "The Simpsons." Radio buys were used in Arizona as well. Collateral materials included temporary tattoos, posters, shoe stickers, and 40,000 bookmarks, which were the product of a youth art contest sponsored by the campaign, distributed through local libraries. According to Behavior Research Associates, 76 percent of Arizonans polled were aware of the campaign and "families with children between the ages of seven and seventeen are most likely to be impressed with the potential efficacy"—a promising indicator of a potential national response.

Aside from education and peer pressure, Reardon says a youth's concept of "monkey see, monkey do" is another major factor. "To the extent that parents and teachers are not lenient in their own health standards, children are likely to set high standards for themselves. To the extent that mass media avoid celebrating health risks, children are likely to avoid celebrating them."

Columbia University research scientists Eleanor Singer and Theresa Rogers joined New York/New Jersey Port Authority statistician Marc Glassman in authoring an AIDS study published in *Public Opinion Quarterly* that put the government under the microscope. The study, not surprisingly, was critical of the government's public information AIDS campaign of the late 1980s:

> The centerpiece of this multimillion dollar campaign, designed by the advertising agency Ogilvy and Mather, was the eight-page brochure, 'Understanding AIDS,' from Surgeon General C. Everett Koop. The brochure was mailed to every household in the country in late May and early June of 1988. The campaign also included radio and television spots and public service announcements aimed at specific subgroups (teenagers, sexually active adults, women at high risk of infections). The pamphlet emphasized the behaviors that put one at risk of contracting AIDS.

The researchers found that the old horse/water adage applies to government brochures. To twist the cliché, you can send the public a brochure, but you can't make them read it. Studying the response to the brochure, along with other government efforts to educate the public about AIDS, particularly efforts to warn young people, singles, nonwhites, or the less well educated, the trio concluded: "We argue that the effects of the campaign on public information were minimal. However, between 1987 and 1988 there was a small but statistically significant increase in reported condom sales. . . . In addition, there was a substantial increase in the number of people expressing concern about AIDS as an epidemic for the population at large. The campaign may well have contributed to both of these changes."

However, the reason cited for the government's overall failure, and the accompanying waste of taxpayers' money, is the same one AIDS activists screamed about at the time. The researchers charge that the government was simply too slow to react to the crisis. By the time it instituted the campaign, the news media had already given substantial attention to the dis-

PRoEthics
LAPD and PR

Situation
The Los Angeles Police Department received a large amount of negative publicity following the Rodney King and O. J. Simpson trials. "Once regarded as the 'Rolls Royce' of law enforcement agencies, the LAPD quickly became identified with wide-spread ineptitude, brutality, racism and sexism."

Response/Approach
An awareness campaign was launched using billboards and city buses. Follow-up research showed that the campaign "generated more positive awareness than any media effort since the department's inception.

"Before creating an effective communications program, the leaders of an organization have to know what it is about themselves that they want to communicate. Building a consensus within a law enforcement agency is especially daunting, for—unlike a public organization—it is largely dependent on the relationship it maintains with elected politicians."

Source: Adapted from Alison Stateman. "LAPD Blues: 'We're Cops. We're Not PR People.'" *Public Relations Tactics* (April 1997): 1, 18, 27.

ease and repeatedly presented the same information that the government would later spend millions to disseminate.

"Had the government campaign been launched earlier, at a time of sparser coverage, its impact might have been more noticeable. Coming when it did, it's incremental effects appear to have negligible, at least so far as changes in knowledge are concerned," the researchers concluded.

Census 2000

It appears the government is trying to get it right this time around with its Census 2000 plan. The plan will establish partnerships with state, local, and tribal governments; private industry; community organizations; businesses; and the media to increase awareness and response rates, especially among the undercounted populations—renters, those who speak different languages, cohabiting couples, migrants, and the homeless.

In 1990, the census used public service announcements to raise awareness; however, researchers found that since the FCC no longer required stations to air them, few people heard them. The Census Bureau hired a private contractor to place paid advertising for Census 2000—a first—to complement its direct mail, celebrity endorsements, and assistance from local officials. Add national media partnerships, using every available medium and language, to the mix and the chances improve that the traditional undercount will shrink.

What's new for Census 2000? A government Web site offering a host of information at www.census.gov with hyperlinks highlighted; the U.S. Postal Service will provide address information; a marketing plan will be implemented by professionals; marketing experts created a new user-friendly questionnaire that is faster and easier to complete; digital capture of forms allows the Bureau to scan responses directly into computers that can read handwriting; and software will give people more ways to respond, for example, at public places and over the telephone.

Corporate-Sponsored Information Campaigns

Many private businesses and corporations have incorporated public information campaigns into their PR or advertising budgets. These generally come in the form of information-heavy advertisements, along with educational materials, provided to schools and community groups. Unfortunately, these companies tend to follow the lemming theory of too many jumping on the same bandwagon. For example, Amtrak, Budweiser, Coca-Cola, Kraft, American Airlines, Miller Brewing Company, Burger King, and McDonald's all have extensive campaigns to connect their company to Black History month.

Although it may be a study in jumping on the bandwagon, how each company went about aligning itself with Black History month in 1990 to 1991 is worth a mention. Amtrak bought ads profiling prominent black inventor Garret A. Morgan, the man who gave us the traffic signal. Budweiser produced posters of "The Great Kings & Queens of Africa." Tenkamenin, King of Ghana from 1037 to 1075, was featured in the 1990s.

Coke employed the image of Martin Luther King, Jr., in its "Share the Dream Scholarship Sweepstakes." The contest offered $25,000 and $10,000 college scholarships to black students. Kraft focused on African American cooking in ads offering a free African American cook booklet. American Airlines purchased print ads honoring modern black leaders, including athletes, business leaders, and politicians.

Miller combined minority recruitment with a public information campaign when it offered calendars to minorities sending in resumés. The arty calendars honored black authors and filmmakers. The calendars have subsequently become collectors items.

Burger King saluted the black children who pushed the integration issue in Topeka, Kansas, in 1951. This is the case that eventually led to the landmark *Brown vs. Board of Education* lawsuit that moved the Supreme Court to strike down the previously used "separate but equal" laws. McDonald's countered with an "African-American Heritage Series" audiotape containing narrations by prominent black Americans telling the stories of famous black pioneers.

In a similar fashion, J. C. Penney, the department store giant, chose to center its efforts around Hispanics. J. C. Penney stages events and contests, usually involving fashion and design, around Hispanic Heritage Month (September 15–October 15), Three Kings Day (January 6), Cinco de Mayo (May 5), Puerto Rican Day (various dates in June), and Dies y Seis Day (September 16).

Why You Need Us

Some information campaigns, especially those centered around the introduction of a new product, are far less altruistic. While most of the budget is spent on basic product advertising, occasionally corporate decision makers seek to educate the public on humanity's need for their product. A classic example was Miller's introduction of Lite Beer, an innovation that shook up the brewing industry. While the bulk of the effort was put into the "Great Taste, Less Filling" theme, there was a notable effort spent to educate the public on what exactly "lite" or low-calorie, beer was, along with its potential health benefits when compared to calorie-laden regular beers.

In addition, products tied to new technology sometimes need more than just an advertising campaign to get them going. The cable television industry, for one, relied on public information campaigns to explain its business. From the beginning, the cable companies had to overcome several consumer questions. Mainly, why should anybody pay for television? And why should homes and cities be wired with hundreds of miles of unsightly, old-fashioned cables? Wasn't this technically regressive?

Despite these initial hurdles, not to mention staggering start-up costs and the almost inconceivable labor involved in wiring individual houses and apartments all across the country, the cable companies were indeed able to convince a majority of Americans to throw away the rabbit ears and rooftop antennas, and say good-bye to free TV, in order to say hello to MTV.

The individual cable channels, of course, also did their part to change the public's attitudes about television. "I want my MTV," the clever slogan of the aforementioned, cable-only music video channel, had people, especially young people, calling the cable companies demanding to get wired.

Cable companies are currently upgrading and rewiring their systems with fiber optics to enable telephone service, instant Internet access, and a range of custom options that will serve their customers well into the twenty-first century.

Stretching the Point

Sometimes when a private enterprise decides to take on an information campaign to benefit its product, the methods can be rather quizzical. The Evian bottled water company's campaign to educate the public on the value of water falls squarely into this category.

Evian's glossy, pull-out ads tell you everything you ever wanted to know about water in general, particularly how vital it is to the human body. The message strategy includes such topics as "More important than food," "You are water," "Good hydration promotes good performance," "We're like cars: water is our coolant," "Water is your body's lubricant for every pump, valve and filter," "The human body is a real drain," "Water: flight insurance," "The more you exercise, the more you should drink," and "Drink in cold weather as well as hot."

It's only at the end of the ad that the company gets to the point and mentions why its particular product, originating in the mountains of France, is the best water around. While the information in the Evian ads and handouts is fascinating, the general-to-specific twist at the end is a bit of a leap.

Existing Product Safety

Another example of a company needing to go beyond advertising is when it's hit with a health or safety problem directly or indirectly related to its product. The pharmaceutical industry in general, and Tylenol in particular, was faced with this after someone purchased bottles of the popular pain reliever, replaced the medicine in the capsules with a poison, and returned the deadly bottles to store shelves to be repurchased. After seven deaths, Johnson & Johnson, the makers of Tylenol, and other companies not only had to scramble to repackage their products in sealed containers but had to explain to the public what they were doing, and warn them not to purchase any bottle with a broken seal.

Similarly, the Genie garage door opener company has for years mounted a strong campaign to educate the public on the danger of automatic doors crushing small children and pets. This effort comes despite the fact that all garage doors made after 1973 contain, by law, a safety feature that forces them to reverse their course when hitting a solid object. Genie wasn't satisfied with just including the reverse movement feature. The company wanted to remind homeowners to frequently test the doors to make sure they're functioning properly, and to warn that most garage door openers made before 1973 remain a hazard. Genie also wanted to discourage parents from allowing their children to play "beat the door," a dangerous game in which a child pushes the wall-mounted button, then races out of the garage and dives under the closing panel.

After several deaths and injuries due to the improper use of child car seats in early 1999, President Clinton announced new federal rules to make car seats safer and protect "our smallest and most vulnerable passengers." The measure was aimed at helping parents and caregivers avoid the confusion that results when using seats or cars of different makes and models. During his weekly radio address, Clinton cited government estimates that more than 70 percent of children who ride in car seats are at risk of injury because their seats are improperly installed. The rule establishes a single standardized system to anchor child safety seats in new cars and trucks by January 2000.

Political Issue Campaigns

Political campaigns are, of course, special cases. PR's founding fathers quickly learned that the same, long-term methods used to introduce a candidate to the public and persuade them to cast their vote his or her way could also be applied to selling commercial products or persuading people to alter their behavior.

Interestingly enough, the political campaign fathered a public information offspring that circled around and ended up right back smack in the political arena. These are the issue campaigns and referendums that have been increasingly showing up on ballots around the nation. California, in particular, has inundated voters with referendums, covering everything from term limits and affirmative action to official English and environmental issues. Without a charismatic candidate to rally around, supporters of various political issues have had to rely on the tried-and-true methods of public information campaigns to get their points across.

Counterattacks

Sometimes a company, industry, or group has no choice but to wage a public information campaign to counter someone else's efforts undermining its product or image. The lumber industry has been forced to battle the environmentalists, various agricultural groups have had to fight back against alarmist campaigns regarding pesticide uses, and the high-profile automotive industry appears to be constantly having to ward off attacks on everything from pollution to safety issues.

In the mid-1990s, the pharmaceutical industry was put back on the hot seat. It came under heavy fire from the Clinton administration for alleged price gouging. The attacks, often emanating directly from the lips of health care–conscious President Bill Clinton and his influential First Lady, had the billion-dollar industry on the ropes. The targeted company's initial tactic of ignoring the charges and hoping that the issue would just blow away is now universally viewed as shortsighted.

"The high price of drugs and the unusually high profit margins of pharmaceutical companies have made drug makers a frequent media scapegoat," summarizes Julie C. Wang, CEO of Wang Associates Health Communications in New York. "To make matters worse, Dr. David A. Kessler, the aggressive head of the Food and Drug Administration [FDA], is on a crusade. . . . The result is that many consumers believe the pharmaceutical companies are getting what they deserve. . . . It's time for public relations experts to speak out."

In an article written for *Public Relations Journal,* Wang anonymously quotes a high-level drug company PR person as admitting that, not unlike the government's own slow response to the AIDS crisis, his industry was far too tortoise-like in responding to the hammering it took from the White House.

"For years, drug companies believed they were beyond reproach and that, because they helped save lives, the way they conducted business was nobody's business but their own," the PR practitioner admitted.

Wang observes that such arrogance finally came home to roost. "This silence, construed as guilt by the average consumer, is compounded by the appearance of hefty price increases for drug products, as well as the industry's glowing annual reports and soaring stock prices. In fact, as industry observers point out, many of the price increases include the introduction of new, more costly drugs that have a major life-enhancing value and actually reduce the overall cost of care by keeping patients out of the hospital. The cost of drugs, they add, represents only 7 percent of the total health care bill."

After relentless attacks from the Clintons, some drug companies finally began to wake up. "Our CEO is making speeches all over the country, meeting with senators on Capitol Hill, and talking to employees to help energize them and give them the information they need to fight back," says Ron Schmid of Lederle Laboratories. "We are organizing a grass-roots response to critics in Washington, D.C., through a series of editorials in 72 newspapers. We are also actively promoting the benefits to society of our R&D [research and development] effort." The moral here is when you're under attack in the public arena, it's imperative to mount an aggressive defense.

The Kettle Fights Back

One of the most ironic "fighting back" public information campaigns has come from the media themselves. With the advent of tabloid television, and the blurring of the lines between traditional journalism and the more sensational tabloid press, the media's credibility has plummeted over the past two decades. With this fall has come a lack of respect and, worse, the ironic phenomenon of the public actually questioning the media's tactics and intrusions into people's lives.

To combat this, the media decided to fight back with a public information campaign of their own. The Society of Professional Journalists (SPJ) joined with the Advertising Council to mount their promedia campaign under the slogan "Project Watchdog."

John S. Detweiler studied the media's subsequent campaign and published his findings in *PR Quarterly*. Detweiler concludes, surprisingly enough, that the media's heavy-handed efforts badly missed the target:

> The [media's] ads carried the theme: 'If the press didn't tell us, who would?' They featured such news stories as Austrian President Kurt Waldheim's ties to the Nazi Party, the space shuttle *Challenger*'s explosion, the Chernobyl disaster and the controversial Marcos-Aquino election in the Philippines. For one thing, the headline on the ads to date is not an invitation to dialogue but a defense of current media practice. Although SPJ claims the project is not designed to be 'self-serving,' the ground rules for dialogue are rather limited. The text of each ad states: 'To get printed information on the role of a free press and how it protects your rights, or to discuss any free press issue, call the First Amendment Center at 1-800-542-1600. This is not a general invitation to discuss press performance. 'Free press issues' suggest maintaining, even expanding, the power and autonomy of the press. There is no hint in the copy that the concept of a 'free and responsible press' is open for discussion. Unrestrained media power is a major concern among a large segment of the public.
>
> The vocabulary of these [media] critics favors such terms as 'the media elite' or 'the establishment media.' Such critics raise a number of questions aimed principally at the television networks, 'Eastern establishment' newspapers, news magazines and major media chains. Who elected them? Why are they so negative? To whom are they accountable? How do you make them responsible? The conventional perception of public service is 'comforting the afflicted.' Journalists put a spin on the term. They regard public service as 'afflicting the comfortable.'

Detweiler says that for these reasons, the media's entry into the public relations field to improve their image was mostly a failure:

> If the imagery of journalist defense of the First Amendment focused upon . . . examples of media responsiveness and responsibility, rather than solely on investigative reporters' exposure of the frailties of others, it would be much easier to establish a dialogue. Openness and willingness to hear others' viewpoints encourage two-way communication. Symbols that journalists actually take pride in such dialogue, rather than repeated mouthing of fears about undue community pressure or conflicts of interest, would establish tangible evidence that journalists consider themselves accountable to their constituencies. It would also reflect upon the motives of journalists: do they enjoy helping or hurting people? A conciliatory attitude would suggest they do indeed enter their profession with the high purpose of being helpful to people rather than as a power trip.

Summary

If the media themselves botch a public information campaign, if the government misses the boat, if buckle up jingles fail to make anyone buckle up, and if crying Native Americans rivet the public but send the wrong message, what's a public information PR practitioner to do? Take the best of each successful campaign, avoid the pitfalls that snagged the ones that failed, and never rest upon one's laurels. Findings also suggest that more attention should be given to understanding the sources and measurement of interest and motivation. Demographic traits, such as age, may also affect success as they may reflect upon how socialization shapes an individual.

QUESTIONS

1. Why has the Smokey Bear Campaign endured?

2. How does tha Ad Council measure effectiveness?

3. What reasons did the Riester Corporation cite for the success of its tobacco prevention campaign aimed at youth?

4. What tactics are the Census Bureau using for Census 2000?

READINGS

Ad Council Web site: www.adcouncil.org/body_research _impact.html.

John S. Detweiler. "Public Relations and the Campaign for Press Freedom." *Public Relations Quarterly 34,* no. 1 (1989); 19–22.

Census 2000 Web site: www.census.gov.

Ronald E. Rice and Charles K. Atkin (eds.). *Public Communication Campaigns* (2nd ed.) Newbury Park, CA: Sage, 1989.

12 The Special Event Campaign

If You Plan It, They Usually Come

CHAPTER OUTLINE

Types of Special Events

The Special Event as a Fund-Raiser

The Planning Process

Planning for a Contingency

Special Events and Their Sponsors

CHAPTER OBJECTIVES

When you have completed this chapter, you should be able to:

- Identify the six characteristics of a special event
- Recognize the potential pitfalls of charity involvement
- List the major topics basic to event planning

Special events. The words imply a festive undertaking of some kind. And in many cases, that is what the public relations strategist has in mind: a social affair that entertains as well as informs; educating the would-be consumer against a backdrop of intrigue and entertainment. However, not all special events serve cake and ice cream; some have no menu at all.

The definition of a special event is broad. It ranges from a corporate open house to a project ground-breaking, a record-breaking marathon to a trivia contest, a department store holiday celebration to a charity fund-raiser. Special events can attract thousands of spectators or participants, or they may be closed to the public. Some last for months; others last perhaps just a minute or two.

Special events are defined or characterized by participation. In most instances, the event planner hopes to deliver a message in person, face-to-face with the target audience, and usually with the opportunity for direct exchange. Said another way, special events reach consumers right where they live. Why is this intimacy so desirable? Why go to the trouble when a simple letter might do? The answer has much to do with the campaign objectives. In their research and interviews with several special event experts, Steven Blackwell and Tara Crihfield identified several key functions, or advantages, of the special event campaign. They contend that the principal element of the special event is its subliminal, embedded communication message. In other words, the special event actually becomes the communications channel, and the result is a subtle but persuasive message that is delivered when its recipient may least expect it.

So the special event—large or small, expensive or without cost, day-long or ongoing —becomes yet another medium to reach a desired audience with one's corporate message. It may stand alone or as one of several communication channels that are utilized. Regardless, the purpose of most special events is to realize some set of predetermined objectives and to evaluate their results.

Types of Special Events

While there are literally hundreds of different kinds of special events, it is quite possible to categorize them into a manageable list of event types. For example, holiday celebrations provide for a lengthy but similar grouping of events, such as Fourth of July extravaganzas, Cinco de Mayo festivals (see Exhibit 12.1), New Year's Day parades, Easter egg hunts, Halloween houses, or Valentine's Day parties.

With that in mind, the following event categories cover most of the special events that public relations managers might encounter with regard to their corporate or client objectives:

- Commemorations/anniversaries
- Holiday celebrations
- Project ground-breaking/topping-off ceremonies
- Grand openings
- Corporate open houses
- Fund-raisers
- Sales and cross-promotions

EXHIBIT **12.1**

Special Events

By the year 2010, people of Hispanic heritage are expected to account for about 13 percent of the U.S. population. Public relations and integrated marketing approaches are being engineered by and for Latinos in various parts of the country, not only to sell mainstream products but also to celebrate the contributions of Hispanics to U.S. society and culture. Many of these campaigns use special events to tie in with Hispanic holidays and celebrations.

- Sporting tie-ins and sponsorships
- Contests, challenges, and record firsts
- Cultural celebrations
- Employee functions

No two events are alike, nor should they be. It is the customization, timing, location, and budget that shape every event and make each slightly different and special in its own way. However, according to Art Stevens of Lobsenz-Stevens, a New York City–based special events agency, there six essential characteristics of the effective special event:

1. The event should have publicity value in its own right. If the event is not of interest, neither the media nor the public will respond.

2. An event should provide the desired positioning for an organization and its product or service. It must be of intrinsic interest to potential customers, who may one day become regular customers.

3. An event works best if it is meaningfully linked to the product or brand name that it is designed to introduce or support. For example, The Playtex Challenge, a weekend athletic competition, linked the Playtex name to women's pursuit of excellence, fitness, and health.

4. The event should run smoothly so that the product link is effective but not intrusive. The program should be interesting, exciting, and meaningful to the public, whether or not the sponsor's name is mentioned.

5. An event should be communicated to the public and media through an effective promotional campaign. Special event promotions should be viewed as focused marketing tools.

6. The event should be innovative, distinctive, and memorable. It should become something that can be owned by its creator or sponsor; in a best-case scenario, the event may become an annual affair.

Later in the chapter, several case studies will demonstrate how these key elements bring an event to life, making what seems like average ideas exceptional communications programs.

The Special Event as a Fund-Raiser

Though raising money is not, and should not be, a prerequisite of every special event, the philanthropic angle tends to be frequently used by many event planners. The strategy is simple: Involve a high-visibility, nonprofit organization in your event, and you undoubtedly will benefit from newfound resources.

First among those resources is the credibility that usually accrues to an event by involving a charity. If it is a well-known and respected charitable organization, its reputation and goodwill carry over to the special event and validate the effort put forth. The charity doesn't necessarily have to be large or national in scope, simply recognized and respected by the local audience where the event is occurring. Examples of such charities would be the local Boys and Girls Clubs, the Salvation Army, food banks, homeless shelters, and even churches.

Another important benefit in involving a charity is the built-in workforce that it can usually lend. Most nonprofits are low on dollars but loaded with volunteers. These individuals come with high commitment and equally high energy; their availability can save an event planner thousands of dollars in manpower costs. One word of warning, however: Do not involve too many well-meaning volunteers without keeping them busy. Volunteers need to be focused and kept busy, or they tend to hamper a planner's efforts, perhaps endanger an event, and inhibit cooperation on future events.

Depending upon the nature of an event, an audience may be important to its success. By naming a charity as benefactor of your event, you are likely to gain a built-in spectator base made up of the charity's regular supporters. This stands to reason as a charity's constituents are going to support a fund-raising event that ultimately benefits their cause with a donation.

Finally, the inclusion of a nonprofit organization in an event can consciously and subconsciously validate the effort taking place. After all, things such as 10K races, record-setting competitions, golf tournaments, black-tie dinners, and the like may or may not be compelling enough to attract participants, spectators, and the media without a charity tie-in. The philanthropic association softens the inevitable commercial overtones that linger from the visible name of an event's corporate sponsor(s).

Before leaving this discussion about special events as fund-raising opportunities, it is important to point out the potential pitfalls of charity involvement:

- Choose as a benefactor for a charity that has at least some relevancy to your organization and its event. Think about why you are including a particular charity and how skeptical consumers and media will view the association. For example, a liquor or cigarette company would not be a good sponsor of an event benefiting a children's charity.

- Involve a charity in your event, especially in the event planning process. This will foster good communications and make both parties clear on who is responsible for what; it will cut down on disappointments or hurt feelings as the event unfolds.

- If a donation or contribution of the proceeds from an event is to be made to your charity, it should be a significant amount. This will prevent potential embarrassment to event planners and their sponsoring organization, particularly if the media covering the event choose to make an issue of the size of the contribution. Event planners would also be wise to discuss the likely contribution with their chosen charity early on so as to prevent any surprise or unnecessary disappointment.

- If your event takes place annually, it makes good marketing sense to maintain an affiliation with the same charitable organization. Rotating benefactors suggests event instability and can be confusing to the marketplace. In fact, many charities are now showing the sophistication to negotiate multiyear contracts with events and their sponsoring corporations to which they lend their names.

The Planning Process

Setting Goals

As with any public relations campaign, the special event planner must clearly establish campaign goals before the planning process can begin. More so than in perhaps any other type of campaign, a special event must have clear focus and meaningful objectives by which its outcome can be measured. Without these parameters, the event planner will be at a loss to explain to a supervisor or client why an event was worth the time and money.

Some basic indicators for measurement of special events might be the number of people attending, the amount and quality of news coverage, the number of business leads generated, or dollars raised (in the case of a fund-raiser).

Without question, the stakes in special event planning are high. Fun or enjoyable as certain events may be, there are almost always important goals that are driving the involvement of the event sponsor, and number one among them is to sell a product, service, or idea. This is why, according to *Special Events Report* publisher Lesa Ukman, more than 5,000 special events are staged annually in North America, attracting more than $850 million in corporate sponsorships.

As many Fortune 500 companies are holding the line on advertising expenditures, dollars seem to be shifting to special event budgets. This is certainly no coincidence. But why?

PRoActive

Celebrating an Anniversary Online

Public relations counselors at Phoenix's America West Arena wanted a unique way to celebrate its fifth anniversary in 1998. The task was to create a unique special event that would create awareness of the Arena's anniversary, launch its Web site, and make an impression on the media—all for $5,000.

The Arena's PR practitioner, Susan Kricun, worked with her staff's marketing coordinator to come up with a solution. The team sponsored an online scavenger hunt on the Arena's Web site. The five-week Web promotion—to reinforce the fifth anniversary—asked visitors to click on the contest icon. After registering, guests were asked to find the answers to five questions scattered throughout the Web site's five pages, in fact forcing participants to click through the pages and thereby become familiar with the information the site offered.

The incentive? The grand prize winner would receive a year-long pass to every music concert at the Arena. Five runners-up would win a $1,000 gift

certificate from CompUSA. For its participation in the online competition, CompUSA gained exposure on the Arena's Web site, in its press materials, and at the halftime ceremonies at a Phoenix Suns game announcing the contest winners.

"Our goal was to come up with an idea that was different, that would have an impact on the media so they would cover the promotion, and offer giveaways that would be valued by our contestants," explained Kricun, now principal partner at Ink! Communications.

The contest was introduced to the media via materials delivered in a mailing tube that played music after being opened. The tube also served as a reminder of the anniversary celebration, with its confetti and streamers heralding the occasion.

The result? Television, radio, and print exposure in addition to the more than 2,000 entries from across the country.

Because a well-conceived and well-executed special event can help its sponsoring organization reach its goal, whether it be increased market share, the opportunity for new product testing, general brand awareness, or simply increased goodwill through community service.

Creating the Planning Team

Once a goal or objectives for an event have been established, the actual planning process can begin. To facilitate such planning, an event planning team should be created. A team is defined as two or more staff members from a company's public relations or marketing department. In the case of an agency conducting an event on behalf of its client, it is not uncommon to find the entire account team involved in the planning process. This approach validates the "two heads are better than one" theory and works to spread the responsibility over several different individuals.

As with any team, there must always be a leader. This individual will direct the planning process, making sure that the creative ideas put forth match the marketing strategies and can be realized from a budgetary standpoint. Then on the day of the event, the designated team leader will act as a field marshal, with all direction coming from him or her. The leader assumes ultimate responsibility for the direction and flow of an event, providing the necessary leadership to staff and volunteers. And, as always, there should be an assistant coordinator on the event project who can step in at a moment's notice and substitute for the original team leader if necessary.

Establishing Action Steps

Sports teams have their playbook; architects work from blueprints; navigators rely on a compass and maps—event planners are no different, or at least they shouldn't be. To produce a successful event that accomplishes what it proposes, the public relations professional must have a strategic plan. And the guts of such a plan are the numerous action steps that cover the infinite details that make up most events. Seldom is there such a phenomenon as overplanning. The problems or failure of an event can usually be traced to oversights in the planning process.

In order to assimilate the myriad of fine details that comprise a special event, the planner should utilize a to-do list or time and action matrix (see Figure 12.1). This simple instrument not only helps pull together the many details associated with a special event, it aids in organizing them into the proper order of execution.

Though not limited to the following checklist, these planning topics comprise the basic areas to consider when planning a major event:

- Selection of a date, researching potential conflicts. Newspapers and citywide magazines, as well as libraries, chambers of commerce, and convention bureaus, may be helpful in uncovering other events that may conflict with your event date.

- Selection of a site. Whether the event is indoors or outside, there are basic questions associated with site selection. Is the site large enough to accommodate all guests? Is it easily accessible? Is there ample parking in close proximity? Must a permit or temporary alcohol license be secured?

Event: Silver Anniversary Suns Fest   **Date:** December 17   , 19 _____

Schedule for: Saturday, January 9, 9:00 a.m.–6:00 p.m.   **Page:** _____2_____ **of** _____2_____

Item No.	Required Action: Description	Delegated to	Date Req'd Comp
16	Coordinate all internal communications to both Phoenix Suns and America West Arena staff.	Harris	
17	Investigate the feasibility of the paper airplane toss for either a free car or Hawaii trips on America West Airlines.	DS/TA	
18	Coordinate the logistics associated with the Kids Clinics (5) and the subsequent involvement of alumni players (Hawkins, Van Arsdale, Adams, etc.).	Haskell/Liz	
19	Coordinate the involvement of radio station(s) related to the pre-promotion of the Kids Clinic and the bands.	DK	
20	Coordinate the contact and setup of the Special Olympics exhibit in the east parking lot.	TA	
21	Coordinate ticket sales, logistics, setup and announcement with Suns ticket office and Dillard's to go on sale week of December 21.	Hart	
22	Develop news materials and distribute press kits to all appropriate local media.	JH/DS	
23	Coordinate in-game and in-Arena promotional announcements by Al McCoy and Jeff Munn, respectively.	Horn	
24	Develop Suns Fest ad to run in January 6 Special Section of the Arizona Republic.	DK	
25	Secure program interviews and Suns Fest plug on 620 Sports Line with Jude LaCava the week of January 4.	Horn	

FIGURE 12.1   Event Planners Rely on Some Type of "To Do" List When Producing Major Activities Such as "Suns Fest"

■ Insurance coverage, minimizing risk. Without insurance, there can be no event. The question then becomes, How much and what kind? Consulting with other public relations practitioners, risk managers, and seasoned insurance agents/brokers can help answer difficult questions about event liability.

■ Creation of an event budget. In many cases, an employer or client will have little or no idea what an event should cost. Consequently, the event planner becomes responsible for ascertaining all costs. This is possible only through in-depth research and vendor bidding.

Seldom will an event sponsor authorize an event prior to the presentation of a detailed income and expense summary.

■ Securing of a photographer. Most special events should be chronicled for their participants and sponsors. Selection of the proper photographer, capable of capturing the desired photos while working within a budget, is easier said than done. Be specific. Tell the photographer what is desired and put it in writing.

■ Security at the event. An event involving any more than a couple dozen people normally requires that a professional security firm be retained. Without such security measures in place, an event may become problematic and is then the full responsibility of its planner.

■ Preparation of the invitation. This is key to a successful event. Does your invitation clearly provide all the pertinent details? Is it attention-getting, memorable, or compelling? Did it arrive in time to give invitees enough notice but not so early that they forget they were ever invited? Finally, do the VIPs and media require a follow-up call to ensure their attendance?

■ Outdoor venues. Outdoor events are typical and comprise some of the best ever produced, yet they pose certain challenges. Planners will need to think about generators to provide electricity, portable toilets, water trucks to keep the dust down, and much, much more.

■ Selection of a caterer. Almost any special event, large or small, inside or outdoors, will call for refreshments. A professional caterer is almost always the solution. Taking this approach will not only ensure that guests enjoy quality food and beverages but will also free the planner from worrying whether the punch bowl is empty.

■ Check-in. Though seemingly elementary, the manner in which event goers are received will go a long way toward shaping the kind of experience they have. Questions range from the use of name tags to advance registration versus pay-at-the-door to table assignments to the use of printed programs. A smooth event is almost always a successful event.

■ Traffic control. For larger events with numerous guests, traffic control must be considered. It is not uncommon to create makeshift parking lots or close streets to accommodate large numbers of people. This will most likely be something that can and should be handled by the local police. Another question to be addressed is self-parking versus valet parking.

■ Audiovisual materials. Nothing can be more embarrassing to an event planner than the malfunction of a slide projector or VCR or a sound system that can't be heard by everyone in attendance. The only insurance against such embarrassment is to pretest all audiovisual and sound equipment, not once but twice.

■ News materials. Assuming an event is to be covered by the local media, there needs to be separate and special planning for this element. Are news kits prepared and complete? Is there someone available to facilitate the media's arrival, answer questions, and ease their ability to cover the event? Juggling the needs of the media (especially television) and the guests is a fine art in and of itself.

■ Rehearsal. Not every event lends itself to a dry run, but whenever possible, practicing the actual program can help ensure the success of an event. Of particular importance is the rehearsal of stage productions, speeches, music, special effects, and the various volunteer roles.

PRoActive
A Blessed Special Event

Situation
"Bobbi McCaughey gave birth to the world's only living septuplets at Iowa Methodist Medical Center in Des Moines. It was a PR practitioner's dream: a media crisis with a happy ending."

Response/Approach
"The communication strategy sessions . . . included representatives from public relations, security, administration, nursing and the medical team. One strategy we all agreed on quickly was that the patient's rights and wishes would always come first. Bobbi and her family would approve any PR tactics prior to implementation."

■ News conferences informed the media of what was happening, but when the family requested that no more be held, the patient's wishes were granted. It was difficult for the hospital to turn down the media. During the wait time, preparations were made.

■ Prepared statements and media training sessions for the physicians, nurses, and administrators who would serve as spokespeople were provided. We prepared a range of comments to be given from best-case to worst-case scenarios.

■ We detailed our "Day of Birth" plan, which included assignments for each of the twelve PR staff members and a telephone notification system.

■ We developed a plan for two centers of operation for the communications staff—one next to the media center and another in the main PR office.

■ We arranged the auditorium for the post-birth news conferences. We worked closely with TV crews who assisted us with lighting, cable, and sound. We also established a media center adjacent to the auditorium and ordered twenty-five additional phone lines to be installed.

■ We detailed the order and specific content of each news conference.

■ We prepared media handouts, fact sheet, physician bios, and B-roll (edited tape ready to be inserted into script) footage of the neonatal intensive care unit.

■ We determined how we would process one-on-one interview requests using our existing media inquiry forms.

■ We assigned a PR staff member to each spokesperson who would schedule interviews. Local media would be our first priority.

■ We credentialed all news media, including producing and distributing media badges and guidelines; assembled a master media list, complete with phone numbers for home or hotel, work, fax, cellular, and pager; and preprogrammed all media fax numbers into two machines in the PR office.

■ We worked with security to determine our needs and assist with media control.

■ We planned for updating the Web site on a regular basis.

■ "Our goals were to provide them [the doctors] with an understanding of the media circus that would likely ensue and the skills to manage themselves in such an environment. We discussed how reporters would behave given competition, deadlines, and zeal for emotion-filled sound bites. To decrease vulnerability, we taught these physicians to identify an audience, develop a premise statement and key supports, and adopt pausing techniques to help them speak more clearly. We provided a 'phases of media coverage model' to help them anticipate how the story would develop."

Source: Adapted from Ann W. Wilson (APR). "The Iowa Septuplets: A Media Crisis with a Happy Ending." *Public Relations Tactics* (February 1998): 1, 7, 19.

Planning for a Contingency

Perhaps the most important word in the event planner's vocabulary is contingency. What would happen in the case of an emergency or unforeseen turn of events? What are the various risks at hand, and how will the planner deal with them? Further, what are the liabilities inherent in an event and who is responsible?

These are the basic questions an event planner must answer. Without adequate answers and planning to address the potential obstacles, a special event is most certainly operating at risk. It could be as obvious but unavoidable as rain or a windstorm (were the weather reports consulted ahead of time?) or as unexpected as a last-minute strike by the unionized band or food servers. The point is simple. Has the worst-case scenario been thought about, and planned for? What are the contingencies? Even in the case of a natural disaster or act of God, if event planners don't have a proposed way out, then they are ultimately to blame for the damage caused to their event.

The best way to properly prepare for the kind of misfortune that can ruin an event is to brainstorm as an account or planning team all those possible and even seemingly impossible problems that could arise. Even though this exercise is not enjoyable and the list may be grim, it is the only way to realistically prepare for the unexpected. More importantly, it is the only way to insulate an event from disaster.

A few examples of cause-and-effect planning are as follows:

Problem or Disruption	*Contingency*
Injury at a sporting competition	On-site medical treatment
Outsiders crashing a private reception	On-site security or police officer available
Slide projector that won't work	Extra projector lightbulbs
Thunderstorms or rain at outdoor event	Cancellation or moving activity indoors

These problem examples are relatively easy ones to foresee and solve. The point is that there is almost nothing that can't be foreseen and overcome with adequate contingency planning. Or as the saying goes, "Fail to plan and you are planning to fail."

Special Events and Their Sponsors

That age-old question comes to mind here: Which did come first, the chicken or the egg? And so too the question arises, Which should come first, events and their need for a sponsor or companies in search of an event to market their product or service?

There really is no right or wrong answer unless one is a purist and believes events should stand on their own creativity and involve a corporate sponsor only in the wake of necessity. But that viewpoint is quickly diminishing. A special event for its own sake is hardly practical, and the chief financial officer will always demand, "Who pays and what's the return on investment?"

The reality of special events is that corporate marketing dollars pave the way for the eventuality of tens of thousands of events all across America. And for good reason—these events sell. With the proliferation and sophistication of events in major markets across America, savvy brand managers have a newfound method of reaching highly targeted audiences with their products or services.

A Visit to the Archives: From Putt-Putt Cars to Fancy Bars

An inside look at two special events may prove enlightening. The client, product, or service is not important here. Rather, the goals, strategies, planning, implementation, and evaluation are what should be observed and considered. The two events are drastically different from each other, yet there is commonality in the areas of event relevancy, creativity, originality, planning, and, most importantly, results.[1]

[1]The two case studies being shared are from the event files of Evans/Artigue Public Relations, a full-service agency in Phoenix, Arizona, that was owned and operated by one of this textbook's authors.

CASE STUDY   Golf Cars Ltd./Melex Golf Cars

Situational Analysis

Golf Cars Ltd. (GCL) in Sun City, Arizona, was in the business of selling street-legal golf carts to seniors living in that upscale retirement community. As a matter of lifestyle, almost every household possessed both a full-size automobile and a golf cart; in fact, the latter were their second cars.

Goals

GCL called upon its public relations agency to help it introduce Melex, its newest line of golf cars. This brand had been in existence but was little known, with minuscule market share in Sun City. Part of the challenge was price resistance by the consumer. The Melex cars were higher quality and also cost more. The only way this cost-conscious market would switch brands and pay more was to get them to test-drive the Melex brand. In this case, seeing would be believing.

The specific client goals were to create name recognition for both Golf Cars Ltd. and the Melex brand, encourage test drives of these new cars, and of course sell the Melex product—all this on what both client and agency agreed was a shoestring introductory budget.

Strategy

As mentioned, the senior market would be slow to respond to switching brands, particularly if it would be more expensive. The strategy was clear: The customers had to get behind the wheel of a Melex and feel the quality for themselves. But how? It would be an uphill battle through usage of traditional advertising and generous product publicity.

Program Planning

Brainstorming by the account team quickly determined that a special event was the solution to this tough product introduction assignment. The situation was ripe for an event. History showed that the Sun City community enjoyed and supported outdoor events. But what type of special event would allow the client to realize its multiple goals? The Melex Grand Prix.

With Phoenix the first stop of the International Grand Prix racing circuit, a seniors' version of a Grand Prix during the same week in March seemed like a natural. This unique race would be run with Melex race cars through the streets of Sun City. There would be eighteen racing teams broken up into three heats, each consisting of a Sun City resident and a well-known community dignitary or

(continued)

media personality. The final piece of the event puzzle benefited a charity with event proceeds, in this case, the seriously or terminally ill children of the Make-a-Wish Foundation.

As with most large events, costs were a primary issue. Golf Cars Ltd. was willing to invest some monies, but in no way could it afford to pay for the entire event. The solution was to approach Melex Inc. and convince it to invest corporate marketing dollars, thus making it the title sponsor. Race car sponsorships were also sold to individual Sun City businesses, creating signage opportunities on the side of each cart.

Implementation

Months of planning culminated on a crisp, weekday morning (spot research showed that seniors stay home or visit relatives on weekends) when Melex carts lined up at the starting line of the Melex Grand Prix. The sight of helmeted grandparents, posing as speedsters, created visuals that were ready-made for television cameras and newspaper photographers, particularly those journalists who were in town to cover the real Grand Prix.

For a first-year event (due to its success, the Melex race became an annual affair), the race drew an impressive spectator base made up of Sun City residents, drivers' families, sponsors, Make-a-Wish representatives, and the media. The forty-five-minute obstacle course ended with a cheering crowd at the finish line; immediately following the race, an awards ceremony honored the top three finishers with trophies. Melex officials were present and, along with all of the event sponsors, were publicly thanked. The Melex and Golf Cars Ltd. representatives also made a check presentation to the charity at that time.

Evaluation

The event was an unquestioned success. Almost overnight the Melex brand name became as well known in the immediate Sun City market as the other more established golf carts. The PR agency created a follow-up promotion to sell the actual carts used in the race at special Grand Prix prices, which in turn spurred visits to the showroom and a major boost in test drives. Those residents who participated in the race told everyone they knew about their experience of driving a Melex, and the participating sportscasters made their experience a part of the six and ten o'clock news. The high level of exposure for Golf Cars Ltd. and Melex, as well as the charitable goodwill, ultimately led to the Melex brand becoming the number one selling cart for the client. Melex Inc. considered developing the Grand Prix concept throughout the country for its other dealerships.

C A S E   S T U D Y   **Scottsdale Plaza Resort/"We're Changing Our Stripes"**

Situational Analysis

This popular, posh Scottsdale resort decided it was time to change its name. After twelve years as a Sheraton affiliate, the owners elected to go independent, dropping the Sheraton name and logo. This action, they reasoned, would allow the resort to more freely compete with the other upscale Scottsdale resorts.

Goal

The client's goal was to effect the name change as quickly and completely as possible without disrupting the flow of business or jeopardizing the long-term standing or success of the resort. This could be accomplished only through an aggressive internal and external marketing communications plan.

Strategy

It was clear that the marketplace would not be sold on the resort's new name until its own staff became comfortable with it and were in a position to sell it to others with clarity and conviction. This meant a dual-pronged communications strategy: speaking to all management and staff, then reaching local and national customers, vendors/suppliers, and the industry at large. Campaign content was simple: To share the new name (actually it was a name modification) and why it was taking place, stressing that the original ownership remained.

Program Planning

The early concern by the account team was that this name change might not be regarded as important by the media or the marketplace. The information needed to be window-dressed and a news hook developed. In essence, a special event was needed.

From the preliminary brainstorming, the theme line, We're Changing Our Stripes, was conceived. This suggested a change was forthcoming and played off the timing of the name-change announcement, which was to take place before the Fourth of July weekend. Because the internal announcement came first, an employee rally was planned in the grand ballroom, complete with indoor fireworks, miniature flags, and of course an official proclamation from the resort owner, who was dressed as George Washington. Even a drum and bugle corps was present to add an authentic, patriotic flavor.

Implementation

Immediately following the red, white, and blue ballroom ceremony, individual department meetings were held so that supervisors could further explain the name change and address themselves to staff questions and concerns. Within a twenty-four-hour period, all resort employees were aware that the resort was in fact changing its stripes. They also understood why and were ready to enthusiastically share the news with customers, suppliers, industry associates, and family.

On that same day, comprehensive news kits were distributed both locally and nationally (with emphasis directed toward the trade magazines). A direct-mail campaign, containing both new business cards from the person writing as well as new Rolodex cards, was also released to all resort constituents that same week. The basic message to be shared was simply that the fine facilities and its owners remained the same; only the name had changed.

Evaluation

Determination of the success or failure of this campaign required little or no research. Seeing would be believing, and the results were felt almost immediately. Hotel operations continued smoothly, and word of the name change was spread by employees with efficiency and enthusiasm. All written notification was made simultaneously throughout the local community and national industry. Media exposure cemented the message and brought certain credibility. Most importantly, not a single advance reservation was canceled, and the sales department continued to meet and exceed its goals.

Summary

At one time, special events were just for fun. Today, they are strictly business—big business.

Whether it be a Jambalaya Festival featuring the world championship cookoff of Cajun food or the Harley-Davidson annual Birthday Reunion that brings together 50,000 motorcyclists on their hogs from all over the country, these kinds of events are marketing-driven. They are meant to retain current customers, cultivate new ones, and win favor and name recognition with almost everyone in between.

There are some corporate sponsorships that are purely altruistic, but they are few and far between. After all, even a contribution to the local art museum is tax-deductible and should provide advertising opportunities in the museum's seasonal program. In a more overt way, companies have been known to underwrite an entire symphony or opera season, thus becoming a marquee or title sponsor. They are then provided numerous spin-off events of their choosing, as well as solid media exposure. Even the media have come to understand the benefit of sponsoring or cosponsoring community events themselves and are reaping the corresponding rewards.

As long as the PR professional or special events manager (as the field allows for additional specialization) can show return for the client's sponsorship dollar, the special event sector will continue to explode and will take its permanent place in the overall marketing mix.

QUESTIONS

1. Event marketing has become extremely popular, replacing some of the more traditional marketing approaches. What are some of the reasons for the success of special events as a marketing channel?

2. Cite four examples of different types of special events, as presented in this chapter.

3. What is a time and action matrix, and how does it contribute to the effectiveness of producing a special event?

4. Cite at least six functions or planning action steps that would apply to almost any special event plan.

5. How can a strategic special event be utilized by marketers to reach a targeted audience segment? Give an example of such targeting and reach.

READINGS

Steven H. Blackwell and Tara S. Crihfield. "Controlling the Communications Impact." *Public Relations Journal* (June 1991): 34–35.

William Souder. "Selling and Marketing: Special Effects." *Inc. Magazine* (October 1984): 161–166.

Art Stevens. "What's Ahead for Special Events." *Public Relations Journal* (June 1984): 30–32.

DEFINITION

time and action matrix: An outline of event details or responsibilities with deadlines that are listed in reverse chronological order, leading up to the start of an event, and assigned to those individuals who are responsible for the implementation of same.

13 The Crisis Campaign

Have You Practiced Your Fire Drill Lately?

CHAPTER OBJECTIVES

When you have completed this chapter, you should be able to:

- Explain how organizations benefit from crisis planning
- Identify crisis themes
- Recognize the stages of a crisis
- Understand the process of crisis communications

Crisis—it can literally make or break an organization. This event, circumstance, or issue can arise with little or no warning, demanding immediate action, and usually resulting in long-term consequences. It can also happen to any company, large or small, public or private. The major keys in effectively planning for a crisis are defining a crisis, monitoring the environment, identifying a crisis, and isolating or limiting its effect.

Defining a Crisis

Crises vary in their nature, magnitude, and intensity, but most can paralyze a corporation's ability to function and erode its credibility and reputation. It is at this critical point when the actions of the public relations professional are pivotal. However, the success of the practitioners' activities, to a large extent, depends upon the corporate leadership's reliance on their counsel long before a crisis arises.

There are a variety of management styles that a chief executive may select. They range from human relations and participatory to authoritarian and oligarchical. The structure used may reveal if the organization is open, closed, or organic in scope. In other words, does the CEO solicit employee suggestions, or are employees expected to obey orders? Is the organization the sum of its workers, or does management believe workers are expendable? Does the organization monitor its environment and change with it, or is it reluctant or resistant to change? The answers to these questions may be at the root of a corporation's life-or-death struggle for survival when a crisis occurs.

If management regards the public relations function as important, then the chances are good that a corporation can successfully emerge from disaster. The chances improve if a crisis communications plan is formulated. Even though most would agree it's basic to plan for contingencies, a full 50 percent of the Fortune 500 companies polled in a 1986 survey admitted they did not have a crisis plan. Ironically, 89 percent of those same respondents felt "a crisis in business is as inevitable as death or taxes." More than a decade later, many major corporations still underestimate the impact of an urgent situation.

Monitoring the Environment

Cutlip and Center have long underscored the necessity for public relations practitioners to act as corporate sentinels. They must watch the horizon, listening for thunder in order to sound the alarm if a corporate storm is brewing. According to Steven Fink, president of Lexicon Communications Corporation, most crises are signaled. But no amount of signaling will be helpful if no one is watching, listening, or keeping score. This corporate inability is a pathology or a sickness within the organization. If too many internal communications elements or goals decay, the disease could become systemic. A crisis is life-threatening and ever-changing, similar to a disease. However, there is a prescription to treat the problem—planning and preparation.

Identifying a Crisis

The ability to identify what might constitute a crisis or an emergency for an organization is obviously the next step in such planning. But it is not always easy to differentiate between a simple problem and a true crisis. Any nonroutine event that could be disruptive to business operations could be classified as a crisis or emergency. Some companies define a crisis as any unusual short-term incident that has a real or perceived negative impact upon the general welfare of their primary constituencies—employees, customers, shareholders, suppliers, or the community—as well as upon the company itself.

Real-world experience has shown that when a disaster occurs, definitions are irrelevant. You instinctively know you have an emergency or crisis on your hands when it hits. Explosions, fires, floods, customer or employee deaths, and scandals present obvious crisis situations.

Isolating Crisis Effects

No organization can anticipate all possible crisis scenarios. That is not the real purpose of emergency planning. The primary objectives are to:

- Assess the organization's overall preparedness—culturally and logistically—for dealing with a disaster
- Identify the public relations department's and management's strengths and weaknesses
- Develop a response game plan that is appropriate for the organization

Crisis Management Preparedness

The ability of an organization's staff to effectively prepare for and cope with an actual disaster will be largely shaped by the existing management structure. Experience has shown that the fundamental strengths and weaknesses of a given company's management approach are both greatly amplified in times of crisis.

For instance, if the organization does not establish close community ties, or if it has a history of maintaining a low profile on certain matters, attitudinal changes may be required prior to, or in unison with, the development of an effective crisis plan that requires community involvement.

Other cultural matters that may need to be taken into consideration in the planning process include the fundamental decision-making process at the organization, the role of internal functions (such as legal, public relations, and risk management) in the decision-making process, the degree of employee participation, staff-management relations, and ownership structure with the city.

Therefore, in assessing the preparedness of the organization to develop and implement a successful crisis management program, it is first necessary to analyze current management policies, organizational structure, communications systems, and attitudes of the management team—and evaluate whether they are compatible with the specific policies and procedures of their crisis response and communications plans.

Planning for the Unplanned

In public relations terms, planning can accomplish two things: It can make something happen or prevent it from happening. In order to control a volatile crisis situation, it is necessary for the practitioner to master both. The planners should keep the organization's mission in mind, as well as preserve corporate assets, both tangible and intangible. The intangibles center around the public relations practitioner's defining task—communicating credibly.

EXHIBIT **13.1**

Disaster Inventory for America West Arena (Phoenix, Arizona)

Operations
Fire
Explosion
Performer Accident
Power Outage
Computer System Failure
Bombing
Terrorism
Severe Work Accident
Other _____

**Employee Safety
& Health**
Fatality
Chronic Safety Problem
Exposure to Carcinogens
Personal Injury Suit
Other _____

Customer Relations
Smoking or Alcohol Policies
Customer Service Complaints
Negative Publicity
Rumors
Other _____

Natural Crises
Flooding
Earthquake
Tornado
Lightning Strikes
Other _____

Labor Relations
Work Stoppages
Organizing Drive
Minority Issues
Handicap Issues
Unfair Labor Practice
Other _____

Management Issues
Temporary Closing
Downsizing/Layoffs
Reorganization
Management Succession
    Following Death of Officers
Executive Kidnapping
Breach of Contract
Competitor Lawsuit
Other _____

**Employee/Management
    Misconduct**
Ticket Scalping
Vendor Kickbacks
Bribery
Sexual Harassment
Slander
Drug Trafficking
Nonpayment of Taxes
Suicide
Murder
Other _____

Government Affairs
State Legislation Impacting Business
National Legislation
Industrial Scandals
Other _____

Organization Issues
Merger, New Owners
Acquisition
Personnel Misconduct
Class Action Suit Against Others
Other _____

This is a discomforting list to contemplate, but the key is to make a reasonable assessment of those crises that could likely happen to this multipurpose, 19,000-seat facility. No organization can plan for all contingencies, but from the above list, the staff should be able to identify the top five or six most likely crisis scenarios.

This credibility can be enhanced if the communicator has a clear idea of how a crisis can disrupt the flow of information. "When a crisis strikes an organization, many outside influences hinder its ability to send its messages," says Lawrence Werner, APR, executive vice president and director, Ketchum Public Relations/Pittsburgh. These "noises" may include confidentiality, deadlines, stress, and human emotion.

Researchers Emery and Trist recognized these distractions "in a turbulent field." From their perspective, the more turbulent the corporate environment, the more collaboration and communication are needed. This is because they serve as a means for arriving at an understanding, a definition of reality. In the case of public relations, the crisis communications plan can help to define reality, serve as a means to reduce uncertainty, and create action.

Today's world is characterized by much higher levels of interdependence and complexity than have ever existed before. This, in turn, has led to what Schon says is the "loss of the stable state." The "loss of the stable state" makes the turbulent environment difficult to know and understand. Planning, then, takes on increasing importance.

In 1984, McCann and Selsky identified another type of environment, which they termed hyperturbulence. It describes a situation in which turbulence has so dangerously accelerated that it has overwhelmed the capacities for some members of the environment or industry to adapt. It ultimately threatens the survival of the rest. McCann and Selsky offer survivalist communities as an example. However, others would include the National Aeronautics and Space Administration's reorganization after the January 1986 *Challenger* disaster, Johnson & Johnson's handling of the cyanide-laced Tylenol deaths, and the savings and loan bailout with the subsequent creation of the Resolution Trust Corporation.

In each case, a period of great instability occurred prior to the actual or feared collapse of the entire entity. In a precollapse environment, the stronger organizations will try to partition the environment into enclaves of less turbulence and unpredictability. For public relations practitioners, this means breaking an organization down into smaller parts so that crises can be limited and therefore made more manageable and survivable.

One way to manage a crisis is through reasoned use of media channels, what researchers Daft and Lengel term information richness. Lengel proposes a continuum to explain how information is processed inside organizations (see Figure 13.1). He theorizes that there are five points along this continuum, ranging from high to low, as to the usefulness of information.

E X H I B I T   **13.2**

Four Risk Strategies

The measurement of perceived risk can be determined through polling and other public opinion research; otherwise, it is often a judgment call. The strategies reflect the balance between real and perceived risk:

- Low real risk; low perceived risk
  In this case, you are often dealing with the "worried well," people who worry about the risks of developing skin cancer after two hours of tanning. All that needs to be done is to communicate individually with those who are concerned.

- Low real risk; high perceived risk
  The case above demonstrated how to allay fears while at the same time communicating a situation of risk. Again, it helps a great deal if the agency doing the communicating has a high degree of credibility.

- High real risk; low perceived risk
  This is the opposite of the above, and calls for a different communication strategy entirely. Antismoking campaigns are the best example of communicating this message. Generally speaking, public indifference has to be overcome, and often is done so only over the long haul, after a sustained and organized communication effort.

- High real risk; high perceived risk
  Get out the crisis communication plan. If you don't have one, there's very little you can do. Again, if you are a credible agency, you are more likely to be believed whatever the situation or the communication strategy.

Value of Information

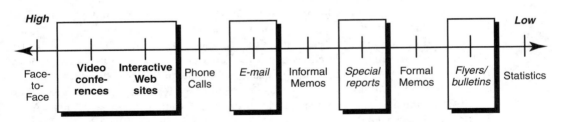

FIGURE 13.1   Information Richness Continuum

Daft and Lengel found that the more critical the information, the more important to communicate face-to-face. This is because we can observe nonverbal cues, such as posture, eye contact, and mannerisms, which provide "richer" or more satisfying communications.

Telephone calls are less rich because they eliminate the nonverbal cues but retain a measure of value via voice tone, intonation, and word selection. Informal memos retain a personal touch but reduce the ability of the listener to pick up cues. Formal memos use highly structured language, which is designed for a wider audience, and "on-the-record" comments, such as mass-produced flyers or bulletins that are impersonal and anonymous.

Numbers or statistics are the least rich because they require context and interpretation to be understood. They have no information-carrying capacity of a natural language, nor do they provide opportunities for visual observation, feedback, or personalization.

Janet Fulk and Charles Steinfeld's work in 1990 offered some additional elements to the continuum—electronic mail, the special report, and the flyer or bulletin. E-mail was viewed as the third richest information medium after telephone calls, with the special report at midrange and the remaining materials at the low end. This updated hierarchy should be reassessed regularly to reflect the expansion of communications media that technology continues to provide, namely, interactive Web sites and Internet and video conferencing. These latest developments would be placed near the high end of the continuum, due to their electronic one-on-one, face-to-face features and rapid and immediate response capabilities.

Armed with this knowledge, a practitioner would be wise to plan for the stages of a crisis. These stages can be termed before, during, after, and follow-up (Occidental Chemical Corporation) or Fink's prodromal (precrisis), acute, chronic, and crisis resolution. It is important to create terms or stages that will be meaningful to your organization. During these stages, the planner can then build in face-to-face communications in the initial phases to reduce uncertainty and progress to formal memos in waning phases, all the while offering the "richest" information possible to a variety of target audiences at a given time.

Themes of a Crisis

According to Laurence Barton (a former professor of management at the University of Nevada, Las Vegas, now an executive with Motorola), four significant themes dominate business and industry in today's globalization, regardless of geography. They are health issues, scientific achievements, consumerism, and nationalism or the demand for reform. These major themes have profound political, economic, and social consequences. For example, HIV has "taxed hospitals, clinics, public and private health providers around the world . . . the projected loss of business from AIDS already exceeds $2 billion in the 1980s."

Scientific advances have given way to dangerous explosions and mishaps. In Bhopal, India, Union Carbide president Warren Anderson arrived to inspect damage caused by a gas leak and its 2,800 casualties and "was arrested by authorities."

According to Barton, consumer issues have mushroomed globally. "Japanese and American fishing interests have all been forced to litigate against serious charges of destruction of wildlife and other endangered species."

And in nationalistic terms, "In Poland, Hungary, East Germany, Romania, the [former] Soviet Union, Korea, Cuba . . . the relaxation of state-controlled rules . . . has created tremendous opportunities for entrepreneurism and profits, terms almost alien for these nations."

Barton's point is that a crisis will have "profound and lasting impacts on business," and emergency plans must be in place to protect "all of its stakeholders: consumers, investors, governments."

PRoActive
Together We're the Best

Problem
In the early 1990s, Los Angeles suffered the blows of a depressed economy, depressed people, fallen real estate values, riots, and crime. From 1990 to 1992, overnight visitors to the City of Angels dropped by 5 million, taking with them $8 million in revenue. Leaders from public and private sectors joined to fund a five-year advertising and public relations campaign under the title of New Los Angeles Marketing Partnership.

Objectives
The objectives were clear—restore the area's image, regain its economic position, and promote it as the right place to live, work, and play. This approach included key international markets as well as those stateside.

Strategy
The strategy gathered together the city's big names with each of the 120 businesses contributing to the campaign war chest. The effort was backed by the City and County of Los Angeles as well as the LA Convention and Visitors Bureau.

Tactics
A three-tiered approach made use of advertising, intensive media relations, and face-to-face meetings with decision makers in the area's twelve industry clusters, including international trade, motion picture and TV production, technology, and health. Boosterism was ditched in favor of a fact-based approach to overcome media skepticism.

Outcome
Over the five-year period—1994 to 1999—27,000 new businesses and 232,000 new jobs were created; real estate values bounced back; and the number of visitors rose steadily. Optimism is also returning to Angelinos, with 72 percent of residents polled saying the next generation will be better off. This is a 20 percent jump from the negative response to this same question in 1995.

The Overall Plan

Although a comprehensive plan is at the very least a self-analysis of your organization, sometimes it is valuable to design an at-a-glance communications blueprint. Lawrence Werner describes such a blueprint as a one-page message action plan (MAP). A MAP "aids strategic planning, represents the overall plan for the project and includes all elements of the crisis communications plan . . . provides an easy reference . . . is flexible."

This communications matrix includes every group to be targeted, concepts to be communicated or a "core message," specific tactics, task responsibilities, timing, and evaluation. Another version of this matrix may be found in Cutlip, Center, and Broom's *Effective Public Relations*; however, it focuses primarily on publicity and promotion as they relate to a campaign or special event.

The crisis communications team is comprised of members who are selected for their areas of expertise. This expertise should be derived from the individuals' experience, resources, and knowledge. This means that a team member may not necessarily be the director of an area within the organization, just the best person for the task. In this way, a positive climate can flourish because it satisfies the equation of authority plus power plus expertise equals leadership.

Leadership can be formal or informal. Within organizations, there are those individuals who may be highly regarded and of whom other employees ask opinions. This person may have no true authority but is influential. In a crisis setting, it may be useful to include these informal leaders to work alongside planners to wield the greatest influence with employees.

If there is a leadership void, the formal or informal actor in the organization may gain power by stepping into the gap. Power can be defined as a "reservoir of potential influence" and, according to Cartwright and Zander, is identified by three separate variables:

1. The degree of uncertainty in the situation
2. The importance of the activity to the larger system of the organization
3. The salience to the individual actor (described by Patchen as a "stake in the decision"; for Hickson, coping with uncertainty is the real basis of power)

Planning will handle many contingencies, but researcher Priscilla Murphy believes that an organization can pretest crisis communications strategies by drawing upon game theory. According to Murphy, "such an approach allows organizations to describe all possible paths that a brewing crisis could take, then analyze hypothetical organizational positions to see which will yield the best response, before committing itself to any public statement." The "players" in this game consider each strategy and analyze their effects mathematically. This quantifiable approach forces public relations practitioners to coordinate the goals of key audiences with their own organizational goals and strategies. "In game theory terms, both players are looking for the minimax position—each is trying to locate the strategy that maximizes his own benefits and minimizes his opponent's," Murphy writes.

Game theory concepts are translated into four basic steps: Identify both players; list all the possible "plays" or strategies open to each player; determine how many points each strategy is worth to the media player; and determine how many points each strategy is worth to the organization ("thus select a communications strategy that maximizes one's own gains and minimizes the media player's gains"). To Murphy, this quantitative decision-making methodology "takes PR one step closer to achieving the status of a substantive profession" as well as eliminating some of the uncertainty that surrounds a crisis.

Groupthink

It must also be noted that the crisis communications coordinator (CCC) should also be aware of a phenomenon that groups are prone to—Janis's groupthink. It is a tendency for groups to arrive at an agreement at the expense of objective, critical thinking. Janis studied various historical fiascoes and determined that groupthink contributed to bad decision making by those who were responsible for U.S. security at Pearl Harbor, the Kennedy administration's mistakes leading to the invasion of the Bay of Pigs in Cuba, and Nixon's underestimation of negative public opinion during the Watergate era.

Groupthink can occur in committees, boards, teams, task forces, and work units. It can be identified by the following symptoms:

- Illusion of invulnerability or the group's willingness to take excessive risks
- The "we feeling," often expressed in shared stereotypes
- Rationalization
- Illusion of morality
- Self-censorship or a tendency by members to censor what they say
- Illusion of unanimity where silence is construed as consensus
- Direct pressure to encourage conformity to the opinions of the group
- Mind guarding, which protects a member from being exposed to disturbing ideas

To avoid this phenomenon, Janis says the primary responsibility falls on the team leader or, in the case of crisis PR, the crisis communications coordinator. This leadership position is called many different things, including emergency response manager. The CCC should allow time for analysis and discussion, promote objectivity, and encourage members to develop and refine listening skills.

The points we have discussed are equally important when the practitioner considers the news media. Barton believes that it is "one of the most crucial areas of crisis management." By studying target audiences, using information richness concepts, and consulting a MAP or crisis plan, practitioners can effectively manage problems as they arise. This is because they have anticipated well and can act. These techniques would be useful in determining if face-to-face communication is needed or if a written statement to the news media may be a more effective course of action. Certainly, honesty should be the practitioner's policy; however, selecting the time, place, source, and method of disseminating a corporate response is vital in a threatening circumstance. These items can be handled if practitioners have prepared and done their homework.

The Planning Process

The planning process is based upon the premise that effective communications—among members of the emergency response team and with the various publics influenced by a disaster—are at the core of effective crisis management.

In implementing a crisis communications plan, it is first necessary to understand the general goals of emergency response planning: Prevent fatalities and injuries to employees and members of the public; provide guidelines for decision making; identify and clarify responsibilities; ensure that valuable time is not lost in implementing or coordinating response efforts; minimize downtime and disruption of business; ensure accurate, consistent, and timely communications; eliminate or minimize confusion and rumors; protect the organization's reputation with employees, customers, and the community; maintain credible relations with the community, local industry officials, and the media; and support rebuilding efforts.

What Should Be Included?

A well-developed crisis plan should clearly state an organization's policies and procedures under emergency conditions and provide the specific information required to carry these out.

Key elements in a crisis communications plan are:

- Purpose of the plan
- The organization's philosophy and policies toward the publics it serves
- Listing of emergency response team members, including titles, work and home phone numbers, and backup personnel
- Explanation of specific responsibilities for each team member
- Listing of all local emergency personnel, local officials, hazardous-materials directors, and other authorities
- Listing of key media personnel
- Physical description of on-site and/or off-site crisis control room and list of required equipment
- Media response plan, including delineation of responsibilities, prepared press materials, location and requirements for press room, and selection of primary spokesperson
- Description of crisis communications network, including telephone pyramid system and other procedures
- A training program, including orientation with the plan manual, emergency response, and communications and/or media training
- A testing program, including periodic testing of communications alert system (internal and external), team assignments, and mock drills
- Inventory of potential disasters and PR vulnerabilities
- Guidelines for communications during a crisis
- Suggested communications activities for follow-up to a crisis

Statement of Purpose

The purpose of a crisis communications plan is to ensure that all management and staff are in a position to contain and manage a given crisis as well as provided with the information they require for a swift and effective resolution of that crisis, and that all other affected people are provided with factual information about the crisis as quickly as possible. This plan minimizes the impact of accidents, natural disasters, extraordinary business events, and related activities upon human life, the environment, the community, the organization's property, and normal business operations.

PRoSpeak

Crisis Communications Planning

The growing interest in crisis communications planning by a variety of corporations and institutions is much desired—and needed. I believe, however, that the payoff stems not from the plans but from the process through which the plans are developed.

Although we regularly assist clients in the preparation of crisis communications plans, we find that it's virtually impossible to prepare a comprehensive plan covering every potential crisis. It's just not possible to look far enough into the future.

Through the planning process, however, our clients gain essential insights, which provide the basis for handling any future crisis. This is the real payoff. Our clients understand, for example, that whether anticipated or unforeseen, major or minor, short-lived or persistent, crises are disruptive. They divert attention from normal operations. They interrupt the status quo. They strip away the comfort and security of our daily routine. They force change upon us. And our natural tendency is to resist change, which is unsettling and unnerving. We're uncertain of the outcome. We fear the unknown consequences.

Thus, crises tend to:

- Undermine confidence
- Spark speculation and rumors
- Strain emotions

Confidence can be maintained by demonstrating through words and actions that you are retaining control of the situation. Leaders must act decisively to show that they are concerned and can be trusted to do the right thing at the right time.

Speculation and rumors can be forestalled through proactive communications. Don't allow others to tell your story. Get out front by reporting what you know when you know it. Go back and fill in the information gaps when additional facts become known. Well-informed audiences have little to fear and no need to speculate nor initiate rumors.

The emotional impact of crises can be alleviated through the style or tone of your communica-

Davis Young, APR
President and Chief Operating Office
Edward Howard & Co.

tions. The pertinent facts of the situation should be reported in a calm, deliberate, and objective manner. Questions should be anticipated and addressed without speculating or drawing conclusions not supported by facts.

As crises unfold, what is apparent today may not be tomorrow. Characteristically, crises go through cycles of good news and bad news, or ups and downs, which strain the emotions of everyone involved. This strain can be exacerbated by holding out false hopes of a fast fix or no hope of any fix. A level-headed approach is essential.

By involving clients in the planning process, it becomes a learning process. With our guidance, they:

- Identify their potential crises
- Identify their internal and external audiences—those who would be affected or may perceive that they would be affected
- Analyze and prioritize the specific concerns of each audience
- Determine the best means to communicate with each audience
- Develop outlines of the messages for each audience

(continued)

PRoSpeak   Continued

While going through this planning process with clients, we have the opportunity to offer advice drawn from our past experiences. For example, I can explain why I firmly believe that nothing beats one-on-one, personal communications. Only then do you have the ability to look each other in the eye and judge if there is a basis for mutual trust.

I also suggest that when such communications are not possible, opt for the next best thing: a group meeting, a telephone call, a video presentation, a personal letter, a memo, a pamphlet or brochure. The means of communication is governed by the priority of the audience and the feasibility considerations.

We like to spend some time discussing the development of messages with our clients. We want them to understand that although their messages may be tailored to meet specific concerns of different audiences, they must be consistent in substance. If not, you lose your credibility and undermine the very confidence you seek.

The planning process also provides an opportunity to guide clients through basic media relations principles. Most organizations dislike and distrust the media. They're unhappy because the media seem to overplay their setbacks and underplay their triumphs.

We remind clients that what is a disaster to them is news to the media; that when you attempt to conceal pertinent information, you challenge the media to expose it. By taking the initiative in bringing a crisis situation to the media's attention, you gain the benefit of using the media to communicate with a massive and widely dispersed audience, such as consumers of an off-the-shelf product.

We suggest that our clients take note of the media coverage of other people's crises. Observe the positive and negative effects of following or ignoring the concepts incorporated in their crisis communications plan.

We find that organizations desiring a crisis communications plan want to do the "right thing." These companies already understand that a crisis can put their image, reputation, and goodwill on the line. They want to be prepared to keep control of the situation and minimize the potential damage. They will accept and embrace the fundamentals of crisis communications. In so doing, they become capable of handling any crisis arising in the future.

The process has paid off.

Many companies base their emergency response policies and procedures on the principles inherent in their companies' philosophy, or mission statement. For example, America West Arena's mission statement suggests that a high level of service is the foundation for a quality entertainment experience. "Through excellence in service and a commitment to integrity, the America West Arena will serve the community by presenting the finest in sports and entertainment events while contributing to the enhancement of downtown Phoenix."

Setting Up an Emergency Response Team

All members of the emergency response team play a critical role in crisis communications. A typical emergency response team might include the following positions:

■ Crisis manager—Functions as highest-ranking on-site manager and is responsible for general coordination, decision making, and communications with top management, disaster recovery managers, and local officials.

■ Assistant crisis manager—Assists crisis manager and assumes management responsibility if crisis manager is unavailable.

- Emergency personnel coordinator—Serves as primary contact and coordinator of emergency personnel only.

- Crisis control room coordinator—Takes responsibility for physical setup of internal communications headquarters.

- Public relations manager—Assumes responsibility for all communications with internal and external audiences, including media and the local community. This person also advises the crisis manager on strategy, prepares press materials and statements, and coordinates media contacts; helps to maintain control over the physical site of the emergency; and assigns special communications duties to other team members for community relations, employee relations, government affairs, press relations, security, marketing/customer relations, and/or press center coordination.

- Media spokesperson—Acts as the central spokesperson during the disaster. This individual should be the primary person who speaks to the media and should have access to management and technical advisers. For a serious crisis situation, the preferred spokesperson would be the highest-ranking officer of the organization. This person may also be the crisis manager.

- Legal adviser—Provides ongoing counsel to the crisis manager, the recovery managers, and public relations personnel.

- Evacuation coordinator(s)—Coordinates evacuation plan with local authorities. This person may also have other team members who are responsible for transportation, communications, and temporary shelter/food.

- External public relations counsel—Works with the organization's internal public relations staff and would work hand-in-hand with the public relations agency executives. The agency staff would serve not only as backup to the internal staff but also as an objective second opinion.

Involving Top Management

One of the most critical decisions to be made in the early moments of a mounting crisis is whether to involve top management, and if so, the role that they should play in the resolution of the crisis. Noninvolvement by the top-ranking officer of an organization can waste time, impair decision making, and jeopardize the company's credibility. On the other hand, involvement of top management demonstrates concern and underscores how seriously the organization regards such incidents. In times of a major disaster, the general manager is also the most appropriate person to deal with elected officials.

If the disaster warrants top management's involvement, it is important that the chief executive officer or the president of the organization immediately take an active and visible role in the resolution of the crisis and function as the primary media spokesperson.

Some companies have established a list of clearly defined emergencies that require top management's involvement (multiple injuries, death from an accident or fire) while others have adopted policies requiring that all "nonroutine" incidents be automatically acted upon, with the authorization of the crisis manager. What works best for your organization will depend upon a variety of factors; however, it is important that this policy be defined in advance and included in the crisis plan.

Establishing a Crisis Communications Network

In order that all "need-to-know" management and staff are alerted to the crisis as soon as possible and that the communications throughout the ordeal remain open and consistent, it is necessary to set up a telephone pyramid calling system. Names of all emergency personnel would be provided to all team members. Each member should be given responsibility for calling two or three additional team members. The critical need is for the channels of communications to be predetermined, which may be easily and effectively established with the organization's existing corporate structure.

Here is how one such network might work. The first person aware of a crisis contacts the emergency personnel coordinator, crisis manager, and all recovery managers. The emergency personnel coordinator contacts emergency personnel only. The crisis manager contacts the assistant crisis manager, crisis control room coordinator, and evacuation coordinator. The assistant crisis manager contacts the public relations manager. The public relations manager contacts the media spokesperson, press relations coordinator, and appropriate outside public relations personnel. Additional members of the public relations team contact other team members.

Important items that crisis team members should have are a wallet card with names and phone numbers of emergency team members and local emergency personnel; a cellular phone; a beeper, paging equipment, or car phone for key personnel; and communications equipment in the crisis control room, including a facsimile machine, portable telephone, and emergency contact instructions for families of key personnel, neighbors, and the telephone answering service.

Setting Up a Crisis Control Room

It is important that a separate area, either offices or a conference room, be equipped to serve as a crisis control center and that all team members are aware of its location. Ideally, the room should be away from the public areas and the executive offices, and be easily accessible to outside personnel. It is also suggested that a separate area be provided for family members and/or community volunteers to gather. The area for families of emergency victims should be away from the media center.

Establishing a Media Center

A predesignated, convenient location for greeting and briefing the media on an ongoing basis during the crisis is critical. This center could also serve as the command center for the organization's public relations personnel. The availability of a number of telephones for the media to use after a briefing is also important. The equipment and materials that should be included in the media center include: laptops or computers with modems, a videotape player and monitor, a microphone or bullhorn, a 35mm slide projector, manual typewriters, the organization's letterhead, updated media directories, prepared press list, paper and pens, press release paper, and name tags.

Identifying "Need-to-Know" Audiences

During and after a crisis, there are a number of people—internal and external—who must be communicated with in a timely manner. For this reason, it is essential that updated names and phone numbers be kept in the crisis response plan and that each team member understands his or her specific communications responsibilities.

The various people who should be contacted depend on the nature of the situation and the priority of the moment. Some crises (such as a fire, for example) would require immediate notification of community authorities.

Monitoring the Attitudes of Our Publics

Ideally, the crisis communications plan should also include some means for gauging the attitudes and opinions of the various publics that could be affected by a disaster: staff, general community, and industry. Many companies routinely conduct employee and community surveys to ensure that they have a current understanding of how these important constituencies perceive them. Such surveys also help to point out potential concerns before they take on crisis proportions.

There are often a variety of circumstances in which documentation of employee and/or community support can prove highly valuable in times of a disaster. The ability to quickly sample community opinions can also prove useful in creating pre- and postevent benchmarks of public attitudes.

Supplying a "SWAT" Team

Emergency situations frequently demand overnight and/or weekend production support from public relations and advertising agencies, typesetters, printers, photographers, artists, media buyers, direct-mail houses, and related communications specialists. Not all vendors are equipped—or willing—to work on such a basis. Much time can be lost trying to track down the private phone numbers of people who can be counted on in an emergency. Therefore, it is a good idea to set up this support network in advance.

Writing and Reviewing the Plan

It is important that the organization's personnel work jointly with outside legal counsel in the development and implementation of the crisis communications plan. Drafts would be reviewed by the executive committee, who would also be involved in the implementation process.

The public relations team would update all names, phone numbers, and addresses immediately upon receipt of changes and issue change notices or reprinted inserts. The plan should be reviewed thoroughly at least once a year.

Training and Testing

Each member of the emergency response team should receive communications training at least twice a year, including a thorough understanding of the organization's policies, familiarization with the crisis plan, review of crisis scenarios and related public relations vulnerabilities, annual team orientation, and participation in mock drills.

These topics could be addressed in an internal crisis prevention and response workshop, which provides the ability to bring department heads together and underscores management's commitment to disaster planning.

The manager or the director of public relations will most likely be responsible for the media relations during a disaster. However, it is recommended that all members of the emergency response team be provided with media training.

Exhibit 13.3 illustrates many of the do's and don'ts of dealing with media interviews and general media relations.

Familiarizing members with the workings of the media will streamline the flow of information during a crisis. This training will also highlight the importance of complete and timely disclosure of available facts in a clear, concise, and understandable manner to the media and the public. The media training process will clarify roles and responsibilities and provide a means for testing the plan under simulated conditions.

Once the plan is approved, it is recommended that each facet of the program be tested. A call-back test of the telephone communications network (pyramid system) should be conducted during both business and nonbusiness hours. Each team member should make his or her prearranged calls, asking contacts to do likewise, and then call the test coordinator to verify completion of calls or report any difficulties encountered.

Team members' knowledge of their specific responsibilities can be tested by telephone inquiries, by written tests, or in group seminars. However, if time allows, the most effective way of testing the plan is with mock crisis drills. A single simulated disaster exercise could be easily conducted in a classroom or workshop setting and based upon previously identified crisis scenarios. Assistance in simulated disaster training may be available through local disaster agencies and emergency personnel organizations.

The written crisis plan should be distributed to all members of the emergency response team, department managers, and supervisors of emergency response team personnel. Copies should be placed in all key locations. All supervisors should be made generally aware of the existence of the manual in the event they need to contact emergency response team members. Distribution and updating should be assigned to the public relations team. Distribution may include the plan being placed on an internal Web site for quick and easy reference by team members.

Risk Communication, Terrorism, and Reputation Management

In recent years, situations have demanded the creation of subspecialties in the area of crisis communications. These spin-offs are risk communication, terrorism, and reputation management. Each follows the basic planning approach, but with some added considerations.

Risk Communication

This form of information flow focuses on warnings to the public. They may include but are not limited to sirens, metal detectors, seat belts, ozone depletion, global warming, or toxic

E X H I B I T **13.3**

Preparing for the Crisis Interview

Corporate communications staffers as well as supervisory field personnel should refer to this checklist of media interview "Dos and Don'ts."

DOs

- Notify top management of the emergency as soon as possible.
- Channel all information inquiries to designated spokespersons.

- Set up communications command post away from the scene where interviews can be conducted
- Find out from top management what the impact of the crisis might be, and use that information to establish communication strategy.

- Be open and honest. Give the media the who, what, when, where, why, and how, to the best of your knowledge at the time. But stick to the facts and avoid speculation.

- Demonstrate the company's concern about the incident, but avoid causing panic.

- Provide as much information as possible, but keep answers brief.
- Write down what you want to say to help focus the response and limit the scope of questioning.

- Have complete information packets available for the media as soon as possible. Have them prepared in advance if possible.
- Work with government and regulatory agencies who might be making announcements about the incident or the company.
- Keep commitments to reporters. Get back to them with the information before the deadline.

- Have a designated spokesperson available to the media 24 hours a day for as many days as necessary until the story fades away.

DON'Ts

- Speculate about circumstances or possible causes of the incident.
- Minimize the problem to the media. If the situation is serious, say so. They'll find out sooner or later anyway.
- Blame anyone for anything. When all of the pertinent facts are known, state them, but avoid passing judgment.
- Release information about people if it will violate their privacy. Respond to the media as quickly as possible. Failure to respond in a timely fashion will lead to negative or incomplete coverage.
- Say "no comment." It will make you look guilty. Instead, explain why you can't discuss the matter at the present time—investigations are not yet complete; legal action is pending; next of kin have not been notified; etc.
- Make off-the-record comments/statements. Everything that is said to a reporter is always on the record.
- Play favorites among the media. It will cause hard feelings and damage your credibility.
- Try to be promotional in news releases or interviews. An emergency is not the time to pitch products or services.
- Ask a reporter not to use something you have said in an interview. That is a sure way to guarantee the comment will be used.
- Answer questions outside your area of expertise. If you don't know an answer, say so.

- Tell a reporter how to write or report a story. He/she will resent your interference. It is appropriate for you to offer to clarify statements or verify facts.
- Answer leading, hypothetical questions. Focus on the actual events as you know them and stick to the facts.

waste. This specialty is felt most in the areas of environmental affairs, health care, technology, and the regulatory process. Risk communication deals with informing people about the existence, nature, severity, or acceptability of risks. It also seeks to quantify risks and to create scenarios to act as a bridge between groups and organizations.

As recommended in this chapter, it is necessary to avoid secrecy; use fact-filled responses; grasp the economic impact of the event; speak in a single, coherent voice; and take the initiative, especially if the information you must disseminate is negative. Other goals in this framework should accept perceptions as reality and take a proenvironment stance. An organization's words and actions must bear this out. Perhaps the most important strategy to implement is to position your company as seeking the truth. One method to accomplish this is to employ independent testing when problems inevitably arise.

PRoEthics

Reputation Management and W. R. Grace

Maintaining a positive corporate reputation can be a never-ending process, even long after the crisis is over. Take the case of W. R. Grace & Co., whose company is the basis of Disney's 1999 movie, *A Civil Action*. The movie once again brings to light the case involving chemical spills and children dying of leukemia, allegedly caused by contaminated well water. Grace has maintained since the beginning that it was not responsible for the contamination, and in 1986 the company paid $8 million to settle the case and end the court battle. Regardless, a best-selling book and a Hollywood movie continue to keep the case in the public eye, and thirteen years later Grace is still fighting for its reputation.

Hollywood's version of the case portrays Grace as the corporate giant that has destroyed the environment and torn families apart. It's an image Grace can't escape, despite the fact that it has spent more than a decade building its reputation and positively contributing to the community.

When the case was brought against Grace in 1982, the company didn't have a crisis strategy and failed in its efforts to communicate with the general public or its own employees. So what was Grace's game plan this time around? How does a company defend itself against Hollywood and Disney's interpretation of the story?

First, the company developed a Web site that offered facts and information that were not presented in the book or movie. Then, the company made sure to inform its 6,300 employees about the film and the upcoming issues. Faxes were sent to staff members, and management spoke to employees at the larger company facilities. Information kits were also sent to employees to describe the background of the situation. By equipping employees with information, they could help answer questions and spread a positive word to the public.

Grace also had plans to contact business and community leaders with its message. On the media side, Grace planned to meet with editorial boards, send press kits to the trade media, and make contact with reporters in the top twenty markets. Also in Grace's long-term PR plan was communications with the community, reminding them of the massive efforts toward environmental cleanup.

PR professionals familiar with the situation say Grace will have to concentrate PR efforts on the recurring problem for years. As long as the book and film receive media attention, Grace will be forced to follow with a reputation management plan and do its own corporate cleanup.

Terrorism

In 1970, there were 298 recorded incidents of terrorism worldwide; by 1992, that number had leaped to 5,404. In 1999, President Clinton voiced concerns that domestic terrorism would be a fact of life in the United States in the next century. The forms terrorism takes range from product tampering, bombing, and hijacking to extortion, arson, and sabotage. These actions can result in lives lost, injuries, property damage, rumors, lawsuits, embarrassment, or simple misunderstandings. What is certain is that terrorism instills fear and creates widespread public attention. It is deliberate and premeditated and is used to achieve a political, social, or religious objective.

A contingency plan to handle this occurrence can mean the success or failure of an organization. Creating a strategy to deal with terrorism can help to contain the situation, allow positive counteractions, and maintain efficiency under fire. A good counterterrorism plan will identify the areas that are vulnerable in your organization, which terrorists may exploit. Once policies and procedures have been agreed upon by management, then specific tactics or action steps can be drawn up to thwart any attempts.

Reputation Management

In the wake of mismanagement of emergencies and crises by major organizations in the 1990s, reputation management evolved as an area ripe for development. From Exxon's handling of the *Valdez* to W. R. Grace's decades-long battle to emerge from a cloud of suspicion, preserving the reputation and credibility of a company and its leadership is now seen as paramount. It falls not to the lawyers but to the public relations practitioners, who are sensitive to the human issues an incident, emergency, or crisis may inspire.

Summary

Preparation—it is perhaps the only assurance that a public relations practitioner has that the flames of crisis may be extinguished before the organization's existence in the marketplace is destroyed. This proactive position is best accomplished through a crisis communications plan. It is a tool that works to protect the integrity and future of an organization and is more than a corporate insurance policy.

As suggested throughout this chapter, the responsibility for such foresight and planning falls to the public relations or communications manager. It is that person's task, if not burden, to anticipate the dreaded episodes that seem unlikely to occur, and then to prepare with vigor and precision as if their eventuality were tomorrow.

Once senior management has endorsed the process and the planning has begun, the remainder of the work lies in the organization and testing of the program. This is where the questions begin. What is most likely to happen in a given company or industry? What will be the response, and who will give it? If the public relations practitioner is wise, what is the contingency when the original approach fails?

Crisis—it is not the fault of the communications professionals within an organization, yet it's the most likely of any assignment that will be faced to demonstrate why public relations practitioners are a vital part of the management team.

QUESTIONS

1. Why do you think firms, even those as sophisticated as Fortune 500 companies, conduct business without a crisis communication plan? How might they best be persuaded to adopt such a plan?

2. What is the single most important attribute an organization must maintain with its public during a corporate crisis?

3. What are the various advantages to employing a message action plan in a crisis communications program?

4. Why is it important to have the involvement of top management in crisis communications planning?

5. In your opinion, what are four or five most "suspect" or vulnerable industries as relating to facing a crisis? What special precautions can they make?

READINGS

Richard A. Barry. "What to Do When the Roof Falls In." *Business Marketing* (March 1984): 96–98, 100.

Laurence Barton. *Crisis in Organizations: Management and Communications in the Heat of Chaos.* Cincinnati, OH: South-West Publishing Co, 1992.

———. "Crisis Management: Selecting Communications Strategy." *Management Decisions* 28, no. 6 (1990): 5–8.

Douglas A. Cooper. "CEOs Must Weigh Legal and Public Relations Approaches." *Public Relations Journal* (January 1992).

Scott M. Cutlip, Allen H. Center, and Glen M. Broom. *Effective Public Relations.* (7th ed.). Englewood Cliffs, NJ: Prentice Hall, 1994.

Steven Fink. *Crisis Management: Planning for the Inevitable.* New York: American Management Association, 1986.

Janet Fulk and Charles Steinfield. *Organizations and Communication Technology.* Newbury Park, CA: Sage Publications, 1990.

David J. Hickson. "A Strategic Contingencies Theory of Intraorganizational Power." *Administrative Science Quarterly* 16 (1971): 216–229.

Irving Janis. "Group Identification Under Conditions of External Danger." *British Journal of Medical Psychology* 36 (1963): 227–238.

Priscilla Murphy. "Using Two-Person Bargaining Games to Plan Communications Strategy." *Public Relations Quarterly* (Summer 1990): 27–32.

Stephen P. Taylor. "Communication is the Key to Containing Crisis." *Hotel and Resort Industry* (December 1990): 48–49, 52.

Lawrence R. Werner. "When Crisis Strikes, Use a Message Action Plan." *Public Relations Journal* (August 1990): 30–31.

DEFINITIONS

crisis: Any nonroutine event that could be disruptive to business operations.

groupthink: The tendency of groups to arrive at an agreement at the expense of objective, critical thinking.

hyperturbulence: A situation in which turbulence has overwhelmed the capacities of some members of the environment or industry to adapt.

information richness: A way to manage crisis through the reasoned use of media channels.

message action plan (MAP): A one-page blueprint that highlights the elements of the crisis communications plan.

publics: Arise when a group of people face a similar indeterminate situation, recognize what is problematic in that situation, and organize to do something about the problem.

telephone pyramid: A crisis team communications method based on a hierarchy of importance.

14 International and Intercultural Realities

Living in a Global Village

CHAPTER OBJECTIVES

When you have completed this chapter, you should be able to:

- Recognize cultural differences
- Recognize difficulties in "translating" messages/campaigns

Of all the world's myriad professions, public relations would appear, at first glance, to be the most uniquely American. After all, what other country could have birthed an army of fast-talking, gold-chain–laden Hollywood press agents? Beyond that stereotype, however, historians agree that America's media-heavy, money-driven capitalistic system was a natural spawning ground for the public relations profession, especially considering that America is often regarded as a place where, to borrow from a popular advertising slogan, image is everything.

The United States, though, isn't the only country whose citizens and businesspersons have a healthy regard for self-image. That's why a study of the practice of public relations in foreign countries proves to be fascinating. It also proves to be, at times, quite frustrating.

Consider the contrasts. It's not unusual to find cases where the PR profession has been used for nearly a century in one nation, while it remains practically nonexistent in the country next door. On top of that, some countries that once knew the value of aggressive, international PR are the same ones that seem lost in understanding it today.

Part of the reason, of course, is political turmoil. New governments and changing governing ideologies frequently alter the face of individual countries. Nations shifting from totalitarian communism to anything-goes capitalism, as in Eastern Europe, naturally experience a sudden need for open communications. These countries have discovered, sometimes rather painfully, that after decades of keeping information from the public, they must instantly develop ways to quickly inform and educate the masses on political and economic reforms.

In turn, when a once lively and thriving nation goes dark—like Cuba in the 1960s or Iran in the 1970s—there's no tolerance for any view outside that expressed by the iron-fisted dictator. The practice of PR dies alongside individual freedom. Still, regardless of the political bent of a country, there's always an undeniable need for some form of PR—even if it's nothing more than pushing the single-minded view of the current dictator down the public's throat.

Countries that try to ignore public relations altogether often meet with disastrous consequences. A Russian public relations intern in the United States, Maria Sevostyanova, dramatized this to a reporter from *The Charlotte Observer*: "During the late 1700s, famine caused the Russian peasants to revolt. The government's response was to import potatoes and spread them among the peasants so they could grow more food. But no one told the peasants that the roots, not the leaves, were the edible part of the plant. People were getting sick and dying from eating just the leaves, while the potatoes rotted in the ground.

"I see public relations as teaching people to eat the potato roots instead of the leaves," Sevostyanova explains. "I've learned that you must communicate from a perspective people appreciate and through methods they understand."

PRoActive
Cultural Missteps

Here are some cases of people who were under the delusion that they had already successfully communicated:

- The owner of a dry-cleaning shop in Bangkok hung out a sign that said, "Drop your trousers here for best results."

- Another cleaners in Rome displayed a sign saying, "Ladies, leave your clothes here and spend the afternoon having a good time."

- The manager of a Paris hotel put a sign on the front desk saying, "Leave your values here before going upstairs."

- The British division of McDonald's was damaged by a persistent rumor that the company supported the IRA. It spent time and money tracing the rumor to its source—a CNN program seen in England reported that McDonald's senior management encouraged its employees to invest in IRAs. IRA in the United States means "Individual Retirement Account," while in Great Britain it means the "Irish Republican Army."

Ferdie's Follies

Primitive communications, combined with lack of public awareness, can be used to forgive the eighteenth-century Russians, but how can one explain what happened in the Philippines in the 1980s? The highly Westernized, PR-savvy, Pacific Island nation was one of the first foreign countries to rely on a well-financed public relations campaign to promote its image. The astute Filipinos hired a prototype American public relations firm, The Hamilton Wright Organization, back in 1905. That foresight helped transform the smattering of islands into a modern, twentieth-century nation while most of its neighbors remained mired in the Stone Age.

With PR woven so tightly into its history, it's hard to comprehend the series of events that led to the crashing fall of the Philippines' powerful Marcos family in 1986. Today, most political scientists agree that war-hero-turned-president Ferdinand Marcos was not overthrown by a political or military coup, or even by a popular uprising. Marcos, one of the world's richest and most powerful rulers, was toppled by bad PR.

"Looking back, many of Marcos's most grievous errors amounted to departures from contemporary views of good basic public relations as open, accurate, two-way communication with diverse publics," notes communications professor Hugh M. Culbertson.

What Culbertson is saying is that Ferdinand messed up—big time. And he got a helping hand from his wife, Imelda. Who can forget the worldwide television shots of Imelda's 3,000 pairs of shoes in stark contrast to so many Filipinos who lived in abject poverty?

Less known among the rest of the world, but well known among Filipinos, were Mrs. Marcos's equally innumerable bra and gown collections. Toss in the Marcos family's twenty luxury vacation homes and the billions of dollars Ferdinand allegedly squirreled away from his nation's treasury, and one begins to see the makings of a public relations disaster.

Yet, even after the snowball of public disdain began rolling down the hill, the Marcos were undeterred. Culbertson, once a visiting professor at De La Salle University in Manila, noted that when President Ronald Reagan announced plans to visit the Marcos palace in Malacanang, there was much concern because Reagan's route would take him past a series of horrible slums. "Rather than improve conditions in the slums, the first lady allegedly built a wall to obscure them from view," Culbertson writes.

The deeper his troubles grew, the more PR blunders Marcos made. Campaign videos of a barefoot Ferdinand pretending to be one of the people by planting rice in the country were so transparent they were met with derision from even the most unsophisticated Filipino. Marcos then made a series of U.S. television appearances during which he proclaimed everything was under control in his island nation, despite news reports that showed hundreds of thousands of people gathered in Manila's Rizal Memorial Park supporting his most hated political rival. "The clear indication was that the president was a liar, a fool, or both," Culbertson observed.

Marcos still didn't get the message. "Forgotten, apparently, was the lesson of history that martyrdom often enhances the popularity and symbolic power of political figures," Culbertson writes. "Many Filipinos saw the death of former Senator Benigno Aquino, widely thought to be engineered by Marcos, as the most disastrous of the president's mistakes."

Aquino's widow, a political novice named Corazon, was promptly swept into power during a remarkable "bloodless revolution" fueled by the fury of the Philippine people—a public which, ironically, once held both Ferdinand and Imelda Marcos in awe. Had the Marcos employed, or heeded, a single relatively skilled public relations adviser, many feel the family could have easily held on to its empire.

Tremendous Growth

Avoiding the repetition of Ferdinand's follies is only one of a score of factors that account for the healthy growth of PR around the world. The unification of the European Community, the explosive economic growth of Asian and Pacific rim countries, and the awakening of many third-world nations all point to a greater need for PR professionals. Experts predict that the PR industry in Europe will quadruple in the near future, eventually topping $5 billion. (That compares with $10 billion in the United States.) London, currently the public relations capital of Europe—if not the world—is expected to generate about a sixth of that total.

This growth is already shaking up the international PR landscape. In 1980, the world's top five public relations agencies were American-owned; in 1990, only one remained in the top five. British firms are now leading the way, with Britain's powerhouse Shandwick the leader in worldwide public relations billings.

Weaker Foundations

Lagging behind, however, is education. Sam Black, former president of the International Public Relations Association, bemoans the fact that foreign colleges and universities have been slow to add PR professors and disciplines to their curriculum. "In Europe, and particularly in Great Britain, the steady growth in public relations practice was not matched by a corresponding development of public relations education," Black notes. That, however, could be viewed as good news for adventurous U.S. PR students. The worldwide demand for those graduating with PR degrees and related skills is expected to remain strong.

China, surprisingly enough, appears to be the exception when it comes to education. Black notes that while public relations was almost nonexistent in the populous Asian nation before 1981, things have changed dramatically since then. "Nearly every Chinese city now has an active public relations society and I think this rapid development has been due to availability of public relations education at universities in many parts of China. There are now public relations programs in more than 100 Chinese universities and colleges."

Following up on Black's research, Ni Chen and Culbertson report in a joint article that "an estimated 750,000 people now practice public relations in various sectors of Chinese society. . . . No other field of study or profession appears to have spread as quickly as public relations in China." The pair attributes the growth to "the death of Mao Zedong in 1976, and the end of the Cultural Revolution that year" marking "a turning point in modern Chinese history. . . . This created new challenges and problems. People became reluctant to follow government instructions slavishly. They demanded, at the very least, information about what was going on in government institutions which formulated policies affecting their lives. That trend gained strength because many felt officials were corrupt and inefficient. The government and the party lost the people's support and trust. A strongly felt need for public participation in decision making—and citizen dialogue with government—resulted."

Another reason for the wide acceptance of PR in China lies in the makeup of the people themselves. "Chinese culture tends to mix personal and public relations," Chen and Culbertson write. "Because of the Confucian concept of i—emphasis on group loyalty—the Chinese find it difficult to accept purely business transactions. The calculated, impersonal, strictly contractual approach of most Western business deals is seen as unnatural and distasteful. While a relationship may exist for purely business reasons, Chinese prefer transactions to be carried out on a more personal, warm, human level."

American Firms Cashing In

All this foreign activity has American firms scrambling to cash in. Such PR giants as Burson-Marsteller, Manning Selvage & Lee International, Bozell & Jacobs Public Relations, Hill and Knowlton, and dozens of others have expanded their foreign operations in the last decade. Even small agencies have jumped into the fray, following the tried-and-true business tradition of going where the money is.

At the start of the foreign PR boom in the mid-1980s, Hill and Knowlton executive Terrence Fane-Saunders explained to magazine writer Alyse Lynn Booth the reasons for the rapid American response: "It is imperative that corporations operating overseas devise patterns of corporate behavior that contribute to the quality of their relationship in those countries. Any U.S. company that is not developing an international public relations program is ensuring its own failure." Fane-Saunders's cryptic warning rings even truer today.

Joe Epley, a former president of the Public Relations Society of America, cites four reasons why international PR will continue to grow:

- Communication technology is driving unprecedented changes in commerce, communications, lifestyles and political systems
- The realignment of economic power
- Major common issues that recognize no political boundary. The biggest of these issues [being] the environment
- The prospect of unprecedented world peace.

All four, he says, come under the umbrella of "our global society growing closer together and the world's people becoming more interdependent upon each other."

Bull Job Markets

PR graduates and professionals eager to jump on the foreign bandwagon are no doubt asking, "Where do I sign up?" Before going any further, it's important to address what is unquestionably the most "foreign" aspect of work in foreign countries—language. While it remains possible to work in, or even head, a foreign branch office of an American PR firm without knowing the native tongue, employers are increasingly looking for applicants who have that special advantage. Public relations is, after all, a medium of communication.

"I think we're finding more of the people who want to be in the public relations business are multilingual," says Peter G. Osgood of Hill and Knowlton. "We look for people who have a second language. It's definitely a benefit."

Burson-Marsteller representatives reveal that 99 percent of those staffing their European offices are bilingual, with half multilingual. At home, Burson-Marsteller also boasts bilingual or multilingual employees. One of the main reasons for this is that it's simply good PR.

"Russians, for example, really appreciate anyone who can even attempt to speak their language because it's an indication to them that you are interested in their country," explains practitioner Paul Brandus, formerly of NBC News in Moscow. "Even if you speak it poorly and you stumble . . . they really extend open arms."

But sometimes, speaking a language poorly can be even worse. Everyone's heard horror stories about Americans giving speeches or addressing foreign business leaders and making terrible linguistic gaffs. That happened to an unfortunate woman in South America when she relayed a story about an embarrassment she suffered. Using the seemingly correct word "embarazada," what she actually told the startled group was that she'd been "made pregnant" by the words of a colleague.

Even when relying on a trained translator, a speaker must be careful. The common U.S. practice of using expressions, slang, puns, or colloquialisms to help make a point is often an invitation to disaster. In Hong Kong, a computer firm failed to get its point across at the press conference because a beaming official mentioned his company's "grass-roots marketing program." The Chinese translation? "Marketing grass roots in Hong Kong."

The same holds true for press releases and other written materials that are selected for translation. Gerry Dempsey, a New York translation expert, warns that "the original text should be written with translation in mind. Metaphors will usually work in other languages, but plays on words are normally impossible to translate. Jokes, jargon, slang and clichés should always be avoided. Aphorisms, on the other hand, can have a good effect, although they don't always remain intact in translation. 'Killing two birds with one stone,' becomes 'catching two pigeons with one bean,' in Italian, 'hitting two flies with one swat,' in German, and 'catching two fish with one rod,' in Korean."

Some companies have learned to combat these problems by translating everything twice—from English to the targeted language, then back to English; this is called back translation. It's only after comparing the original English with the posttranslated version that a document is deemed ready for distribution.

For those looking for a language major or minor, Dempsey adds that "the most popular languages in corporate America are French, Spanish, German, Italian, Japanese and Chinese. A second tier would include Portuguese, Dutch, Swedish and Korean."

Regrettably, sometimes fluency in a country's native tongue is not enough when it comes to the tightrope act of image building. Dizzying differences in dialects can be dramatic. Consider Dempsey's linguistic coup de grace: "French has two main dialects, Parisian and Quebecois, while German has three (spoken in Germany, Switzerland and Austria). Portuguese has two (Continental and Brazilian) and Dutch has a twin sister called Flemish, which is spoken in Belgium. Spanish is used in scores of countries and territories all over the world."

As an example of how different dialects of the same language can be, consider U.S. English. Yuri Galitzine of Galitzine & Partners, LTD, London, points out that American press releases and brochures are worthless in Britain if the writers don't realize that a truck is a lorry and can't distinguish between a wrench and a spanner.

John Freivalds of the Corporate Word, Inc., Minneapolis, Minnesota, weighs in with his own mind-bender: "As far as language is concerned, in the Baltic Republics, Moldova and the Ukraine, it would be highly offensive to conduct business in Russian, rather than the language of the republic. In other areas, Russian may be considered an acceptable 'lingua franca' for the time being. However, it would be greatly to your advantage, especially in areas such as Armenia and Georgia, to acknowledge in conversation that Russian is only being used for expedience." It's easy to see why so many foreign PR firms are forced to rely heavily upon good native hires.

Culture, Culture, Culture

To turn a cliché (which we'd never do if this were to be translated), the three most important things a foreign service PR professional must learn about the assigned country are culture, culture, and culture. To put it another way, once you've survived the pitfalls of language, watch out for the potholes of culture. Researchers Kevin Avruch and Peter Black describe culture as shared meaning, permitting members of a group "to perceive, interpret, evaluate, and act on and in both external and internal reality"; the keys to cultural identity are language and custom.

Does all this give you a headache? Pop a few aspirin tablets—but only if you're American, of course. John M. Reed, writing for *Public Relations Quarterly,* explains that you should avoid offering your pain pills to Chinese, Latin Americans, Italians, Spanish, or French. Chinese use topical applications to rub in their medicines. Latin Americans, Italians, and the Spanish quizzically go for injections; the French prefer suppositories. "Same product. Same need. Same effect. Delivered differently," Reed reiterates.

"The delivery or distribution of public relations messages through the media follows the same proposition. . . . International PR requires that you bridge a cultural or linguistic gap, or both. That's the trick, the challenge, the key and the success of it in a nutshell. . . . For all intents and purposes, the basic program elements do not change cross-culturally. Research, objectives, methods, programming, and message development remain very much the same. The variable is audience. In media relations, the audience is of a type you must get into the shoes of, and walk in for a while, in order to understand what works, how to operate. With new audience values, you as a professional need new ways of working."

Once you've walked in your target audience's shoes, getting the message to them through the local media can also be a cultural nightmare. "Even 'reporter' must be defined precisely in each nation before media relations can be effective," Reed emphasizes. "Reporter here [America] means a paid employee of a media outlet. Reporters elsewhere fall into three classes":

- Sophisticated journalists—as in Germany and Japan—with whom veracity and the importance of the story dictate the coverage
- Unsophisticated hacks—as in hot-weather countries in the Mediterranean, Middle East, Africa, South Asia and most of Latin America—for whom reporting may be a second or third source of income, and for whom personal gain and their editors' biases are most important
- Government writers—in the state-controlled environments—for whom compliance with government-approved story lines is mandatory.

PRoSpeak

Multiculturalism: The World at Large
Remarks to the Public Relations Society of America (Excerpts)

Peter Cummings
Neilsen Research Worldwide

The greatest single barrier to successful communication is the delusion that it has already occurred. That delusion can be fueled by a number of different factors: by impatience; by arrogance; by ignorance; or simply by the assumption that the rest of the world is just a slightly larger version of ourselves.

There's a corollary to that point: It is that the second biggest obstacle to communication in the world market is the delusion that there are shortcuts. Oh sure, you can take speed courses in foreign languages. But communication is more than just language.

But that is sometimes a hard lesson for us Americans. When we are confronted with challenges, we like to think that there must be some sort of technological fix.

After all, if satellites can beam CNN to small villages in San Salvador and Siberia . . . if astronauts can make house calls in outer space to try to fix telescopes that are malfunctioning . . . if technology can reduce the entire Library of Congress to a small stack of compact discs—we wonder why that same technological genius can't be applied to the problems of missed intercultural communications, and to the challenge of international misunderstanding.

No wonder, then, that about thirty years ago we latched on to the theories of an otherwise obscure professor of English named Marshall McLuhan. McLuhan was so impressed by the ways that the technology of communication was tying the world together that he coined the phrase, "the global village." That striking image suggested that we would all soon live next door in a cozy international neighborhood, where we could chat with each other electronically as easily as if we were gossiping over our backyard fences.

And in many ways McLuhan's predictions have come true. For example, suppose I were to tell you that last Saturday night a young Frenchman picked up his Chinese girl in his German car and took her to an Indian restaurant. After dinner they went to the theater to see *Miss Saigon,* a musical that first opened in London about American soldiers in Viet Nam, based on an opera by an Italian composer about an American soldier and a Japanese woman. After the theater, they went to a Kuwaiti-owned nightclub where they so enjoyed dancing to the Latin beat of the music that they forgot to look at their Swiss watches and only realized that it was time to go home when the leather on their stylish British shoes began to wear thin. The point is that you couldn't know, just from my description, whether it took place in Hong Kong, Geneva, Rome, Mexico City, Paris, or Buenos Aires.

Or consider this other example: Suppose you suffered a spell of amnesia and woke up in an office somewhere in Europe, the United States, or Japan— an office humming with personal computers, fax machines, modems, telephones, voice mail, and all the rest. You would not know where you were without consulting something that told you which language was being spoken there.

Those two examples show just how much of McLuhan's predictions have come true. But the concept of "the global village" always implied more than just a global shopping mall and a nexus of electronic tools. It also suggested that somehow intercultural misunderstanding would tend to dissolve in a flood of electronically enabled communication, that hostilities rooted in differences would naturally dissipate through electronically enhanced dialogue.

But in that larger sense of the term, we now know that a funny thing happened on the way to "the global village." From Bosnia to Beirut, from Mogadishu to Miami Beach, it is painfully clear that the more optimistic reading of McLuhan is, to say the least, premature.

In many ways, a more fitting image of our world today is that supplied by the historian who wrote that "We spin out as from a centrifuge, flying apart socially and politically, at the same time that enormous centripetal forces press us all into more and more of a single mass every year. The world is more concentrated and more diffuse than ever before."

To be sure, technology can improve the logistics of communication, in that way serving as the centrifugal force pulling the world together. But technology cannot, by itself, overcome all the cultural, historical, and economic forces that simultaneously push us apart.

I'm sure you remember Henry David Thoreau's response to the fellow who ran up to him breathlessly and said, "Isn't it exciting that with the new telegraph Maine can now talk to Texas!!" Thoreau replied, "But what if Maine doesn't have anything to say to Texas?" Technology can make communication possible. But it cannot, by itself, overcome the centripetal forces that also split the world apart. It cannot answer Thoreau's question. It cannot ensure that the right messages are formulated, that they are successfully translated, or that they are correctly understood.

The differences that result from cultural differences are often at their most powerful exactly when they are at their most subtle and unexpected. Consider the example of Winston Churchill. You've all seen the old newsreel pictures of Churchill heroically tromping around the bombed-out sections of London, defying enemy aircraft in order to rally the British people to what he called their "finest hour." In all those risky strolls, Churchill never suffered a scratch. Churchill also flew on some missions with the Royal Air Force, sometimes right into clouds of anti-aircraft fire. Again, never a scratch. Finally, when the war was over, Churchill came to the United States for a kind of victory lap and vacation. But while he was here, Churchill failed to reckon with the fact that Americans drive on the opposite side of the street from Britons. So he stepped off a curb after looking the wrong way. Wham! He was immediately hit by a car he never even saw.

And so it often is in a multicultural world. You're often unaware of your ignorance till it hits you from your blind side. Consider the case of the American sent to Tokyo for four days to negotiate a joint venture with a Japanese company.

After three and one-half days of small talk and chitchat, he figured he'd better push things along. So he blurted out, "Can we finally get down to business, please?" Wham! He was hit by a custom he never even saw—a custom that showing impatience will kill your deal in Japan.

Or consider the American businessman who arrived for a meeting with a Saudi executive. After the Saudi asked several questions about the American's flight and his hotel accommodations, the American tried to return the courtesy by asking after the Saudi's wife. Wham! He was hit by a custom he never even saw—the custom that it's considered indecent to ask about a man's wife in Saudi Arabia.

Differences matter. A lot. It seems built into our nature. Differences cause fear and, too often, contempt. Complicating the fact is that our identities and our differences are in large part defined by others. For example, an Ibo may be an Owweri Ibo or an Onitsha Ibo in what was the eastern region of Nigeria. In Lagos, he is simply an Ibo. In London, he is a Nigerian; in New York, he is an African.

Whether we like it or not, our ethnic identity is in part established by others. As I've thought about that incident, by the way, it seems to me to rather neatly sum up both the strengths and weaknesses of the American approach to managing the new global marketplace.

The strength is that we are such a diverse culture in America that in a limited way we are a microcosm of the global cultural diversity. That's part of our strength. The corresponding weakness is that we can too easily mistake that microcosm for the macrocosm.

Reed's second commandment after "know thy reporters" is "know thy publication." "To have an impact in Panama on the political and business elite, what's the optimum choice? The choice is from three TV channels, several radio stations, newspapers in English for the white community, English for the Black community, and Spanish for the rest of the community. The correct answer? None of the above. The ideal outlet is a monthly newsletter of the golf and country club. Anyone who is anyone belongs to the golf and country club, and carefully reads the newsletter."

More interesting examples from Reed:

> In France, business people read national business publications. One hit hits all of France. Business people in Italy read regional business papers, so you cannot go just to one publication. More than any secret of success is the often forgotten fact that the largest concentration of international media personnel in the world is right here in the United States. Centered in Washington, New York and elsewhere (Chicago, San Francisco, Los Angeles and Miami principally), the international press is a ready resource that saves time, money and frustration in dealing with the selection variables.

Playing to the international press in America is a good suggestion. Sometimes, however, even when the mountain's already been brought to you, it's still best to go to the mountain. Experts universally agree that any client who has a long-term commitment in a foreign country should have a PR staff, consultant, or agency situated in that country—which brings us back to the issue of cultural differences.

"Do public relations scholars accept the fact that public relations' basic philosophies and principles are not the same in different societies, and that there may be different types of public relations?" asks Abduirahman H. Al-Enad. "Or do they insist that public relations is public relations, a profession which is expected to behave on the basis of preset values and philosophies that do not change across time or place?"

Al-Enad drives his point home with a simple, eye-opening, matter of semantics: "Public relations is labeled and known as 'general relations' in the Arab world. The term 'public' as it means in the semantics of the English term 'public relations' is not used at all in Arabic, not even in public relations or 'general relations' text books. . . . The political sensitivity of the term 'public' and its association with another sensitive term, 'public opinion,' could be one reason for the intentional mistranslation of it. . . . Public opinion, which was once an essential factor in the evolution of public relations, does not have the same power today in most of these [Third World] countries. The labor force is unorganized and [in some countries] is not allowed to do so. 'The public be damned' is an authoritative living rule in many places."

So why does "general relations" exist in third-world Arab countries at all? Al-Enad says it's because PR "works as an information office in ministries and other governmental agencies. It communicates with the public to achieve mainly one or both of two goals":

- To educate the public on subjects related to client field of work and increase its knowledge about pertinent issues, and persuade it to behave or act differently (e.g., go to school, immunize, obey traffic rules)
- To publicize achievements of client and/or society as a whole, and make the public feel satisfied.

In India, a PR practitioner might need a good dose of aspirin—in all its forms—just to begin understanding that country's diverse culture. Consider what Bombay PR professional Cerena de Souza advises:

> To understand communication problems better, perhaps one needs to understand the vast Indian canvas. India's internal problems are truly complex. A country of more than 850 million, possessing 25 distinct ethnic identities, 1,652 mother tongues of which 15 are officially

recognized; myriad dialects; a stratified caste system; enormous income gaps between the elite and the poor; a bustling middle class of over 100 million; an entrenched trade union; Marxist political parties refusing to disband in spite of changes in Russia; and a population comprising Muslim, Sikh and other smaller minorities alongside the Hindu majority create a truly mind-boggling picture.

How would one begin? Souza says computers are one way. They're surprisingly popular in a country where the bullock cart is still a common means of transportation. "Apple and Macintosh are household names," Souza notes. "So where do communicators fit in today's [India] scene?" she continues. "A tremendous need for professionals exists as never before. Good communicators are rare. Industry is continuously on the search for them. And there is a felt need for professionals in government, and other avenues of service."

Farther east, a PR man or woman in Japan often finds that the first, and most difficult, obstacle to overcome is the Japanese cultural bias toward extreme modesty. "Many Japanese regard public relations as a kind of self-promotion or self-propaganda," Professor Toshio Matsuoka of Kanagawa University explains. "They regard it as the opposite of modesty, a traditionally admired virtue. Modesty requires good deeds be done in silence. To talk about good deeds and success would, therefore, be very rude, a form of self-propaganda." Matsuoka says Japanese firms instead focus their efforts inward on what they consider their two most important publics—their employees and their customers. That, of course, translates into detailed internal employee communication networks and diligent customer relations—both cousins of traditional public relations.

White Cats

On the other hand, the Japanese certainly know how to use, or try to use, public relations in other countries. A classic World War II story from Burma points this out. It also illustrates how damaging a cultural mistake can be, and how easily it can be rectified once an understanding of the problem is reached.

Cleveland Amory recalls, in his book *The Cat Who Came for Christmas,* that the Burmese people hold white cats sacred. The Japanese used this knowledge to mount a PR campaign aimed at turning Burmese road workers against the British Army. The Japanese did this by spreading rumors that the Brits had no respect for white cats. The offended road builders began walking off the job in waves, grinding the critical building projects to a halt.

An equally clever English colonel fought back. He scoured the countryside for all the white cats he could find and scattered them around the worksites. He then ordered the creation of a white cat logo, which he emblazoned on every jeep, truck, and tank in the area. The word spread among the Burmese that the British aerodromes, roads, and even the army itself were invincible. Why? Because they were all protected by the white cat.

Returning to Latin America, where cats are just cats, some see Reed's harsh indictment of the Spanish media's "payment for placement" culture as a fading relic of the past. "Latin journalism has made tremendous strides," counters practitioner Ruben Aguilar. "While it's still possible to find journalists with their hands out. . . . Increasingly it is the news content of the material and the veracity of the source that determine coverage. . . . Treat the media in Latin America as you would media in the U.S. You'll be pleasantly surprised by your reception."

Ketchum Public Relations Worldwide's Raymond Kotcher writes: "The media in Latin America is increasingly sophisticated, reflecting a new generation of professional journalists." Aguilar adds that another positive in Latin America is that they're generally understanding about language. "Latin Americans are used to hearing CEOs who aren't fluent in Spanish and especially, Portuguese."

But don't go overboard, in Latin America or anywhere else. Former PRSA president Epley reminds us that the view of the Ugly American remains alive and well overseas. "[Some] in our country and elsewhere feel that Americans are too arrogant and elitist. We may think we invented public relations, but developing nations are using the same tools we do and, in many respects, are doing a better job than we are."

Around the World in Eighteen Minutes

So, with all these language and cultural problems, is anybody out there getting it right? Of course. Public relations is, if anything, resilient and adaptable. A quick trip around the world makes this clear.

Melvin L. Sharpe, writing in *Public Relations Review,* starts us on our global journey. In Brazil, PR practitioners must have both a university degree and a professional license before they can write their first release, giving the profession a respect it lacks even in the United States. Turkey, an Arab country in a region known for harsh traditions that strangle professional women, nonetheless has a healthy number of women in PR leadership roles. Canada has a streamlined PR industry that no doubt grew out of the fact that the country boasts a few national newspapers instead of thousands of smaller "hometown" presses. The Netherlands has seen fit to weave ethical issues into most of its PR practices; Dutch PR students, in particular, are taught to weigh social benefit against organizations' profit.

Nigeria, surrounded by a virtual PR wasteland, credits its long business relationship with Britain for its astoundingly advanced PR industry. According to Sharpe, the African nation "has a strong national public relations association, an excellent code of ethics, a professionally controlled licensing process, entry level education requirements and continuing education requirements for practitioners, and a cabinet minister in government with public relations responsibilities for the country."

Continuing our travels, one discovers that Hong Kong has a bustling PR industry. "Hong Kong is the center of a vast geographic, cultural, political and economic region," says Alan Mole of Shandwick Asia/Pacific. "And it is increasingly becoming the center of choice for international PR covering the People's Republic of China, Taiwan, Indonesia, Malaysia, the Philippines, South Korea, and in some cases, even Australia."

In Spain, the profession has made the jump from publicity and financial services to the more advanced areas of crisis management, the environment, high technology, and health care. In France, private PR firms are growing faster than corporate or government internal departments, which is always a positive sign of widespread use and acceptance. French PR professionals have also branched out into the graduate school level of "crisis managers, issue managers, public affairs experts, lobbyists, investor relations and financial specialists."

In Slovenia, following a dark period when PR professionals were classified as "sociopolitical workers" and chained into the service of the ruling ideology, things have begun to open up. A PR course is now part of the curriculum of Ljubljana University. "The nineties are flourishing years for Slovenian business communications," decrees Brane Gruban of Pristop Communication Group, Ljubljana, Slovenia. "PR in Slovenia has developed into a professional field, which in terms of quality and technical equipment is, comparatively speaking, closer to the U.S. than to neighboring European countries."

Private Firms' Successes

Private firms that have invested time, money, and effort in studying the international PR landscape have found it fiscally rewarding. American Express, with its famous "If they're lost or stolen, we'll replace them" motto leading the way, has always been tuned in to good international PR. Conducting business in more than thirty-two languages, the credit card company relies heavily upon local PR executives to avoid language and cultural problems.

Other companies that have used strong PR campaigns to fuel their overseas expansion include Whirlpool, Upjohn, Honeywell, AT&T, and Avon cosmetics, just to name a few.

Avon's case is particularly interesting. In the early 1980s, when the cosmetic giant entered new countries like China, executives discovered that cultural hurdles in a few nations made it difficult to rely upon their famous door-to-door, "Avon calling," direct-marketing technique. The natives simply weren't used to that kind of doorstep sales approach. Forced to sell retail, Avon had to develop a less personal method of publicizing its products to get the word out. To accomplish this, Avon decided to build name recognition, and in turn publicize its retail products, through the creation and sponsorship of the International Women's Running Circuit. The races, staged in seventeen countries, have been so successful that Avon has gained enough acceptance to start going door-to-door in countries where that marketing technique was previously unheard of.

"Many times, we were told that the press would not carry news of our events unless we bought paid advertising or worked out some financial arrangement, but we found this not to be true," says Avon's then PR director William J. Corbett. "It was impossible for the press to ignore a truly newsworthy event with thousands of women running through the main streets of a sizable city. The Running Circuit not only increases our visibility in our host countries, it carries the message of fitness, health and beauty to tens of million of people."

War and Amnesia

The activities of Israel's tourist ministry following the Persian Gulf War are a good illustration of crisis PR at work overseas. Faced with making up for the loss of $700 million in tourist revenue in less than a year because of the war, Israel decided to both ignore and rewrite history. Avoiding the volatile term Middle East, Israel began promoting itself as part of the peaceful Eastern Mediterranean. That enabled the country to dance around concerns tourists might have about renewed hostilities or terrorism.

"We don't need to tell people that security has been tightened," explains Barry Biederman of Biederman, Kelly & Schaffer Inc., Israel's U.S. representative. "We don't want to expose raw nerves. We implicitly answer people's questions and fears by portraying Israel as an attractive, warm place, and also as a country with a rich, historical background." As with PR everywhere, Israel's motto appears to be "whatever works."

Mohammed Coming to the Mountain

So far, we've focused our discussion on the PR explosion in foreign countries. A sister phenomenon is the rapid increase in the number of foreign countries promoting themselves inside America and around the world. One needs only to look at legendary boxer Mohammed Ali's bank account to realize one way this has been accomplished in the past quarter-century. When the famed American boxer was at the top of this game, his fights were so huge they exceeded the boundaries of sport and became international events. Countries around the world began clamoring to stage the matches, not because of a passion for the sport but to take advantage of the mountain of publicity showered upon the host city. Ali was such an effective promotional tool that a single forty-five-minute boxing match could result in decades of name recognition for a previously unknown city or country.

Zaire, Africa, a previously obscure city, remains indelibly etched in the world's consciousness because of that exhilarating moment nearly three decades ago when Ali came off the ropes to knock out the previously invincible George Foreman. And who can forget the thunderous "Thrilla in Manila," a raging war in which a battered Ali prevailed over his nemesis, Smoking Joe Frazier? Regrettably, no single human holds the magical allure that Ali once held. However, that doesn't mean it's impossible to duplicate the recognition Ali brought to various countries. It's just harder and more expensive.

Getting the Olympics

Today, the best, albeit very expensive, way to gain worldwide recognition for a city or country is to host the Olympic Games. For two weeks—regardless of whether it's the Summer or Winter Games—the eyes of America and the rest of the world are focused on whatever city is playing host. This can bring enormous benefits to a city and country, especially a previously unknown one.

While the advantages of all that publicity are obvious, a number of academic studies have been undertaken to try and measure the Olympian effect. One of the most extensive was undertaken by Israel D. Nebenzahl of Bar-Ilan University, Israel, and Eugene D. Jaffe, Baruch College, City University of New York. The pair charted consumer acceptance of Korean-manufactured electronics before and after the 1988 Olympic Games in Seoul.

Quoting *The Economist,* the professors began their data-rich study by stating that the Koreans had specific goals in mind when bidding for the Games: "South Korea has invested $3.5 billion in staging them [the Games], but the government expects twice that to come back in higher exports. . . . South Korean businessmen hope the rest of the world will see them not just as makers of cheap footwear and textiles, or even of cars and ships, but advanced goods like semiconductors and computers too." Not surprisingly, Nebenzahl and Jaffe conclude that hosting the Olympics did indeed "improve respondents' attitudes towards the electronic products made in Korea." On top of that, the professors discovered that "respondents who viewed the Games with relatively high frequency were willing to pay more for each of the four [Korean-made] products [two different brands of videocassette recorders and microwave ovens]."

However, and it's a big "however," the professors warn that hosting an Olympics can be a $3.5-billion dice roll. A positive outcome, especially in today's violent world, can never be ensured. One need only recall the disaster of the Munich Games to see how quickly things can backfire: Munich, Germany—a city and nation still trying to recover from the inhumanity of the Holocaust—coping with a band of terrorists who murdered Jewish athletes in the Olympic Village. Then, when German officials cut a deal with the terrorists that allowed them to escape, it was seen by many around the world as further evidence of Germany's continuing hatred of Jews. What began as Germany's sincere attempt to repair its image ended up, at the very least, merely reminding the world of its past.

Similarly, but to a much lesser extent, the 1994 Winter Games in Lillehammer, Norway, were overshadowed by the tabloid frenzy surrounding the story of U.S. ice skaters Tonya Harding and Nancy Kerrigan. To summarize, associates of Harding admitted that they conspired to disable Kerrigan, Harding's rival, in order to give Harding a better chance of winning an Olympic medal and cashing in on post-Olympic endorsement gold. A hired hitman clubbed Kerrigan in the knee, knocking her out of the U.S. Figure Stating Championships. The injury ultimately failed to keep Kerrigan out of the Olympics. Riding a wave of public sympathy, Kerrigan skated, won the silver medal, and was showered with the endorsements Harding's associates coveted.

Lost in the melodrama were Lillehammer and Norway, the city and country that had spent billions for the windfall of publicity, which ended up being dominated by Harding and Kerrigan. "The sponsor may not be able to ensure that the event he or she is sponsoring has a positive image," Nebenzahl and Jaffe reiterate. "This is a real worry attested to by sports-related violence during European soccer games."

In 1999, the Olympic spirit dimmed anew in the wake of a bribery scandal that alleged that the organizers of the Salt Lake City Games gave International Olympic Committee (IOC) members more than $1 million in cash, gifts, scholarships, and other favors in order to win the 2002 Winter Games. The worst scandal in the modern Olympics' 105-year history resulted in closed-door sessions with the IOC and major corporate sponsors that feared their $50 million investment each was quickly losing value. The companies were concerned that the scandal would snuff out the halo effect of the Olympic rings logo as a promotional tool if the problems persisted. Ten of the eleven companies in the Olympic Program—the highest level of sponsorship—met with the IOC in February 1999 to demand reform. The group included *Sports Illustrated,* McDonald's, John Hancock, Samsung, Coca-Cola, IBM, Visa, United Parcel Service, Xerox, and Eastman Kodak; Panasonic did not send a representative. In a move to pressure the IOC to make changes, John Hancock insurance broke off negotiations with NBC on $20 million in Olympic ads for the 2000 Sydney Olympics. David D'Alessandro, company president, said he was trying to save the Olympics' good name, not force a price reduction. Reforms cover four points: a change in top management, expulsion of any IOC member linked to the scandal (which spread to the Nagano and Sydney Games), permanent changes in voting for host cities, and open financial records.

Getting the Ink

The examples above are admittedly extreme. Not every nation can host an Olympics, positive or negative. Most foreign public relations efforts consist of much more modest efforts. Like any other individual or business seeking to position its name in front of a specified public, the countries hiring U.S. firms to push them inside America simply want to reap the benefits of some good ink or video. According to Amelia Lobsenz, writing in *Public Relations Journal,* "Foreign governments retain American public relations firms largely for tourism, trade, investments, industrial development and image building."

American PR firms eagerly accept this business because it's both interesting and lucrative. More than a hundred foreign countries regularly contract with U.S. PR firms on an annual basis, providing a major source of income for the PR industry.

"More and more public relations firms are competing for foreign assignments, and we can expect to see more diversity in this area," Lobsenz continues. "The reason is clear. The international public relations practitioner today must be a consultant not only in public relations, but also in business management, marketing, economics, law, government, sociology, politics, science, technology and international affairs."

Once again, however, taking on a foreign client is not without risk. A significant chapter of PR history covers the downfall of major PR firms and individual PR pioneers who hitched their wagons to turbulent foreign governments. The reason PR firms and practitioners are so vulnerable harkens back to PR itself. If you live by PR, you can die by it. In other words, there is nothing more ironic than a PR firm destroyed by bad public opinion resulting from the representation of a foreign client who suddenly becomes a major American enemy.

That is exactly what has happened numerous times in the past. Pioneer PR practitioners Ivy Lee and Carl Byoir were rocked in the 1930s when one of their clients, Germany, came under the internal influence of the Nazi party. As Germany began instituting racist policies and moved closer to world war, Lee in particular was called into question. He was subsequently dubbed "Poison Ivy" in the halls of Congress. Although Lee denied having anything to do with the German government or German war machine, the catchy "Poison Ivy" tag stuck with him until his death in 1934. Had Ivy Lee lived through the decade and into World War II in the 1940s, the situation no doubt would have worsened.

Similarly, another pioneering PR firm, The Hamilton Wright Organization (founded in 1908), was brought down in part after a Senate committee questioned the company's activities while representing Nationalist China and apartheid South Africa.

Hamilton Wright II, the son of the firm's founder, eloquently argued in letters to researchers and historians, and in his Congressional testimony, that his company specifically avoided the quagmire of international politics. "We have never contracted for 'political propaganda' in any manner, shape or form," Wright stated in a letter to Scott Cutlip of the University of Georgia.

Speaking before Congress, Wright explained his company's policies further: "The contract [with China] was bull's-eyed to publicizing the way of life of Free China and this was brought down to a pinpoint exposé of their agriculture, their industry and their way of life to show the American people the problems they had. We also sought to bring into sharp focus how foreign aid money was being spent by the Chinese, and particularly to show that they were getting more mileage out of the dollar than many other countries."

Another Wright executive explained its entire foreign operation thus: "To sum up—we believe that the people of the United States want and need to know about the peoples of the rest of the world. They can do so largely by having access to legitimate news and/or pictures that authentically transmit how our overseas friends live, work, play. In a constantly expanding world of modern communications—radio or television, the daily and Sunday newspa-

PRoEthics

Nike on the Run

Situation

The Nike Corporation has been criticized for its practice of using third-world labor.

Response/Approach

According to Gerald Meyers, the former CEO of American Motors Company, "Nike abused its own brand name and that is contrary to what is taught in every marketing organization and business school . . . They believed their own press clippings." A risky approach.

Nike has "to put themselves on the side of the public interest of the countries involved and take some credit for their growing prosperity. Then they should fix what's wrong, develop some minimum standards and stick by them. And don't employ children. You can't perfume a pig."

Nike's original approach seemed to be a defensive one. Nike didn't take the opportunity to admit a wrong and thank people for bringing the issue to the table. "The misstep means that Nike now has to go that extra mile."

Nike used the Internet to tell its side of the story and "sent representatives to college campuses in an attempt to convince young opinion-makers that Nike's treatment of foreign labor is fair, even generous."

Source: Adapted from Chris Cobb. "Courting Controversy: Nike Takes the Heat for Their World Labor Practices." *Public Relations Tactics* (June 1998): 1, 17, 27.

---

pers, the illustrated magazines or 'slick' publications, the trade journals and to some extent the house organs of our major corporations—there is no limit except professional talent and good taste plus a sense of integrity in all undertakings."

The hearings did not unearth traitorous activities, but the PR damage to Wright's firm was nonetheless severe. "The U.S. Senate Foreign Relations Committee hearings developed into nothing more than a public smear. . . . There was no finale to his [Senator William Fulbright's] hearing—no censure—no nothing," Hamilton Wright II charged.

Complicating matters was the fact that the Senate investigation uncovered questionable business practices in the Wrights' company. Specifically, the company had guaranteed publicity results. Such a guarantee was, and remains, a violation of the Public Relations Society of America's Code of Professional Standards. (Article 13—"A member shall not guarantee the achievement of specified results beyond a member's direct control.") PRSA used the hearings to suspend and censure H. Wright III, who was a member at the time.

Hamilton Wright II was incensed by PRSA's action, saying the guarantees were a cultural matter that PRSA didn't understand: "In the foreign field, it is virtually impossible to secure a contract (Egypt, Morocco, Ceylon, Turkey, Pakistan and other governments) without making specific guarantees. The PRSA requested us to delete these guarantees from our contracts. We refused."

Cutlip, dean emeritus of the University of Georgia's Henry W. Grady School of Journalism and Mass Communication, undertook an extensive study of the rise and fall of The Hamilton Wright Organization in 1987. Cutlip came away with a far more sympathetic attitude toward the Wrights.

"Hamilton Wright knew the ways and mores of foreign governments better than any American counselor, and his word that many of these governments insisted on guarantees must be accepted as a fact of life in the representation of foreign clients, at least in his day," Cutlip writes.

Cutlip points out that getting in hot water over foreign representation is hardly a thing of the distant past. Michael Deaver, a former PR adviser to President Ronald Reagan, came under extensive review and criticism in the mid-1980s. Deaver "stubbed his toe on greed for a quick buck after leaving the White House in May 1985," Cutlip asserts. "Deaver's blatant use of his 'access' to the Reagans and the Administration prompted a congressional probe of his contracts with foreign governments, and [resulted in] efforts to tighten laws affecting lobbying for foreign governments."

Again, these are extremes. The overwhelming majority of American PR firms that sign foreign clients report that the relationship is both educational and mutually beneficial.

Some countries, and individuals, know the PR profession so well that they can, and have, taught us a thing or two. One of the best examples is former Soviet Union president Mikhail Gorbachev. Imagine the seemingly insurmountable problem facing Gorbachev on his numerous American visits. The balding Russian was the leader of America's biggest political and ideological enemy. While he expected to be treated with respect during political functions, how would he be received with anything but disdain by the American public?

Gorbachev was keenly aware of the American public's fascination with celebrity. So instead of coming across as the leader of one of the most oppressive governments in the earth's history, he and his wife, Raisa, positioned themselves as media stars. And it worked. Wherever they went during their U.S. visit, the Gorbachevs were treated like movie stars.

"Minnesotans grew up with the ebullient charisma of Hubert Humphrey, who was renowned for his ability to connect with crowd members in a way which made each one feel a personal bond with the senator," observed Minneapolis PR man Kevin O'Connor after the Gorbachevs visited his city in 1990. "Gorbachev sparked this same electricity. The Soviet president is a case study in effective use of nonverbal communication—using hand gestures, facial expressions, eye contact, posture and walking style to portray a likable, trustworthy friend. These nonverbal skills are particularly valuable in the international arena. Universal symbols, such as a smile, speak volumes, and favorable public opinion in the host country can pave the way toward favorable relations with that country's political leaders." In a classic case of "you scratch my back, I'll scratch yours," Minnesota jumped on the Gorbachev visit to flood the accompanying international press corps with information on Minnesota's economy, industry, agriculture, technology, attractions, and long-standing ties to international business.

Getting the Vacationers

A strong, and pleasantly simplistic, aspect of foreign public relations is the job of moving bodies (i.e., moving tourist bodies) to host countries. With the fall of the Iron Curtain and the crumbling of the Soviet empire, countries like former East Germany and the former members of the disbanded Soviet Union (the areas currently or formally known as Czechoslovakia, Bulgaria, Poland, Romania, Yugoslavia, and Hungary) are experiencing huge booms in tourism.

Aside from their natural and man-made attractions, these countries use U.S. and international PR firms to inform tourists of the relatively low costs of visiting their countries and the cooling of any political instability. As an example, for years one of the biggest bargains in the world's downhill skiing industry was the Olympic-class slopes in the former Yugoslavia. An eight-day stay (including airfare, hotel accommodations, and two meals a day) cost less than a similar stay in America. The price remains a bargain today, but travelers are advised to monitor the sweeping political changes and divisions in the area before planning a ski trip.

Low-Context/High-Context Cultures

Beyond the gulfs of language and culture that separate people and nations, is there a fundamental problem in the way we comprehend messages and their corresponding intent? Yes, according to researcher Lorand Szalay, the problem arises between different viewpoints: the individualistic versus the communal (the collectivistic or the relationship-oriented), the low-context versus the high-context.

"Individualistic cultures, of which the United States is a paradigm, hold freedom, the development of the individual personality, self-expression and personal enterprise and achievement as supreme values," writes Cohen. Individual rights, mobility, equality, and life by contract are paramount. Authority may be questioned, and conflict is resolved via the courts rather than by consensus.

Conversely, a communal attitude is based on the need for a partnership or a village, and on the primacy of the family, clan, or caste. The welfare of the group subordinates the wishes of the individual. "Face must be preserved at all costs . . . dishonor is a fate worse than death . . . group affiliation is acquired by birth," says Cohen. Law is meaningless, and personal contact replaces the business contract. Cohen also explains how these different constructs affect communication across cultures (Westerners and non-Westerners) with regard to the role of language and concepts of time.

Stella Ting-Toomey characterizes these interactions between high-context and low-context cultures as particularly prone to confusion. "High-context communication is associated with key elements in the communal ethic . . . maintaining face and group harmony," writes Cohen. It communicates allusively rather than directly, they weigh words carefully, and lying is acceptable if it avoids unpleasantness. High-context cultures must also cultivate personal relationships as a foundation for future business partnership. Cohen notes that the relationship is regarded as an end in itself.

Timing is also vital to high-context speakers. Since embarrassment is to be avoided, small talk is elevated to an art form. "To an outsider, the high-context individual may appear insincere, suspicious, and devious, but these traits are simply part of the veneer of courtesy and indirection essential to preserve social harmony," writes Cohen. Low-context cultures, such as the United States, dislike subtlety. There language is punctuated with "bottom lines," "straight talk," and "cutting to the chase." Accuracy is virtuous, and little importance is placed on face, hidden meanings, context, or nonverbal gestures in order to do business.

Unlike their counterparts in the United States, traditional societies move at the pace of the natural world, paying scant attention to the 24/7 rationale. Schedules, deadlines, planning, and agendas are the vocabulary of Westerners. Edward Hall writes that Americans "are oriented almost entirely toward the future." By contrast, high-context cultures revere the past.

Summary

The PR profession continues to experience a healthy, and sometimes explosive, growth overseas. Adventurous practitioners willing to overcome language and cultural challenges, as well as media restrictions, should find the foreign market—inside and outside the United States—interesting, educational, and profitable. Technology, especially the Internet and the World Wide Web, will assist the PR practitioner in creating greater access to international audiences, dissolving barriers, discovering hidden dimensions, and bridging gaps throughout the twenty-first century.

Q U E S T I O N S

1. What are the four reasons public relations will continue to grow?

2. What specific considerations do international campaigns pose?

3. What is meant by high-context and low-context?

4. What problems does the International Olympic Committee face in the wake of scandal?

R E A D I N G S

Kevin Avruch and Peter Black. "The Culture Question and Conflict Resolution." *Peace and Change* 16 (1991): 27–30.

Raymond Cohen. *Negotiating Across Cultures. International Communication in an Interdependent World.* Washington, DC: United States Institute of Peace Press, 1997.

Edward T. Hall. *Beyond Culture.* New York: Anchor Books, 1976.

Raymond L. Kotcher. "The Changing Role of PR in Latin America." *Public Relations Tactics* (March 1998): 26.

Larry Siddons. "Reform or Revolt for Olympics." *Associated Press,* February 13, 1999.

Lorand Szalay. "Intercultural Communications: A Process Model." *International Journal of Intercultural Relations* 5 (1981): 133–146.

Stella Ting-Toomey. "Toward a Theory of Conflict and Culture." *International and Intercultural Communication Annual* 9 (1985): 71–86.

15 Campaign Analysis and Measurement

Has Anyone Seen My Yardstick?

CHAPTER OUTLINE

Role of Measurement

Pseudo-Evaluation

Evaluation Styles

Essentials of Campaign Evaluation

CHAPTER OBJECTIVES

When you have completed this chapter, you should be able to:

- Understand the value of systematic evaluation
- Distinguish the difference between results and impact
- Identify evaluation styles applicable to public relations

Accountability. Contributing to the bottom line. Documenting success. Each has been used to define how the public relations campaign is deemed effective for a corporation or client. However, arriving at this assessment is far from precise. In fact, it varies from program to program, campaign to campaign, organization to organization. Bill Adams, a professor at Florida International University, admits there are no "foolproof ways to measure one's PR campaign." Practitioners Nicholas Tortorello and Ed Dowgiallo write that measurement "is not a cut-and-dried technical activity."

Role of Measurement

So, are public relations professionals forced to rely solely on the traditional clipping files and video placements to determine results? No. Although there are no universal criteria, that does not mean scientific or measurable results are not possible to gauge. Tortorello and Dowgiallo say that standards "must be defined for each program in relation to its goals. The art lies in knowing what criteria should be examined and how measurements should be made." That means that evaluation should actually be addressed and defined during program planning, not left as an afterthought.

This seems like sound, straightforward thinking; however, Cutlip, Center, and Broom note that planning and evaluation are regarded by many as the two weakest steps in the public relations problem-solving method. So rather than regard a PR campaign as a series of discrete stages, it is clear that a more integrated approach in the preparation phase is warranted.

Katherine Delahaye Paine, founder of The Delahaye Group (a world leader in PR measurement), notes that when she started the firm in 1987, "nobody wanted to pay for PR measurement. . . . Surveys found that people spent 1 percent of the PR budget on measurement and research. About five years ago it was up to 3 percent, inching up toward 5 percent. So we've seen a huge shift." She notes that since the mid-1990s, the practitioner who used to just "worry about counting clips is now looking to do message analysis, branding, investor relations, internal communications measurement, reputation measurement, Internet measurement, international measurement. Responsibilities have grown."

It's clear that analysis and measurement techniques are strategic parts of the process as well as being mainstream. The shift is also being felt across international borders and, according to Walter Lindenmann of Ketchum Public Relations Worldwide, "is growing in importance on a global basis. . . . There is a growing surge of interest . . . throughout the world to measure public relations effectiveness from a bottom-line perspective." He notes that Ketchum clients are asking for effectiveness measures "not in just one country, but often in several countries in which they operate." The era of planning and implementing public relations based on hunches, guesswork, and gut feelings is virtually over, he contends.

Nager and Allen claim that "CEOs demand that all managers be held accountable for what they produce. This is true of all departments. Public relations is no exception." Top management requires objective information and statistics to prove how public relations contributes to the bottom line. "With the mass audience breaking down into far narrower segments, each with its own interests and concerns, research is the only certain method for knowing that a communications program will reach its target," write Finn and Harrity.

However, for all the practitioners who support the blending of scientific research and program evaluation, there are others who object to the integration. They claim public relations is as much an art as a science and, as such, cannot be measured.

Pseudo-Evaluation

When faced with the demand for objective information and statistics that show how public relations efforts contribute to organizational effectiveness and corporate coffers, Dozier says too often pseudo-planning and pseudo-evaluation have been the response. "True public relations planning links specified program activities to specified outcomes regarding attitudes, knowledge levels and behavior of targeted publics. True evaluation measures changes in attitudes, knowledge levels, and behavior of targeted publics." Dozier explains that true evaluation also involves measures where "the cause of changes in publics can be reasonably

PRoActive

Measuring Impact

If research is going to be part of the process, it needs to start before the campaign kicks off. In order to evaluate a public relations project, goals and objectives should be set. Technology has greatly affected the speed and accuracy of producing results. Today, there are computer programs that can "chart and tabulate data to spot trends, identify areas of opportunity or problems and summarize results." In the past, practitioners could arrange for clipping services but had to do much of the content analysis via qualitative rather than quantitative methods, researchers note. With companies and services like Nexis and Lexis, people looking for articles can simply type in what they need, and a listing appears.

Researchers may want to identify some of the following variables to profile media coverage for their clients:

- Name of the media outlet
- Outlet's city of origin
- Type of publication (daily or weekly newspaper, magazine, trade publication, wire service, and so on)
- Type of coverage (news, editorial, opinion, or letter to the editor)
- Favorability, in terms of the client's point of view
- Ranking of articles as favorable, unfavorable, or neutral compared to the client's position
- Sources quoted from the client's side as compared to the competitor's side
- Name of journalist/writer
- Pertinent issues that appear in the story, including pro- or anti-client arguments or messages
- All news sources that may appear in an article (public officials, company spokespersons, products, others)
- Points the client is trying to communicate

- Impact competitors' quotes have in communicating or hindering the coverage of client's points
- How the client company and the competition are positioned by the media on key issues
- Which audiences are being reached
- What messages they are receiving
- What subjects the media are following most closely

"Many firms can also extrapolate details by cross-tabulating geographic coverage, favorability, circulation reports and reporter's attitudes or biases. The next tier in public relations research may well be active measurement versus passive measurement. Active measurement equals the information targeted to specific audiences. Passive includes information given to a general audience."

According to a poll conducted by *Public Relations Journal,* respondents note that "Demand from top management for measurable, bottom-line results and accountability has caused a shift toward a more structured way of measuring results of public relations campaigns and programs." According to the same poll, here are some ways to conduct research and evaluation:

- Implementing smaller, statistically correct mini-surveys
- Linking messages with an 800 number to capture responses
- Identifying a specific department in the return address on all press releases, so that the number of callers per release can be tracked
- Using a database search to find/confirm media pickups
- Sending a survey/thank-you note to all customers after a major campaign
- Collecting response cards
- Using desktop mapping software

Source: Adapted from Deborah Hauss. "Measuring the Impact of Public Relations: New Electronic Research Methods Improve Campaign Evaluation." *Public Relations Journal* (February 1993): 14–21.

PRoSpeak

A Tale of Two Cities
or
Ain't It a Dickens?

Public relations campaigns can be analyzed and measured in many different ways, simple and complex, inexpensive and expensive, meaningful and meaningless.

Most people want to see tangible results from their efforts and expense. Measurement of the results of public relations programs need not be problematic. The key is deciding what to measure.

The county seat of Polk County, Florida, is Bartow, about halfway between Tampa and Orlando, fifteen miles south of Interstate 4. Polk County is a large county in area, fourth in the state, eighth in population (415,000). Despite being a big phosphate mining and citrus-growing area, the population is relatively low on the income scale. Lots of retirees. Lots of trailer homes.

In 1991, workers in the new Polk County Courthouse began reporting an increase in respiratory and other illnesses. Suspicion fell on the building itself as the source of the illnesses, and that was later confirmed by environmental and medical examinations. Sick Building Syndrome.

A thorough inspection of the building found increased levels of mold and mildew in the air inside the building, particularly on the lower floors. Damp spots were widespread. Construction irregularities were identified, such as a faulty air conditioning system. Windows and brickwork had been installed improperly. It was determined that elimination of the problem would require a massive reconstruction project costing $17 million, on a building which cost $34 million to build four years earlier. The populace was shocked and outraged. The news media had a field day.

One editorial headed "Courthouse of Horrors" called it "a 10-story monument to bungling" and referred to the building as "The Nightmare on Broadway." Most media coverage was in the same vein.

People continued to get sick.

Public relations counsel was sought. On advise of counsel, direct communication with county employees was stepped up, especially in the

James Tolley
The James Tolley Company
Sarasota, Florida

Courthouse; relocation of building employees was accelerated; a full-page advertisement explaining the situation was placed in the local newspaper; and residents (taxpayers!) were invited to inspect the problems for themselves at an open house.

Lawsuits were filed against contractors, subcontractors, architects, and engineers. They were answered by countersuits, but residents knew the county was attempting to recover funds from those at fault.

Did the campaign work? Yes, it did. The newspaper decided to run the advertisement as a public service. One newspaper columnist changed her tune and praised the County Commissioners for the open-house idea. Employees appreciated receiving more information faster and direct from supervisors. The County Commissioners could not escape the wrath of the electorate, however, and some of the incumbents were reelected.

From Bartow, Florida, we go halfway across the country to a better-known city and a better-known, but in many ways similar, crisis campaign. The city is St. Louis; the campaign is the Chrysler odometer scandal. A federal grand jury indicted Chrysler and two of its St. Louis assembly plant executives on charges relating to alleged odometer tampering.

Management personnel at the plant were required to randomly select a vehicle from each day's production and drive it home at night as a spot check. Test reports were completed about each drive. To make sure the car's new owner got full benefit from Chrysler's mileage-related warranty, the test drivers routinely disconnected the odometers for the road test and reconnected them on return to the plant. This was the "odometer tampering" cited in the indictment. Chrysler manufacturing personnel defended the practice; Chrysler lawyers said nothing done was illegal.

The charge, issued by the federal attorney at a press conference, was front-page news across the country and the lead item on the national evening TV news programs.

Chrysler at first issued a statement saying that it had acted in the best interests of its customers and had done nothing illegal. Key dealers reported little customer concern and advised Chrysler management to let the issue die out.

Several executives were not so sure that it would "die out" without severe harm to the company. A crisis response was planned, and a telephone survey of nationwide opinion was conducted.

The survey, representative of the entire adult population of the United States, showed that 69 percent, or 166 million adults, were aware of the government's charges and 55 percent of those, or 91 million, thought Chrysler was in serious trouble. Boxcar numbers!

Chrysler's response was to apologize, offer compensation to anyone who was hurt by the practice, stop the practice, and reassure customers and the public of Chrysler's concern for quality and reliability. A press conference was held in which Lee Iacocca, Chrysler's CEO, announced Chrysler's plan and said the practice had been "stupid," forget whether it was legal. Letters were sent to dealers and owners; ads were placed in newspapers from coast to coast. Another survey of public opinion was conducted.

Did the response work? Yes.

News media accurately reported Chrysler's action plan. How did the company measure? There was no drop in sales trends. Stock price was not affected. Iacocca's mail changed from 98 percent anti to 2 percent anti. The public opinion survey showed that 53 percent of adult Americans, 127 million, were aware of Chrysler's corrective actions, and 67 percent of those, 85 million, thought Chrysler had dealt adequately and correctly with the problem and put it behind them.

In both Bartow and St. Louis, strong, effective (and expensive) remedial action was taken. Those affected were assured of both concern and recompense.

Results were measured by a turn in media articles and editorial coverage, and by the results of public polling. Public understanding, and perhaps forgiveness to some extent, was achieved. In Chrysler's case, sales and stock price did not falter. In Polk County's case, the County Commissioners were reelected.

There were simple and incontrovertible measures of the success of the campaigns.

---

attributed to program efforts." If planning and evaluation are not linked, then nothing can be measured. "Measurement of programs without goals is form without substance."

How can one distinguish true planning and evaluation from the pseudo variety? According to Dozier, "Pseudo evaluation is wedded to pseudo planning . . . the problem . . . is that means and ends are confused." So counting news release placements or clips and garnering awards for employee publications fall short of measuring the outcome of a successful PR program. "Communication is not the outcome, the measurable impact. . . . Communication is important only in the effects it achieves among publics." To Dozier, true planning and evaluation are distinguished by "specifying effects and measuring them."

Tortorello and Dowgiallo use the words results and impact to draw the distinction. "By results . . . we mean the publicity it generates. . . . The right messages must be seen by adequate numbers of the target audience, or no significant impact can be expected. . . . The key is how it affects the audience's awareness, knowledge, attitudes or behavior. . . . The real goals are impacting the hearts and minds of people."

Impact can be micro or macro. Micro-evaluation may take the form of a follow-up survey of attendees at a seminar to measure attitudes as to a specific topic or speaker, or readers may be interviewed to check awareness of a media placement or to monitor understanding. Focus groups may also be helpful to aid in gauging reaction to an event. Macro-approaches measure changes in attitudes of a target public over a period of time, both pre- and postprogram or pre- and postcampaign. Tools to measure changes may take the form of buying patterns, telephone surveys, employee surveys, or core message tracking in public relations media only. By isolating PR messages, practitioners can verify the effectiveness of their techniques as opposed to those items or issues covered via advertising or marketing.

Evaluation Styles

What is, as Kendall says, "convincing proof" of a campaign's or program's effectiveness? Among public relations practitioners, Dozier cites "three evaluation styles" that may prove helpful in answering that question: scientific evaluation, seat-of-the-pants evaluation, and scientific dissemination evaluation.

Scientific evaluation uses counting and social science methods to gather data before and after a program is implemented. Samples, surveys, opinion polls, and message content analysis are hallmarks of this style. Seat-of-the-pants evaluation relies upon personal, subjective assessment in which anecdotes or observation is the preferred approach and whose effectiveness is proved in the opinions of peers or the number of awards won. Scientific dissemination evaluation is based on the "numeric analysis of clip files, a log of column inches or air time, the reach of the media used, or the content analysis of those clips," says Dozier. Practitioners may use a combination of the three styles.

These styles may link together a range of categories that might serve to prove the effectiveness of the campaigns undertaken (see Exhibit 15.1). Kendall identifies them as goal attainment, measurement of improvement, measurement of results, cost-efficiency, organizational change, unplanned results, and unarticulated hopes. But rather than just the identification of categories, focus on why a program is initiated in the first place.

The National Academy of Sciences offers the different purposes of evaluation. They include, but are no means limited to, needs assessment, basic research, small-scale testing, field evaluation, policy analysis, fiscal accountability, coverage accountability, impact assessment, and economic analysis. It is clear that, whatever the intent, it is the manifest outgrowth of the initial stages of the PR problem-solving process—identifying the problem and setting specific, measurable goals and objectives.

With regard to campaigns, public relations practitioners most often employ measures of goal achievement, improvement, or results. The pretest/posttest approach allows for benchmarking, regarded by many as the optimal way to score campaign success. Kendall defines goal achievement as "determined from a careful analysis of the situation, that research identified the true nature of the problem confronting the organization, and the goal and the criterion for its achievement were based on these results."

The "careful analysis" description could emerge after a situational analysis is conducted using Cutlip, Center, and Broom's guidelines; however, the goal must be arrived at

---

EXHIBIT **15.1**

Evaluation Types Applicable to Public Relations

Appropriateness Evaluation:	Investigates the nature and depth of information the publics should be receiving.
Awareness Focus:	Determines who knows about a program or issue and what they know.
Criterion-Referenced Evaluation:	Is similar to goal achievement evaluation; criterion may be from sources other than problem identification research.
Descriptive Evaluation:	Is a nonjudgmental effort to find out what happens or happened in a campaign, apart from its goals.
Effectiveness Evaluation:	Looks at goal achievement and the degree of its success.
Effort Evaluation:	Appraises personnel, staff, and time as indications of investment in a campaign.
Extensiveness Evaluation:	Asks to what degree the campaign solved the problems identified.
Formative Evaluation:	Asks, either during or afterward, how the campaign can be improved.
Goal-Based Evaluation:	Measures the attainment of the goal.
Impact Evaluation:	Determines the direct and indirect effects of the campaign.
Performance Evaluation:	Appraises the change in behavior of the target publics.

Source: Adapted from Michael Q. Patton. *Practical Evaluation.* Beverly Hills: Sage, 1982, pp. 45–47; and Robert Kendall. *Public Relations Campaign Strategies.* New York: HarperCollins, 1996, pp. 413–414.

---

based on honest assessment and ethical considerations. If goals are simply set by those who know they can be attained in order to reach an MBO target activity, then achieving the goal may be hollow. Success on paper may give way to an actual displacement of goals, where survival within the organization or the industry is ensured, but little else. To overcome this potential abuse, Kendall suggests that "evaluation should seldom be confined to one procedure."

Improvement implies a benchmark used to calculate the effects of a campaign. "A benchmark may be a survey taken before the campaign against which results of a postcampaign survey will be measured to determine 'success,'" writes Kendall. Benchmarks, or compass points, may include sales, profits, traffic, stock prices, ratings, circulation figures, or any measurable element of a program or campaign. James Grunig, however, asserts that any spike on the needle must recognize a "theory of publics," which takes into account passive and active audiences. "To plan a program or campaign, practitioners must know the kind of publics they are dealing with. To evaluate the program, they must know the likelihood of success for each objective. A realistic objective for an active public [who seeks out information] will be totally unrealistic for a passive [transitory] public."

PRoEthics

Political Perspectives

Ethics, in relation to the public relations field, is viewed by some as absent and by others as necessary. The author's purpose is to "sketch a framework to help organizational ombudspeople analyze ethical dilemmas from both an organizational and a stakeholder perspective."

According to Cavanagh, Moberg, and Velasquez (1981), there are three approaches to ethics: utilitarian, theory of rights, and theory of justice. "Classic utilitarian approaches are based on an evaluation of the act or decision. Moral evaluations of the greatest good are determined by assessing the consequences of the action taken," Spicer writes.

"The best example of a theory of right is the American Bill of Rights, a document that guarantees certain inalienable rights thought to be held by all people. In an ethical system based on rights, decisions are judged ethical if they do not infringe on another's rights. . . . The importance of the rights philosophy to organizational interactions with external stakeholders is determining who has the right to be included in the decision process."

Equity, fairness, and impartiality should guide those working under the theory of justice. "The first principle, distributive justice, states that similar individuals should be treated similarly. Second, rules should be clearly stated, understood by all, and administered fairly, thereby avoiding expressions of partiality." Finally, a theory of justice says that if people don't have control over a situation, they should not be held responsible for the situation.

"Although all three theories—utilitarian, rights, and justice—are available for managers, including organizational public relations practitioners, to use, research indicates a particular fondness for utilitarian approaches." Organizations and stakeholders will invoke different moral theories in their attempts to analyze and resolve issues. These differences emanate from differences in assessments of responsibility. "Organizational members—insiders—actors—are more likely to focus pragmatically on an issue and to attempt a resolution from previously established ways of doing.

"Insider-actors perceive themselves to have limited discretionary power or control because of their allegiance to the system in which they work—its culture, its rules, its historical approaches, its policy, and so on. In essence, the insider perspective binds the organizational manager, thereby limiting his or her discretion in decision making and action. This insider-actor perspective forces limits on the acceptance of responsibility, especially when moral issues are approached from the perspective of act utilitarianism. Those issues for which the insiders accept responsibility are those that can be controlled by management." In this view, organizations are not responsible for those issues that fall outside the realm of managerial practice, pragmatics, and policy.

"Outsider-observers [stakeholders] are far more likely to make assessments of organizational actions based on their perception of organization sensitivity and responsiveness to their needs. Given the broader viewpoint of the outsiders, they are more likely to impute responsibility to the organizational actor than are the organizational actors themselves. In this manner, then, stakeholders are more likely to perceive that the organization has more discretion or volition than the organization either has, claims, or acknowledges."

Source: Adapted from Christopher Spicer. *Organizational Public Relations: A Political Perspective.* Mahwah, N.J.: Lawrence Erlbaum Associates, 1997.

Improvement also implies that change for the better occurs. The role of the change agent is particularly apropos for the public relations practitioner. Change agents, as do practitioners, monitor their environment and build relationships internally and externally; they adjust organizations to environments and environments to organizations. They negotiate multiple realities, craft messages, evaluate progress of an organization's programs and campaigns, and then chart the future.

Results do not imply that pre- and/or postmeasures are at work, simply that a positive shift has taken place. They may be most apparent during the course of a program or campaign in which monitoring of current conditions takes place. These in-process results may offer insight into program adjustments at critical points in the life of a campaign and aid in the course corrections that planning affords.

Essentials of Campaign Evaluation

Kendall suggests three essentials in choosing a campaign evaluation strategy: in-process, internal, and external. "In-process evaluation monitors the campaign while it is being implemented," Kendall writes, and it would also incorporate contingency plans should unexpected issues or emergencies arise. The methods a practitioner would employ are "keeping a campaign diary [to record facts, impressions, relationships, observations], holding staff meetings, . . . debriefing sessions." Internal evaluation examines the campaign after it has been executed. Although the methods used to arrive at the evaluation may be the same as in-process or external approaches, internal assessment is designed to focus on outcomes. Internal evaluations are useful in assigning weights to "individual performance of team members or project personnel. . . . Evaluations may be based on assigned duties, projects, achievements, performance, quality of work produced, or a combination of these," Kendall explains. External evaluation turns the lens outside the organization to examine target audiences, media, other organizations, competitors, and public opinion. The external exercise gets to the heart of the systems perspective that Grunig and Hunt advance in that "it encourages practitioners to systematically monitor their environment, to formulate solutions to problems identified in this manner, to design programs as part of these solutions, and to monitor these programs on their effectiveness."

Summary

Analysis or evaluation may take the form of quantitative or qualitative assessment or, ideally, a combination of the two. Together, they offer context and scope of the personnel, decisions, goals, objectives, audiences, messages, and communication vehicles involved in a public relations campaign. As Crabble and Vibbert explain, "Well-planned evaluation is cost-efficient, contributes to public persuasion research, reduces confusion, and sets up a framework by which public relations can become a more understood and valuable function within an organization." Like all good research, evaluation should take place before, during, and after a program or campaign, and it must be agreed upon in advance as to how the data will be used to guide public relations efforts in the future. The guideposts or benchmarks that evaluation provides enable a practitioner and organization to use strategic planning to be responsive to changes in the internal and external environments and in their relationships with their publics.

QUESTIONS

1. Why are evaluation measures valuable to the client as well as to the public relations counselor?

2. What is the general attitude of CEOs toward analysis and measurement?

3. How can you distinguish between true and pseudo-evaluation?

4. What are the categories of evaluation that are applicable to the public relations practitioner?

READINGS

William Adams. "Ask the Professor." *Public Relations Tactics* (August 1995).

Deborah Holloway. "How to Select a Measurement System That's Right for You." *Public Relations Quarterly* 37, no. 3 (Fall 1992): 15–17.

Robert Kendall. *Public Relations Campaign Strategies.* New York: HarperCollins, 1996.

Walter K. Lindenmann. "Trendwatch." *Public Relations Tactics* (July 1996).

———. "Research, Evaluation and Measurement: A National Perspective." *Public Relations Review* 16, no. 2 (Summer 1990): 3–16.

Katherine Delahaye Paine. "Escape from 'Measure-Not Land.' " *Public Relations Tactics* (July 1997).

Jennie M. Piekos and Edna F. Einsiedel. "Roles and Program Evaluation Techniques Among Canadian Public Relations Practitioners." In *Public Relations Research Annual.* Ed. Larissa A. Grunig and James E. Grunig. Hillsdale, NJ: Lawrence Erlbaum Associates, 1990.

Joan Schneider. "Developing PR Launches That Sizzle, Not Fizzle." *Public Relations Tactics* (January 1996).

Nicholas Tortorello and Ed Dowgiallo. "Evaluating the Impact of Public Relations." *Public Relations Journal* 46, no. 11 (November 1990): 34–37.

REFERENCES

Ackley, Dennis. "The Secret of Communicating Bad News to Employees." *IABC Communication World* 9, no. 8 (1992): 27–29.

Affeldt, D. "Electronic Mail: Using the Computer to Communicate Electronically." In *New Technology and Public Relations,* ed. Kalman B. Druck. Foundation for Public Relations Research and Education, 1986.

Al-Enad, Abdulrahman H. "Public Relations' Roles in Developing Countries." *Public Relations Quarterly* 35, no. 1 (1990): 24–26.

"All the News That Fits the Budget." *Broadcasting* (September 23, 1991): 15–16.

Allan, Michael J. "Quake '89: Observations from the Front." *Public Relations Journal* 46, no. 4 (1990): 25–26.

"America at the Crossroads." *Public Relations Journal* 48, no. 12 (1992): 10–15.

Andrews, Michael C. "Today the Goodyear Blimp, Tomorrow the Moon." *Public Relations Quarterly* 38, no. 1 (1993): 39–40.

Antrobus, Edmund. "Back in the U.S.S.R. and Eastern Europe." *Public Relations Journal* 46, no. 5 (1990): 20–26.

Auclair, Marcel. "Out of Africa: Going Where No Communicator Has Gone Before." *IABC Communication World* 9, no. 3 (1992): 43–45.

Babbie, Earl R. *Social Research for Consumers.* Belmont, CA: Wadsworth Publishing Company, 1982.

Baer, Daniel H. "Selling Management on Public Relations Research." *Public Relations Quarterly* 28, no. 3 (1983): 9–11.

Baig, Edward C. "Ready, Set—Go Online." *Business Week: The Info Revolution* (1994): 124–133.

Baker, W. Randolph. "Counsel to Counsel." *Public Relations Journal* 44, no. 2 (1988): 24–26.

Ballard, Jan. "Your Crisis Communications Plan." *Trends* 9, no. 2 (1993): 18–19.

Beardsley, John. "The Gorbachev Visit: Lessons and Themes in Public Relations." *Public Relations Journal* 46, no. 8 (1990): 9–12.

Behunin, R. Alan. "Post-War Business Prospects Bloom in Middle East." *Public Relations Journal* 47, no. 5 (1991): 10.

Bellack, Daniel W. "Exploiting EEC Marketing Potential." *Public Relations Journal* 46, no. 1 (1990): 14–15.

Bergner, Douglas. "The Role of Strategic Planning in International Public Affairs." *Public Relations Journal* 38, no. 6 (1982): 32.

Bernays, Edward L. *Crystalizing Public Opinion.* New York: Boni and Liveright, 1923.

————. "Research and Evaluation." *Public Relations Quarterly* 28, no. 4 (1983): 14.

Bernbach, William. "Some Things Can't Be Planned," a speech at the Western Regional Meeting of the American Association of Advertising Agencies, Pebble Beach, CA, November 3, 1965.

Bivins, Thomas H. "Applying Ethical Theory to Public Relations." *Journal of Business Ethics* 6 (1987): 195–200.

Black, Sam. "Widening the Education Panorama in Europe." *Public Relations Quarterly* 35, no. 1 (1990): 15–16.

————. "Public Relations in China Today." *Public Relations Quarterly* 35, no. 4 (1991): 29–39.

Blankinship, Steve. "Issues Management." *IABC Communication World* 10, no. 7 (1993): 24–27.

Blyler, Nancy Roundy. "Teaching Persuasion as Consensus in Business Communication." *The Bulletin* 56, no. 1 (1993): 26–31.

Boehike, William. "How Computers Are Reshaping PR." *O'Dwyer's PR Services* 7, no. 7 (1993): 22–23.

Bok, Sissela. *Lying, Moral Choice in Public and Private Life.* New York: Vintage Books, 1978.

Bolland, Eric J. "Advertising v. Public Relations." *Public Relations Quarterly* 34, no. 3 (1989): 10–12.

Book, Albert C., and C. Dennis Schick. *Fundamentals of Copy and Layout.* Chicago: Crain Books, 1984.

Booth, Alyse Lynn. "Going Global." *Public Relations Journal* 42, no. 2 (1986): 22–27.

Botan, Carl. "International Public Relations: Critique and Reformulation." *Public Relations Review* 18, no. 2 (1992): 149–159.

Bouchard, André. "Freak Explosion Jolts Baie des Ha! Ha!" *Public Relations Journal* 48, no. 10 (1992): 44.

Bovet, Susan Fry. "Trends in the 'New' Europe." *Public Relations Journal* 49, no. 9 (1993): 18–24.

Briggs, William. "Intercepting Interlopers." *Public Relations Journal* 46, no. 2 (1990): 40.

————, and Thomas Bernal. "Validating the Code of Ethics." *IABC Communication World* 9, no. 6 (1992): 40–43.

————, and Marilen Tuason. "Let the Games Begin! PR vs Marketing." *IABC Communication World* 10, no. 3 (1993): 16–20.

Broom, Glen M., and David M. Dozier. "An Overview: Evaluation Research in Public Relations." *Public Relations Quarterly* 28, no. 3 (1983): 5–8.

————. *Using Research in Public Relations: Applications to Program Management.* Englewood Cliffs, NJ: Prentice-Hall, 1990.

Brown, Guy E. II. "Building Momentum After Delayed Response." *Public Relations Journal* 46, no. 12 (1990): 40.

Bucher, J., ed. *Philosophical Writings of [Charles] Pierce.* New York: Dover, 1955.

Burgess, John. "Wire War: Putting America Online." *Washington Post,* 22 October 1989, C3.

Burnett, Leo. "Keep Listening to That Wee Small Voice." [1961] in *Exploring Advertising, ed.* Otto Kleppner and Irving Settel. Englewood Cliffs, NJ: Prentice Hall, 1970.

Burns, John. "As Reporters Close In, Execs Learn to Exhibit Grace Under Pressure." *Modern Healthcare* 22, no. 49 (7 December 1992): 33–34.

Calloway, L. K. "Survival of the Fastest: Information Tech and Corporate Crisis." *Public Relations Review* 17, no. 1 (Spring 1991): 85–92.

Cameron, Glen T., and Patricia A. Curtin. "An Expert Systems Approach for PR Campaigns Research." *Journalism Educator* 47, no. 2 (1992): 13–18.

Capps, Ian. "What the 'New Tech' Really Means for Commercial Profits." *Public Relations Quarterly* (Summer 1993): 24–25.

Carney, Bill. "Communicating Risk." *IABC Communication World* 10, no. 5 (1993): 13–15.

Center, Allen H., and Glenn M. Broom. "Evaluation Research." *Public Relations Quarterly* 28, no. 3 (1983): 2–3.

"CEO: Managing Expectations Is Key to Global Public Affairs." *Public Relations Journal* 49, no. 7 (1993): 6.

Chapman, Ray. "Measurement: It Is Alive and Well in Chicago." *Public Relations Journal* 38, no. 5 (1982): 28–29.

Chard, David. "Taiwan Communicators Growing in Status." *IABC Communication World* 10, no. 6 (1993): 43.

Chase, W. Howard. *Issue Management: Origins of the Future.* Stamford, CT: IAP, 1985.

Chen, Ni, and Hugh M. Culbertson. "Two Contrasting Approaches of Government Public Relations in Mainland China." *Public Relations Quarterly* 37, no. 3 (1992): 36–42.

Chess, Caron, Alex Saville, Michal Tamuz, and Michael Greenberg. "The Organizational Links Between Risk Communication and Risk Management: The Case of Sybron Chemicals Inc." *Risk Analysis* 12, no. 3 (1992): 431–438.

Cialdini, Robert B. "Littering: When Every Litter Bit Hurts," in ed. Ronald E. Rice and William J. Paisley Newbury Park, CA: Sage, 1989.

Cipalla, Rita. "Dealing with Crisis the United Way." *IABC Communication World* 9, no. 9 (1992): 23–26.

———. "Coping with Crisis." *IABC Communication World* 10, no. 7 (1993): 28–30.

Clampitt, Philip G., and Cal W. Downs. "Employee Perceptions of the Relationship Between Communication and Productivity: A Field Study." *Journal of Business Communication* 30, no. 1 (1993): 5–28.

Cohen, Alan, in "NBC and Kellogg Co-star," Joe Mandere, *Advertising Age* (19 July 1993): 32.

Collins, Erik L., and Robert J. Cornet. "Public Relations and Libel Law." *Public Relations Review* 16, no. 4 (1990): 36–47.

"Communications Revolution Reaches China." *Public Relations Journal* 49, no. 7 (1993): 4.

Computers in the Workplace: Selected Issues. Washington, DC: National Commission for Employment and Policy, 1986.

"Conflict Resolution, Common Sense Rules." *Public Relations Journal* 44, no. 2 (1988): 19–20.

Corbet, William J. "Realities and Perception of International Public Relations." *Public Relations Journal* 39, no. 1 (1983): 20–22.

———. "International Consumerism: Threat or Opportunity?" *Public Relations Journal* 40, no. 8 (1984): 18–20.

Crable, Richard E., and Steven L. Vibbert. "Managing Issues and Influencing Public Policy." *Public Relations Review* 11, no. 2: 3–16.

Culbertson, Hugh M. "Public Relations, A Big Part of the 1986 Filipino Story." *Public Relations Quarterly* 32, no. 2 (1987): 14–16.

———, and Ni Chen. "Communitarianism: A Foundation for Communication Symmetry." *Public Relations Quarterly* 42, no. 2 (Summer 1997): 36–41.

Cushman, Aaron. "Why Marketing Directors Are Listening Now." *Public Relations Journal* (May 1990): 17–19.

Cutlip, Scott M. "Attendant Responsibility: Public Relations and the SEC." *Public Relations Journal* 41, no. 1 (1985): 26–31.

———. "Pioneering Public Relations for Foreign Governments." *Public Relations Review* 13, no. 1 (1987): 13–34.

———. "Lithuania's First Independence Battle: A PR Footnote." *Public Relations Review* 16, no. 4 (1990): 12–16.

———. *The Unseen Power: Public Relations History: From the 17th to the 20th Century.* Hillsdale, NJ: Lawrence Erlbaum Associates, 1995.

———, Allen H. Center, and Glen M. Broom. *Effective Public Relations,* 7th ed. Englewood Cliffs, NJ: Prentice Hall, 1994.

D'Alessandro, David. "Event Marketing Winners: Olympics, Local, Causes." *Brandweek* (12 July 1993): 16.

Dalsass, Diana. "Prelude to a Launch." *Public Relations Quarterly* 38, no. 1 (1993): 10–11.

Darman, John, in "Cooperation Between Client and Firm Yields Successful 19-Country Product Launch." *Public Relations Journal* (August 1993): 24.

David, Meryl. "Persuasion, Fitting In." *Public Relations Journal* 44, no. 2 (1988): 20.

Dempsey, Gerry. "Global Communication Comes Into Its Own." *IABC Communication World* 9, no. 12 (1992): 21–23.

de Souza, Cerena. "Communicators in India Transcend Cultural Diversity." *IABC Communication World* 10, no. 6 (1993): 44–46.

Detweiler, John S. "Public Relations and the Campaign for Press Freedom." *Public Relations Quarterly* 34, no. 1 (1989): 19–22.

"Developing a Winning Global Strategy." *Public Relations Journal* 46, no. 12 (1990): 14.

Dilenschneider, Robert L. "You: Ready for Trouble?" *Public Relations Quarterly* 38, no. 1 (1993): 29–30.

Dillard, James Price. "Persuasion Past and Present: Attitudes Aren't What They Used to Be." *Communication Monographs* 60, no. 1 (1993): 90–97.

Dillman, Don A. *Mail and Telephone Surveys.* New York: John Wiley and Sons, 1978.

"Diverse Work Force Contributes to Healthy Organizations." *Public Relations Journal* 46, no. 12 (1990): 12.

"Doing PR in South America Has Its Worries and Its Rewards." *O'Dwyer's PR Services* 7, no. 7 (1993): 18–19.

Dowling, James H. "Public Relations in the Year 2000." *Public Relations Journal* 46, no. 1 (1990): 6.

Dozier, David M. "Program Evaluation and the Role of Practitioners." *Public Relations Review* 10, no. 2 (1984): 13–21.

———. "Planning and Evaluation in PR Practice." *Public Relations Review* 11, no. 2 (1985): 17–25.

———, Larissa A. Grunig, and James E. Grunig. *Manager's Guide to Excellence in Public Relations and Communication Management.* Mahwah, NJ: Lawrence Erlbaum Associates, 1995.

Drucker, George. "PR Finds New Niche Promoting Promotions." *Inside PR,* February 1991, 25.

Drucker, Peter. "Management's New Paradigms." *Forbes* (October 5, 1998); 152–176.

Duffy, Robert A., and Michael J. Palmer. "How Multimedia Technologies Will Influence Public Relations Practice." *Public Relations Quarterly* (Spring 1994): 25–29.

Duncan, Thomas R., and Stephen E. Everett. "Client Perceptions of Integrated Marketing Communication." *Journal of Advertising Research* 33, no. 3 (1993): 30–39.

Dyer, Samuel Coad Jr., M. Mark Miller, and Jeff Boone. "Wire Service Coverage of the Exxon Valdez Crisis." *Public Relations Review* 17, no. 1 (1991): 27–36.

Ehling, William D., and Michael B. Hesse. "Use of Issue Management in Public Relations." *Public Relations Review* 9, no. 2 (1983): 8–35.

Epley, Joe S. "Public Relations in the Global Village: An American Perspective." *Public Relations Review* 18, no. 2 (1992): 109–116.

———. "Russian Interns Go Off to Work." *Public Relations Journal* 49, no. 5 (1993): 4–5.

Erlank, Milner. "South African Communicators Face Challenge." *IABC Communication World* 9, no. 3 (1992): 50–52.

"Ethical Values Reflect Responsibility to Client, Organization and Self." *Public Relations Journal* 48, no. 1 (1992): 10.

"Europe 1992: A Threat to Mid-Sized Firms?" *Public Relations Journal* 45, no. 6 (1989): 8.

Evans, Fred J. "Business and the Press: Conflicts over Roles, Fairness." *Public Relations Review* 10, no. 4 (1984): 33–42.

Farinelli, Jean L. "Needed: A New U.S. Perspective on Global Public Relations." *Public Relations Journal* 46, no. 1 (1990): 18–19.

"FCC Report Concedes TV's Future to Cable." *Broadcasting* (1 July 1991): 19–20.

"Field Should Promote Public Relations' Ability to Outperform Advertising." *Public Relations Journal* 45, no. 6 (1989): 13–14.

Fine, Marlene G. "New Voices in the Workplace: Research Directions in Multicultural Communication." *Journal of Business Communication* 28, no. 3 (1991): 259–275.

Fink, Conrad C. *Media Ethics.* Boston: Allyn and Bacon, 1995.

Finn, D. and M. K. Harrity. Research in B. Cantor (ed.) *Inside Public Relations.* New York: Longman, 1984, 273–287.

Fitzgerald, Mark. "Planning for Disaster." *Editor & Publisher* (19 June 1993): 44.

Flay, Brian R., and Thomas P. Cook. "Three Models for Summative Evaluation of Prevention Campaigns with a Mass Media Component," in *Public Communication Campaigns,* ed. Ronald E. Rice and Charles K. Atkins. Newbury Park, CA: Sage, 1989.

"Florida Utility Wins Top Silver Anvil for Crisis Work During Hurricane." *Public Relations Journal* 49, no. 7 (1993): 6.

Forbes, Paul S. *PRSA White Paper: Revitalizing Business Ethics.* New York: Public Policy Committee of the Public Relations Society of America, 1989.

Forrest, Anne B. "The Continental Divide: Coping with Cultural Gaps." *IABC Communication World* 5, no. 7 (1988): 20–22.

———. "Communicators in Hong Kong Adjusting to Change." *IABC Communication World* 10, no. 6 (1993): 35–37.

Foster, Lawrence G. "The CEO Connection: Pivotal for the '90s." *Public Relations Journal* 46, no. 1 (1990): 24–25.

———. "10 CEOs Send a Message to Public Relations." *Public Relations Strategist* 1, no. 1 (Spring 1995): 4–12.

Freivalds, John. "Six Strategies for Doing Business in the Former Soviet Republics." *IABC Communication World* 9, no. 7 (1992): 20–23.

Friedel, Stuart Lee, and Michael C. Lasky. "Legal Implications of Public Relations for Unapproved Drugs." *Public Relations Quarterly* 38, no. 1 (1993): 15–17.

Fry, Susan L. "How to Succeed in the New Europe." *Public Relations Journal* 47, no. 1 (1991): 17–21.

———. "Reaching Hispanic Publics with Special Events." *Public Relations Journal* 47, no. 2 (1991): 12–13.

"German Firms Seek Ties with U.S. Counselors." *Public Relations Journal* 49, no. 7 (1993): 8.

Goldberg, Nancy, in "Benchmarking 101." *Corporate Community Relations Letter,* The Center for Corporate Community Relations at Boston College, 7, no. 9 (June 1993): 3.

Goldman, Elaine. "Dinosaur or Rocket?" *Public Relations Journal* 40, no. 10 (1984): 12–13.

Gollner, A. B. *Social Change and Corporate Strategy: The Expanding Role of Public Affairs.* Stamford, CT: Issue Action Press, 1983.

Goltz, G. "The Workforce Reorganization." *Presstime* (September 1989): 18–23.

Gonring, Matthew P. "Communication Makes Employee Involvement Work." *Public Relations Journal* 47, no. 11 (November 1991): 38–39, 40.

Gore, Robert. "In a High-Profile, Crisis-Laden Business, Insurance CEOs Rely on Public Relations." *Public Relations Journal* 49, no. 5 (1993): 21.

Gould, Richard A. "How to Prosper under the New Tax Law." *Public Relations Journal* 43, no. 1 (1987): 27–30.

Graham, Gerald H., Jeanne Unruh, and Paul Jennings. "The Impact of Nonverbal Communication in Organizations: A Survey of Perceptions." *Journal of Business Communication* 28, no. 1 (1991): 45–62.

Grant, David M. "Cross-Cultural Crossed Signals." *Public Relations Journal* 44, no. 10 (1988): 48.

Green, Rick. "Who Are We Talking To About Employee Communication?" *IABC Communication World* 10, no. 6 (1993): 26–28.

Gruban, Brane. "Slovenia—Catching the Wave of Communication Internationalism." *IABC Communication World* 10, no. 6 (1993): 40–42.

Grunig, James. "Basic Research Provides Knowledge That Makes Evaluation Possible." *Public Relations Quarterly* 28, no. 3 (1983): 28–32.

Grunig, Larissa A. "Strategic Public Relations Constituencies on a Global Scale." *Public Relations Review* 18, no. 2 (1992): 127–136.

Hainsworth, Brad, and Max Meng. "How Corporations Define Issues Management." *Public Relations Review* 14, no. 4 (1988): 18–30.

Harris, Thomas L. "Why Your Company Needs Marketing Public Relations." *Public Relations Journal* (September 1991): 26–27.

Harrison, E. Bruce. "Assessing the Damage, Practitioner Perspectives on the Valdez." *Public Relations Journal* 45, no. 10 (1989): 40–45.

Harrison, Stanley L. "Pedagogical Ethics for Public Relations and Advertising." *Journal of Media Ethics* 5, no. 4 (1990): 256–262.

Harrison, Thomas A. "Six PR Trends That Will Shape Your Future." *Nonprofit World* 9, no. 2 (1991): 21–25.

Heger, Kyle. "Exploring the Inner Space of Employee Communication." *IABC Communication World* 10, no. 5 (1993): 28–31.

Helfer, Edward. "Intercontinental Communication." *Public Relations Journal* 39, no. 2 (1983): 24–26.

Hervo, Pierre. "France Is on Its Way." *IABC Communication World* 10, no. 6 (1993): 53–54.

Holland, Robert. "Face-to-Face Communication Comes Face-to-Face." *IABC Communication World* 10, 1 (1993): 24–26.

Holloway, Deborah. "How to Select a Measurement System That's Right for You." *Public Relations Quarterly* 37, no. 3 (1992): 15–17.

Holst, Gull-May. "Is the World of the Communicator Shrinking or Expanding?" *IABC Communication World* 9, no. 3 (1992): 48–49.

Horaney, Michele. "The Russian President Is Coming . . . No He's Not!" *Public Relations Journal* 46, no. 8 (1990): 11.

Hoskins, Robert L. "Annual Reports: Difficult Reading and Getting More So." *Public Relations Review* 10, no. 2 (1984): 49–62.

"Hospitals Top List of Crisis-prone Industries." *Public Relations Journal* 47, no. 1 (1991): 13–14.

Huttenstine, Marian. "New Roles, New Problems, New Concerns, New Law." *Southern Public Relations Journal* 1, no. 1 (1993): 5–11.

Jacobs, Lou Jr. "Photograph Rights—A Negotiable Issue." *Public Relations Journal* 41, no. 2 (1985): 38–39.

"JC Penney Ties Model Search Finals to Hispanic Heritage Month." *Public Relations Journal* 47, no. 2 (1991): 14.

Joffe, Bruce H. "Law, Ethics and Public Relations Writers." *Public Relations Journal* 45, no. 7 (1989): 40.

Josephs, Ray. "Japan Booms with Public Relations Ventures." *Public Relations Journal* 46, no. 12 (1990): 18–20.

———. "Hong Kong, Public Relations Capital of Asia?" *Public Relations Journal* 47, no. 9 (1991): 20–25.

———. "Public Relations in France." *Public Relations Journal* 49, no. 7 (1993): 20–26.

Judd, Larry R. "Credibility, Public Relations and Social Responsibility." *Public Relations Review* 15 (Summer 1989): 34–40.

———. "Importance and Use of Formal Research and Evaluation." *Public Relations Review* 16, no. 4 (1990): 18–28.

Jung, C. L., and Douglas C. West. "Advertising Budgeting Methods in Canada, the UK and the USA." *International Journal of Advertising* 10, no. 3 (1991): 239–250.

Kastiel, Diane Lynn. "PR's Value: More Than Just the Numbers." *Business Marketing* 72 (May 1987): 48.

Katz, Anthony R. "Checklist: 10 Steps to Complete Crisis Planning." *Public Relations Journal* 43, no. 11 (1987): 45–47.

Katz, Marcia, and Ken Rabin. "Prescription for New Product Introductions." *Public Relations Quarterly* 38, no. 1 (1993): 12–14.

Kauffman, James. "NASA's PR Campaign on Behalf of Manned Space Flight, 1961–63." *Public Relations Review* 17, no. 1 (1991): 57–68.

Kearns, David, in "Benchmarking 101." *Corporate Community Relations Letter,* The Center for Corporate Community Relations at Boston College, 7, no. 9 (June 1993): 3.

Kemper, Ben. "Face-to-Face Feedback Works." *IABC Communication World* 10, no. 7 (1993): 20–23.

Kerlinger, Fred N. *Foundations of Behavioral Research,* 3rd ed. New York: Holt, Rinehart and Winston, 1986.

Kern-Foxworth, Marilyn. "Victory Together Coalition Plays Major Role in Arizona Vote Establishing Statewide King Holiday." *Public Relations Journal* 48, no. 12 (1992): 7–9.

Kessler, David A., in "FDA Writing Tougher Rx for Pharmaceutical Marketing." Marilyn L. Castaldi, *Public Relations Journal* 47, no. 8 (August 1991): 14–16, 19.

Kinkead, Robert W., and Dena Winokur. "How Public Relations Professionals Help CEOs Make the Right Moves." *Public Relations Journal* 48, no. 10 (1992): 18–23.

Kirban, Lloyd. "Showing What We Do Makes a Difference." *Public Relations Quarterly* 28, no. 3 (1983): 22–27.

Kotcher, Raymond L. "The Changing Role of PR in Latin America." *Public Relations Tactics* (March 1998): 26.

Kruckeberg, Dean. "The Need for an International Code of Ethics." *Public Relations Review* 14, no. 2 (1988): 6–18.

Larson, Mark A., and Karen L. Massetti-Miller. "Measuring Change after a Public Education Campaign." *Public Relations Review* 10, no. 4 (1984): 23–42.

Leahigh, Alan K. "Marketing Communications: If You Can't Count It, Does It Count?" *Public Relations Quarterly* 30, no. 4 (1985): 23–27.

Lesly, Philip. "Multiple Measurements of Public Relations." *Public Relations Review* 11, no. 2 (1985): 38.

———. "Public Relations in the Turbulent New Human Climate." *Public Relations Review* 17, no. 1 (1991): 1–8.

Levin, Carl. "Representing Foreign Interests." *Public Relations Journal* 38, no. 6 (1982): 22–24.

Levin, Donald M. "Helping Entrepreneurs Succeed." *Public Relations Journal* 47, no. 1 (1991): 30–31.

Levine, Joshua. "Selling the Sultan." *Forbes* 144, no. 2 (1989): 264–265.

Levins, Ilyssa. "Can Public Relations Actually Move Product?" *Public Relations Quarterly* 38, no. 1 (1993): 18–19.

Leyland, Adam, in "MACH3 Launch." *PR Week* (April 1999).

Limaye, Mohan R. "Cross-Cultural Business Communication Research: State of the Art and Hypotheses for the 1990s." *Journal of Business Communication* 28, no. 3 (1991): 277–299.

Lindenmann, Walter K. "Dealing with the Major Obstacles to Implementing Public Relations Research." *Public Relations Quarterly* 28, no. 3 (1983): 12–16.

———. "Beyond the Clipbook." *Public Relations Journal* 44, no. 12 (1988): 22–26.

———. "Research, Evaluation and Measurement: A National Perspective." *Public Relations Review* 16, no. 2 (1990): 3–16.

———. "An 'Effective Yardstick' to Measure Public Relations Success." *Public Relations Quarterly* 38, no. 1 (1993): 7–9.

———. "Going International—a Public Relations Trendwatch." *Public Relations Tactics* (July 1996).

Lobsenz, Amelia. "Representing a Foreign Government." *Public Relations Journal* 40, no. 8 (1984): 21–24.

Lorez, F. Michael. "Focus Group Research in a Winning Campaign." *Public Relations Review* 10, no. 2 (1984): 28–38.

Lukaszewski, James E. "Checklist: Anatomy of a Crisis Response." *Public Relations Journal* 45–47.

Major, Michael J. "Sun Sets Pace in Work Force Diversity." *Public Relations Journal* 49, no. 6 (1993): 12.

Maloff, Joel. "The Business of Internetworking." *Internet World* (July/August 1994): 34–39.

"Managing a Crisis with Advertorials, VNRs and Satellite News Conferences." *Public Relations Journal* 46, no. 10 (1990): 13.

Markoff, J. "Here Comes the Fiber-Optic Home." *The New York Times* (November 5, 1989): Sections 3, 1, 15.

Martinson, David. "How Should the PR Practitioner Respond When Confronted with Unethical Journalistic Behavior?" *Public Relations Quarterly* 36, no. 2 (1991): 18–21.

Masterton, John. "Discovering Databases: Online Services Put Research at Practitioner's Fingertips." *Public Relations Journal* 12 (November 1992): 17–19, 27.

McElreath, Mark P. "Dealing with Ethical Dilemmas." *IABC Communication World* 10, no. 3 (1993): 11–15.

———. "Who Cares." *IABC Communication World* 10, no. 4 (1993): 10–13.

———. "Ethics by Committee?" *IABC Communication World* 10, no. 5 (1993): 35–37.

———. "Going One-on-One." *IABC Communication World* 10, no. 7 (1993): 17–19.

McEwen, Laura. "Communicating Under Fire—Using the Media to Promote Peace." *IABC Communication World* 10, no. 7 (1993): 9–12.

McGoon, Cliff. "Putting the Employee Newsletter On-Line." *IABC Communication World* 9, no. 4 (1992): 16–18.

McKeand, Patrick, "GM Division Builds a Classic System to Share Internal Information." *Public Relations Journal* 46, no. 11 (November 1990): 22–25, 41.

"Measuring Results Adds Value to PR Field." *O'Dwyer's PR Services* 7, no. 7 (1993): 36.

Merrill, John C. *Journalism Ethics: Philosophical Foundations for News Media.* New York: St. Martin's Press, 1997.

Miller, Alan, in "PR Finds New Niche Promoting Promotions." *Inside PR* (February 1991): 25.

Miller, Karen. "Smoking Up a Storm, Public Relations and Advertising in the Construction of the Cigarette Problem, 1953–1954." *Journalism Monographs* 136 (December 1992): 1–35.

Milmo, Sean. "Demand Mounts for International PR Agencies." *Business Marketing* 70 (1985): 21.

Montagna, Catherine. "Nonprofits Survive Scandals, Budget Crunch." *Public Relations Journal* 49, no. 5 (1993): 8–9.

Moore, Richard. "Insiders Look at Ethics and Relationships." *Public Relations Journal* 46, no. 7 (1990): 29–30.

Moriarty, Sandra E. *Creative Advertising: Theory and Practice.* Englewood Cliffs, NJ: Prentice-Hall, 1986.

Mulholland, Gerry. "When Times Are Tough, Australians Get Tougher." *IABC Communication World* 9, no. 3 (1992): 46–47.

Mullins, Ronald Gift. "Employee Communications—Fracture for Success and Security." *IABC Communication World* 9, no. 9 (1992): 18–21.

"Multilingual Communication: Results of a *Communication World* Poll." *IABC Communication World* 10, no. 6 (1993): 46.

Murphy, Priscilla. "Using Two-Person Bargaining Games to Plan Communications Strategy." *Public Relations Quarterly* 35, no. 2 (1990): 27–32.

Myers, Adele, in "MACH3 Launch." *PR Week* (April 1999).

Nebenzahl, Israel D., and Eugene D. Jaffe. "The Effectiveness of Sponsored Events in Promoting a Country's Image." *International Journal of Advertising* 10, no. 3 (1991): 223–237.

Netteburg, Kermit. "Evaluating Change: A Church Publication Studies Its Readers." *Public Relations Review* 10, no. 2 (1984): 63–71.

Newlin, Patricia. "A Public Relations Measurement and Evaluation Mode That Finds the Movement of the Needle." *Public Relations Quarterly* 36, no. 1 (1991): 40–41.

Newsom, Doug, and Bob Carrell. *Public Relations Writing: Form and Style,* 5th ed. Belmont, CA: Wadsworth Publishing Company, 1998.

Niederquell, Michael O. "Integrating the Strategic Benefits of Public Relations into the Marketing Mix." *Public Relations Quarterly* 36, no. 1 (Spring 1991): 23–24.

"Nine Ways PR Contributes to the Bottom Line." *Trends* 9, no. 2 (1993): 32–33.

Novelli, William D. "You Can Produce Effective PSAs." *Public Relations Journal* 38, no. 5 (1982): 30–32.

———. "One-Stop Shopping: Some Thoughts on Integrated Marketing Communications." *Public Relations Quarterly* 34, no. 4 (Winter 1990): 7–9.

O'Connor, Kevin. "Public Relations . . . Soviet Style." *Public Relations Journal* 46, no. 8 (1990): 10.

O'Donnell, R. "Using Telecom to Complement the Personal Touch." In Kalman B. Druck (ed.), *New Technologies and Public Relations.* New York: Foundation for Public Relations Research and Education, 1986.

Ogbondah, Chris. "Internationalizing U.S. Public Relations: Educating for the Global Economy." *Public Relations Quarterly* 36, no. 4 (1991–92).

Ogilvy, David. *Confessions of an Advertising Man.* New York: Ballantine Books, 1971.

O'Leary, Timothy J., and Linda O'Leary. *Computing Essentials.* New York: McGraw-Hill, 1995.

O'Neill, Harry W. "How Opinion Surveys Can Help Public Relations Strategy." *Public Relations Review* 10, no. 2 (1984): 3–12.

O'Neill, Kathleen, and Adam Shell. "Trying to Get Tourists to Forget the War." *Public Relations Journal* 47, no. 5 (1991): 10–11.

Paine, Katherine D. "Escape from 'Measure-not Land.'" *Public Relations Tactics* (July 1997).

Parker, Robert A. "Employee Publications—Dying? Flourishing?" *IABC Communication World* 10, no. 1 (1993): 31–37.

Parlik, J. V. *Public Relations: What Research Tells Us.* Newbury Park, CA: Sage, 1987.

Parnell, Myrtle, and Jo Vanderkloot. "How to Build Cross-Cultural Bridges." *IABC Communication World* 6, no. 7 (1989): 40–42.

Parsons, Talcott. *Structure and Process in Modern Societies.* Glencoe, IL: Free Press, 1960.

Pasadeos, Yorgo, R. Bruce Renfro, and Mary Lynn Hanily. "Influential Authors and Works of the PR Scholarly Literature: A Network of Recent Research." *Journal of Public Relations Research* 11, no. 1 (1999): 29–52.

Patterson, Philip, and Lee Wilkins. *Media Ethics.* Dubuque, IA: Wm. C. Brown Publishers, 1997.

Pear, Marcia J. "Conference Workshop Focuses on Learning to Communicate Across Cultural Chasms." *IABC Communication World* 9, no. 5 (1992): 7–9.

Pearson, Ron. "Beyond Ethical Relativism in Public Relations: Coorientation, Rules, and the Idea of Communication Symmetry." In *Public Relations Research Annual Vol. 2,* ed. Larissa A. Grunig and James E. Grunig. Hillsdale, NJ: Lawrence Erlbaum Associates, 1989.

————. "Reviewing Albert J. Sullivan's Theory of Public Relations Ethics." *Public Relations Review* 15, no. 2 (Summer 1989): 52–62.

————. "Ethical Values or Strategic Values? The Two Faces of Systems Theory of Public Relations." In *Public Relations Research Annual Vol. 2,* ed. Larissa A. Grunig and James E. Grunig. Hillsdale, NJ: Lawrence Erlbaum Associates, 1990.

Peirce, Charles. In *Philosophical Writings of Peirce,* ed. J. Buchler. New York: Dover, 1955.

Piekos, Jennie M., and Edna F. Einsiedel. "Roles and Program Evaluation Techniques among Canadian Public Relations Practitioners." In *Public Relations Research Annual Vol. 2,* ed. Larissa A. Grunig and James E. Grunig. Hillsdale, NJ: Lawrence Erlbaum Associates, 1990.

Pinsdorf, Marion K. "Flying Different Skies: How Cultures Respond to Airline Disasters." *Public Relations Review* 17, no. 1 (1991): 37–56.

Plumley, Joseph P. Jr., and Jim Wilson. "The Relationship between PR Counsel and Legal Counsel in the Corporate Environment: What Are They Saying?" *Southern Public Relations Journal* 1, no. 1 (1993): 12–17.

Poincaré, H. *Science and Hypothesis.* New York: Dover, 1952.

"PR Sells Goods Better Than Ads in Eastern Bloc." *O'Dwyer's PR Services* 7, no. 7 (1993): 1.

Pratt, Cornelius. "Public Relations in the Third World, The African Context." *Public Relations Journal* 41, no. 2 (1985): 11–16.

————. "PRSA Members' Perceptions of Public Relations Ethics." *Public Relations Review* 17, no. 2 (1991): 145–159.

————. "Public Relations: The Empirical Research on Practitioner Ethics." *Journal of Business Ethics* 10, no. 3 (1991): 229–236.

"Preparing for 'The Real Thing.'" *Public Relations Journal* 46, no. 5 (1990): 14.

Procter, Jo. "Packaging Integrity." *Public Relations Journal* 40, no. 12 (1984): 24–28.

"Public Opinion Makers Must Promote Global Harmony: U. N.'s Sevigny." *Public Relations Journal* 46, no. 12 (1990): 14.

"Public Relations Must Pave the Way for Developing Diversified Work Force." *Public Relations Journal* 48, no. 1 (1992): 12–13.

Puntila, Tuula. "Finnish Communicators Are Helpers Both in Good and Bad Times." *IABC Communication World* 10, no. 6 (1993): 47–48.

Quella, James. "Defining Knowledge Management." *Public Relations Strategist* 4, no. 2 (Summer 1998).

Rayfield, Robert, Lalit Acharya, J. David Pincus, and Donn E. Silvis. *Public Relations Writing: Strategies and Skills.* Dubuque, IA: William C. Brown Publishers, 1991.

Reardon, Kathleen K. "The Potential Role of Persuasion in Adolescent AIDS Prevention," In ed. Ronald E. Rice and William J. Paisley. Newbury Park, CA: Sage, 1989.

Reed, John M. "International Media Relations: Avoid Self-Binding." *Public Relations Quarterly* 34, no. 2 (1989): 12–15.

Reeves, Byron. "Now You See Them, Now You Don't: Demonstrating Effects of Communication Programs." *Public Relations Quarterly* 28, no. 3 (1983): 17–2.

Reeves, Rosser. *Reality in Advertising.* New York: Ted Bates, 1960.

Reinhardt, Claudia. "How to Handle a Crisis." *Public Relations Journal* 43, no. 11 (1987): 43–44.

Reisman, Joan. "Global Affiliates Challenge the Big Guys." *Public Relations Journal* 46, no. 3 (1990): 20–24.

————. "Taking on the World." *Public Relations Journal* 46, no. 3 (1990): 18–19.

Rice, Ronald E. Adaptation of "Communication Efforts to Prevent Forest Fires," from first edition by Eugene F. McNamara, Troy Kurth, and Donald Hansen. *Public Communication Campaigns,* 2nd ed. Ronald E. Rice and William J. Paisley. Newbury Park, CA: Sage, 1989.

Ritchie, Eugene P., and Shelley J. Spector. "Making a Marriage Last, What Qualities Strengthen Client-Firm Bonds?" *Public Relations Journal* 46, no. 10 (1990): 16–21.

Roman, Anne. "Ohio Firm Breaks International Ice." *Public Relations Journal* 47, no. 5 (1991): 40.

Rosser, Connie, June A. Flora, Steven H. Chaffee, and John W. Farquhar. "Using Research to Predict Learning from a PR Campaign." *Public Relations Review* 16, no. 2 (1990): 61–77.

Rubenstein, Lauren. "How Lawyers See Public Relations." *Public Relations Journal* 42, no. 12 (1986): 35.

Ryan, Michael, and David L. Martinson. "Ethical Values, the Flow of Journalistic Information and Public Relations Persons." *Journalism Quarterly* 61, no. 2 (Spring 1984): 27–34.

Schuler, Joseph F. Jr. "Trivet! Kak U Tebya?" *Public Relations Journal* 46, no. 11 (1990): 10.

Schwartz, Bill, and Dennis Lewis. "Global Roundup: High-Tech Public Relations." *Public Relations Journal* 40, no. 8 (1984): 25–27.

Segal, Alan F. "Close Encounters with IRS." *Public Relations Journal* 43, no. 11 (1987): 10–14.

Seitel, Fraser. *The Practice of Public Relations,* 5th ed. Columbus, OH: Merrill, 1992.

Sen, Falguni, and William G. Egelhoff. "Six Years and Counting: Learning from Crisis Management at Bhopal." *Public Relations Review* 17, no. 1 (1991): 69–83.

Sendiri, Fatimah Yeop. "The Malaysian Perspective One of Dynamic Growth." *IABC Communication World* 10, no. 6 (1993): 51–52.

Serafin, Ray. "Saturn Recall a Plus—for Saturn." *Advertising Age* (August 16, 1993): 4.

Shamir, Jacob, Barbara Straus Reed, and Steven Connell. "Individual Differences in Ethical Values of Public Relations Practitioners." *Journalism Quarterly* 67, no. 4 (1990): 956–963.

Sharlach, Jeffrey R. "A New Era in Latin America." *Public Relations Journal* 49, no. 9 (September 1993): 26–28.

Sharpe, Melvin L. "The Impact of Social and Cultural Conditioning on Global Public Relations." *Public Relations Review* 18, no. 2 (1992): 103–107.

Shauffer, Jim. "The Maxi-Communication Audit—A Precision Instrument for Change." *IABC Communication World* 10, no. 1 (1993): 20–23.

Shell, Adam. "Client Views: Affiliates v. Multinationals." *Public Relations Journal* 46, no. 3 (1990): 23.

———. "Crises Caused by Executive Miscues on Rise." *Public Relations Journal* 48, no. 10 (1992): 8–9.

———. "New Breed of Speakers Represent Diversity, New Ideas." *Public Relations Journal* 49, no. 5 (1993): 10–14.

———, ed. "Employees Go Overseas to Survey Competition." *Public Relations Journal* 46, no. 10 (1989): 10.

Shelton, Christina M. "The Bloomington Hospital Public Relations Department, A Case Study." *Public Relations Quarterly* 38, no. 1 (1993): 25–28.

Shewchuk, Ron. "Green Gold?" *IABC Communication World* 10, no. 5 (1993): 16–19.

Simon, Raymond. *Publicity and Public Relations Worktext,* 5th ed. New York: Macmillan, 1986.

Singer, Eleanor, Theresa F. Rogers, and Marc B. Glassman. "Public Opinion About AIDS Before and After the 1988 U.S. Government Public Information Campaign." *Public Opinion Quarterly* 55, no. 2 (1991): 161–179.

Singletary, Michael W., Susan Caudill, Edward Caudill, and Allen White. "Motives for Ethical Decision-Making." *Journalism Quarterly* 67, no. 4 (1990): 964–972.

Sinickas, Angela D. "Supervisors are Not the Preferred Communicators!" *IABC Communication World* 9, no. 11 (1992): 25–28.

Skillman, Juanita M. "A PR Plan for Records Managers." *Records Management Quarterly* 26, no. 3 (1993): 30.

Small, William J. "Exxon Valdez: How to Spend Billions and Still Get a Black Eye." *Public Relations Review* 17, no. 1 (1991): 9–25.

Small, William. "The Changing Face of Network News." *Television Quarterly* 25, no. 1 (1991): 105–106.

Smith, Alvie L. "Bridging the Gap Between Employees and Management." *Public Relations Journal* 46, no. 11 (November 1990): 20–21, 41.

Smith, Ralph Lee. *The Wired Nation: Cable TV—The Electronic Communications Highway.* New York: Harper and Row, 1972.

Sneed, Dan K., Tim Wulfemeyer, and Harry W. Stonecipher. "Public Relations News Releases and Libel: Extending First Amendment Protections." *Public Relations Review* 17, no. 2 (1991): 131–144.

Spaniel, Bill. "In Riot's Wake, L.A. Chapter Steps Up Multicultural Efforts." *IABC Communication World* 9, no. 8 (1992): 18–22.

Spiers, Paul. "Public Relations in Egypt and the Middle East." *IABC Communication World* 9, no. 3 (1992): 40–42.

Stanley, Guy. "Free Trade Agreement: Its Implications for Public Relations." *Canadian Business Review* 16, no. 1 (1989): 47–49.

Staughan, Dulcie, Bill Chamberlin, and Carol Reuss. "For Corporate Libel Plaintiffs: Life After Gertz." *Public Relations Review* 10, no. 3 (1984): 47–60.

Stocking, S. Holly. "Packaging Risk: Lessons for Students in PR and Journalism." *Journalism Educator* 47, no. 2 (1992): 26–31.

Strenski, James B. "Techniques for Measuring Public Relations Effectiveness." *Public Relations Quarterly* 27, no. 1 (1982): 21–24.

———. "International Networking Tailors Communications Programs Across the Globe." *Public Relations Quarterly* 30, no. 1 (1985): 28–29.

———. "Understanding of Culture Essential to Success in Japanese Market." *Public Relations Quarterly* 31, no. 2 (1986): 9.

———. "Measuring the ROI of Public Relations." *Chief Executive* (January/February 1988): 36–41.

"Study: Emphasis on Ethics Reaches Lower Rungs of Corporate Ladder." *Public Relations Journal* 48, no. 1 (1992): 10–11.

"Targeting Black Consumers." *Public Relations Journal* 47, no. 2 (1991): 20–21.

Taylor, Frederick. *The Principles of Scientific Management.* New York: Harper, 1911.

"The Town of Lloyd vs. Texaco." *Public Relations Journal* 45, no. 10 (1989): 29.

Todd, Mike. "Helping Internal Audiences Cope." *Public Relations Journal* 45, no. 6 (1989): 40.

Toer, Juan Carlos. "Argentine Communicators Finding Their Niche." *IABC Communication World* 10, no. 6 (1993): 37–39.

Tortorello, Nicholas, and Ed Dowgiallo. "Evaluating the Impact of Public Relations." *Public Relations Journal* 46, no. 11 (1990): 34–37.

Traverso, Debra K. "Opening a Credible Dialogue with Your Community." *Public Relations Journal* 48, no. 8 (1992): 32.

Trout, Jack. " 'Positioning' Is a Game People Play in Today's Me-Too Market Place." *Industrial Marketing* (June 1969): 51–55.

Troy, Kathryn. "Internal Communication Restructures for the '90s." *IABC Communications World* (February 1989).

Tuggle, Charlie. "Media Relations during Crisis Coverage." *Public Relations Quarterly* 36, no. 2 (1991): 23–28.

Tyler, Lisa. "Ecological Disaster and Rhetorical Response." *Journal of Business and Technical Communication* 6, no. 2 (1992): 149–171.

Unger, Lonnie. In *Getting New Clients,* ed. Kalman D. Druck. 1986.

United Way Strategic Institute. "Nine Forces Reshaping America." *The Futurist* 24, no. 4 (July–August 1990): 9–16.

"U.S. Firms Take Varied Approaches to Japanese Market." *Public Relations Journal* 46, no. 12 (1990): 21–24.

U.S. Department of Commerce and Trade and the International Trade Administration. *Dataquest, April 1998.* OH: McGraw-Hill.

van Riel, C. B. M. "Corporate Communication in European Financial Institutions." *Public Relations Review* 18, no. 2 (1992): 161–175.

Vogl, Frank. "Closing the Gap, New Approaches to International Media Relations." *Public Relations Journal* 46, no. 7 (1990): 18–20.

Wallace, Ward. "Reflections on PR/Communication in Spain." *IABC Communication World* 10, no. 6 (1993): 49–50.

Walsh, Frank E. "Corporate Election Campaigns: In Conflict with the Law or Not?" *Public Relations Review* 9, no. 2 (1983): 7–16.

———. "Fundamentals of First Amendment Protection." *Public Relations Journal* 39, no. 1 (1983): 37.

———. "Public Relations Firm Charged with Insider Trading." *Public Relations Journal* 42, no. 2 (1986): 10.

———. "Commercial Speech." *Public Relations Journal* 42, no. 9 (1986): 9–10.

Wang, Julie C., in "FDA Writing Tougher Rx for Pharmaceutical Marketing." Marilyn L. Castaldi. *Public Relations Journal* 47, no. 8 (August 1991): 14–16, 19.

Warner, Fara. "In the Fast Lane." *Brandweek* (5 July 1993): 21–24.

"Ways to Avoid Ethical Problems." *Public Relations Journal* 49, no. 6 (1993): 9.

Weaver, Ruth Ann, and Theodore L. Glasser. "Survey Research for Legislative Relations." *Public Relations Review* 10, no. 2 (1984): 39–48.

Werner, Lawrence R. "When Crisis Strikes Use a Message Action Plan." *Public Relations Journal* 46, no. 9 (1990): 30–31.

———. "Marketing Strategies for the Recession." *Management Review* 80, no. 8 (1991): 29–30.

Westerbeck, Tim. "A Hospital's Worst Nightmare." *Public Relations Journal* 47, no. 11 (1991): 8.

White, Rene. "Beyond Berlitz: How to Penetrate Foreign Markets through Effective Communications." *Public Relations Quarterly* 31, no. 2 (1986): 12–16.

Wicks, Andrew C. "Norman Bowie and Richard Rorty on Multinationals: Does Business Ethics Need 'Metaphysical Comfort'?" *Journal of Business Ethics* 9 (1990): 191–200.

Wiesendanger, Betsy. "Plug into a World of Information." *Public Relations Journal* 50, no. 2 (February 1994): 20–23.

Wilcox, Dennis L., and Lawrence W. Nolte. *Public Relations Writing and Media Techniques.* New York: Harper and Row, 1990.

Wilkinson, Ann. "Globalization: Are We Up to the Challenges?" *Public Relations Journal* 46, no. 1 (1990): 12–13.

Will, Gavin. "Church in a State." *This Magazine* 25, no. 5 (1992): 11–12.

Wind, Yorum, in "Flops: Too Many Products Fail. Here's Why." *Business Week* (August 16, 1993): 77.

Winokur, Dena, and Robert W. Kinkead. "How Public Relations Fits into the Corporate Strategy." *Public Relations Journal* 49, no. 5 (May 1993): 16–23.

Wise, Jim. "Tracking Legislation." *Public Relations Journal* 45, no. 9 (1989): 43–44.

Wittenberg, Ernest. "Getting It Done Overseas." *Public Relations Journal* 38, no. 6 (1982): 14–15.

Wright, Donald K. "Implications of the IPRA 'Gold Paper'." *Public Relations Review* 9, no. 2 (1983): 3–6.

———. "Examining Ethical and Moral Values of Public Relations People." *Public Relations Review* 14, no. 2 (1988): 19–33.

Wulfemeyer, K. Tim, and Lowell Frazier. "The Ethics of Video News Releases: A Qualitative Analysis." *Journal of Mass Media Ethics* 7, no. 3 (1992): 151–168.

Wylie, Frank Winston. "Business and Ethics and Long-Term Planning." *Public Relations Quarterly* 36, no. 2 (1991): 7–12.

———, and Simeon P. Slovacek. "PR Evaluation: Myth, Option or Necessity?" *Public Relations Review* 10, no. 2 (1984): 22–27.

Wylie, Kenneth. "Integration Is the Wave in Recharged $816.6 Million Industry." *Advertising Age* (May 17 1993): S-1, S-7.

Young, Davis. "Reputation and Ethics in a Cynical Age." *Public Relations Journal* 49, no. 5 (1993): 32.

INDEX